REPRESENTING
POST-REVOLUTIONARY IRAN

REPRESENTING POST-REVOLUTIONARY IRAN

Captivity, Neo-Orientalism, and Resistance In Iranian-American Life Writing

Hossein Nazari

I.B. TAURIS
LONDON • NEW YORK • OXFORD • NEW DELHI • SYDNEY

I.B. TAURIS
Bloomsbury Publishing Plc
50 Bedford Square, London, WC1B 3DP, UK
1385 Broadway, New York, NY 10018, USA
29 Earlsfort Terrace, Dublin 2, Ireland

BLOOMSBURY, I.B. TAURIS and the I.B. Tauris logo are trademarks of
Bloomsbury Publishing Plc

First published in Great Britain 2022
This paperback edition published 2024

Copyright © Hossein Nazari, University of Tehran, email: nazarih@ut.ac.ir, 2022

Hossein Nazari has asserted his right under the Copyright, Designs and
Patents Act, 1988, to be identified as Author of this work.

For legal purposes the Acknowledgments on p. viii constitute an extension
of this copyright page.

Series design by Adriana Brioso
Cover image © Dominika Zarzycka/NurPhoto/Getty Images

All rights reserved. No part of this publication may be reproduced or transmitted
in any form or by any means, electronic or mechanical, including photocopying,
recording, or any information storage or retrieval system, without prior
permission in writing from the publishers.

Bloomsbury Publishing Plc does not have any control over, or responsibility for, any third-party websites referred to or in this book. All internet addresses given in this book were correct at the time of going to press. The author and publisher regret any inconvenience caused if addresses have changed or sites have ceased to exist, but can accept no responsibility for any such changes.

A catalogue record for this book is available from the British Library.

A catalog record for this book is available from the Library of Congress.

ISBN: HB: 978-0-7556-1736-4
PB: 978-0-7556-4808-5
ePDF: 978-0-7556-1737-1
eBook: 978-0-7556-1738-8

Typeset by Deanta Global Publishing Services, Chennai, India

To find out more about our authors and books visit www.bloomsbury.com and
sign up for our newsletters.

For:
Sara and Saba

CONTENTS

Acknowledgments   viii

Chapter 1
INTRODUCTION: IRAN IN WESTERN IMAGINARY   1

Chapter 2
NOT WITHOUT MY DAUGHTER: THE MOTHER OF NEO-ORIENTALIST BESTSELLERS   33

Chapter 3
READING LOLITA IN TEHRAN: MANUFACTURING MUSLIM LOLITAS FOR THE WEST   83

Chapter 4
SIGHTING PERSIAN STARS IN THE WESTERN SKY: THE DAWN OF A DISCOURSE OF RESISTANCE IN *JASMINE AND STARS*   151

Chapter 5
TOWARD AN AMBIVALENT FUTURE   189

Notes   195
Bibliography   206
Index   219

ACKNOWLEDGMENTS

This book would not have been possible without the encouragement and contribution of those whose support kept me going during the process. I am most grateful to my wife, Sara, for her unwavering support. Had it not been for her love and understanding, this book might have never come to conclusion.

In writing this book, I have benefited from the scholarly contribution of my colleagues at the University of Canterbury. I am forever indebted to Professor Paul Millar, whose friendship has been nothing short of a privilege for me. Drs. Nicholas Wright and Daniel Bedggood provided prompt and insightful feedback on the manuscript; for this, and for all their succor and support, I cannot thank them enough. I am grateful to Dr. Maureen Montgomery for her constructive comments on the second chapter of this book and for all her other contributions. The late Professor Howard McNaughton also offered valuable feedback on the second chapter. *Requiescat in pace*!

Professor Hossein Pirnajmuddin remained as true a friend and mentor during the process of writing this book as he has always been, and Amir Khadem was always there, his encouragement and support as nourishing as ever. I am also genuinely grateful to Rory Gormley and Yasmin Garcha at Bloomsbury for all their help, feedback, and patience from the very first contact through to the publication of the book.

Finally, I would like to express my heartfelt gratitude to all family members, friends, and colleagues who, in one way or another, have either contributed to this project or made life a bit easier in hectic times. God bless them all.

Chapter 1

INTRODUCTION

IRAN IN WESTERN IMAGINARY

In the introduction to her travelogue, *Two Wings of a Nightingale: Persian Soul, Islamic Heart* (2011), the New Zealand author Jill Worrall writes that "Iran is probably the most misunderstood country in the world, and its people are among the most feared" (Worrall). This statement alone is a testament to the significance of Iran, as a major locus in the Muslim Orient, in the Western imaginary, particularly in the mainstream Western discourse apropos the Oriental/Muslim Other. It also bespeaks the power of the representational regime through which the country, its people, and particularly its main religion, Islam, have been subject to constant tropes of Othering, demonization, marginalization, and negation in the West, not least in the United States.

It is the dominance, ubiquity, authority, and serious cultural and political implications of such representations that lend urgency to a methodical analysis and critique of such regimes of knowledge production about the Oriental Other. This book, therefore, seeks to critique literary representations of Iran, which were part of the proliferation of literary productions informed by the two defining historical junctures of the 1979 Islamic Revolution in Iran—and within that context the Iran–Iraq War (1980–8) and the Hostage Crisis (1979–81)—and what is now commonly referred to as 9/11. The corpus of literary texts dealing specifically with Iranian contexts has expanded exceedingly since the revolution and reached its apex in what Professor Hamid Dabashi has dubbed "the haymarket of post 9/11 anxieties" (*Post-Orientalism* 276). Sanaz Fotouhi has recorded that while between 1980 and 2001, no more than sixteen memoirs had been published by Iranians residing in the West, from 2001 to early 2012 at least fifty more memoirs were published (99), excluding works of fiction and poetry volumes—a trend that still continues.

This book provides a much-needed analysis of this literary phenomenon in Iranian-American self-narratives, undertaking a critical perusal of three paramount memoirs penned by Iranian-American women, which are deemed to be paradigmatic works in their representations of Iran and Islam. The three texts are Betty Mahmoody's *Not without My Daughter* (1987), as the quintessential pre-9/11 example of captivity narratives; Azar Nafisi's *Reading Lolita in Tehran: A*

Memoir in Books (2003), as the iconic neo-Orientalist post-9/11 Iranian-American, and by extension Middle Eastern, memoir; and Professor Fatemeh Keshavarz's *Jasmine and Stars: Reading More than Lolita in Tehran* (2007), as the paramount counter-narrative. While there also exist memoirs written by hyphenated Iranian-European women, none of them share the iconic status of the three memoirs in question, in terms of their popular reception, their impact on the perception of Iran and Islam, their engagement with political agendas, and the celebrity status of their authors. Furthermore, the ongoing tension in US-Iran relations lends a sense of urgency and topicality to Iranian-American memoirs, which is rather lacking in other memoirs.

The critical exegesis of the texts in question is built primarily upon Edward Said's theorization and critique of the concept of Orientalism in his seminal 1978 book of the same title, and its latter-day manifestation, that is, post-9/11 neo-Orientalism. The analysis of the three iconic texts seeks to reveal that notwithstanding their formal and, to a lesser extent, thematic differences, the narratives in question represent Iran and Islam within a long-established Orientalist frame of reference and through similar representational apparatus. Furthermore, even though these texts are products of two different eras, that is, pre- and post-9/11, the similarities in the social, political, and historical contexts of their production have significantly contributed to their promotion, dissemination, and reception in the United States, and more broadly in the West.

In my perusal of the three narratives, I will demonstrate how the dominant Western representations of Iran and Islam can be read as manifestations of a sustained and long-standing Orientalist discourse formulated in and popularized by the West. Such discursive continuity is a fact that Edward Said bemoans in his Preface to the twenty-fifth-anniversary edition of his *Orientalism*. Said laments the lack of any evident change in the manner in which American and European representations of the Middle East portray contemporary Muslim societies primarily in terms of what they see as "their backwardness, lack of democracy and abrogation of women's rights" (xviii). He then goes on to demonstrate how the overall understanding of the Middle East and Islam has deteriorated in the United States since the first publication of his *Orientalism* in 1978:

> I wish I could say, however, that general understanding of the Middle East, the Arabs and Islam in the United States has improved somewhat, but alas, it really hasn't ... In the US, the hardening of attitudes, the tightening of the grip of demeaning generalization and triumphalist cliché, the dominance of crude power allied with simplistic contempt for dissenters and "others," has found a fitting correlative in the looting, the pillaging, and destruction of Iraq's libraries and museums. (xviii)

Therefore, my critique of the three narratives engages not only with the representational tropes of othering vis-à-vis Iranian people, their culture, main religion, and politics but also with a counter-narrative that seeks to challenge and offer an alternative to the dominant Orientalist discourse via which Iran is often represented and understood. Through an in-depth analysis of the three texts, I will demonstrate how the dominant Western representations of Iran conditioned by certain historical junctures are informed by an Orientalist episteme. Within this regime of knowledge production, the Iranian/Muslim Other, in general, is represented as inferior, and Iranian/Muslim women, in particular, are depicted as oppressed, victimized, passive, and in need of liberation. Such a rendition corresponds with the official view of the United States toward Iran—regardless of which party may be in power—which represents the country not only as its archnemesis but often as *the* greatest threat to world stability. Such representations have, indeed, disturbing political implications in the context of the continuing tensions between Iran and the United States. I will also illustrate, in my discussion of the last narrative, how through an intervening discourse of resistance, hyphenated authors and artists can construct a space that can enable a mode of writing back to the hegemony of Orientalist representations, and can lend greater visibility to the voices that are perpetually dehumanized, marginalized, and silenced in the dominant Western narratives.

Any attempt at investigating certain selective representations of any subject must take account of the historical context that underlies the subject of representation and in which the subject is constantly re-conceptualized and recycled. This is because, in all their normative selectivity, particular conceptualizations of any given country, culture, or people are always informed by a historicity that is definitive of the image represented. Hence, without such contextualization, neither the subject of representation nor its (mis)representations can be fully appreciated. It is only apt, therefore, to briefly demonstrate first the historical significance of Iran to the West and then the historicity of its representations.

Earliest Figurations: The Lavish Nemesis

Although Worrall's observation, quoted at the beginning of this section, about the endemic misconceptions of Iran clearly encapsulates the current Irano-Islamophobic zeitgeist in the West, representations of Iran in the Western imaginary extend as far back as classical antiquity. With Iran, formerly known as Persia, occupying one of the most significant geostrategic loci on the world stage throughout history, the image of the country has always remained central to the Western imaginary. As Lila Azam Zanganeh has observed, "[w]hether as a haven of exotic sensuality or a stronghold of fanatic religiosity, Iran has, since ancient times, inflamed the popular imagination" (xi). From 550 BC, when it was deemed the world's preeminent empire during the Achaemenid era, right through to when it fell subject to the colonial whims of Russia, Britain, the Ottoman Empire, the USSR, and the United States, and, later, the 1979 Islamic Revolution that toppled the Pahlavi dynasty, ending twenty-five centuries of monarchy, Iran has always been of considerable geopolitical significance to its immediate neighbors and dominant world powers alike.

The earliest imaginings of Persia[1] as the realm of luxury, excess, despotism, and arrogance were primarily inspired by the rise, reign, and decline of the Persian Empire as the world's largest ancient empire and civilization hitherto, and the archrival of its Occidental counterparts. That the Persian Empire became the subject of much obsession, awe, and apprehension in the European collective consciousness is evident in the figurations of Persia in the literary imaginary of the Occident throughout centuries. This reflects the importance of Persia as an immediate neighbor and antagonist of the Greek states in this period, and the lasting centrality of the Greek and Roman classical period in the West. Some of the most ancient representations of Persia appeared in the earliest of Aeschylus's surviving plays, *The Persians* (472 BC), which, according to Edward Said, is the earliest, and the quintessential, text in which "Europe . . . articulates the Orient" (*Orientalism* 57). In this historical tragedy about the Greek defeat of the Persians in the Battle of Salamis (480 BC), the Persians are made distinct from their Greek counterparts through their indulgence in such "Eastern excesses"[2] (*Orientalism* 57) as extravagance, hubris, sensuality, despotism, and irrationality (Pirnajmuddin 21).

In his pioneering study of the literary representations of Persia, Hossein Pirnajmuddin has meticulously demonstrated how the foregoing figurations were also circulated in the canonical and non-canonical works of such English Renaissance texts as Christopher Marlowe's *Tamburlaine the Great* (1587), Edmund Spencer's *The Faerie Queene* (1590), and John Milton's *Paradise Lost* (1667) and *Paradise Regained* (1671), to name but a few (4). Thanks to the Romantic poets' interest in and appropriation of the matter of the Orient, images of Persia as a land of exoticism, mystery, indulgence, and unbridled sexuality appeared more than ever before in the English literary tradition, especially in the works of such Romantic poets as Lord Byron and Robert Southey. Such an interest is clearly exemplified in such works as Thomas Moore's Oriental romance, *Lalla Rookh* (1817), as well as the late-eighteenth- and early-nineteenth-century "Persian poetry fad" in England. John D. Yohannan has attributed the Romantic interest in Persia to "the establishment, in England, of a genuine, firsthand study of the languages of Persia, Arabia, Turkey, and India," among other things (137).

Foundational to the Occidental imagining of Persia is the text popularly known in the West as *One Thousand and One Nights* (or alternatively, *Arabian Nights*). Arguably, no other work has contributed as widely to the exoticization and eroticization of Persia in the Western imaginary. With the harem—as a site where pleasure and peril are curiously intertwined—lying at the heart of the narrative, *One Thousand and One Nights* represents Persia as a locus of unbridled sensuality and cruelty and has significantly shaped the European view of the licentious, misogynistic, and murderous Persian, best epitomized in the character of the Persian King Shahriar and his treatment of his many doomed wives. Regardless of such figurations of Persia (or the greater Orient), and consistent with an Orientalist view of Oriental philistinism, Said draws attention to how in his *Eothen* (1844), Alexander William Kinglake concludes that "the *Arabian Nights* is too lively and inventive a work to have been created by a 'mere

Oriental, who, for creative purposes, is a thing dead and dry—a mental mummy'" (*Orientalism* 193).[3]

It was, however, in the Oriental travelogues penned by European travelers, missionaries, and delegates mostly during the age of European, and particularly British, colonialism that representations of Persia as uncivilized, backward, primitive, decadent, and unfit-for-self-governance pervaded the mainstream Western discourse on the Orient in earnest. Prominent in this category is James Morier's *The Adventures of Hajji Baba of Ispahan* (1824). Written by a British imperial diplomat,[4] the novel has been considered "the most popular Oriental novel in the English language and a highly influential stereotype of the so-called 'Persian national character' in modern times" (Amanat 561). Such colonial accounts are characterized by overwhelmingly negative representations of Persia and its peoples. *The Adventures of Hajji Baba of Ispahan*, for instance, "lampoons Persians as rascals, cowards, puerile villains, and downright fools, depicting their culture as scandalously dishonest and decadent, and their society as violent" (Amanat 561). The opening passage from another one of Morier's works, *The Mirza* (1841), a collection of tales about Persia, encapsulates the dominant discourse of the British Empire concerning both its Persian Other and itself. The passage bears quoting in full:

> Although the Persians cannot be complimented upon their morality, as a nation, yet no one can deny that they abound in a lively wit, a social disposition, and in qualities which fit them to be agreeable companions. The Englishman, bred up in reverence of truth, in love of justice, and in admiration of every thing that constitutes good government, with a strict sense of honour, and a quick impulse to uphold his rights as an independant man, remains perfectly astonished and incredulous at all he sees and hears, when first he finds himself an inhabitant of an Asiatic state. In Persia particularly, where truth and falsehood are upon equal terms, where a man to live, must practice deceit, where the meaning of the word honour is not to be defined, and where there is no government but such as emanates from caprice or despotism, there his astonishment and disgust are complete, although, at the same time, should he have any turn for humour, he cannot help being amused at the ingenuity of the wiles exercised, at the light-hearted levity, and apparent clown and pantaloon philosophy with which evils, such as the Englishman would call great, are supported. (1–2)

Such depictions would be best understood if read against the backdrop of an expanding British imperialism in its heyday. In the colonial context of their own time, such accounts served as "soft weapons," to borrow Gillian Whitlock's phrase (*Soft Weapons* 3), deployed to justify and perpetuate colonial domination that pledged the civilizing of the Oriental subject. Such nationalistic chauvinism is also applied to other countries (including European ones) and at times to the British, too. Nevertheless, the British, and other colonial European powers' accounts become more dominant as other aspects of imperialism support their ascendancy.

As far as representations of Iran in the United States are concerned, it is imperative to contextualize such representations within the historico-political context of the last century. In the second half of the twentieth century, the role played by the United States in Iran's political landscape became increasingly more dominant. The US intervention in Iranian internal affairs reached its climax when in 1953 the new US administration decided to execute a coup d'état that overthrew Iran's first democratically elected prime minister—Dr. Mohammad Mosaddeq, who had nationalized Iran's oil and incurred the wrath of the British— and reinstated the second Pahlavi Shah. Following the coup, which was to become Iranians' most painful collective memory of the United States for decades, the shah set out to consolidate his power, and in so doing sought the backing of the United States, to which he now owed his throne. The United States had now a much stronger presence in Iran, partly justified by its fear of Iran's Communist neighbor. As a result, the official relations between the two countries strengthened. The US presence was both justified and solidified through such factors as the alliance whereby the United States assisted in the buildup of Iran's military and the notorious SAVAK (Iran's intelligence and security organization), and the creation of diplomatic immunity, known commonly in Iran as "capitulation", granted to all US military personnel stationed in Iran. Such displays of American dominance and superiority were among a variety of factors that fueled the anti-American sentiment, which, in turn, played a significant role in setting the ground for the 1979 Islamic Revolution. With the collapse of the last Pahlavi dynasty and the advent of a new era for Iran, characterized by an Islamic system of governance and strong opposition to any form of foreign intervention, the severely strained relationship between the two countries grew ever more troubled. The tensions reached a climax when on November 4, 1979, a group of revolutionary students seized the US Embassy in Tehran, which they dubbed "the nest of spies," and took fifty-two American diplomats and citizens hostages for 444 days. The hostage-taking was inspired by several major factors: espionage charges against the US embassy staff, preventing another US-engineered coup d'état, and demanding the extradition of the shah, who was in the United States. This landmark juncture in the history of the relationship between the two countries will be further elaborated in the following chapter.

Fabricating an "Axis of Evil"

Much of Iran's geopolitical significance to the West over the past century owes to its rich oil reserves and its strategic location for the dominant Western, as well as Eastern, powers. The British exploitation of Iran's oil at the turn of the twentieth century and Iran's geostrategic importance to the dominant world powers during the First and Second World Wars are some of the better-known instances of Western interest in Iran as a major economic and geopolitical locus. Even though Iran was never an official colony of Western powers, as Richard Cottam has observed, there existed "a bizarre situation in which a form of indirect colonial control existed in the hands of two imperial powers whose relative positions were in constant flux" (9).

Nevertheless, since the 1979 Islamic Revolution, one of the most important decolonizing movements of the twentieth century, the position of Iran in geopolitical equations has undergone considerable mutations. Almost all Western countries, primarily the United States, who had exerted overwhelming sway over Iran's political, economic, and cultural landscapes, lost their vested interests and had to grapple with a post-revolutionary Iran defined by ideas of independence and resistance to foreign hegemony. It was against this backdrop that Iran went from being, in the words of Jimmy Carter, the West's "island of stability" in the Middle East to its chief "enemy." This metamorphosis partly fueled the persistent tropes of Othering and vilification that were soon enormously intensified by the Hostage Crisis, the representation of which in Western media served to further associate Iranians with such phrases as "non-rational," "hungry for martyrdom," and "unwilling to compromise" (Mobasher 49). A 2020 Gallup Poll shows that 88 percent of Americans have a mostly/very unfavorable opinion of Iran and Iran ranks third on the list of the countries considered to be the greatest enemy of the United States today (down from first in 2011 and 2012), after Russia and China and before North Korea. Regardless of the validity and the controversial nature of such polls, one cannot but concur with Danny Schechter that "Iran is being used again as a symbol of the menacing 'bad guy.'" Schechter goes on to argue that "Iran is almost tailor made to play the role of a contrived enemy. The nation is an Islamic Republic; and, has a history of disagreements with the US. It refuses to bow down to American cultural or political demands and insists on playing an independent role in the world at large, according to its own customs and values."

With the advent of the 1979 revolution and what in the West was perceived as the resurgence of Islam,[5] a whole new phase of writings on Iran, mostly travel narratives, began to emerge. These works borrow from and build upon the Oriental travel-writing genre and regurgitate similar topoi and motifs popularized by European emissaries of the nineteenth century. However, they focus more on what they purport to be the workings of the revolution and Islam in post-revolutionary Iran. Paramount in this genre are the two "Islamic" travelogues of the Trinidad-born British writer, V. S. Naipaul, *Among the Believers* (1981) and *Beyond Belief* (1998), which recount the author's excursions in the four Muslim countries of Iran, Pakistan, Indonesia, and Malaysia[6] and portray Muslims predominantly as backward, frozen-in-the-past, ignorant, and fanatical (Marandi and Nazari 2017; Nazari 2016).[7] Even so, such travel accounts of Iran by Westerners, or Westoxicated authors (to borrow Jalal Al-e Ahmad's term), were few and far between and often not very consequential.

Similarly, although the Islamic Revolution of 1979 initiated the migration of many Iranians to the West, particularly to the United States, the exodus did not produce a substantial body of literature in English by first-generation Iranian-American authors either in the memoir genre or in fictional modes of writing.[8] In fact, in the review printed on the back cover of the first anthology of Iranian-American writings, *A World Between*, Michael Beard observes that the stories of Iranian-Americans "never really became public and Iranians often seemed the most invisible of new Americans."

The September 11 events marked a watershed in contemporary world history and, coupled with the subsequent US "War on Terror," gave rise to an unprecedented Islamophobic zeitgeist that posited Islam as the greatest threat to the "civilized" world.[9] In his January 29, 2002 State of the Union Address, George W. Bush opened his speech by warning that "the civilized world faces unprecedented dangers" (Bush "State of the Union Address"). He then went on to brand North Korea, Iran, and Iraq as major enemies of the United States, asserting that "[s]tates like these and their terrorist allies constitute an axis of evil, arming to threaten the peace of the world." Most ironically, however, none of the terrorists purportedly involved in 9/11 were citizens of the three countries comprising Bush's axis of evil. Furthermore, even though Iran was not, by any stretch of the imagination, implicated in 9/11, the branding of Iran by the US president as part of the axis of evil attached an Iranophobic element to the rampant post-9/11 Islamophobia. This Iranophobia also owes much to the prevalent public mindset that does not distinguish between Iran and its Arab neighbors and rather treats the whole gamut of countries in the Middle East as monolithically "Islamic." With the "threat" of "Islamic fundamentalism" looming large in the West, knowing the Muslim Other became a *sine qua non* for the US public. In the words of Fatemeh Keshavarz, "[s]ince 9/11, knowing about the Muslim Middle East is not a luxury, it is a matter of life and death" (*Jasmine and Stars* 2).

Central to the United States' definition of itself as a civilized nation has been the position of (white) women, as exemplified by the early Suffragists (Elkholy). Traditionally, within US civilizational discourse, the exploitation and oppression of women have been projected as a characteristic of "uncivilized"/"savage" cultures, perhaps best observed in the tradition of American captivity narratives. It is, therefore, no surprise that since the 1979 Islamic Revolution the status of women has been part of a US neoconservative agenda (Ernst 13) as a means of measuring other nations' civilized status. As Carl W. Ernst points out, "neo-conservative attacks on Islam generally include a gender egalitarian and women's rights perspective" (13). It was mostly in this context that the veil and other Islamic laws regarding women assumed a highly publicized place in the anti-Islamic rhetoric in the West. In the same vein, essential to the post-9/11 Islamophobic discourse and the justification of US wars in Iraq and Afghanistan was the rhetoric of "liberating" Muslim women, or, to borrow Spivak's *locus classicus*, the notion of "white men saving brown women from brown men" (93).

The "oppression" of women in Afghanistan, for instance, played a major role in the pre-invasion rhetoric after 9/11. In the same 2002 State of the Union Address—which more than anything else encapsulates the Bush administration's American exceptionalist mindset—the US president declared triumphantly that "[t]he last time we met in this chamber, the mothers and daughters of Afghanistan were captives in their own homes, forbidden from working or going to school. Today women are free and are part of Afghanistan's new government" (Bush "State of the Union Address"). In other words, while the United States was persistently obsessed with the "threat" of the Muslim world, the post-9/11 outlook placed the question of Muslim women on center stage. As Christina Ho has observed, concurrent with the United States waging its "War on Terror" first in Afghanistan and then in Iraq, "the liberation of women from barbaric regimes became a powerful rationale for intervention" (432). The irony is that in Iraq especially, military intervention has indeed set back such goals (Al-Ali and Pratt). Bush's assertion sounds even more extraordinary with hindsight, taking into account the fact that, according to a UN report, in 2019 the number of civilian casualties in the aftermath of the invasion of Afghanistan had surpassed 100,000, many of them women and children (UN News 2020). Also, a 2018 study by Brown University researchers found that the post-9/11 US wars in Afghanistan, Iraq, and Pakistan have killed at least half a million people and left at least 37 million others displaced.

Writing Iran in America

In the same manner that white middle-class Western women were recruited to join the "civilizing mission" of European colonial powers, a significant number of Middle Eastern/"Muslim" women have produced a corpus of literary works focusing on what they purport to be the oppression of Muslim women. Even though the majority of these authors identify as feminists and women's rights activists, Bahramitash has dubbed this coterie of authors "Orientalist feminists" ("Orientalist Feminism" 108). As the critique of Betty Mahmoody's and Azar Nafisi's narratives would reveal, the feminist ethos through which the Iranian/Muslim women have been presented is predicated upon the presumption that the experience of white, middle-class, and relatively well-educated Western women can be universally representative of Muslim, "third world," or other minority women. Although such a simplistic idea has been vigorously contested by a whole array of women-of-color feminists—such as Gayatri Chakravorty Spivak, Toni Morrison, Chandra Talpade Mohanty, Gloria Jean Watkins (bell hooks), and Sharin N. Elkholy—Orientalist feminism continues to function on this false premise. Nevertheless, as the chapter on Fatemeh Keshavarz's *Jasmine and Stars* will illustrate, Orientalist feminism is far from uncontested and is often challenged by Middle Eastern, Muslim, and women-of-color feminists questioning the ethos of a brand of feminism that they deem to be shortsightedly white, Western, and universalist.

Post-9/11 Islamophobia and the question of Muslim women are definitive to the production and Western reception of "Muslim" and Middle Eastern memoirs by female authors, since almost all such accounts are highly critical of the authors' countries of origin and the status of Muslim women. It is largely due to this particular historical juncture that what is now considered a phenomenon in the American literary landscape transpired. The post-9/11 US literary market witnessed the burgeoning of Iranian-American self-narratives unprecedented by any other minority group in North America. Sanaz Fotouhi has recorded that only between 2003 and 2011 Iranian women published more than forty books with major publishers, with most offering a belated "yet timely account of the Islamic revolution and its traumatic consequences in hindsight of conflicts between Iran and America" (127). In fact, Fotouhi's exhaustive list of Iranian-American writings includes about 140 works of memoir and fiction produced, predominantly by Iranian women, after 9/11 to early 2012 (229-37).

I should hasten to add that the designation of Azar Nafisi's *Reading Lolita in Tehran* (2003) and Fatemeh Keshavarz's *Jasmine and Stars* (2007) as "post-9/11" memoirs transcends their analysis as merely products of a specific juncture in US history. In other words, the two paradigmatic texts were not merely produced after 9/11, but also display thematic and contextual denominators that distinguish them as literary products of the Iranian diaspora in that particular period in US history. As such, the two texts in question are part of the proliferation of Iranian-American memoirs and belong to the category of academic and journalistic memoirs. They also share the overarching topoi (most importantly the question of Iranian womanhood), the dominant literary genre, and the target Western audience, especially women, that they each attempt to address and educate. Furthermore, they display similar narrative strategies in terms of their investment in the power of firsthand, personal narratives and eyewitness accounts. Both texts also evince strong association with the West (especially through the authors' academic education in the United States and Europe), and position the authors as expert authorities through their academic affiliation with top US universities.

The question of authorial authenticity and authority plays a paramount role in the production, reception, and promotion of these memoirs. In the context of post-9/11 apprehensions and curiosity about the Muslim Other, coupled with widespread public ignorance regarding Islam, these memoirs are often read as "true" accounts. In these narratives, the authors cast themselves as latter-day Scheherazades who, through their storytelling, both recount the "threat" and "depravity" of the Muslim world and manage to "save" themselves (and by extension other "victims"). Thus, the texts in question go beyond their temporal specificity. They are informed by denominators that owed much to the post-9/11 atmosphere which brought the question of Muslim women to the fore of public and political discussions and in the aftermath of which "experts" and "natives" claiming firsthand knowledge of the Muslim Other were in high demand.

The Iranian-American literary landscape, especially after 9/11, is characterized by the predominance of women and, with few exceptions, the absence of men. One such exception is Afshin Molavi, who published two narratives after 9/11: *Persian Pilgrimages: Journeys across Iran* (2002) and *The Soul of Iran* (2005). Nevertheless, owing largely to the controversial 2009 presidential election that brought Iran back to the headlines, a few memoirs by Iranian men have emerged and have been rather well-received in the United States since 2010. *Letters to My Torturer* (2010) by Houshang Asadi (translated into English by Nushin Arabzadeh), *A Time to Betray: The Astonishing Double Life of a CIA Agent Inside the Revolutionary Guards of Iran*

(2010) by Reza Kahlili, and *The Gaze of the Gazelle: The Story of a Generation* (2011) by Arash Hejazi are some of the better-known titles in this latest trend.

The predominance of women in the Iranian-American literary scene after 9/11 can be traced to several factors. Persis M. Karim, who has anthologized three collections of Iranian-American writings,[10] maintains that fulfilling parental expectations and "the exigencies of immigrant life" have left little space for Iranian men in America to pursue literary and poetic aspirations (xx). Also, the rise in the number of Iranian-American women writers is seen as an "outgrowth of Iranian women's specific experiences," in terms of both the special circumstances brought about by migration, which requires reshaping their identities to befit their new context, and the need "to respond to the view of Iranian women purveyed by both the Islamic Republic and the Western media" (Karim xx).

While the reasons offered by Karim sound tenable, there are other factors that have less to do with the actual lives of Iranian-Americans in the United States. One such factor is the high demand in the US literary and media markets for exotic tales from Muslim countries, driven by what Jasmin Darznik has described as "an insatiable curiosity for both the intimate details of [Muslim women's] lives and descriptions of forbidden and alien landscape" ("The Perils" 56). In addition, the sense of urgency and necessity attached to any form of knowledge about the "threat" of Islam and the Middle East in the post-9/11 milieu has been instrumental in the production and reception of such narratives. In this context, the question of Muslim women has been brought to fore by Western feminists who employ "the language of human rights in their struggles to compel states and international organizations to address questions of gender inequality and women's rights" (Fernandes 33). However, when the contextual and historical situatedness and specificity of Muslim women's lives, experiences, and struggles are overlooked, the campaign against the "oppression" of Muslim women, as Chandra Mohanty has effectively argued, results in divesting them of their social and political agency (71).

Memoiring Iran

Equally significant in the discussion of the post-9/11 wave of Iranian-American literary productions is the predominance of the memoir as the genre in which the works of Iranian-American authors have most frequently appeared. What makes the consideration of such texts warranted is the fact that autobiographical writing by women, as we know it today, has never flourished in earnest in the Iranian literary tradition (Milani "Iranian Women" 130; Najmabadi et al.; Whitlock *Soft Weapons* 164). This absence has been mainly attributed to a cultural context that "values and strongly institutionalizes a sharp separation between the inner and the outer, the private and the public," where self-revelation is not normally encouraged (Milani, Iranian Women" 130). This self-censorship, as Milani argues, bespeaks a personal and social internalization of the censorship imposed on Iranian social, political, and literary landscapes for centuries, which manifests itself, among many other things, in the absence of an established autobiographical tradition, not least among women, in contemporary Iran. Concomitant with the notion of self-censorship was the high rate of illiteracy among Iranian women prior to the 1979 revolution, which further impeded any literary self-representation. Nevertheless, this does not mean a total absence of autobiographical writing in Iran; rather, most such instances of life writing were penned by prominent male figures who mostly recounted important historical or political junctures and whose accounts contain little or no information about their private lives.[11]

Some critics have attributed the preference in the Iranian-American literature for the memoir genre partly to the fact that, unlike autobiography, memoir writing is mostly a female domain (Fuchs; Larson 12; Simons). The distinction, however, remains contested, as there are other scholars who maintain that the separation of these terms is elastic, with only recently a distinction on the narrower scope of focus being a parameter that sets a memoir apart from a sometimes longer life representation in autobiography. Nima Naghibi, for instance, has used the terms interchangeably, arguing that "the contemporary abundance of nonfictional self-reflexive narratives tend to challenge the traditional generic and gendered distinctions between the two categories" (80). Naghibi has argued that while the genre of autobiography operated "within an evolutionary model of personal development and was generally understood as a superior form of self-reflexive exercise," memoirs were "perceived to make fewer intellectual demands of the reflecting subject" (79-80).[12] Therefore, given that most Iranian-American memoirs are centered upon specific historical junctures in Iran or on exilic female experiences (or on occasions, a combination of both), the female authors have chosen to articulate their narratives within the framework of a genre that is perceived to be less male-dominated.

One of the most significant theorizations of the memoir genre revolves around the "therapeutic and revelatory" qualities attributed to self-writing (Olson). Suzette A. Henke has designated this mode of writing as "scripto-therapy," which she defines as "the process of writing out and writing through traumatic experiences in the mode of therapeutic reenactment" (xii). This feature, therefore, can partly explain the proliferation of Iranian-American memoirs as part of a larger trend invigorated by an unprecedented number of novice memoirists in the United States. As the majority of Iranian-American memoirists (or their parents) migrated to the United States in the aftermath of the revolution, their accounts are replete with expressions of nostalgic reminiscences, trauma, the desire to return to a "lost" homeland, and the vicissitudes of exilic life. In this light, the memoir constructs a discursive site proffering the potential for self-expression, within which the exilic subject can both maintain and renegotiate her identity. It is through the very process of writing about a traumatic past, the pangs of exile, and often a challenging and ambivalent exilic existence, that the diasporic subject can negotiate their agency and subjectivity. As Henke has observed

> Autobiography has always offered the tantalizing possibility of reinviting the self and reconstructing the subject ideologically inflected by language, history, and

social imbrication. As a genre, life-writing encourages the author/narrator to reassess the past and to reinterpret the intertextual codes inscribed on personal consciousness by society and culture. (xv)

Most Iranian-American authors invest heavily in the articulations of the revolution as a traumatic encounter and a crucial moment in the (re)construction of their identities. As such, they have opted for writing memoirs as a process of therapeutic engagement conducive to the recovery and redefinition of their identities, while often simultaneously envisaging the promise of a better future in their adopted home.

It is precisely because of such potentialities that the memoir genre has also lent itself to being adopted as a site of discursive resistance and a space through which the author can transcend established generic and thematic frontiers by enunciating alternative modes of exilic subjectivity and by writing back to mainstream narratives. In the context of Iranian-American self-narratives, such possibilities enable Keshavarz to articulate a very different Muslim, female, and hyphenated subjectivity than those of dominant Iranian-American memoirs. As Fotouhi has remarked, "[t]he memoir allows for the voices of the marginal to regain their agency and subjectivity through very personal and remembered experiences by transcending boundaries of public/private, dominant/dominated, colonized/colonizer and offering multiplicities of alternative social narratives" (106). As the author of a rare, hence "marginal," Iranian-American memoir, Keshavarz effectively capitalizes on the multiple potentials offered by the genre to craft a memoir which, while working within the established norms of Iranian-American life-writing, manages to challenge and subvert the mainstream representations of Iran and Islam that pervade the accounts of other Iranian-American memoirists.

Paramount in the production and promotion of a memoir is also its perceived truth value, which plays a significant role in its public and critical reception. Paula S. Fass has observed that historians see the memoir as "an important historical tool" (107). She further argues that the contemporary boom in memoir writing is partly "an expression of the widespread engagement with history in the contemporary world" (108). Furthermore, she attributes the genre's appeal to "a growing sense of the speed of change and the declining importance of distance on our planet" (108). Along the same lines, George W. Egerton has proposed that the attractions of the memoir appear "to derive from its capacity to personalize and dramatize political and historical phenomena, while often offering up a fare of sophisticated entertainment" (346).

That memoirs often do offer historical and political insight is beyond question. In the case of post-9/11 Middle Eastern/Muslim memoirs, the fact that the version or selection of the history they recount has significant political implications for their Western audience, and is often in line with the grand narratives promoted by Western governments, lends an additional air of urgency and authority to them. Nevertheless, it is the engagement with the memoir as a "true account" proffering social, historical, and political "facts"—as almost always advertised by the publishers and claimed by the authors—which seems to play the most significant role in the reception and appreciation of memoirs. Capitalizing on their truth claims and written primarily for a Western audience, these memoirs "promise the Western reader access to the East, a promise that invokes a long history of colonial desire to unveil the simultaneously eroticized and abject Muslim woman" (Naghibi 81). An apt example to illustrate the importance of the authenticity factor is the case of Norma Khouri's *Forbidden Love* (Random House, 2003),[13] which recounts the tragic story of the murder of the author's friend, Dalia, in an act of honor killing in Jordan. According to Malcolm Knox, literary editor of the *Sydney Morning Herald*,

> Her tragic story stole readers' hearts and triggered an international outcry. She became a best-selling author in the same league as J. K. Rowling and Michael Moore. She petitioned the United Nations personally, was published in 15 countries, and Australians voted her memoir into their favourite 100 books of all time.

However, Khouri's narrative, as Knox revealed, turned out to be entirely fictitious, as Knox discovered that the author had left Jordan when she was three years old and, therefore, had not been living in the country during the timeframe of her story. The Australian readers, who had purchased 200,000 copies of the book by the time it turned out to be a complete hoax, were, indeed, disappointed and outraged when the truth about the author's highly questionable character and her spurious narrative came to light.

One can perhaps concur with André Gide's observation in his autobiography, *If It Die*, that "[m]emoirs are never more than half sincere, however great the desire for truth. Everything is always more complicated than one makes out" (248). It is against this backdrop that Fatemeh Keshavarz's *Jasmine and Stars* demonstrates the complexities of the genre beyond a simplistic tell-all, "true account" façade. Through an in-depth analysis of the mechanisms of the genre as well as by crafting her own resistant memoir, Keshavarz produces a narrative that operates on a more nuanced and complex level than most other narratives about life in the Middle East, especially the lives of Muslim women.

As yet another testament to the pivotal role of 9/11 in the emergence and reception of Middle Eastern life-writing, some scholars have proposed that the attention paid to Iranian-American memoirs owes mostly to their pertinence to the broader political context of Islam and the Middle East rather than the literary merits of the texts (Adams; Vanzan). Read in this context, the hyphenated authors serve as mediators whose "true" accounts are meant to familiarize Western readers with the "realities" of the Muslim world, especially as regards the status of women. As Ali Behdad has argued,

> That such neo-Orientalist texts are produced, published, and disseminated mainly in the United States and Western Europe suggests that their authors' investment in politics must be understood not as an oppositional demand for human rights or democracy by a subaltern subject but in relation to the neo-imperial interests and interventions of the United States in the region. (288)

I should hasten to add that although the pivotal role of 9/11 and the construction of Iran as an "axis of evil" has been fundamental to the proliferation of Iranian-American memoirs and to securing their success and reception in the West, the role of other significant factors should not be underestimated. One such factor is the rise of the second generation of Iranian-Americans, the majority of whom were either born or grew up in the United States. As such, their language proficiency and fuller immersion in the Western context have enabled them to assume more substantial roles in the production and presentation of their "native" cultures.[14]

While catering to the post-9/11 atmosphere in the United States is often regarded as one of the primary reasons for the burgeoning of Iranian-American memoirs, the urge to write about the vicissitudes of exile, double-marginality, identity crisis, cultural rootlessness, and unbelonging, or what M. Persis Karim (1999) has tersely called "the tension of belonging to both—and neither—Iranian and US cultures" (25), experienced by the second-generation writers, can go a long way toward accounting for the boom in Iranian-American literary productions. The feeling of social ostracism and marginalization experienced by Iranian-American writers was at its peak during the post-revolutionary years, most specifically during the Hostage Crisis. While such accounts of displacement and exilic life are considered more genuine and less controversial, they pale in comparison to the ones with overtly political overtones and implications. Nor are these accounts even remotely as well-received as their neo-Orientalist counterparts, since they do not often conform to the mainstream representations of Iran in the United States and, as such, the expectations of the average Western reader. Indeed, the role of the publishing industry, news media, and associated agencies can hardly be overemphasized in the reception of such memoirs. From a media perspective, such accounts are not often deemed newsworthy. In an interview, Firoozeh Dumas, the only Iranian-American female author who has opted for the medium of humor in her memoirs, *Funny in Farsi: A Memoir of Growing Up Iranian in America* (2003), *Laughing Without an Accent: Adventures of an Iranian American, at Home and Abroad* (2009), and *It Ain't so Awful, Falafel* (2016), summarized the attitude of the media toward Middle Eastern memoirs that do not correspond with the mainstream representations of the Middle East in the United States:

> I have been travelling the country for five and half years, giving speeches. I give keynotes, I speak in colleges, and I have never had national press . . . The truth is what I do is considered "soft news" . . . It's not scary, that's the problem. Shared humanity is considered soft news. But if I had written a book about hating a group of people, I guarantee you would've seen me by now on television. In fact, a few years ago, when *Funny in Farsi*, my first book, was a finalist for Thurber Prize for American Humor, I was scheduled to be on CNN . . . and then the day before I got dumped. And I tuned in the next day because I wanted to know who they had dumped me for. And they dumped me for an author who had written a book about female suicide bombers . . . and I thought here we go again, having something about the Middle East that is frightening. (ForaTv)

The same attitude toward representations of Iran, Islam, and the Middle East in general can be observed across the Western world. The award-winning New Zealand author Jill Worrall thus describes the very difficult experience she had with the publishing industry when trying to publish her 2011 travel narrative, *Two Wings of a Nightingale: Persian Soul, Islamic Heart*:

> This [book] was turned down by so many publishers. One thing that is really depressing is that I had an agent who buffered me from the rejection slips, but once she said, "This publisher said if she'd been arrested or assaulted by a border guard we would've been interested", and that was another rejection. There is no danger in there. I thought publishers would be interested in breaking down stereotypes and what I discovered was most publishers wanted books that reinforced the stereotypes, and that was so difficult. (Nazari, "A Labor of Love" 327)

Another sociocultural factor conducive to the post-9/11 wave of Iranian-American memoirs is the shift in recent decades in the United States toward what Ali Behdad has called

> disclosure as a dominant mode of social relations—a shift evident not only in the rhetoric of the war on terror, which encourages the willing surrender of civil rights for the supposed security of surveillance, but also in the ascendance of reality TV and other tell-tale genres to a position of pop culture dominance. (295)

The tendency for self-disclosure and articulations of one's private life can be observed in a whole array of cultural productions ranging from autoethnographic literary forms to popular American TV series or talk shows[15] wherein people are encouraged to reveal the most private aspects of their personal lives. Similarly, the increasing role that social media networks such as Facebook, Twitter, Instagram, YouTube, and a host of similar online platforms play in people's lives, encouraging constant status updating and photo and video sharing, has significantly contributed to the disclosure trend. The success of neo-Orientalist memoirs, therefore, can also be construed as part of the ascendance of popular genres centering on claims of reality and authenticity.

Undoubtedly, the memoirs produced in the past two decades have been instrumental in making Iranian-American female writers more visible not only in the literary domain, but also in the public and media domains, so much so that automotive manufacturer Audi used an image of Azar Nafisi in one of its famous advertisements, where she is suspended in the air in front of a shelf of books. Besides the vast readership that the major works in the trend in question have attracted, the myriad interviews, book tours, television appearances, book-reading sessions, awards, interviews, and other manners of publicity have certainly lent unprecedented visibility and currency to Iranian-American women authors. Nevertheless, since the preponderance of such narratives operate within a well-established Western (neo-)

Orientalist frame of reference, they have arguably led to even further misrepresentation, marginalization, and, at times demonization, of the people, especially women, living inside Iran. This marginalization is carried out via an Orientalist-feminist outlook that persistently portrays Iranian/Muslim women as veiled, oppressed, and passive victims of a patriarchal culture and deems their liberation possible only through the abandonment of their Islamic faith (exemplified, more than anything else, by the shedding of the veil) and embracing the sociocultural norms of the West.

Ironically, while such works are often deemed to be conducive to the greater visibility of Iranian women living in Iran, by focusing on decontextualized and simplistic accounts of their challenges and religio-cultural norms and values— especially "veiling"— they serve to render them even more "invisible" and "veiled." Throughout her *Jasmine and Stars* (2007), Fatemeh Keshavarz thoroughly demonstrates how the visibility and celebrity of authors like Azar Nafisi in the West are often achieved at the cost of greater invisibility of and disregard for many towering Iranian women in social, political, cultural, and scientific spheres. Such discursive disenfranchisement of Iranian women is carried out through the negation of the multiplicity, vibrancy, and dynamism of Iranian women's lives and their sociopolitical and cultural agency. The established topoi vis-à-vis Iranian/Muslim women obliterate the variegated tapestry of a lively female culture not only of social participation and activism but also of resistance in Iran. This is carried out mostly through denying the many significant improvements in almost every aspect of Iranian women's lives and positing their Western counterparts as a liberated, hence superior, model to aspire to. Such strategies of negation as well as the many manners in which Iranian women continue to assert their pivotal role in the fabric of Iranian society will be elaborated in detail in the exegesis of each text in the following chapters.

From Orientalism to Neo-Orientalism

The main critical framework within which the three selected texts are analyzed derives mainly from Edward Said's critique of Orientalism. In his classic *Orientalism* (1978), Said expounds the dominant attitudes of the West toward the Orient, especially the Muslim and Arab Orient. Such attitudes are exemplified in the enormous corpus of scholarship produced by prominent Western writers within such diverse fields as philology, literature, anthropology, history, geography, philosophy, and psychology. According to Said, in the discourse of Orientalism, the Orient and, by extension Orientals, are viewed as possessing such characteristics as "despotism," "splendor," "cruelty," "sensuality," "irrationality," "depravity," "childlikeness," "difference," "strangeness," "separateness," "eccentricity," "backwardness," "silent indifference," "feminine penetrability," "supine manipulability," "exotic sensuousness," and "inability to self-govern," to mention only a few.

Said proposes several definitions for the concept of Orientalism, each of which tends to focus on one facet of the Orientalist regime of knowledge production and representation. To begin with, Said defines Orientalism as "a way of coming to terms with the Orient that is based on the Orient's special place in European Western experience" (1). He further articulates the concept as "a style of thought based upon an ontological and epistemological distinction made between 'the Orient' and (most of the time) 'the Occident'" (2), and proceeds to elaborate on his formulation of the concept through what he deems to be its hegemonic attributes:

> Orientalism can be discussed and analyzed as the corporate institution for dealing with the Orient—dealing with it by making statements about it, authorizing views of it, describing it, by teaching it, settling it, ruling over it: in short, Orientalism as a Western style for dominating, restructuring, and having authority over the Orient. (3)

Another one of Said's various conceptualizations of Orientalism defines the term as "a manner of regularized (or Orientalized) writing, vision and study, dominated by imperatives, perspectives and ideological biases ostensibly suited to the Orient. The Orient is taught, researched, administered, and pronounced upon in certain discrete ways" (202).

In his conceptualization of Orientalism, Said capitalizes upon Foucault's theorization of the nexus between knowledge and power, demonstrating how the West's modus operandi of producing and promoting knowledge about its Oriental Other is implicated in Western colonization and imperialism in the Orient. Thus, Said's *locus classicus* has it that Orientalist texts "can *create* not only knowledge but also the very reality that they appear to describe" (94). As such, he views Orientalism as "a kind of Western projection onto and will to govern over the Orient" (95). In other words, as Said avers along the same Foucauldian lines,

> Ideas, cultures, and histories cannot seriously be understood or studied without their force, or more precisely their configurations of power, also being studied ... The relationship between Occident and Orient is a relationship of power, of domination, of varying degrees of a complex hegemony. (5)

It is precisely because of the nexus between discourse and power that the texts chosen in this book are situated in the broader historico-political contexts of their production. These texts are investigated with attention to the manner in which they serve to reinforce certain political agendas pursued by different US governments apropos the Middle East and, in particular, Iran.

As seminal and groundbreaking as Said's theorization of Orientalism, in its many modes, functions, and manifestations, has been, it has had its fair share of criticisms and counter-responses. One common criticism leveled against Said is that he does not sufficiently acknowledge previous scholarship on Orientalism in earlier studies of such disciplinary areas as philology, Islamic Studies, anthropology, history, philosophy, and sociology. This, as Ziauddin Sardar avers, makes Said's contribution seem "to have emerged ready-made and fully-fledged, as though from nowhere, and proceeded to shape and dominate the debate"

(66). In fact, Sardar goes as far as insinuating that Said's contribution to the field, on purely scholarly terms, is neither unique nor more substantial than his predecessors. However, he does admit that Said's work enkindled a vigorous and long-standing debate "focused specifically on something called 'the Orient'" (67).

Perhaps the main criticism of Said's Orientalism, however, is the most ironic one: that like the Western discourse it criticizes, Said's treatment of Orientalism is monolithic and overlooks diversities, pluralities, eclecticism, and nuances. In "Orientalism and its Problems" (1994), for instance, Dennis Porter argues that

> Unlike Foucault, who posits not a continuous discourse over time but epistemological breaks between different periods, Said asserts the unified character of Western discourse on the Orient over some two millennia, a unity derived from a common and continuous experience of fascination with and threat from the East, of its irreducible otherness. (130)

Inasmuch as the current study is concerned, even though Said makes a few references to the images of ancient Persia in Aeschylus's *The Persians*, there is an almost total absence of modern Iran in *Orientalism*. This is significant since, due to the reasons mentioned earlier, Iran has always occupied a paramount locus in the geopolitics of the Middle East both prior to and after the 1979 Islamic Revolution and has always figured prominently in the Western imaginary. In this light, one could argue that Said's Orient is mostly trammeled by the geographical specificity of the so-called Arab world. This can be partly attributed to Said's own Arab/Palestinian background and, ipso facto, his greater familiarity with Arab territories and their figurations.

Nevertheless, Said partially remedies this lacuna first in a series of articles published on the Islamic Revolution and the Hostage Crisis in Iran[16] and then in his *Covering Islam: How the Media and the Experts Determine How We See the Rest of the World* (1981), which deals extensively with US media representations of the 1979 Islamic Revolution and the Hostage Crisis. In this important work, Said draws attention to and questions broadcast and press media images of Iranians, among others, as a violent, "anonymous," "deindividualized," and "dehumanized" mob (6, 35, 43, 48, 86, 87, 95, 101), and the revolution as driven primarily by "Islamic fanaticism." Significantly, such stereotypes pervade the first two texts critiqued in this book.

The criticisms of Said's model of Orientalism notwithstanding, his theorization of the concept proves particularly instrumental in constructing a theoretical framework within which to probe representations of Iran and Islam in the West. Although Said does not deal with modern Iran in his magnum opus, his meticulous observations on Islam and other Muslim nations are greatly useful in providing a critical vocabulary with which to investigate representations of Iran in post-9/11 Iranian-American literature.

Against the backdrop of what some critics have perceived to be Said's overlooking of the heterogeneities of the subjects of representation, Homi K. Bhabha has theorized the notions of "ambivalence" and "mimicry" in colonial discourse, which serve to undermine Said's dichotomous epistemology by crafting a space for resisting the hegemony of colonial discourses. "The question of the representation of difference," Bhabha contends in his influential *The Location of Culture* (1994), "is always also a problem of authority" (89). In this light, Bhabha's notion of "mimicry" can be helpful in understanding some of the questions of authority, authenticity, and authorial positionality—what I will be calling "double-situatedness"—in Iranian-American memoirs. Bhabha defines colonial mimicry as "the desire for a reformed, recognizable Other, as *a subject of a difference that is almost the same, but not quite*. Which is to say, that the discourse of mimicry is constructed around an ambivalence" (86). He proceeds to further elaborate on the notion, remarking that mimicry is "the sign of a double articulation; a complex strategy of reform, regulation and discipline, which 'appropriates' the Other as it visualizes power" (86). In the context of the current study, the "hybrid" or hyphenated subjectivity of Iranian-American authors makes it possible to somewhat view their positionality in light of Bhabha's theorizations of mimicry and ambivalence in (self-)representations of colonial subjects.

Other derivatives of Orientalism have proven particularly expedient in shedding light on certain aspects of the texts under study. One such offshoot of Orientalism is the concept of auto-Orientalism. Put succinctly, auto-Orientalism is self-discourse about Orientals by themselves (Carrier 36; Lie 5), mirrored in the representing subject's deployment of "a native or seminative insider tone" (Keshavarz, *Jasmine and Stars* 3). In the current study, the concept has been employed to illuminate the situatedness and authority of the author in the exegesis of *Reading Lolita in Tehran* and *Jasmine and Stars*. In a similar fashion, the concept of strategic auto-Orientalism has been adopted from Gayatri Spivak's theorization of a "strategic" employment of "essentialism" (183). Such strategic intervention is conducted through finessing the fluid nature of particular "essences" to discursively intervene in and negotiate constructions of the Other without necessarily consolidating them. This useful concept is instrumental in the discussions of resistance against the discursive hegemony of Orientalist narratives in the chapter on *Jasmine and Stars*.

Given the centrality of representations of women in both Western and Middle Eastern narratives on Iran and Islam, postcolonial and "Third World" feminist scholars have paid particular critical attention to such representations. In her *Inessential Woman: Problems of Exclusion in Feminist Thought* (1988), Elizabeth V. Spelman avers that "the real problem" of certain brands of Western feminism is how they have "confused the condition of one group of women with the condition of all" (4). In other words, much of Western scholarship on "Third World" women is informed by the "universalism it assumes in encoding and representing all third world women as victims of an ahistorical and decontextualized notion of patriarchy that results in a homogenous notion of the oppressed third world women" (Elkholy).

The irony in such a universalist feminist discourse is that such homogenization and essentialization of womanhood, as Chandra Mohanty has also argued, "colonizes and appropriates the pluralities of the simultaneous location of different groups of women in social class and ethnic frameworks" (72). There lies, nonetheless, a greater irony in both the vocabulary of the universalist Western feminism that insists on representing Muslim women as "oppressed" and victims of "Islamic" violence—images that only serve to further Orientalize and "oppress" them. The irony is further compounded by interventionist US policies in the Middle East, which, among other things, are perpetrated under the pretext of "liberating" Muslim women. This irony is the "blindness of first world complicity in various forms of third world oppressions" (Elkholy) best exemplified in the role of the United States in aiding and abetting regimes that commit the violence (Fernandes 34). This is most obvious in the case of such countries as Saudi Arabia, which remains a key US ally in the region but possesses an abysmal record on human, and especially women's, rights.

While the general theoretical scaffolding of this book is informed by Said's theorization of Orientalism, it is within the framework of what scholars have termed a "Neo/New Orientalist" discourse that the works critiqued in this study can be best understood. Succinctly defined, neo-Orientalism, according to Behdad and Williams, is "a mode of representation that while indebted to classical Orientalism, engenders new tropes of othering" (284).

A latter-day version of its nineteenth-century European forebear, neo-Orientalism displays distinctive characteristics that serve to distinguish it from its classical predecessor. In the following, I will first enumerate some of the similarities between the two concepts and proceed to articulate some of their differences, as proposed by two prominent Iranian-American critics, Professors Fatemeh Keshavarz and Ali Behdad. Following Behdad, I opt for the term *neo-*Orientalism (rather than Keshavarz's *New* Orientalism) to highlight the discursive continuity and internal consistency between the classical and more recent modes of Orientalist representation.

What Said has called the "internal consistency" (*Orientalism* 5) of Orientalism can be observed in the fact that, although conditioned by very different historico-political contexts and produced by natives/semi-natives, the neo-Orientalist Middle Eastern narratives are as "monolithic, totalizing, reliant on a binary logic, and based on an assumption of moral and cultural superiority over the Oriental other" as their classical Western precursors (Behdad and Williams 284). Ironically, indeed, such narratives have proven to be as, if not more, silencing, polarizing, and oppressive as the "primitive" cultures and societies they denigrate. Within this course, the multiplicity, heterogeneity, and nuances of the subjects of representation are often stifled under the authoritative, dominant voice of the author who, more often than not, appropriates and rehashes Orientalist tropes in representing the Oriental Other. As in classical Orientalist narratives, the essentialization of the Other is carried out through the deployment of discursive strategies such as negation, affirmation, oversimplification, dehistoricization, decontextualization, feminization, infantilization, exoticization, and eroticization. These discursive strategies produce a monochromatic image of the Other, which completely obliterates what Keshavarz has termed the "multihued tapestry of human voice and experience" in the lives of Middle Eastern subjects (*Jasmine and Stars* 5).

In a similar vein, like its classical precedent, as a major strategy for constructing an inferior Other, the neo-Orientalist discourse attributes anything that is "too impressive to be considered inferior . . . to a glorious but discontinued past" (Keshavarz *Jasmine and Stars* 3). In the case of Iran—and Islam, too—this discursive strategy is practiced much more frequently, given the country's ancient history as one of the world's greatest empires and civilizations. This strategy is most obvious in Nafisi's *Reading Lolita in Tehran* where the contemporary Iranian society is portrayed as devoid of any literary tradition and Persian classical literary masterpieces are rendered anachronistic and attributed to an irretrievable, irrelevant, and long-bygone past.

There are, however, significant features that distinguish neo-Orientalist narratives from their precursors. First, the provenance of neo-Orientalism is often located in the United States, rather than in Europe, yet the phenomenon transcends the geographical boundaries of the United States to include other European countries, especially England, France, and Germany, albeit to a lesser extent. Likewise, in distinction to classical Orientalism, neo-Orientalist narratives are not predominantly produced by Western subjects. Rather, they are mainly authored by Middle Eastern writers, intellectuals, "experts," non-professional writers, or fake authors producing out-and-out hoaxes (as in the case of Norma Khouri's *Forbidden Love*), many of whom have become celebrities or pursued political or academic positions after the publication of their narratives. Also, whereas classical Orientalists were commonly male European intelligentsia, missionaries, and scholars, neo-Orientalist authors tend to be predominantly female "natives" whose assumption of authenticity authorizes their discourse. Moreover, their investment in the "moral authority" and "special immunity" they often enjoy as "heroes" and ostensible survivors of "Islamic fundamentalism," "patriarchy," "discrimination," and "violence" often renders them almost "impervious to critique" in their popular reception (Behdad and Williams 295). This fact is reflected, among other things, in the disproportionate praise lavished on such narratives in the extraordinary number of rave reviews published on them.

What further distinguishes classical Orientalism from its contemporary counterpart is the popularity, immediacy, and accessibility of the neo-Orientalist discourse made possible by the ascendancy of the age of information technology in its multifarious forms such as news, video, and social media platforms (Behdad and Williams 284). Furthermore, both the self-proclaimed authenticity and the accessibility of neo-Orientalist accounts, or what Behdad has called "a journalistic pretense of direct access to truth and the real" (284), contrasts the "will to knowledge" of classical Orientalism (Said *Orientalism* 272). Insofar as the historical specificity of such accounts is concerned, one could safely claim that with very few exceptions, the neo-Orientalist narratives—whether authored by Iranian-Americans or other Middle Easterners—have been published in the United States in the aftermath of 9/11, and informed by the urgency and yearning to represent the "threat" of the Muslim Other often represented in the prevalent figure of the terrorist or fundamentalist.

The other significant characteristic of neo-Orientalist narratives is their open and "unapologetic investment in and engagement with the politics of the Middle

East" (Behdad and Williams 285). While Orientalist narratives served to justify the colonial presence of Europe in the Orient, this purpose was mostly achieved through a narration that rendered the natives as essentially inferior to their Western colonizers and, therefore, in need of being "civilized" and "liberated" (Keshavarz, *Jasmine and Stars* 2). Not only do neo-Orientalist authors partake openly in the politics of their countries, but they are also at times recruited and promoted by Western political establishments that benefit from such representations. This is evident in the case of Azar Nafisi's alignment with the neoconservative coterie in the United States, which will be elaborated in greater detail in the chapter on *Reading Lolita in Tehran*.

Equally important in the construction of neo-Orientalist discourses is what Behdad and Williams have termed "ahistorical historicism." In essence, the term entails various modes of historical misrepresentation and falsification of current historico-political events in the Middle East coupled with the denial of the United States' neo-imperialistic agendas in the region (285). Thus, for example, while both Mahmoody and Nafisi misrepresent such landmark events in contemporary Iranian history as the Islamic Revolution and the Iran–Iraq War, they simultaneously engage in the utter negation of the role of the United States and the West in both events. Such blatant instances of negation are made all the more expedient by the general Western readers' unfamiliarity with the history and politics of the Middle East, on the one hand, and Islam, on the other.

Apropos the major tropes of Othering, the neo-Orientalist discourse capitalizes on the whole array of essentialist Orientalist motifs, such as the barbarism, violence, primitiveness, backwardness, licentiousness, animality, ignorance, and philistinism of the Oriental Other, but is most specifically obsessed with a re-appropriation of the topos of the veil as the key signifier of Muslim women's "oppression" and "victimization." While the classical Orientalist discourse employed the veil primarily to exoticize the Oriental woman and metonymize images of the harem as a space charged with Oriental mysteriousness, sensuality, and inaccessibility (à la *One Thousand and One Nights*), the neo-Orientalist discourse deploys the veil as the emblem of Muslim women's alleged oppression and invisibility (Behdad and Williams 285). In their Orientalist-feminist frame of reference, such accounts represent the veil as the principal impediment to Muslim women's visibility, mobility, and the realization of their "true" subjectivity. As a result, they reinforce the binary opposition between a free, civilized, secular, and democratic West vis-à-vis an oppressed, primitive, and tyrannical Orient. In other words, the veil functions as a discursive site within which a civilizing relationship is forged between the West and its Muslim Other and "sanctions a paternalistic and neo-imperial relation between the west and Muslim societies by enabling a discourse of rescue" (Behdad and Williams 294).

Unlike their classical counterparts, some of the neo-Orientalist narratives, particularly *Reading Lolita in Tehran*, are characterized by a hybrid nature in that they adopt an informal tone, often in the form of addressing the reader directly, while at times engaging simultaneously in academic or literary commentary to further establish the "expert" status of the author. However, this does not mean that the first-person narration or the employment of an informal tone is unique to neo-Orientalist discourses, as they are often quite common denominators of a variety of other autobiographical modes of writing. Rather, they are features that both characterize neo-Orientalist writings and partially set them apart from their classical predecessors. While this feature is not shared by all neo-Orientalist memoirs, it does figure prominently in the memoirs by Nafisi and Keshavarz. Nevertheless, as Keshavarz has demonstrated, almost all neo-Orientalist narratives capitalize on "the power of personal voice, nostalgia in exilic literature, the assurance that comes with insider knowledge, and the certainty of eyewitness accounts" (*Jasmine and Stars* 4). These features, indeed, go a long way toward explaining the popularity and truth value of such texts in the West.

The truth claim of neo-Orientalist narratives can help account for another one of their common denominators. Despite their unprecedented popularity in the West, the neo-Orientalist accounts are rarely translated into the native language of their authors. In the case of Iranian-American memoirs, the only exceptions are Firouzeh Dumas's *Funny in Farsi: A Memoir of Growing Up Iranian in America* (2003) and *Laughing without an Accent: Adventures of a Global Citizen* (2008), which seem to have been published mostly on account of their effective employment of humor in a personal narrative that does not capitalize on demonization of its subject for its popular reception. Besides their highly contested truth value, the unavailability of such translations in native tongues may be attributed to their lack of literary and artistic merits compared with indigenous and foreign literary productions, their formulation within and prioritization of a Western frame of reference with which few native readers would identify, their unapologetic demonization of Middle Eastern and Islamic cultures, as well as state censorship.

Representing Iran: A Tour D'horizon

Since this book navigates a whole array of concepts such as Orientalism, feminism, captivity narratives, reception, and resistance to hegemonic discourses, a vast body of literature on the mentioned subjects has been drawn upon in the critique of the selected narratives. Some of the most significant critical studies referenced in the book provide a general framework for critiquing Western representations of the Iranian/Muslim Other, such as the works of Said, Bhabha, Keshavarz, and Behdad, some of which were briefly discussed in the foregoing discussions of the book's theoretical frameworks. There are other significant texts, such as Edward Said's *Culture and Imperialism* (1993), which similarly furnish a critical apparatus in discussions of resistance against the hegemony of the colonial/Orientalist discourse. Also, Parvin Paidar's seminal study, *Women and the Political Process in Twentieth Century Iran* (1995), builds on Said's theorization of Orientalism to formulate the interconnected lineaments of Orientalist feminism. The following offers an overview of some of the major literature most apposite to the subject of each chapter.

Despite the enormous popularity of Betty Mahmoody's *Not without My Daughter*, very few critical analyses of the memoir have been conducted. In fact, responses to the book were mostly restricted to highly acclamatory book (and film) reviews and passing references in discussions of broader relevant issues. The only major work has been Deborah Cunningham Walker's Master of Arts thesis, *Veiled Images: Eurocentrism in "Not without My Daughter"* (1999), which examines Eurocentric media stereotypes in the cinematic adaptation of the book. While Walker's study does offer some valuable insights to Western readers, what is particularly ironic in her analysis is that it betrays the author's unfamiliarity with some basic sociocultural facts about the country and religion she sets out to demystify. For instance, Walker's analysis suffers from a persistent Western conflation of Iranians with Arabs. Even though the author provides a historical overview of the country from the Persian Empire down to the Iran–Iraq War, she employs the term "Arabic" interchangeably with Persian, Iranian, and Muslim, and often contextualizes many contemporary Iranian cultural traditions in terms of tribal and Bedouin, no less, Arab mores (62, 67, 69, 72, 73, 94).[17] Such instances of confusion and misinformation are a further testament not only to the prevalence of misrepresentations of Iran in Western media and popular culture but, woefully, also to an inexcusable negligence and inaccuracy in academic and scholarly studies of Iran and Islam.

Until not very long ago the existing literature on Iranian-American narratives was unsurprisingly scant—a fact that is consistent with the meager contribution of Iranian-Americans to the pre-9/11 US literary market. However, as the body of Iranian-American literature has been rapidly expanding, more critical responses, mostly by Iranian scholars or hyphenated Iranians in the West, have begun to dominate the landscape of Iranian-American literary scholarship. This book, therefore, is situated within a rather nascent critical terrain in a way that is in dialogue with the scholarship in the field. It also addresses lacunae and areas underexplored by other scholars, not only through its engagement with the issue of representation, but also by devoting two of the three chapters to works that remain either pitifully understudied (as in the case of Mahmoody's memoir) or that have not received the critical attention they deserve (as is the case of *Jasmine and Stars*). Therefore, it is both through its methodology and the selection of texts that this book asserts a distinct place in the ongoing scholarship on Iranian-American memoirs.

One major cluster of studies on Iranian-American literary productions addresses broader issues of autobiographical writing and analyzes such works primarily in terms of the conditions of exile, trauma, nostalgia, memory, identity, coming of age, displacement, and homecoming.[18] Even though such critical studies have at times been drawn upon in this book and do serve to contextualize and demonstrate the heterogeneity of the Iranian-American autobiographical landscape, they do not feature significantly in this study for their lack of engagement with the problematics of representation, especially Orientalist representation, and their broader implications in the context of the post-9/11 era.

Owing to the multifaceted narrative quality of *Reading Lolita in Tehran*, which interweaves social and political commentary, personal anecdotes, and literary discussions, not to mention the many highly contentious assertions and assumptions made in the text, Nafisi's memoir has elicited far more critical responses than any other Iranian-American memoir to date. The titles of most such responses imitate or are variations on the title of Nafisi's memoir—a fact that further testifies to the controversial nature of a text the contentiousness of which, as the chapter on *Reading Lolita in Tehran* will illustrate, begins from its very title and cover image.[19] While some of the critical responses to *Reading Lolita in Tehran* engage more specifically with the question of (teaching English) literature in the memoir,[20] others focus on a variety of feminist representational politics. Interestingly, all studies focusing specifically on the politics of teaching English literature and its implications are carried out by Western scholars, as opposed to studies on the politics of representation and identity that are conducted predominantly by Iranian and hyphenated Iranian academics.

The most significant and exhaustive critique of *Reading Lolita in Tehran* is Professor Fatemeh Keshavarz's *Jasmine and Stars: Reading More Than Lolita in Tehran* (2007). In her memoir, which blends personal reminiscences, social commentary, and meticulous literary analyses of prominent Persian literary texts with a critique of Nafisi's *Reading Lolita in Tehran*, Keshavarz posits *Reading Lolita in Tehran* as the "New Orientalist" memoir *par excellence*. The text also resembles Nafisi's narrative thematically more than any other Iranian-American memoir. Keshavarz criticizes what she terms the "New Orientalist" discourse, epitomized by Nafisi's memoir, for its lack of specificity, demonization of Muslim cultures, and almost total negation of indigenous literary, artistic, social, and political dynamism in Iran. In so doing, she also constructs her own counterhegemonic discourse by highlighting what the "New Orientalist" narratives characteristically tend to disregard and marginalize. In foregrounding her authorial voice, Keshavarz capitalizes on personal reminiscences, her identification with both Eastern and Western cultures and civilizations, and her knowledge of both Persian and English literatures to effectively construct a narrative that is as counter-Orientalist as Nafisi's is (neo-)Orientalist.

Professor Hamid Dabashi's 2007 *Native Informers and the Making of the American Empire* also bears noting as the most controversial and astringent response to Nafisi's memoir. In his critique of the memoir, published on Al-Ahram Weekly, Dabashi expounds the "politically expedited collective amnesia --of manufacturing consent" in the West for US military interventionism in a period he characterizes as the most belligerent in US history. He effectively demonstrates how Nafisi's *Reading Lolita in Tehran* and a host of kindred memoirs and works of fiction are implicated in US (neo-)imperialism and in cultivating US public opinion against Iran, and by extension the broader Middle East, by cannibalizing the predicament of Muslim women and placing it "squarely at the service of the US ideological psy-op, militarily stipulated in the US global warmongering." He further buttresses his hypothesis by revealing Nafisi's political links to major American neoconservative figures such as Bernard Lewis and Paul Wolfowitz, both of whom were major proponents of the US wars in Iraq and Afghanistan. Also, Dabashi excoriates Nafisi for what he deems to be her total elimination of the contemporary literary tradition in Iran and "positing English literature yet again as a modus operandi of manufacturing trans-regional cultural consent to Euro-American global domination" after the fashion of nineteenth-century British colonialism. While some scholars contend that Dabashi has gone too far in his criticism of Nafisi (Byrne "A Collision"), his article is useful in highlighting the interface between literature—and more broadly, culture—and hegemony/imperialism. In so doing, indeed, Dabashi is following in the footsteps of his late colleague at Colombia University, Edward Said.

Contrary to Nafisi's memoir, due to its much less controversial and more even-handed treatment of the vast range of cultural, political, and social issues it covers, *Jasmine and Stars* has elicited far fewer critical responses. Manijeh Mannani's *Reading beyond Jasmine and Stars: Reading More than Lolita in Tehran* (2009) remains the major critical response to Keshavarz's memoir hitherto. In her criticism of Keshavarz's memoir, Mannani fulminates against Keshavarz for what she perceives to be her alleged possession of "an infallible memory," her "beautification of the Iranian culture," and a criticism of Nafisi's memoir that is "far from objective and realistic" (322-3). Eventually, though, Mannani's whitewashing of Nafisi's numerous exaggerations, sociohistorical falsifications, and distaste for things Iranian and Islamic, coupled with her vitriol against *Jasmine and Stars*, reduces her response to an ad hominem attack on Keshavarz and her work.

Apart from the foregoing studies, a number of important theses and dissertations on Iranian-American memoirs have also been written, again mostly by Iranian or hyphenated Iranian scholars. Like other critical responses mentioned earlier, such academic attention to the phenomenon of post-9/11 Iranian-American literary productions has been largely on account of the sudden visibility of Iranian-American memoirs and their authors' newfound agency as cultural and political "mediators" and "experts" on issues related to Iran and Islam. Also, such studies have occasionally been framed as a way of writing back to the blinkered representations and the dominance of such narratives in the West. Some of the major academic studies are Sara Saljoughi's *Whiteness, Orientalism and Immigration: A Critique of Two Iranian Exilic Memoirs* (2008),[21] Katayoun Zarei Toossi's *Dislodging (New) Orientalist Frames of Reference: Muslim Women in Diasporic and Immigrant Muslim Anglophone Narratives* (2012),[22] Cyrus Amiri's *Two Thousand and One Scheherazades: Images of the Father and "Fatherland" in Post-9/11 Novels and Memoirs by Women of the Iranian Diaspora* (2013),[23] Zeinab Ghasemi Tari's *The Politics of Knowledge and Post-Revolutionary Iran: An Analysis of the Iranian Studies Journal and Iranian-American Memoirs (1979-2012)* (2015),[24] Jasmin Darznik's *Writing Outside the Veil: Literature by Women of the Iranian Diaspora* (2007),[25] and Sanaz Fotouhi's *Ways of Being, Lines of Becoming: A Study of Post-Revolutionary Diasporic Iranian Literature in English* (2012).[26]

One important study that this book draws upon in the discussion of auto-Orientalism is Martina Koegeler's *American Scheherazades—Auto-orientalism, Literature and the Representations of Muslim Women in a Post 9/11 U.S. Context* (2012). Koegeler's study offers a comparative juxtaposition of two works by Arab-American writer Mohja Kahf—her novel *The Girl in the Tangerine Scarf* (2006) and her volume of poetry, *Emails from Scheherazad* (2003)—with Nafisi's memoir.

In this important study, Koegeler sets out to demonstrate how "Arab/Muslim American women writers employ varying forms of auto-orientalism to gain access to the US literary market via the citation of orientalist tropes and thus actively participate in the majority discourses surrounding Islam, Muslim women and Americanness" (iii).

What distinguishes the current study from its predecessors is that it is the first study that focuses specifically on paradigmatic representations of Iran (rather than random texts) both pre- and post-9/11 and also engages with the question of resistance to the neo-Orientalist discourse in Iranian-American self-narratives. It is also the only substantial piece of research hitherto that offers an in-depth textual critique of the works of Betty Mahmoody and Fatemeh Keshavarz. Also, even though critiques of *Reading Lolita in Tehran* figure in some of the studies mentioned above, they are mostly focused on one particular aspect of the memoir, whereas this book attempts to cover as many facets of Nafisi's narrative as the space of this work allows. These distinctive features are further explained in the following organization of the study.

Organization of the book

This book is organized in five chapters. Besides the opening and closing chapters, the main textual and contextual analyses of the narratives under study are organized in a three-tier design, dealing respectively with Betty Mahmoody's *Not without My Daughter* (1987), Azar Nafisi's *Reading Lolita in Tehran: A Memoir in Books* (2003), and Fatemeh Keshavarz's *Jasmine and Stars: Reading Beyond Lolita in Tehran* (2007). These texts share a number of characteristics that explain their selection for the purposes of this book. First, all three texts enjoy an iconic status in their significance to the Western discourse vis-à-vis Iran and Islam, their reception by the Western readership, the (neo-)Orientalist (and counter-Orientalist in the case of *Jasmin and Stars*) discourse that each exemplifies, and their broader implications both for the Iranian Other they tend to represent and for the American audiences they intend to reach. Thus, Betty Mahmoody's bestselling *Not without My Daughter*, critiqued in Chapter 2, epitomizes representations of post-revolutionary Iran before 9/11. The third chapter engages in a critical exegesis of Azar Nafisi's highly contentious *Reading Lolita in Tehran*, as the quintessential post-9/11 Iranian-American memoir.[27] Fatemeh Keshavarz's *Jasmine and Stars* is the topic of the fourth chapter, which is selected as the most significant memoir to date that both diverges from the (neo-)Orientalist discourse exemplified by the first two texts and simultaneously seeks to subvert it.

In addition to the iconic status these texts enjoy, they all rely in their representations on thematic commonalities specific to post-revolutionary Iran: the 1979 Islamic Revolution, the 1980 Iraqi-imposed war on Iran, the Islamic faith, and the question of Iranian/Muslim women, particularly the veil. Similarly, even though they are at times referred to broadly as autobiographical writings by Iranian-American women, the texts under study fall more specifically within the genre of memoir writing. As such, each of the three texts focuses principally on particular junctures in the life of the autobiographical narrator. While Mahmoody's account chronicles her "captivity" in Iran in the mid-1980s (a few years after the Islamic Revolution and amid the Iran–Iraq War), Nafisi's memoir recounts the same turbulent period of revolution and war in the longer span of almost two decades. In a similar vein, Keshavarz's narrative engages with the questions of the revolution and war, returning to them on different occasions, but also frequently draws on recollections of her childhood and early youth and her experience of life in Europe and the United States. In this sense, one could say that Keshavarz's narrative is characterized by a more dispersed and disjointed temporality than the other two memoirs, mostly due to the fact that she has organized her narrative based on particular prominent figures in her life—the titular "stars"—rather than specific historical junctures.

The three chosen memoirs also share another significant feature. All three texts are written by women whose claims of belonging to both the Western and Eastern worlds, through birth, education, and having lived in both hemispheres, go a long way toward qualifying them for representing Iran and Islam and imparting a certain (implicit and explicit) authority and authenticity to their authorial voice and their representations. In this light, the works of all three authors can be broadly defined as belonging to the body of Iranian-American literature in English and published in the United States.

Besides the denominators all three texts share, there are also contextual elements that are shared alternately between two of the texts. For instance, both *Not without My Daughter* and *Reading Lolita in Tehran* achieved bestseller status on *The New York Times* bestseller list ("Paperback Best Sellers"). This bears particular significance, since it further corroborates the iconic status of each text and its enthusiastic reception in the West, thereby further justifying their selection as paradigmatic texts operating within a (neo-)Orientalist paradigm. Furthermore, both *Reading Lolita in Tehran* and *Jasmine and Stars* can be designated as academic memoirs, not only because both authors are academics by profession, but also because they are both literature professors and their works engage in serious and in-depth discussions of English and Persian literatures, respectively. In addition, both authors belong to the "first-generation" women of the Iranian-American diaspora—a fact that renders the comparative analysis of their works more warranted. In this light, one could argue that Nafisi's memoir is well placed as the intermediate body chapter of the book, since, on the one hand, it best exemplifies the consummation of an Orientalist discourse vis-à-vis Iran initiated in earnest after the Islamic Revolution by *Not without My Daughter*; on the other hand, due to the many thematic and structural commonalities between Nafisi's memoir and that of Keshavarz, it serves as a bridge between *Not without My Daughter* and *Jasmine and Stars*, making for a smooth transition from discussions of (neo-)Orientalist discourse and Western hegemony toward a different narrative of resistance and subversion.

The choice of Mahmoody's memoir along with other (more strictly) "Iranian-American" memoirs needs to be further qualified. The initial idea for this book was to investigate specifically the upsurge in the production of Iranian-American memoirs written by female authors of the Iranian diaspora in the post-9/11 United States and to focus on representations of Iran in some of the bestselling titles. Nevertheless, as the extensive preliminary readings of the existing literature progressed, the thematic and conceptual impress of Mahmoody's memoir revealed itself. Hence, owing both to its pioneering status in Western representations of post-revolutionary Iran and to the striking similarity between the representational modus operandi of the post-9/11 memoirs with this text, the scope of the study was extended to include *Not without My Daughter* (1987),[28] a modern American captivity narrative *par excellence*, which remains "the most popular book ever published in the US about Iran" to date (Milani "On Women's Captivity" 43).

Beside its paradigmatic status in Western literary representations of post-revolutionary Iran, there were other factors that justified the choice of Mahmoody's memoir. Even though Mahmoody may not strictly belong to the category of "Iranian-American," the US-born author was married to an Iranian doctor and spent about two years in the country. Hence, like all Iranian-American memoirs, the purchase of this dual-situatedness—that is, the compradorial, intermediary position—serves to sanction the assumption of "privileged" access to inside information. This serves to authorize Mahmoody's consideration along with the other two Iranian-American authors whose hyphenated identity allegedly empowers them to represent, or rather produce, their native country for the consumption of their Western audience. Also, Mahmoody's work shares the majority of the thematic and formal lineaments of the memoirs that would emerge in the post-9/11 milieu. Another major factor—and a major challenge, indeed—in the choice of Mahmoody's work was the fact that, as previously mentioned, no significant scholarly critique of Mahmoody's book was found at the time of writing this book and discussions of the book were confined to book reviews and passing references in the analysis of other texts and broader concepts. This limitation made the effort all the more worthwhile to critique *the* paradigmatic contemporary Western text in representations of post-revolutionary Iran, shedding light on its rhetoric of Orientalist Othering as well as its reception in the West. It is, therefore, only apt to initiate the analysis of literary representations of post-revolutionary Iran by critiquing Mahmoody's memoir.

Throughout her memoir, Mahmoody draws heavily on what she postulates as irresolvable differences between Eastern and Western cultures and, as is characteristic of Orientalist writings, her text reinforces the idea of such essential differences by positioning them on a value-laden binary of a "civilized" West vis-à-vis its "primitive" Oriental Other. By virtue of the authority vested in her, due to her Westernness, as someone able to allegedly see through the Muslim, Oriental psyche,[29] and her access to private Iranian spaces, Mahmoody sees it fit to conclude that Iranians are filthy (15, 23, 27, 28, 31, 32, 36, 37, 65, 85, 231, 335), scheming (220), corrupt (17), violent (21), hostile (342), lazy (429), eager to kill (203), unorganized (35), unpredictable (342), animal-like (41), and strange (45). Through such representations, Mahmoody forges an Iranian Other that best corresponds with the image of the Iranian enemy that the United States has been promulgating since the 1979 Islamic Revolution. It is, therefore, little wonder that the American judge who eventually issued the divorce decree said in an interview that "If I were in control of this country, there'd be a lot of dead Iranians."

The trajectory from the critique of Mahmoody's memoir to Nafisi's is informed by an Orientalist discursive continuity which regurgitates many of the underlying motifs of *Not without My Daughter* against a similar sociopolitical background, but discussed through the lens of British and American literary classics and published in the post-9/11 age. This "internal consistency of Orientalist discourse," as Jamal Eddine Benhayoun has argued, "is meant to perpetuate and naturalise the practice of polarizing the world in terms of Manichean categories such as Self and Other, Orient and Occident, and Western and anti-Western" (119). Furthermore, both narratives are characterized by a blurring of the boundaries of fact and fiction, where history is perpetually dehistoricized, decontextualized, and fictionalized and fiction and myths are historicized and passed as facts. The chapter on *Reading Lolita in Tehran*, thus, offers a brief synopsis of Nafisi's bestselling memoir and proceeds to examine both its popular and critical reception in the West. In my critique of Nafisi's memoir, I have attempted to cover the wide range of issues the text capitalizes on in its neo-Orientalist construction of post-revolutionary Iran. Thus, the chapter offers an in-depth reading of the representations of Iranian/Muslim women as "damsels in distress" and focuses on the topos of the veil in the context of the Orientalist feminism conducive to the perpetuation of such images. Taking into account the political zeitgeist of the memoir's release time (i.e., the post-9/11 atmosphere), the chapter also demonstrates the interface between representations of Iran and Islam and the US neoconservative political agenda in the Middle East. Furthermore, a discussion of the text's controversial front cover as well as the appropriation of Western literature as a "liberating" medium for Iranian/Muslim women is proffered to survey as many of the highly contentious issues put forward in the memoir as possible.

From the discussion of Nafisi's memoir as the paradigmatic neo-Orientalist narrative, the trajectory of the study moves to a counterhegemonic representation of Iran and Islam in Fatemeh Keshavarz's memoir. In this section, an analysis of Keshavarz's memoir is presented whereby the author's discursive strategies of resistance and constructing a counter-narrative are elucidated. Besides Nafisi's, Keshavarz's memoir is the only other academic memoir and is similarly qualified by a confluence of the academic, the personal, and the literary. Like Nafisi, Keshavarz interweaves the accounts of her academic career, her personal stories, and the analysis of iconic texts from Persian literature to formulate her narrative. Unlike Nafisi, however, she does so to arrive at a counterhegemonic and counter-Orientalist representation of her native country and religion, which she deems to be conspicuously absent from the body of Orientalist representations promoted by Iranian-American memoirs:

> Portraits of people or of social and cultural conditions should be like tapestries woven out of a hundred different threads, or like mosaics made of many tiles. When there are holes in the tapestry or tiles missing, the entire picture is

> distorted. Like many works contributing to the New Orientalist narrative, *RLT* contains a few patches of truth. In its entirety, however, it is a tapestry with many holes, a mosaic that has every other piece missing. (*Jasmine and Stars* 18)

As different as Keshavarz's memoir of the missing Iranian story is in its authorial intention and analysis, it is presented through fairly similar thematic and formal frameworks and, as such, operates within the same boundaries set by the dominant body of Iranian-American memoirs. This, in turn, lends greater effectiveness to Keshavarz's arguments and strikes a ready chord with her intended audience, since the text is located within the same structural and thematic formulations as those with which the audience are already familiar. Throughout the chapter, I have sought to demonstrate the ways in which Keshavarz provides an alternative lens through which to view Iranian society and literature. She achieves this mostly through capitalizing on prominent Persian literary giants such as Rumi and Attar, and by drawing on her personal narratives which serve to counterpoise those of the "New Orientalist" memoirs. Finally, the Conclusion presents a brief overview of the study along with some concluding remarks.

Chapter 2

NOT WITHOUT MY DAUGHTER

THE MOTHER OF NEO-ORIENTALIST BESTSELLERS

> Twenty years before Sen. John McCain (R-AZ) would sing, "Bomb, bomb, bomb, bomb, bomb Iran," to the old Beach Boys tune "Barbara Ann," the idea was proposed in the most popular book ever published in the US about Iran.
>
> Farzaneh Milani, "On Women's Captivity in the Islamic World"

The most recent polls available on Americans' overall opinion of Iran reveal that the majority of Americans still harbor a largely unfavorable view of the country, while only 6 percent regard Iran as the United States' "greatest enemy." This figure is significantly lower than that of the previous polls conducted earlier, perhaps mostly owing to such facts as Iran's abiding by the 2015 nuclear agreement known as JCPOA (The Joint Comprehensive Plan of Action) while Donald Trump unilaterally withdrew from it, the war in Syria, and the rise of ISIS in the Middle East.

It is safe to claim that US public opinion on Iran is more often than not colored by ongoing saber-rattling about an impending war against Iran not only by such notorious US hawks as John Bolton but also by successive US presidents. In 2002, George W. Bush infamously called Iran part of "an axis of evil," and Barack Obama's official stance that, if the prolonged nuclear negotiations failed, the United States had no qualms about bombing Iran was best expressed in his (in)famous "All options are on the table" and "I don't bluff" rhetoric. More recently, Donald Trump who, in October 2017, had called a nation of over eighty million people "a terrorist nation," threatened to destroy fifty-two Iranian cultural sites if Iran retaliated for his murder of General Soleimani. Also, almost all Republican candidates of the last US presidential election insisted that the "military option" must remain on the proverbial "negotiating table" as the only viable alternative out of Iran's "nuclear issue," even after a historic deal was reached with Iran.

It is a fact well known that the prospect of a war against Iran, as many international political pundits contend, would be little short of an Armageddon, or, as Michel Chossudovsky has argued, a "World War III scenario" (46). In this context, it is particularly important to observe how the image of the United States' "enemy" is constructed and promoted. The past two decades have witnessed the ever-increasing advancement of technology and the proliferation of digital and online platforms, which have in turn made the dissemination of, and access to, information significantly more convenient. Such technologies are often characterized by a sense of immediacy made possible by the instantaneous publishing and broadcasting of news, particularly facilitated through such social media platforms as Facebook, YouTube, Twitter, Instagram, and the like. In the context of this discussion, the ubiquity of such media and similar modes of communication has also significantly contributed to a much greater exposure to representations of the Other, through news, documentaries, and footage of the so-called Third World being instantly available in diverse virtual environments. The upsurge of interest after 9/11 in getting to know the "Muslim enemy" brought both representations and the "threat" of the so-called Muslim world into sharper focus.

As far as representations of Iran in the United States are concerned, when the digital era had not yet fully developed and the majority of present-day online information sources were either nonexistent or far from ubiquitous, Betty Mahmoody's trend-setting international bestseller, *Not without My Daughter* (1987),[1] was the first major work of popular literature on Iran. The book, and its eponymous 1991 Hollywood adaptation, introduced Americans, and by extension the Western world, to post-revolutionary Iran and played a major role in promoting Iranophobia and Islamophobia in the 1980s and for decades to come.

In short, *NWMD* chronicles Betty Mahmoody's marriage-gone-wrong to a US-educated Iranian-born anesthesiologist, Dr. Sayed Bozorg Mahmoody—known in the book by the nickname Moody—who had lived in the United States for more than two decades. According to the book, in August 1984, at the time of Iraq's war[2] against the fledgling Islamic Republic of Iran, Betty Mahmoody encouraged her husband to travel to Iran for what the author claims was meant to be a two-week holiday (50). The holiday, we are told, stretches into an eighteen-month "entrapment" from which the American "heroine" liberates herself when she allegedly puts her life, and that of her six-year-old daughter, on the line by fleeing the country through the mountains on the border between Iran and Turkey in the dead of winter.

The book, however, is no typical action-and-suspense thriller. While on the surface Mahmoody's text narrates the account of a failed intermarriage between a white American woman and her Iranian husband, as Roksana Bahramitash, an Iranian-Canadian professor of gender and Islamic Studies has suggested, it is "presented in a sensational narrative that portrays Iran of the mid-1980s and Islam as essentially brutal, frightening, and exceptionally misogynist" ("The War on Terror" 227). Given the book's unprecedented popularity and its manner of representing Iran, one could argue that no single work of literature has ever tarnished the public image of Iran and the average Iranian on a global scale as Mahmoody's memoir (and its movie adaptation). The book, in other words, can be considered the classic Orientalist narrative of the late twentieth century; one that served as the pioneer of a generation of neo-Orientalist memoirs on Iran to emerge in the first decade of the new millennium, particularly post 9/11.

In the following sections, after discussing the book's reception, I will examine how Mahmoody's narrative operates within the well-established framework of a fully fledged tradition of American captivity narratives. I will then demonstrate how the foundation of this allegedly "true account" of a white American woman and "her" daughter's alleged captivity in Iran is constructed upon an overtly "manifest Orientalism"—as opposed to "latent Orientalism"—defined by Edward Said as "the various stated views about Oriental society, languages, literatures, history, sociology, and so forth" (*Orientalism* 206). This manifest Orientalism is characterized by the recurring tropes of a colonial discourse that informs Mahmoody's representations of Iran. Against this backdrop, the picture that emerges of Iran is one of a land that seems to be irremediably primitive, misogynistic, fanatical, and contaminated.

Reception: Rolling out the red carpet

Not that it's inflammatory or anything, but "Not Without My Daughter" makes you want to set off for Iran with an atomic rolling pin.

Rita Kempley, *The Washington Post*

Before embarking on a critique of Mahmoody's text, it is important to establish the influence and the reach of the text (which partly serves to exemplify its "iconic" status) through its reception in the West. *Not without My Daughter* has earned the title of "the most popular book ever published in the U.S. about Iran" (Milani, "On Women's Captivity" 43). Almost immediately after its publication, the book emerged as an international bestseller "on three continents" (Australia, North America, and Europe), was translated into more than twenty languages, and sold about twelve million copies (Mahmoody and Dunchock 245).[3] The book's sales record was unprecedented in the history of French nonfiction, as noted in the 1990 Guinness Book of Records, but "the greatest wave of all," according to Mahmoody herself, was in "Germany, where more than 4 million copies had been purchased and the book topped the bestseller list for more than two years" (Mahmoody and Dunchock 245). Selected as a Literary Guild alternate, *NWMD* was nominated for a Pulitzer Prize in 1987, and finally, the book's extraordinary success inspired the publication of no less than thirteen similar "true stories" between 1987 and 1998 (De Hart 51). On some of the most popular and widely used online book databases (such as *We Read*, *goodreads*, *Google Books*, and *Amazon*), the book enjoys an average rating of more than 4 out of 5, and the number of reviewers and comments on the foregoing online platforms indicates the extent to which the book has been, and continues to be, read as an "authentic" story some three decades after its publication.

In a similar vein, the critical reception of the book in popular media, such as newspapers and websites, remains overwhelmingly laudatory, with almost all reviews putting the American "heroine" on a pedestal and castigating Iranian culture and Islam. Melani McAlister has observed that when the book first appeared in 1987, "it was reviewed positively and prominently in the major book publications; reviewers called it a 'compelling drama' and a 'riveting inside look at everyday life in Ayatollah Khomeini's revolutionary paradise'" (162). In the almost total absence of academic critiques of the work[4] and the predominantly enthusiastic reviews of it, objection to Mahmoody's work was voiced mainly from diasporic Iranian intellectuals or binational organizations that suffered the demonization of the Iranian/Muslim culture and intercultural relationships. Also, Iranian women, as well as women married to Iranian men, protested against the stereotypical and simplistic representations of Iran, Islam, and intermarriages (De Hart 53).

The publication of Mahmoody's book also launched her meteoric rise to fame and fortune, earning her a place in national and international halls of fame. In her book, Mahmoody makes no secret of her utter disdain for her husband and literally anything reminiscent of Iran; notwithstanding, she has preserved her husband's Iranian family name to this date. This paradoxical act of preservation is significant to the reception of Mahmoody and her book. On the one hand, it functions as an umbilical cord through which the author stays connected to and is remembered by her much-despised time in Iran. On the other, it is through the selfsame Iranian name that she is known around the world and can sustain her successful profile. The surname, therefore, operates as a double signifier, invoking at once a feeling of xenophobia and infuriation at things Iranian (and by extension admiration for Betty's "American" bravery and defiance), as well as her international celebrity. At home, Mahmoody received the American Freedom Award in 1991 and was lionized by Oakland University in Michigan as "Outstanding Woman of the Year" (Mahmoody and Dunchock 246). Also, an honorary doctorate was conferred on her by her Michigan alma mater, Alma College. Internationally, she was celebrated as both the "Most Courageous Woman of the Year" and "Woman of the Year" in Germany for 1990. In 1992, *NWMD* won the Dutch readers' prize for best book and a Dutch newspaper entitled Mahmoody "Mother of All Mothers" (De Hart 52). Among her many awards and honors, Mahmoody also takes pride in the fact that she was "asked to stand in for former British Prime Minister Margaret Thatcher," in the same ceremony in which "she was chosen to receive the American Freedom Award in Provo, Utah for the July, 4, 1991, festival" (Mahmoody and Dunchock 246).

The publication of *NWMD* soon posited Mahmoody as a cognoscente on Iran, Islam, intercultural marriage, as well as international abduction cases. In no time, she appeared on the most popular American television talk shows as well as on national and international radio programs and started lecturing on these issues. Her "expertise" was also employed in the US political and judicial systems. In her second book, *For the Love of a Child* (1992), Mahmoody explains that she acts "as an ongoing consultant to the State Department on the subject," has served as the chief investigator for legislation passed in Michigan relating to international kidnapping, and has appeared "as an expert witness" in divorce trials (254). Mahmoody is also the president and co-founder of "One World: For Children," an organization designed, among other things to promote intercultural understanding (and, as we will see, the irony should not be lost).

In 1992, Mahmoody, with a second ghost author, Arnold D. Dunchock, wrote *For the Love of a Child*, "part autobiographical sequel to her first book, part collection of stories (compilation) of other parents who have suffered the international abduction of their children, and part survey of the laws currently affecting these parents and children" ("For the Love of a Child (Review)"). Perhaps in response to the objections by Iranian-American and Muslim organizations to the misrepresentations in the book, Mahmoody reaffirms in this sequel that "[m]y life with my husband and my daughter was exactly as I recount it in my book. I stand by my story in every detail" (268). Unsurprisingly, her second book falls within very similar thematic patterns and the rhetoric of cultural stereotyping of different "foreigners," reaffirming the alleged moral superiority of Americans and concluding implicitly that intermarriage is a no-go zone.

In her second book, Mahmoody attributes the success of *NWMD*, what made it a "worldwide phenomenon," to "the universality of its subject: the bond between parent and child, and the extreme to which people will go when the bond is threatened" (245). She also maintains that the book's cause célèbre owes much to its "concern for the ordinary," its focus on the minute, everyday particularities of Iranian lives: "No matter what people's status, we all have an everyday home life and a natural interest in the routines of others" (245). Furthermore, she attributes the phenomenal success of her book to the fact that her story struck a ready chord with many fellow-sufferers. She observed that her story elicited responses from those who had suffered in silence and inspired them to step out of the dark and tell their own stories (247).

Despite Mahmoody's attempt to frame the appeal of her narrative in terms of the "universality" of its topic and its engagement with "the ordinary," one would be hard-pressed to acknowledge Mahmoody's reasons behind the success of her book. For one thing, a survey of the many reviews on the book reveals that it was never promoted as a story revolving around the natural bond between a mother and her daughter; nor does the book evince any "interest" in the ordinary daily lives of Iranian women. If anything, the narrative portrays those lives as mundane, pathetic, and miserable. One could argue that the major appeal of Mahmoody's story is rooted in its all-too-familiar plot: a white American Christian woman trapped in the land of the "enemy." Mahmoody's account appeals to her intended American audience by drawing on a long-established tradition of American captivity narratives with which many American readers are already familiar. At the time of its publication, this appeal was further reinforced by the lingering memory of the Hostage Crisis which was still fresh in the collective consciousness of the American public, thanks to its daily coverage in the US media. Betty De Hart argues that the story's appeal also owes to the "ongoing ancient animosity of Christianity towards Islam" (53)—an observation that might seem warranted in light of the considerably greater success of the book in the predominantly Christian West, and the popularity of "the clash of civilizations" rhetoric among the general Western public. However, as the following section will demonstrate, there is a predominantly white, American, Christian iconography at play in the text which engenders a bipolarity that persistently pits white American Christian ideals and values against Iranian/Islamic ones, at once commending the former and denigrating the latter.

Resurrecting the American Captivity Narrative

Stories of captivity and incarceration grow popular neither overnight, nor without good reason. In fact, the continued popularity and the wide readership of American captivity narratives are rooted in a variety of sociocultural, political, and historical dynamics. Far from developing in a vacuum, the tradition's genesis and development owed much to the deep-seated roots in the literary and political collective consciousness of the American public. *Not without My Daughter*, the modern-day embodiment of such narratives, draws extensively on two seemingly different, but closely interconnected, traditions. More specifically, it perfectly exemplifies that category of literary writing known as "hostage narratives," which, according to Brian T. Edwards, are "sensationalistic accounts in the mainstream press that . . . reincorporate a period two centuries or more ago in the vocabulary and logic of the period" (340).

Classical captivity narratives were often stereotypical accounts of white people, predominantly women, ensnared by "savage" foes. Be that as it may, the genre's malleability has allowed it to be employed circumstantially to align with the dominant zeitgeist of different eras in which the narratives have been produced. Owing to their often amateur authorship, being expressions of some form of desperation, and their deep roots in history, culture, and religion, captivity narratives have come to occupy a prominent place in American "low literature" (Colley 199). These narratives are part of a well-established literary genre, which was particularly popular from the seventeenth to the nineteenth centuries. The plots of such narratives were often far from convoluted and mostly composed of a foreseeable concatenation of events, predominantly in the form of reversals and twists of fate. The thrust of such stories can usually be encapsulated as a white American woman captured by "Indians" who snatch her away from a life of luxury and liberty and who becomes entrapped in the clutches of "savages." Whether the "innocent" captive walks into her solitary confinement unwittingly or is abducted against her will, she is made to suffer harrowing conditions and to endure barbarous torments. No matter what tribulations she undergoes, the white captive eventually works her way out of the ordeal and is rescued by a combination of her tenacity, bravery, and God's grace. In the end, good always triumphs over evil and the "victim" returns home to tell the story of her survival, which is "all the more riveting for being true" (Milani, "On Women's Captivity" 45).

For centuries, the predominant view of captivity narratives has been that of a rather monolithic genre, constructed upon certain well-established principles of diegesis and content. Richard Vanderbeets has defined captivity narratives as "a single genre" whose "fundamental informing and unifying principle" is a ritualistic journey through the archetypal separation, transformation, and return phases (549). However, as the genre gradually became a subject of academic scholarship and criticism, its perception as a unified literary tradition came into question. Tracing the development of captivity narratives across the past few centuries made it clear that the substantial corpus of captivity narratives could neither be encapsulated into a single genre, nor could it be considered exclusively American.[5]

Captivity as the Pilgrim's Progress

Analyzing the wide-ranging body of captivity narratives, Roy Harvey Pearce has categorized them into three main genres. He has argued that despite their "natural basic unity of content," captivity narratives have developed and changed course over centuries and the genre has "shape[d] and reshape[d] itself according to varying cultural needs" (1). Penned mostly by early Puritan frontierspeople, the first and the greater share of captivity narratives were what Pearce calls "simple, direct religious documents" (2). They comprised a classic religious pattern of abduction (or "removal"), affliction, and redemption. Tapping into deeply ingrained perceptions of history and Puritan ideological traditions, these narratives placed the familiar story of "providential deliverance" into the novel context of "the American Indian frontier" (Minter 337).

Captivity was no far-fetched concept to the sixteenth- and seventeenth-century American Christians. In fact, it was a well-established part of their religious credo to view the entire human existence as a pilgrimage through various imprisonments: from the "welbelov'd" in utero imprisonment, man is cast out into the "lower prisons" of this "fallen world" only to find their soul imprisoned within the confines of the flesh (Minter 338). Similarly, they envisioned heaven and hell in terms of their spatial physicality: the former was characterized by an open spaciousness, whereas the latter was described in carceral terms. In a similar fashion, they defined "the life of sin as a terrible enslavement and the life of faith in a fallen world as servitude, a 'sweet captivitie to God'" (Minter 339).

In his *Regeneration through Violence: The Mythology of the American Frontier 1600-1860* (1974), Richard Slotkin spells out the strong religious and ideological underpinnings of captivity narratives, where often the faithful white American was cast as a figure whose predicament and affliction served to caution and salvage the lives of other potential victims: "The ordeal is at once threatful of pain and evil and promising of ultimate salvation. Through the captive's proxy, the promise of a similar salvation could be offered to the faithful among the reading public, while the captive's torments remained to harrow the hearts of those not yet awakened to their fallen nature" (94).

Two doctrinal traditions underlie the first category of captivity narratives. First, such narratives are steeped in the ideology of Providentialism: they chronicle the vicissitudes of the captives' traumatizing ordeals and their eventual salvation by "the gracious providence of God" (Pearce 2). In such Puritan narratives, the captivity experience assumes symbolic significance. No matter how harrowing, what befalls the captives is part of a greater divine scheme and nothing but "evidences of God's inscrutable wisdom" (2). As villainous as the Indians may be in such stories, they are merely God's instruments, "actors in a divine drama" (Minter 337).

Second, underwritten in these narratives is "a doctrine of afflictions that welcomed suffering and adversity by defining them as corrective, instructive, and profitable" (Minter 337). Both the captivity experience *in toto* and the specific traumas the victims suffer signify the captive's "elect" status: separation, captivity, and torment signify the captives' "chosenness" (Minter 337). The notion of "election" is originally mentioned in the Bible as "whom the lord loveth he chasteneth" (Hebrews 12.6) and it has been internalized by certain Christian sects. This, in fact, indicates another characteristic feature of such early captivity narratives: the familiar Puritan medium of drawing on biblical symbolism and allusions. Captivity narratives are "saturated in biblical language" (Colley 202), and such references function as a vicarious medium, connecting the individual's journey and her destiny to that of a nation (Minter 342).

Propagandizing Captivity

Linda Colley has demonstrated how the gradual transition from the Age of Faith to the Age of Enlightenment occasioned a shift away from the spiritual roots of captivity narratives (202). Gradually, the straightforward, firsthand, and religious nature of captivity narratives gave way to a novel development within the genre. The captives' personal experiences were exploited for social and political purposes which, in turn, gave rise to narratives of a propagandistic nature. One of the significant characteristics of these narratives is what Pearce has termed "stylization"—the concern with a verbatim recounting of the ordeal and faithfulness to its particularities begin to dissipate and writing the story by an external literary agent comes to find "a kind of journalistic premium" (3). Hence, firsthand personal experiences of devout Puritan captives are gradually supplanted by "the writing of the hack and the journalist" (Pearce 6). However, even though the initial authors of such accounts were not men and women of letters, it would be naïve to assume that they were literary virgins, "bringing pure and unadulterated stories to a corrupting print market" (Colley 210). The captives' own responses to their ordeal were also shaped by fictions to which they had been exposed. In propagandistic narratives, the experience turns into an instrument principally at the service of promoting both loathing and fear of the Other, with the intent of the typical writer being "to register as much hatred of the . . . Indians as possible" (Pearce 6), rather than illusrating the workings of God's all-encompassing providential design.

The Out-and-Out Sensational

There is a "natural" shift from captivity narratives as propagandistic tracts to the third subgenre: the "out-and-out sensational" (Pearce 3). Like propaganda narratives, the outright melodramatic narratives were penned mostly by authors other than those directly involved in and affected by the experience of captivity. The more captivity narratives steered away from the initial, more "truthful," direct, and personal accounts, the more they grew in stylization, and thus the latest category of captivity narratives is characterized by a "journalistic extremity of language and style" (Pearce 9). From the mid-eighteenth century onward, it had become common practice to spice up the narratives and "stylize" them by interpolating as much fictional padding as possible to render them more journalistically worthwhile. Greater stylization in these later narratives came, indeed, at the cost of an almost total lack of concern for accuracy and authenticity, as the only thing their derivative authors were concerned with was the "salability of penny dreadful" (Pearce 9). These later narratives of captivity are notorious mélanges of fact and fiction. Even though, according to Pearce, many such narratives might be true in substance, they are "built up out of a mass of crude, sensationally presented details" (9). The greater share of such narratives exists to illustrate Indian atrocities, and their significance is mainly "vulgar, fictional, and pathological" (Pearce 9).

Eventually, in the latest subcategory of captivity narratives so much liberty was taken with the original stories that a great many of them evince little or no pretense at authenticity. By this time (mid- to late-eighteenth century), the publication of such stories had become, more than anything, what Pearce has dubbed "an occasion for an exercise in blood and thunder and sensibility" (12). The predominance of pulp thriller captivity narratives and the almost totally absent concept of verisimilitude in such narratives led to a few authors appending a truth-swearing affidavit to the later editions of their stories (Pearce 12).

The progressive course of captivity narratives does not end with the sensational thriller. Captivity narratives, and especially the second and third subgenres, are characterized by a persistent interlacing of preexisting fiction and lived experience and are usually deemed to contain some measure of substance, however slight it might be. This is one of the features that problematize the study of captivity narratives through a single disciplinary lens—be it literature, history, religion, ethnography, or politics—and that exemplifies the "porous boundary between history and imaginative literature" (Colley 201). Out of the sensational shockers grew narratives that were published as genuine and truthful accounts but were, in actuality, "out-and-out fakes" (Pearce 13). However, the blood-and-thunder narratives had strayed to such a wild extremity of language and content that they differed from the outright hoax narratives only "in the degree of their absurdity" (13). In short, the shift from one type of captivity narrative to another signified a progressive secularization. This secularization paved the way for a new kind of propaganda and sensationalism, which, in turn, meant "increasing exploitation—increasing disregard for the particularities of the experience recounted as well as for the language of its appropriation" (Minter 347).

Captivity narratives have been described as "persistent, protean, profusely distributed over time and space and often downright plebeian" (Colley 200). Embedded in the archetypal captivity narratives, like any other context-specific phenomenon, is a built-in obsolescence. Thus, to transcend the restrictions of temporal and historical specificity, the genre has survived and regenerated through various adaptive strategies and has reappeared in novel forms. Both as a mode of writing and as a mode of thinking, the malleable nature of captivity narratives enables them to be readapted and remolded to suit different cultural and political landscapes and zeitgeists. That is why with each new US adventure abroad, narratives of new frontiers and foes have followed, although the classic topoi persist and remain essentially similar.

It is within the framework of the trajectory of captivity narratives and the genre's appropriation for different purposes at different times that *NWMD* can be read as an archetypal latter-day captivity narrative which comes to share the literary denominators of its progenitors. Like many later classical captivity narratives, *NWMD* is a text wherein the three subgenres of captivity narratives converge. It is informed by an undergirding religiosity in the sense that it draws on the Puritan ideas of punishment and salvation; it is a propagandistic tract in the sense that it promulgates popular and political propaganda about Iran, Islam, the Islamic Revolution, and the Iran–Iraq War; and numerous instances of exaggeration, myth, and disinformation qualify it as a highly sensationalized pulp thriller.

There is a religious underpinning and vocabulary at work in Mahmoody's memoir, which makes the perusal of the story as a religious captivity narrative, or a purgation narrative, feasible. The first stage in this pilgrimage is removal. Describing her "first remove," Mary Rowlandson explains in her narrative how she was taken away from "house and home and all our comforts within door and without" (10). In a similar vein, Betty, the white American Christian woman, flies from her "fallen world" of American luxury and privilege into the "trap" that would be her "cell" for the next eighteen months to come. She is held "captive" (42, 94, 204) not only by her "tormentor" but by the entire "backward" nation (55) and is allegedly forced to suffer the most extraordinary afflictions. Nevertheless, the story tells us that Betty does not weaken in her resolve in the face of adversity, constantly seeking help and redemption from God, and her staunch faithfulness along with her stamina come to fruition when at long last she manages to escape and tell her "true" story to other people.

It was customary for captive-writers, or later hack writers, to describe the place of their captivity as "hell." In one of the earliest and best-known prototypical captivity narratives, Mrs. Mary Rowlandson's *The Sovereignty and Goodness of God* (1682),[6] the locale and the setting of captivity, along with the captors' rituals, make the place "a lively resemblance of hell" (10). Similarly, the infernal imagery utilized in Mahmoody's account highlights the religiosity of the experience. The summer heat is "hellish" (11), Betty's ordeal is described as going through "hell" (322), and the whole country is also described as "hell" (22, 64, 308, 417).

Even though the afflictions that captives undergo become more meaningful when placed in the framework of God's providence and omniscience, Betty's torment seems to be caused also by her betrayal of her faith by marrying a Muslim, and perhaps her neglect of not attending the Free Methodist Church (105). The ordeal, however, reunites Betty with her faith. In times of distress, her recourse is her regained religious faith, exemplified in her many prayers to God and her wish to read the Bible: "God was my only companion through the tedious days and nights. I spoke with Him constantly" (212). For early American Christians, despair was a grave sin, "born of failure of confidence of election" (Minter 340). In captivity narratives, the captives constantly oscillate between near despair and hope, but never completely surrender. The same pattern is evident in *NWMD*. Despite many moments of crushing "despair" (108, 168, 208, 217, 219, 289, 293, 359, 361), Betty always manages to find rays of hope in her faith and never acquiesces.

Mahmoody makes it very clear that her predicament was also compounded by her religious faith—the fact that she was a non-Muslim "trapped" in a Muslim country. However, strengthened by her regained faith, she puts her trust in God's judgment:

> Moody centered much of his wrath upon the fact that I was not Moslem.
>
> "You will burn in the fires of hell," he screamed at me. "And I am going to heaven. Why do you not wake up?"
>
> "I don't know what's going to happen," I replied softly, trying to appease him. "I'm not a judge. Only God is a judge." (230)

The text includes other occasions when Moody treats Betty harshly apparently for no other ascertainable reason than being a Christian. When Betty, quoting a verse from the Holy Quran, declares that "Both of our families should help us with our problems," Moody retorts: "Your family is not Muslim. They do not count" (58). Similarly, when she objects to Moody keeping her away from her dying father, Moody replies:

> Is your father Moslem, he asked sarcastically?
> No, of course not.
> Then it does not matter, Moody said. He does not count. (144)

While Mahmoody's descriptions of Islam in her narrative convey the sense that Islam is an exclusionist religion and that Muslims are openly hostile to Christians, such representations stand in stark contrast to Islam's view of the people of other faiths, explicitly spelled out in different passages in the Quran: "Those who believe (in the Qur'an), and those who follow the Jewish (scriptures), and the Christians and the Sabaeans—any who believe in God and the Last Day, and work righteousness—shall have their reward with their Lord; on them shall be no fear, nor shall they grieve" (2:62). In fact, not only does Islam not preach religious exclusionism, it forbids the imposition of faith on non-Muslims[7] and considers Christians "nearest in love" to Muslims (Cole).[8]

The preceding examples illustrate the seemingly unbridgeable gap between Muslims and Christians, or between the broader East and West, reinforced by Muslim "apathy" toward non-Muslims—a fallacy that contradicts the most basic tenets of Islam. In fact, Islamic teachings are strongly averse to any form of discrimination against human beings. Islam's insistence on deracialization and equality of people of all races, colors, and walks of life threatened the very existence of the religion at its inception by the affluent ruling elite in a highly stratified Arab society where slavery, especially of the people of color, was common practice. Unsurprisingly, Mahmoody's account makes no mention of the peaceful coexistence of such religious minorities as Christians, Jews, and Zoroastrians in

Iran, which have always been part of the fabric of Iranian society for more than two millennia.[9] However, the insistence in Islam on egalitarianism does not necessarily indicate that all the followers of the religion abide by this ideal, as is also the case with the followers of any other religion or secular ideology. In other words, one cannot rule out the possibility that Mahmoody might have faced some exclusionary behavior from some people she met in Iran. However, what renders such claims problematic is that, together with other unfavorable representations of Muslim men and women, and the often inaccurate references to Islamic practices and teachings, they paint a profoundly negative picture of Islam, which is not only highly distorted but also feeds into the Islam-as-the-enemy-of-Christianity narrative.

The same religious underpinning and the sharp contrast created between Islam and Christianity figure prominently in the movie as well, which has also led to some reviewers' reaffirming such religious binarism. A review published on the Movieguide.org, for instance, notes that "[t]he film shows the true horrors and evils of Islam, from the denial of female sexuality in husband/wife relationships[10] to the fanatical religiosity which drives this people," and goes on to point out the significance of the movie for its intended Western Christian audience:

> Sally Field, who plays Betty Mahmoody, gives a strong witness for Christ. In the film, the work of this believer stands the test of fire; and, for Christian viewers, it has the effect of building one's faith . . . [I]t is shown through one woman's dynamic, personal relationship with the Lord is she able to overcome her circumstances. This is, after all, what Christianity is all about. (Movieguide)

Betty's eventual deliverance is not different from that of traditional captivity narratives, either. In classic captivity narratives, especially in the early narratives, the captives invariably attribute their redemption to God's "grace," "mercy," or "wisdom": "Mahtob and I pray[ed] our thanks to God for survival and renew[ed] our desperate pleas for deliverance" (239). In a similar vein, Mahmoody writes in her second book that "[t]here is no explanation for what happened. I believed we were saved by the grace of God" (6). The idea of deliverance is fundamental to some captivity narratives and the double position of the captive-author as survivor-savior characterizes Mahmoody's narrative, too. The following section will demonstrate how captivity narratives function as cautionary tales that are meant to be redemptive for Western Christian readers.

Tales of Caution and the Mixed Marriage Menace

Not without My Daughter enjoys a significant cautionary underpinning of a rather didactic quality, which is continued and elaborated at greater length in Mahmoody's second book. Readers are invited to exercise caution against the often "veiled threats" that the "primitive East" and the Other pose. Like any other major leitmotif of such narratives, the cautionary element can also be traced to the American captivity narrative tradition. In this light, the (white, Western,

Christian) readership's reception of *NWMD* and kindred narratives can be partly accounted for in terms of the cautionary and redemptive nature of these narratives.

Authors of early American captivity narratives narrated their stories not only as a means of coming to terms with the indelible agonies and traumas they claimed they experienced, but, *a fortiori*, as a way of cautioning others, too. They took it upon themselves to awaken and enlighten the readers. This role is both socially and religiously significant. It is both assumed by the authors for themselves as dutiful, devout Christians, and also conferred upon them by their audience by virtue of the position of authority and authenticity they came to establish through the narration and reception of their stories. In her epistolary captivity novel, *The History of Maria Kittle* (1779), Ann Eliza Bleecker declares her intention in writing her story to be opening "the sluice gates of her readers' eyes" (qtd. in Pearce 14)—an expression which conflates the benevolent intention of the author in awakening her readers with the extent of horror to be exposed in the story.

Classic captivity narratives spoke to two potential spiritual dangers simultaneously: one was the danger of hubris and self-contentment bred by the awareness of one's elect status, and the other was the danger of despair brought about by the "failure of confidence of election" (Minter 339). Remaining vigilant and unbeleaguered by these dangers necessitated that good Puritans retain an "imperfect assurance" and remain in a constant in-betweenness. This prompted a dual necessity: the need to familiarize oneself with "the noble operations of the blessed Spirit" against which they could judge their own experiences, and the need to produce one's own account, to narrate one's own spiritual journey, as a sign that "one's own name, too, was listed among the elect" (Minter 339). As Minter maintains, embedded in the very act of writing is "the conviction ... that for others her story can be exemplary, that it can enter their ongoing struggles with salvation" (341). The acts of reading, hearing about, and writing such narratives are made extensions of that "imperfect certainty," junctures in the eternal drama of salvation which for Puritans held no promise of a closure before death. It is noteworthy that the legacy of this Puritan worldview has somehow been translated into political action and is manifest in the US history of not only constructing enemies but also promoting an image of the country as one constantly prone to be attacked by foreign nations such as Japan, the former Soviet Union, China, Russia, North Korea, and, most recently, Iran—a drama that appears to have no end in view.

The act of writing also promotes the American heroine-writer as a Christ-like figure whose suffering is meant to be redemptive for the readers—a role that, according to her second book, Mahmoody assumes by attempting to "save" other American women undergoing similar circumstances. This redemption, however, cannot happen if the story remains untold. It is through verbalizing the experience and conveying the message to the audience that the author can both reflect on her ordeal and learn from it in retrospect, while simultaneously cautioning and informing her readers. In a similar vein, authors of more recent captivity narratives have sought solace in the act of writing as a way of surmounting their past predicaments.[11] Mahmoody, for instance, writes in *For the Love of a Child* of the therapeutic effect of composing her story: "I was angry when I wrote the book. It was like therapy for me" (12).

Authors of captivity narratives have also taken it upon themselves to warn their readers against venturing across normative racial, cultural, and religious frontiers, especially when mixed marriages are concerned. Modern captivity narratives of the last few decades, as Vron Ware has observed, are marked with a growing obsession with the intermarriage of Western *women*, dominated by a discourse revolving around the "menace" of cross-cultural romances, which are allegedly bound to culminate in a doomed cul-de-sac (62). In such narratives, embedded in the intercultural marriage is an alarming sense of foreboding that is bound to materialize when the captivity, or whatever other tragedy awaits the Western woman (such as the abduction of children), at long last transpires. Such marriages are depicted not only as endangering Western women alone; by extension, they put the entire society to which they belong at risk. By virtue of their sexuality, Western women function as gateways to the Western world and, therefore, their marriages to non-Westerners are deemed as posing a threat to the idea of Western civilization. Consequently, Western women who transgress the bounds of the "colour line of love" are deemed to compromise Western nation states. The authors' "mistake" should make their audiences wary of mixed marriages and dissuade them from treading the "wrong" path. In this light, the authors are cast as "cultural reproducers of the West," empowered through their experience to pass judgment on the propriety of social behavior and to "exert control over other women who are constructed as deviants" (Yuval-Davis 37). Finally, the freedom of choice manifested in the possibility of committing the "mistake" of intermarriage is, in fact, one of the main factors that distinguish the involuntary captivity of white Western Christian women in classic accounts from the relatively conscious "transgression" of later "learned Foolhardies" (Ware 62).

Myth-making in Not without My Daughter

Even though a religious underpinning does inform Mahmoody's narrative, the propagandistic and sensational features of captivity narratives figure more prominently in the text. Not only is the narrative ridden with propaganda of all sorts against Iran, its culture, and main religion, the instant celebrity it yielded provided Mahmoody with numerous platforms to continue disseminating such propaganda against Iran and Islam. This propagandization is carried out, among other things, through perpetuating a panoply of myths, half-truths, and rumors, some of which have grown so popular as to recur in many later neo-Orientalist writings on Iran. One such myth is the existence of an apparently summary capital punishment code in Iran. In Mahmoody's Iran, all crimes and offences, no matter how minor, seem to be punishable by execution.[12] Repeatedly, Mahmoody claims that birth control is illegal in Iran and women can be put to death by merely using contraception of any kind (256). Thus, the IUD she carries within herself is presented as nothing short of a death warrant: "Suddenly, there in my hand was the bit of plastic and copper that could condemn me to death" (231). The fact of the matter, however, is that even though the use of contraception has been at times religiously controversial in the past, it has never been illegal and, despite capital punishment being legal in Iran, it is reserved only for such major felonies as murder, rape, and heavy drug trafficking. Indeed, in a country where she claims one can be "sentenced to six years in prison" for "thinking against the government" (314)—a claim that simply defies reason—it should come as no surprise if someone were executed for using contraception, or fleeing across the border illegally.

Another myth popularized through the book is the abduction of underage boys to fight in the war front. Mahmoody quotes a friend of hers as saying, "[w]hen they [the revolutionary guards] see a group of boys, they pick them up and take them to the war . . . They do this at school, too. Sometimes they take a truck to a boy's school and take away the boys to be soldiers. Their families never see them again" (161). However, despite Mahmoody's claim, the defense against the 1980 Iraqi-imposed war was so popularly supported throughout the war that hundreds of thousands of volunteers constituted the majority of Iranian forces, especially since in the aftermath of the revolution the Iranian army was still a fledgling one (Dugdale-Pointon). Accounts of many young Iranian boys who tampered with their IDs to look eligible to fight as volunteers in the war—and many such accounts have been documented—are quite well-known among Iranian families. One famous example is a 2015 memoir (and its 2019 movie adaptation) published in Iran, whose title can be translated into *Those 23 People*, which narrates the memories of twenty-three teenagers, some of whom had gone to great lengths to pass as legitimate volunteers.

One other fiction that Mahmoody draws heavily upon, and is also regurgitated in other neo-Orientalist texts, is the myth of raping virgin girls before execution. Betty thus summarizes the myth: "Inevitably they [the revolutionary guards] raped their women victims—young girls too—before they killed them. I shuddered as I remembered their horrid saying: 'A woman should not die a virgin'" (394). This accusation also appears in other passages in the book (294). However, as Marandi and Pirnajmuddin have demonstrated, such systematic acts of rape have never occurred, as the philosophy behind them is simply nonexistent (35). Quite the contrary, rape itself is a first-degree felony in Iran for which the rapist can be sentenced to capital punishment. Mahmoody's text is fraught with more than a few such myths, fabrications, contradictions, inaccuracies, and apocryphal tales.[13] Colley has interpreted the existence of such untruths in captivity narratives as a sign of the lack of authenticity in such narratives and has concluded that "narratives which draw on an individual's genuine exposure to captivity rarely make this kind of mistake" (206).

Characteristically, captivity narratives stemmed from some sort of reality and were worked up in various ways into something horrific and absurd (Pearce 16). Quite similar to these classic sensational narratives, *NWMD* is packed with overly sensational details, which match Pearce's description of the "noisomely visceral thriller" category of American captivity narratives (1). Pearce argues that many such narratives are informed by an "American Gothicism," as they seem to "delight in gruesomeness." The authors of such narratives capitalize on "the luxury of sorrow," "the luxury of horror," and "all that such narratives had come to mean for American readers—a meaning which rose out of emphasis on physical terror, suffering and sensationalism" (15). The following passage is one among many instances in *NWMD*, which exemplifies the emphasis on gruesomeness, horror, pain, and sensationalism:

> Moody grabbed me, threw me to the floor, and pounced upon me. He seized my head in his hands and banged it repeatedly against the floor . . . Moody bit into my arm deeply, drawing blood. I screamed, wriggled free from his grasp, and managed to kick him in the side. But this produced anger more than pain. He grabbed me with his two mighty arms and threw me to the hard floor. I landed on my spine and felt pains shoot the entire length of my body. Now I could barely move. For many minutes he stood over me cursing violently, kicking at me, bending over to slap me. He yanked me across the floor by pulling at my hair. Tufts came loose in his hand. (200)

The second reservoir of tropes that *NWMD* taps into is the political collective consciousness of her Western, particularly American, audiences, especially those of the 1980s. To this date, *NWMD* remains the prototype of "hostage narratives," rehashing the all-too-familiar stereotype of the white Western woman entrapped in the Orient. From a historico-political perspective, the narrative can be traced back to what is commonly known as the "Hostage Crisis" in the West. Less than a year after the Islamic Revolution, on the fourth of November 1979, a group of revolutionary university students took fifty-two American hostages from the US Embassy in Tehran, in reaction to the presence of the deposed shah in the United States and in exchange for his extradition. On a deeper level, however, the hostage-taking was the outward expression of a more profound and long-standing Iranian apprehension: that just like the 1953 CIA-orchestrated coup d'état that removed Iran's first democratically elected prime minister, Dr. Mohammad Mosaddeq, and reinstated the increasingly unpopular shah, the United States would engineer another putsch and squelch the fledgling revolution at its inception. While President Carter referred to the coup as "ancient history," when asked by a reporter if he thought the intervention was justified, for Iranians the coup remains, to this day, anything but history. Professor Vali Nasr has argued how "[i]n the popular mind, the hostage crisis was seen as justified by what had happened in 1953 . . . People saw it as an act of national assertiveness, of Iran standing up and taking charge of its own destiny. The humiliation of 1953 was exorcised by the taking of American hostages in 1979" (Snider). In the aftermath of the crisis, all relations between the two countries were severed and remain as such to this day.

In the realm of media and literature, hostage-taking was made the most recurrent leitmotif in all Iran-related broadcasts as well as works of literature and cinema of the time.[14] The representation and reception of this crisis in the United States owed greatly to the tradition of American captivity narratives. As Melani McAlister has argued, "the discourse of terrorist threat formed in the context of the Iran hostage crisis depended on the underlying structure of a captivity narrative—those stories of whites taken by Indians that had dominated the literature of early America" (199).

The Hostage Crisis remains paramount in understanding the complexities of the strained relationship between Iran and the United States and is essential in analyzing representations of Iran and the Western public view of Iran. One could argue that the incident has become as deeply ingrained in Americans' political collective consciousness as the 1953 CIA-engineered coup is in Iranians' minds. Stephen Kinzer, an American author who has thoroughly researched and written on the history of Iran–US relationship, especially the coup d'état in question, contends that "[t]o this day we are still living under the emotional overhang of the hostage crisis of 1979" (Kinzer).[15] He further contends that Americans are still "caught in this emotional prison" and explains how the humiliating memory of the coup has remained with the Iranians as well.[16]

As a fully-fledged captivity/hostage narrative, *NWMD* operates at two parallel levels: at one level it recounts the story of the white American woman trapped in the land of the "enemy." Expressions of this mode of entrapment start on the front cover of almost all versions of the book and continue on its back cover. The publisher's blurb on one edition urges the reader to "[i]magine yourself alone and vulnerable. Imagine yourself . . . trapped by a husband you thought you trusted, and held prisoner in his native Iran, a land where women have no rights and Americans are despised." In a short declaration, the blurb achieves much: it establishes the image of the white American woman as innocent, vulnerable, and betrayed; it portrays the Other as minatory and untrustworthy; it draws on the patriotic sentiments of American readers by telling them of another country's hatred toward them and earning their hatred back; and, finally, it reiterates the shopworn cliché of the oppressed Muslim woman, deprived of all her rights.

The back cover of another edition reads: "Mother and daughter became prisoners of an alien culture, hostages of an increasingly tyrannical and violent man." As demonstrated above, the choice of the word "hostage," and its synonyms, which are reiterated throughout the book,[17] is anything but coincidental. They are, quite the contrary, *mots justes* chosen with careful calculation to take the reader a few years back to the Hostage Crisis and to catalyze emotional engagement with the melodrama. In an early soliloquy Mahmoody thus expresses her state of captivity: "Was this real? Were Mahtob and I prisoners? Hostages? Captives of the venomous stranger who had once been a loving husband and father?" (42). Elsewhere, she ponders that if she leaves Iran without her daughter, "Mahtob would be trapped in this crazy country with her insane father" (191).

Betty's captivity and entrapment operate on two interconnected planes. On a domestic scale, Betty is imprisoned in her sister-in-law's, Essey's, and later her own home respectively, either because, according to her, she has done something that has incurred her husband's wrath or for no particular reason at all. This is how she describes her state of captivity in her home when her husband would leave the house or would go to hospital to work: "[The window] was unlocked, sliding open to my touch. I poked my head through and gauged the possibilities. I could scramble through this window easily enough and reach the landing, but I would still be held captive by the heavy iron street door, which was always locked" (204).

It looks as though she is entirely cut off from the outside world and even if she attempted to break away from the confines of her "prison," "dutiful Islamic spies" (126) would inform on her to her husband. All the places she lives in are described in the book in carceral terms. Similarly, her sister-in-law and her family, along with Essey, Nasserine, and her own husband, are described as her captors, kidnappers, jailers, and hostage-takers (56, 72, 81, 117, 25).

On a larger plane yet the entire city of Tehran mutates into a metropolitan prison, circumscribed by the mountain ranges that serve as its towering walls: "The countryside was beautiful, to be sure, but the beauty was the result of gargantuan mountain ranges rising higher and standing out in sharper relief than the Rockies of the western United States. They ringed Tehran on all sides, turning the entire city into a trap" (167). Mahmoody's description of the mountains surrounding Tehran resonates with the Puritan view of nature as "sinister captivity" and the "vast, desolate howling wilderness . . . as most formidably the devil's own" (Minter 345). Even when she is out of her prison-home, she is trapped in the sprawling city and it is not only her husband or his relatives whom she views as her prison guards—the city's entire populace plays the paradoxical double role of her captors and, as we will see later, her fellow inmates.

On a yet more macroscopic level, the country in its entirety transmutes into a massive prison-nation from which Betty strives to escape. Even when she manages to break out of her prison-home, and away from the prison-city, she is still behind the greater bars of the prison-country. This hostage imagery pervades the entire text. In one notable instance, Betty describes her "entrapment" in "a country that, to me, had seemed populated almost totally with villains" (334). This insistence on being "entrapped" in a society of "villains" is underpinned by a Puritan ideology that viewed the society as a "lesser prison of this lower world, but also as man's proper home, as scene of saintly pilgrimage" (Minter 345).

The second parallel that underlies *NWMD* is when it dawns on Betty, as if in a flash of realization, that she is not a lone sufferer in her predicament. In fact, she discovers that all Iranian women are her fellow-sufferers. Betty shares the harrowing experience of her captivity with her "cellmates," all Iranian women (whom she also paradoxically depicts as her captors and jailors): "Now I realized anew that these women were caught in a trap just as surely as I, subject to the rules of a man's world, disgruntled but obedient" (118). In another passage, when negotiating her escape with a liaison to smugglers and pondering the "professional network" of human smugglers and the history and reasons behind its development, she concludes: "I was not the only one trapped in Iran. If life here was intolerable for me, surely there were millions of people all around me who shared the same sentiments" (175). Nevertheless, even in finding fellow-sufferers in Iranian women, she casts herself as totally distinct from her "cellmates." While she is presented as actively resisting and challenging the system in which she finds herself captive, Iranian women are presented as not only merely acquiescent to it but also as reinforcing and legitimizing it through their alleged silence, which, for Betty, makes them complicit in the system that holds them both captive.

What is significant in analyzing the depiction of Iranian women's alleged literal and figurative incarceration in *NWMD* is the fact that their "imprisonment," on both domestic and broader scales, transpires in a more holistic and ideological framework. In Mahmoody's eyes, lying at the root of Iranian woman's physical, spiritual, and domestic incarceration is the same rationale that justifies the "barbarous" Iranian/Muslim man's cruelty and the government's fanaticism. Mahmoody's narrative makes it increasingly clear that the culprit is none other than the now-all-too-familiar root of all evils: Islam.

According to Betty, before being imprisoned in her house or country, the Muslim woman is shackled by her immobilizing faith, "locked up inside her mandatory veil—a mobile prison shrunk to the size of her body" (Milani "On Women's Captivity" 40). In a variety of its different forms and synonyms,[18] the trope of the veil resurfaces in almost every other page of the story. This omnipresence, however, is anything but merely descriptive. The veil, and especially the chador, is exploited to the fullest to rehash and reinforce the idea of the invisibility of Muslim Iranian women and to portray them as suppressed by their "restrictive" faith, "cloaked in the omnipresent heavy black chador" (9). Invited to a family gathering, Betty cannot but notice how all around her "hovered insolent, superior-looking men" while "women wrapped in chadors sat in quiet subservience" (34).

Interestingly, even the definition Betty gives of the chador is erroneous and misleading: "A chador is a large, half-moon-shaped cloth entwined around the shoulders, forehead, and chin to reveal only eyes, nose, and mouth" (5). In reality, however, the chador neither covers the forehead and chin, nor is it supposed to; nor is it meant to "reveal only eyes, nose, and mouth." The definition of the chador, only one of the common forms of hejab in Muslim countries, seems purposely distorted to reinforce the alleged oppression, invisibility, and incarceration of Iranian Muslim women. Betty adds that "the effect [of the chador] is reminiscent of a nun's habit in times past" (5), thus invoking the Orientalist trope of the backwardness and medievalism of Muslim cultures, while representing the chador as anachronistic and Iran as a country frozen in a dark, primitive past. The chador-clad women Mahmoody describes are not only "backward" by virtue of their "antiquated and even unhealthy dress code" (35)—although it is not clear how the garment is "unhealthy"— their manners and bearing as well as their physical appearances are all the more uncouth and uncivilized. Upon his arrival in Tehran, Moody is "engulfed" by "a mob of robed veiled humanity that clawed at his business suit and wailed in ecstasy" (9). Once again, one can see the image of a "mob," the denial of identity and individuality, and the bestialization of the Other all in one picture— tropes that will be discussed in greater detail in the following sections. Wondering why she is wearing "this stupid scarf" (9), Betty worries that she "must smell like the rest of them by now" (9). The chador seems to be the culprit for all that she deems wrong with the "veiled mob," from their countenance and their "stench" to their manners. Betty does not want her "American" daughter to be raised in a country where not only women's "beauty" but also their "spirit" and "soul" are "cloaked."

She does not want her daughter to become "one of them" (103). As David Spurr has pointed out, "[t]he fear of contamination that begins by the biological thus expands, through a scale of progression that moves both metaphorically and metonymically, into anxiety over psychological perils of going native and finally into the dystopian view of vast social movements that threaten civilization itself" (91).

Mahmoody does not make any efforts to conceal her imperious disdain and abhorrence for the chador. Not only does she profess to loathe the garment, she also expresses her strong aversion to and disgust for the Iranian women who don it. Musing upon the education system in Iran and concluding that the system is designed so as to produce subservient women, she reveals her feelings for Iranians, in particular, women, saying that she "hate[s] the sight of all Iranians, especially meek women in chadors" (115), thus legitimizing it for her Western audience to hate anyone who looks different.

In short, it can be concluded that it is not only the physical space of the house, the city, or the country that binds Iranian women, nor is it merely the presence of their tyrannical husbands or any other "superior-looking" (34) males. According to Mahmoody, it is the observance of religious faith that restrains their very existence.[19] In this light, the chador, Mahmoody's much-loathed reminder of the "cloaked" Iranian woman, is anything but a symbol of religious observance. It transmogrifies, in Betty's phantasmagoric world, into shackles chained to Iranian women's bodies, and, as she claims, their souls, too. In her second book, Mahmoody explains her reaction to shedding her "hated chador, the black fabric designed to cloak Iranian women from head to toe" (17). According to her, not only is this imprisonment the fate of Iranian women, anyone who sets foot on the turf of the country is also bound to suffer the same lot. When Ellen, Betty's American friend who has converted to Islam, tells her on the phone that she thinks Betty should tell Moody about her plan "out of her love for me and concern for my welfare and that of my daughter" (182), she hangs up the phone, "feeling an Islamic noose around her neck" (183)—a description that both signifies Ellen's betrayal of "American" and "Christian" values, and also reinforces the idea that Iranian women's fate is not exclusive to them; rather, if one lives among them—for no matter how short a period of time—one is bound to be cloaked, abused, beaten, and "noosed."

Thus, according to Mahmoody, no matter where the Muslim woman stands in the world, regardless of what country she resides in or what she does, as long as she is loyal to the observance of her religion, she remains eternally subjugated, dominated, harnessed, and cooped up. Even though Mahmoody sees Islam as the root of the "plight" of Iranian women, and the nation at large, as evidenced by many instances of myth and inaccuracies vis-à-vis Islam, her (and her ghost writer's) grasp of the religion and her understanding of the Islamic history and tradition are at best minimal.

Ghosting Ghastly Narratives

One of the significant components often neglected or underestimated in analyses of both classic and modern captivity narratives is the role of co-authors, or ghosts, in the process of narrative pelection and composition. Like much else about captivity narratives, the role of ghost authors in the construction of such narratives is anything but a novelty. As early as the early eighteenth century, narratives of a more journalistic and propagandistic character were written in more acceptably "literary" styles, somehow inflecting from the didacticism of the narratives of God's providence and devout religiosity to the natives' "savagery." These narratives were primarily produced or ghostwritten by the hack and the journalist to enhance the conventional stylistic features of the narrative (hence the term "stylization") and to make the story more compelling and, as a result, more readily marketable.

In this light, the role of the ghost author in Mahmoody's narrative bears noting. William Hoffer, who co-authored the book with Mahmoody, has been described as an author who "has been spinning out international bestsellers for more than 20 years" ("William Hoffer"). In his track record, Hoffer has such works as *Midnight Express* (1977), which could be considered the most recent predecessor of *NWMD*. Unsurprisingly, *Midnight Express* is another tale of incarceration, only this time with a young white American man as the protagonist, in what the book blurb describe as yet another "environment of hellish squalor": Turkey. Except for the transformation of the fabled Turkish harems into a hideous dungeon where torture, rape, and murder prevail, there is nothing in *Midnight Express* that is not typical of the brand of Orientalism applied to Turkey. Carol Stocker has argued that the book-cum-movie is only another tale that "depict[s] the Middle East as a malignant nightmare" (Stocker).[20] The following lines from the movie adaptation of the book, uttered by Billy, the American protagonist, to the Turkish judge in court, neatly summarize the dominant attitude of the story toward Turkish people: "For a nation of pigs, it sure is funny you don't eat them. Jesus Christ forgave the bastards. But I can't. I hate them. I hate you, I hate your nation and I hate your people."[21]

It should come as no surprise that a few years later *NWMD* resonated with strikingly similar passages and depictions of the Muslim Iranian Other. In *For the Love of a Child*, Mahmoody recounts how she came to choose Hoffer as her collaborator:

> While in Tehran, I had heard about street demonstrations against *Midnight Express*, though the book and the movie based on it were banned there. I wanted to write with a person who had had such a profound effect on ordinary people in Iran—the people who had had such total control over my own life . . . If this writer could move the Iranian fundamentalists so strongly in absentia, I thought, he must be very effective. (21)

William Hoffer was, in a sense, "very effective." As an American author of melodramatic thrillers, Hoffer surely knew too well the marketing logistics as well as the political zeitgeist of the time that had largely shaped the popular taste of the 1980s and 1990s United States. Even though *NWMD* fails to live up to standard literary conventions of narrative composition and stops at the level of the sensational and the propagandistic, Hoffer has certainly m"stylized" the raw story, and the book does owe much of its success to Hoffer's contribution. Also, as far as offending the religious and national sensibilities of "fundamentalist"[22] Iranians is concerned, Mahmoody and Hoffer seem to have achieved that goal, since, as Bahramitash has observed, the book "helped to incite racist, anti-Muslim, and anti-Iranian feelings across Europe and North America" ("The War on Terror" 227).

West Meets East: The Clash of Civilization and Un-civilization

Mahmoody takes every opportunity to draw on Iranian people's airing of their grievances toward the US government's antagonistic policies against the Islamic Republic of Iran. It is no secret that the 1980s were troubled times of escalating friction between Iran and the United States. The tension had officially commenced and come to the fore almost from the very beginning of the establishment of an Islamic Republic in Iran in 1979. With the collapse of American leverage and hegemony in the post–revolution Iran, American influence and interference were anything but welcome.

In order, however, to make sense of the anti–US government sentiments in Iran of the 1980s—and the stress on the word *government* is a legitimate one[23]—it helps to analyze the narrative against the backdrop in which it has been written. During the time span that the events in the book transpire, August 1984 to February 1986, tension was particularly exacerbated between Iran and the United States. The official presence of the United States had formally ceased to exist in the aftermath of the Islamic Revolution and the subsequent takeover of the US Embassy in Tehran by revolutionary university students. Lured by the United States into attacking Iran (Paul), Iraq imposed an all-out war against Iran and invaded parts of the country for eight years, leaving hundreds of thousands of people dead, millions displaced, and entire cities destroyed. There is now a plethora of irrefutable evidence that the United States did not stop merely at seducing Iraq into the catastrophic war with Iran—one that has earned the title of the longest war of the century (Hiro). It also aided and abetted Iraq, supplying then-president Saddam Hussein with battlefield intelligence, chemical weapons, and poison gas, which he used against Iranian soldiers and civilians, as well as civilian Kurds of his own country. These facts have been articulated by many prominent American figures, including Congressman Ron Paul (Paul), Noam Chomsky ("Rogue States"), and Stephen Kinzer (Goodman).[24]

It was in the midst of such extremely strained relations that Betty Mahmoody set foot in Iran. There are many passages in the book (as well as episodes in the film) that depict the bombing raids on civilians and the havoc wrought on the capital city of Tehran as well as other cities (55, 58, 59, 61, 76, 154, 241, 307). However, Mahmoody never acknowledges in her account, and in fact insistently denies, the fact that the air raids had anything to do with the United States. Instead, she tries to depict a country where people fanatically despise Americans apparently for no good reason except their inherent zealotry bred by the fact that they are "Shiite Moslems, still glorying in the success of their revolution, clad in the self-righteous robes of fanaticism" (58). Writing on the history of Iran–US relations, Ted Snider argues that

[w]hen it comes to Iran, most North Americans are historical creationists. They believe that current events regarding Iran did not evolve, but emerged *ex nihilo*, out of nothing ... But that North Americans have no historical memory of the causal events that led to the current events of today does not mean that they didn't happen. The people of Iran remember them (Snider).

Although Snider's essay is written in the context of the prolonged nuclear negotiations between Iran and the P5+1, which resulted in a deal that was eventually shredded by Donald Trump, his point rings true for almost any conflict between the two countries since 1979.

The anti-US sentiment Mahmoody constantly mentions is nowhere better crystallized than in the character of her allegedly American-turned-Iranian husband. When the Hostage Crisis erupts, Mahmoody tells us, Moody does not conceal his "elation" over the incident, "clearly gleeful that America was emasculated before the world" (223). Elsewhere, claiming to have been ferociously beaten by Moody, Betty reports that Moody threatened to kill her "with a big knife": "I am going to cut you up in pieces. I am going to send your nose and your ear back to your folks. They will never see you again, I will send them the ashes of a burned American flag along with your casket" (188). Read against the historical backdrop mentioned earlier, such statements strike a ready chord with the American audience at a time when the traumatizing memory of the Hostage Crisis was still fresh in their minds and tensions between the two countries were running particularly high. In fact, such depictions tapped into the "New Patriotism" of the 1980s (Hoberman 320), which inspired many American cultural productions of the period. The trope was especially popular in the Hollywood industry of the time, which, according to James Hoberman, was characterized by a "mad cacophony of patriotic symbols" (271). Deborah Cunningham Walker has demonstrated that such productions, including the book, "unabashedly affirm traditional American social values and institutions and negate all things 'un-American'" (30). In the same light, Andrew Busch writes that, according to Martin E. Marty, there is "too intimate a connection between the new patriotism and attitudes of superiority, egotism, and militarism" (54). This patriotic symbolism also permeates Mahmoody's second book, *For the Love of a Child*, with many references to the Stars and Stripes. Taking refuge in the American Embassy in Ankara, Betty finds herself "just where I wanted to be, safe in the shadow of our flag" (5). Similarly, as she flies into New York, she notices that "the Statue of Liberty had never looked so beautiful. There she stood proudly and I had a new appreciation for what she symbolized" (15). Also early in the book, Mahmoody describes an occasion when "[o]n the Fourth of July, Bill's [William Hoffer, the co-author of *NWMD*] wife and son joined us to celebrate the holiday. Bill held Mahtob up to hang the American flag, ever so proudly, on the pole to the side of our house. Mahtob was one patriotic six-year-old who truly understood the meaning of freedom" (23).

While Mahmoody seems to be much beleaguered by Iranian people's anti-American government sentiments, she believes that such sentiments are disingenuous: "Although Moody's countrymen officially hate Americans, they venerate the American educational system" (3). Furthermore, she informs us that despite their "hatred" of the West, there are "many Iranians who retain an appreciation of the western style of life and who bristle at the present government's official contempt for America" (106). In fact, through decontextualizing the anti-US government sentiments of the time and failing to differentiate between both the American and Iranian people and their governments, Mahmoody misinforms her readers, while simultaneously justifying her own enmity toward Iranians as well as preaching hatred and insisting on difference.

In his discussion of the scope of Orientalism, Edward Said delineates how Harold W. Glidden's assertion that on the Western and Oriental scale of values "the relative position of elements is quite different" epitomizes what he calls the "Orientalist confidence" (*Orientalism* 49). Said then goes on to argue how, within the dominant Orientalist discourse, what constitutes an Oriental is different from that of a Westerner in essence:

> No merely asserted generality is denied the dignity of truth; no theoretical list of Oriental attributes is without application to the behavior of Orientals in the real world. On the one hand there are Westerners, and on the other there are Arab-Orientals; the former are (in no particular order) rational, peaceful, liberal, logical, capable of holding real values, without natural suspicion; the latter are none of these things (49).

It is, therefore, within this Orientalist paradigm that Mahmoody paints an Iran that seems to be intrinsically and systematically different from her country. This difference, far from being neutral or natural, is heavily charged and culminates in what Said has designated as "the essence of Orientalism: the ineradicable distinction between Western superiority and Oriental inferiority" (*Orientalism* 42).

In her depiction of Iran and its constant juxtaposition with the United States, Mahmoody exploits every possible means at her disposal to demonize Iran. She taps into Western, especially American, political, religious, social, and even racial distinctions to exemplify how anything Iranian is not only radically different from but also averse and inferior to its American counterpart. What is more, such differences across cultural and religious frontiers are not represented as worth exploring, engaging with, relating to, or comprehending. By dint of Iranian people's "inferiority", such differences should make every Westerner wary of engaging with Iranians, and by extension all Muslims, while appreciating the unquestionable "superiority" of their own culture. The narrative's investment in the extremely tense relationship between Iran and the United States in the 1980s seems primarily intended to reinforce the idea that Iranian people are resentful of all Americans. By contrast, this homogenizing attitude seems mostly absent in other protagonists in Mahmoody's second book. In *For the Love of a Child* (1992), we hear from one of the female American "heroines" who had spent some time in Iraq that "[t]hey [the Iraqis] made a big distinction between the US government and the American people. They had no stereotypical American in mind—and they wanted to convince me that the Iraqi people are not our enemies" (192).

No such distinctions are reserved for Iranians in *NWMD*, though. At one point in her book, she literally defines herself as the "enemy" of Iranian people when she wonders: "Do the [Iranian] Kurds hate Americans, too? Or are we allies, common enemies of the Shiite majority?" (388). This annunciation is more than Mahmoody simply venting her indignation at Iranians. When contextualized and placed into a historico-political framework, it can be translated into a corollary of the longstanding disposition toward, and its need for, fabricating enemies and defining itself against them, which spans from well before the "red menace" of the Cold War era to the present-day Iran (Schechter). This proclivity, exemplified nowhere more aptly than in George W. Bush's informal fallacy "[y]ou are either with us or against us" ("Address to a Joint Session"), can be observed here in the character of Betty, whose insistence on defining herself against her "enemies" resurfaces throughout the text. What is also noteworthy in the aforementioned quote is the fact that Mahmoody resorts to another myth, that is, Shia–Sunni animosity, by implicitly referring to the Sunni-majority Kurdish population of Iran with whom, in an instance of wishful thinking, she hopes to forge an alliance against the Shia-majority.

Betty's "American superiority" versus "Iranian inferiority" binary allows for no exceptions. Ranging from the physical to more complex phenomena such as culture, religion, social etiquette, and lifestyle, Iranians are persistently denigrated throughout the narrative. Such descriptions serve to reinforce the Orientalist binary and arouse in Western readers a certain disgust at and fear of an entire nation. In spite of such monolithic representations, in her second book, Mahmoody, most surprisingly, disavows any attempts to paint the relationship in absolutist terms: "Although I have said that our worlds are vastly different, I've never suggested that Iranian culture is bad and western culture is good" (277).

Betty makes sure the minutest cultural differences or traditions are not exempted from her racist diatribes against things Iranian and Islamic. Her reductionist characterizations include highly selective portrayals of the city landscape or domestic spaces, the sweeping attribution of certain characteristics to people or places, or preaching hatred against the Iranian nation in general. What is yet more astonishing is Mahmoody's assertion in *For the Love of a Child*, in response to objections to the biased and racist depictions in the book and the film: "I always understood that my ordeal in Iran was created by one individual—my husband. I never generalized about Iranians" (277). In the next sections, I will refute this assertion by analyzing Mahmoody's representations of Iran, focusing on major colonial tropes through which she represents the country and its people as well as the manner in which she juxtaposes the two countries to reinforce the binary of "American superiority" vis-à-vis "Iranian/Muslim inferiority."

Colonial Discourse in Not without My Daughter

In his Foucauldian theorization of the nexus between knowledge and power, Edward Said effectively demonstrates that Orientalism (as a discourse) and colonialism coexist symbiotically, mutually reinforcing each other and investing one another with meaning. In a similar vein, in his seminal study of colonial tropes, *The Rhetoric of Empire* (1993), David Spurr identifies a binarism in which "[t]he colonizer's traditional insistence on difference from the colonized establishes a notion of the savage as *other*, the antithesis of civilized value" (7). Spurr's influential study identifies and analyzes twelve fundamental rhetorical tropes that figure prominently in colonial discourses. He also investigates the manner in which such rhetorical topoi have been deployed in the modern period of European and American colonization, and the more recent period of decolonization (1). In *NWMD*, Mahmoody draws extensively on an essentialist binary between the United States and Iran and widely employs the Othering tropes of colonial discourse. In the context of this discussion, the tropes of "debasement," "affirmation," and "negation" are some of the more significant and recurring modes of writing about the Iranian Other. "Taken together," Spurr argues, "these constitute a kind of repertoire for colonial discourse, a range of tropes, conceptual categories, and logical operations available for purposes of representation" (3). In the following, some of the most recurring instances and dominant tropes of colonial discourse in *NWMD* will be elaborated.

Debasement: The Corrupt, Contaminated Other

As a major trope in colonial discourse, contamination resurfaces throughout Mahmoody's narrative and, by contributing to the "primitivism" of Iranians, reinforces the idea of their inferiority to, and their essential difference from, their American counterparts. In his analysis of the trope of *debasement*, Spurr argues that "[i]n colonial discourse, every individual weakness has its political counterpart—uncivilized society according to this logic being little more than the uncivilized mind and body writ large" (76). Hence, the many instances of physical contamination and defilement depicted in the text—regardless of how authentic they might be in the first place—are far from mere descriptions of bodily or spatial attributes; rather, they are directly linked to moral judgments made by the white Western woman about her Oriental Others.

In Mahmoody's Iran, filth, squalor, and stench seem to prevail. From the physical descriptions of Iranians to the descriptions of private and public spaces, cars, and foods, everything is depicted through images that create a sense of disgust and revolt the reader. From the very moment Mahmoody steps into "this alien world," she is "struck . . . by the overpowering stench of body odor" (5). Almost everyone she meets in and outside the airport reeks of perspiration. Although they may vary in their degree of "filthiness," the fact that all Iranians she meets are "foul-smelling" (250, 318) is presented as indubitable. Stinking seems to be such a distinctive feature of Iranians that when she meets Zia, "one of an innumerable multitude of young male relatives" of Moody, she likes him not only because of his courtesy and sophistication or his being "taller than most of the small-statured Iranian men," but "best of all," because "he was clean" (7). Once in Iran, Mahmoody worries immediately that having worn the scarf for a few minutes, she "must smell like the rest of them by now" (9). It is not the "hellish" summer heat or the crowded airport that may explain the stench of body odor; Mahmoody insists that it is because the most basic concepts of hygiene are alien to Iranians and simply beyond them.

One example of such "disregard" for hygiene, which Mahmoody is always quick to point out, is bathing. "Once a year," she proclaims, "everyone in Iran takes a bath" and that is for the occasion of Nowruz, the Persian New Year (163). Mahmoody's "discovery," however, is contradicted by her reference to the Islamic practice of ablution after sex. Nevertheless, she claims, quite oddly, that even when Iranians shower after having sex, it is not for hygiene reasons, as she dismisses such concepts as alien to Iranian culture; rather, the ritual ablution is meant "to wash away the taint of sex" (85)—a concept that has more to do with the medieval Roman Catholic view of sex as a "necessary evil" than with Islam. Ironically, the practice she refers to (called the "major ablution" in Islamic terminology) is only one of the numerous instances in Muslim hygienical jurisprudence, such as the (minor) ablution before the daily prayers and other mandatory or optional major ablutions for different occasions. Mahmoody further juxtaposes this "Iranian" proclivity with her own insistence on the "western custom" (29) of personal hygiene, when she recounts how, when staying in her sister-in-law's house in Tehran, she was the only one who "continued to shower daily" while "Ameh Bozorg [Moody's elder sister] and the rest of her clan continued to stink" and were "dressed in the same filthy clothes day after day, despite the drenching heat" (27). This obsession with the corporeal resonates with a well-established colonial discourse vis-à-vis the natives. In colonial discourse, Spurr argues, "the body of the primitive becomes as much the object of examination, commentary, and valorization as the landscape of the primitive. Under Western eyes, the body is that which is most proper to be primitive, the sign by which the primitive is represented" (22).

Not without My Daughter is packed with images of "Iranian" contamination and defilement, which are too numerous to list in their entirety here. However, as the examples cited earlier demonstrate, Mahmoody's insistence on the physical contamination of Iranians serves to reinforce their alleged primitivism, which she then posits against "American" notions of personal hygiene. In Mahmoody's Iran, the corporeal and the moral often converge to construct an image of Iranians, which represents them to be as morally corrupt as they are physically repulsive. This is especially true of Iranian men's alleged misogyny and sexual perversion. Mahmoody persistently depicts the average Iranian man as a macho misogynist and a molester. One bus driver, for instance, who is described as "a particularly pungent Iranian" (275), and one of the few Iranians whom Mahmoody does not immediately hate (and who actually helps her when she is trying to find the right bus home), turns out to be no more than an opportunistic groper when he "presses his horrid, foul-smelling body" up against her (276). In a similar vein, Moody's family members, both male and female, almost all of whom are denigrated for smelling and being dirty, are also represented as given to lying, spying, hypocrisy, misogyny, and violence. The narrative, therefore, can be said to serve as a site where physical contamination and moral corruption converge to construct the ultimate image of the Iranian Other.

The Cult of "Iranian" Domesticities

The trope of defilement does not stop at the level of the corporeal. Rather, it spills over into the interior of Iranians' domesticities. Like the obsession with the somatic, the scrutiny of the natives' interior spaces constitutes a major lineament of colonial discourses. Spurr argues that in Western literature there is a whole tradition "from colonial American captivity narratives to the novels of Forster and Marlaux" constructed on "this trial of penetration into the interior spaces of non-European peoples" (19). It is in these spaces, he maintains, that "the confrontation of cultures takes place face to face, or rather eye to eye, and it is here, at close range, that the gaze of the writer can have its most powerful effect" (20). In *NWMD*, the descriptions of Iranian interior spaces enhance the overall effect of primitivism and alienation that is produced throughout the narrative.

There seems to be no dearth of evidence in *NWMD* to "prove" how alien the concepts of cleanliness and orderliness are to Iranians. There are "no handkerchief or tissues" in Iran, Mahmoody proclaims. Rather, what she observes is "the women using these veils instead. The smell was repulsive" (24). Similarly, even though Mahmoody tells us that Iranian women are brought up to be submissive and "dutiful" housewives with no freedom at all (213–14), they seem not to be good at even the most rudimentary duties of housewifery. At their best, Mahmoody asserts, they are "haphazard housekeepers" (79). Almost all the Iranian houses that Mahmoody visits are represented as being in utter disarray and chaos. The kitchen walls of Ammeh Bozorg's house, for instance, are "coated with the accumulated grease of decades" (20); Nasserine is "amazed to learn that walls could be washed and that hers were originally white instead of grey" (93); and "Essey's kitchen, though filthy, was nonetheless sterile in comparison to Ameh Bozorg's" (32).

Mahmoody's representations of Iranian household politics resonate with some of the most famous passages of Harriet Beecher Stowe's *Uncle Tom's Cabin* (1852) depicting Southern kitchens. Similar to Miss Ophelia, who tries to instill a sense of Northern discipline and efficiency in Dinah's Southern kitchen, Mahmoody attempts to familiarize her husband's relatives with a sense of "American" order and hygiene. In a similar vein, Moody's elder sister, Ammeh Bozorg, strongly resembles Aunt Dinah, who is represented as "a dreadfully untidy old woman" (Stowe 297). The lack of any semblance of order in Mahmoody's image of Iranian women's kitchen government is reminiscent of Aunt Dinah's kitchen in Little Eva St. Clare's New Orleans home, which looks "as if it had been arranged by a hurricane blowing through it" (311) with "the rolling-pin under her bed, and the nutmeg-grater in her pocket with her tobacco" and "sixty-five different sugar bowls, one in every hole in the house" (317). Thus, both Iranian women and African-American women slaves are characterized as primitive and uncivilized through their lack of "civilized" American values as reflected in domestic discipline and order.

Similar pejoratively descriptive vocabulary is employed by Mahmoody to represent Iranian culinary practices and table manners. According to Mahmoody, Iranians do not seem to care much about cleaning or washing food ingredients, which are almost always described as infested with "bugs" and "worms" (74, 83, 97). Of Nasserine, Mahmoody says that she was "an atrocious cook, neither knowing nor caring much about hygiene, nutrition, or palatability" and her supply of rice "was the filthiest I had seen, contaminated not only by tiny black bugs but also wriggling white worms. She did not bother to wash it prior to cooking"

(83). Just as Iranians' perceived lack of hygiene drives Mahmoody to proclaim her "loathing" for Iran (35), the alleged contamination and poor organization of interior spaces drive her toward the same conclusion: "I hate her [Ammeh Bozorg]. She is dirty, filthy. Every time you go into the kitchen, somebody is eating over the stove and the food is dribbling back into the pot. They serve tea and they don't wash the cups and there are bugs in the food and worms in the rice and the house stinks" (74).

Mahmoody's descriptions of the domestic politics of Iranian households invoke the "Cult of Domesticity" or "Cult of True Womanhood", ingrained in the minds of nineteenth-century Americans (Brown 507). The cult emphasized cleanliness, arrangement, and organization of household environments and paraphernalia as well as proper wifely/womanly skills deemed necessary to run a perfect household. Moreover, as Gillian Brown has pointed out, "since kitchens both provide for families and display the systems of political economy with which domestic economy intersects, the responsible housekeeper observes the significance of kitchen things and seeks the best governing system for an orderly domesticity" (90). Mahmoody's descriptions of Iranian domesticities can also be read as part of a longer tradition of women travelers comparing domestic environments, and many more who used the domestic scene as a device for Orientalist denigration. It should be noted, however, that some female travelers, such as Mary Wollstonecraft and Lady Mary Wortley Montagu, though exoticist in some ways, tended to be more positive of other cultural practices than their home culture.

Characteristically, Mahmoody establishes herself as embodying the ideal domestic government whose household management and concomitant skills are the antithesis of Iranian women's allegedly slipshod grasp of household politics and domestic management. Unlike the Iranian women she encounters, Mahmoody is represented as clean, frugal, and well-organized to a fault and, as such, she embodies the character of a true American woman *par excellence*. Even Iranians seem to be aware of this "essential" difference between Mahmoody and themselves. The local supermarket owner, for instance, acknowledges Mahmoody's prudent domestic management in contrast to Iranian women's profligacy, commenting: "You are the best woman in Iran. Most Iranian women are wasteful" (273). Thus, descriptions of Iranian domestic spaces and household management become occasions for reinforcing the civilized West vs. primitive East binarism and for highlighting the moral "superiority" of the West. As McClintock (1995) has argued, "[h]ousework is a semiotics of boundary maintenance. Cleaning is not inherently meaningful; it creates meaning through the demarcation of boundaries. Domestic labour create[s] social value, segregating dirt from hygiene, order from disorder, meaning from confusion" (170). The alleged profligacy, contamination, and disorganization of Iranian households, therefore, serve as signifiers of their broader moral degeneracy and turpitude. Nasserine, whose alleged utter lack of any sense of order and hygiene is described in great detail, is also represented as an "Islamic spy" (126) who has no will of her own, has to report on Betty's activities, and who does not intervene when Betty is being battered by her husband. The same holds true for the teachers at Mahtob's school, who are accused of silently standing by and only watching when Moody is claimed to attack and almost kill Betty in the school corridor (185).

Furthermore, one could argue that Mahmoody's descriptions constitute a kind of projection, via the Other, of an image of an idealized Americanness, revealed as an ideal of white American femininity and offer an occasion for using the Other as a kind of mirror—a way of constructing a self-image. As such, similar to the stark contrast between the lifestyles of the black Miss Ophelia and Aunt Dinah in *Uncle Tom's Cabin*, the notorious "Iranian" housekeeping scandalizes the white American woman, offending her sense of domestic propriety (Brown 503). In addition, similar to the political connection established between kitchen economy and slavery in Stowe's book, Mahmoody's representations of Iranian women's chaotic domesticity culminate in a discussion of what she deems to be the abject, multitiered slaveries of Iranian women: to their husbands, to their traditions and, above all, to their religion.

Affirming the "Self," Negating the "Other," and Bestialization

Two other major rhetorical strategies in colonial discourse, *negation* and *affirmation*, are apposite to the discursive analysis of Mahmoody's *NWMD*. Succinctly defined, *negation* is the strategy through which "Western writing conceives of the Other as absence, emptiness, nothingness, or death" (Spurr 92). It is the act of marginalizing, or rather effacing, the Other, and treating them as a nonentity. The process of negation assigns less or no value at all to non-Western cultures, thus, "negating" their worth (Walker 84). Negation spans a wide gamut of issues, ranging from the space, history, culture, religion, and language with which the Other is associated to their identity and their very existence. Therefore, every aspect of the Other's life can potentially become subject to this strategy. The Oriental subject, as well as all the attributes that are deemed to constitute their character, are constantly nullified, negated, and silenced in colonial discourses.

Affirmation, on the other hand, is the validation of the cultural, political, religious, linguistic, and imperial presence of the Western subject/writer and a reaffirmation of the value of their presence in the face of the Other's engulfing nothingness. In other words, it is the gesture in which "the subject actually constitutes itself through repetition, allies itself with the law, and strengthens itself against imminent danger from without or within" (Spurr 110). The primary function of affirmation in colonial discourse is to justify, by dint of demonstrations of moral superiority, the authority and legitimacy of those in control of the discourse (110). As is evident from this definition, affirmation is deeply rooted in Rudyard Kipling's notion of "The White Man's Burden"—the idea that the "superior" white race should take it upon itself, due to its perceived moral and cultural ascendancy, to rule over and "better" the colored races. This civilizing mission requires the constant negation of the Other to open up a space for the affirmation of the Western subject, made all the more stronger by means of iteration and recurrence. *Affirmation* and *negation* constitute two of the most inextricably interwoven rhetorical figures in colonial discourse, as one always necessitates the other: in negating any aspect of the Other, the Western subject affirms their own sovereign position either explicitly or by implication.

In *NWMD*, Mahmoody devotes much of her narrative to the "primitivism" that characterizes Iranian manners. One prominent example is "Iranian" eating etiquette. "Eating," Mahmoody declares, "is the primary social activity of these people" (183), thus imparting the "backwardness" and "lack of sophistication" of Iranians, who, in her eyes, are not least acquainted with the most basic forms of socialization and social decorum. In fact, almost all modes of socialization by Iranians are negated in the narrative and reduced to the level of the animalistic.

Characteristically, Mahmoody juxtaposes the alleged absence of any social sophistication in Iranian culture with instances of the gatherings she and her husband used to attend in the United States, thus contrasting their "sophisticated" socializations with the well-to-do and the elite in the United States to "uncivilized" Iranian gatherings which, she claims, primarily focused on eating. To Mahmoody, indeed, only gatherings of their American friends qualify as proper socialization. The Iranian students' meetings in Mahmoody's US home to discuss politics and the upcoming revolution in Iran—even though not for the mere purpose of eating—are dismissed as fanatical and suspicious.

The use of animal imagery and metaphors is common practice within the domain of colonial discourse. It is, therefore, little surprise that one can often find in *NWMD* the bestialization of the Iranian Other at work as a descriptive strategy. Hugh Henry Brackenridge, a famous editor of American captivity narratives and one of the "great Indian haters," wrote in his prefatory note to *Narrative of a Late Expedition* (1783) of the necessity of eliminating entirely those "animals, vulgarly called Indians" (qtd. in Pearce 10). This animalization of the colonized Other has been used to dehumanize not only Native Americans and people of color, but also the inhabitants of white colonies (although they were still considered superior to the brown and black natives). Helen Carr has observed that the Irish, for instance, were often identified as "squalid apes" (75)—an epithet that emphasizes both bestiality and contaminatedness simultaneously. Such bestialization, in turn, renders the colonized Other as inferior and in need of being tamed, civilized or outright annihilated. In a similar vein, Mahmoody employs the same vocabulary to describe both the physical appearance and behavior of Iranians. "The moment we entered the house," Betty notes, "Moody's hawk-nosed sister came running. She shrieked with delight and fell upon him, showering him with kisses" (164). As in this example, and much like descriptions of contamination, the physical and the behavioral often come together to highlight the coarse animality of Iranians in the narrative.

In a similar fashion, Iranian eating manners are described in tellingly animalistic terms: "Sitting on the floor cross-legged or perched on one knee, the Iranians attacked the meal like a herd of untamed animals desperate for food" (15). The fact that some Iranians, among people from many other cultures, prefer to sit on the floor and spread a *sofreh* (usually an oilcloth spread on the floor for eating) on which they arrange the foods is not regarded as a signifier of cultural diversity. Rather, its difference from the cultural norms of the white Western writer renders it uncivilized and bizarre, thereby deserving condescension and derision.

Almost all descriptions of family gatherings and parties in the text, except when the host is a Westerner or a Westernized Iranian, depict Iranians "shoveling" food "indiscriminately into their chattering mouths that spilled and dribbled bits and pieces all over the sofrays[25] and carpets and back into the serving bowls" (15). Characteristically, Mahmoody pits her own socially "sophisticated" manners against those of Iranians, thus reaffirming her American civility and superiority vis-à-vis Iranians. Her invitation of Moody's family for dinner is only one such instance: "Within moments my dining room was a mess. Bits of food flew all about the table and onto the floor as the guests plunged in with their hands and, occasionally, a spoon. Moody, Mahtob, and I ate quietly, using the proper utensils . . . I knew I would be up late that night cleaning grains of rice and other scraps of food from the walls and out of the carpet" (292). Besides the bizarrely animalistic imagery deployed to describe Mahmoody's guests, unlike many Asian countries, eating with hands is not a common practice in Iran and anyone slightly familiar with Iranian culture would be astonished by such willful misrepresentation, the primary purpose of which seems to be the accentuation of images of primitivism and incivility. What makes such descriptions even more extraordinary is Mahmoody's references to the fact that Moody's family were by no means average Iranians and, in fact, belonged to the upper crust of the society (2, 27,191, 248): "In the midst of this strange society . . . we were counted among the elite. We bore the prestige of a respected family that, compared to the norm, was far advanced in sophistication and culture . . . and we were, in relative terms, rich" (27).

The aforementioned examples go a long way toward highlighting the interconnectedness of the tropes of debasement, animalization, negation, and affirmation and the manner in which they reoccur and reinforce one another and serve to represent a dehumanized, primitive Other. At the other end of the Orientalizing gaze—and in contrast to the land where people "accepted the squalor as the norm" (259)—lies Mahmoody's America, which appears utterly devoid of such "Iranian" characteristics and is unadulterated, sophisticated, and civilized. Such dichotomization could signify a kind of purging reflex—a projection of a utopia via the squalor of the Other, a Puritan cleansing of Otherness within and without.[26]

Mahmoody explains that even those "exceptional" Iranians who seem to appreciate hygiene and cleanliness go to the United States to relish them. Early on in the narrative, she juxtaposes Iran and America sharply by contrasting the ideas of hygiene and social justice. On several occasions, she claims that the highest level of cleanliness on the Iranian scale is still considered "filthy" by American standards—an assertion that serves multiple purposes instantly: debasing what she sees as belonging to the Other and therefore as different from her native culture; negating the diversity and heterogeneity of an entire nation and squeezing them into pigeonholes; and affirming the superiority of "American" cultural values. She contrasts the two countries again, when she hopes that Moody would come to his senses and "realize that his professional future was in America, not in a backward nation that had yet to learn the lessons of basic hygiene and social justice" (49).[27] Those very few "cultured" Iranians whom she encounters are those who are, in one way or another, linked with the United States either via their education or moving between the two countries, or are simply among those who "retain an appreciation of the western style of life" (106). Dr. Najafee, a family friend, for example, divides his time between the two countries, "coming here [to Iran] to earn exorbitant fees in his private practice, and spending six months of the year in California attending seminars, studying, and appreciating freedom and cleanliness" (245). Lack of hygiene is presented as such an essential "Iranian" characteristic that when Betty encounters "clean" Iranians, she tends to identify them as Americans. She does not conceal her surprise at having encountered "a whole new circle of wonderful loving people, who delighted in civilized living, who were, regardless of the circumstances of their birth, far more American than Iranian" (305). It is not only the American author who tends to identify the "civilized" Iranians as Americans. The "civilized" and "cultured" Iranians themselves do not seem to wish to be associated with Iran, either. Of two of her "civilized" friends Mahmoody learns "the wonderful fact that both Chamsey and Zaree lived ten months of each year in America . . . Zaree was about fifteen years older than Chamsey. A widow, she now lived with her sister. Her English was not as polished as Chamsey's, but she, too, was very friendly to me. Both women considered themselves Americans" (245).

Also, Mahmoody remembers how her friend "Chamsey was excited about severing most of her ties to Iran and eager to return to California" (279). Betty's descriptions of this Westernized Iranian elite resonates with Bhabha's concept of colonial mimicry as "the desire for a reformed, recognizable Other, as *a subject of a difference that is almost the same, but not quite*" (*The Location of Culture* 86). In the same light, Spurr has also argued that in colonial discourses, "[t]he desire for Western styles of consumption . . . is seen as a natural aspiration toward a better life, while it is also treated as a sign of weakness. There is a certain contempt for non-Western peoples who appear so ready to abandon their traditions" (86). Mahmoody's sympathy and association with the Westernized Iranian elite is only to the extent that they embrace and affirm "American" values. However, even in doing so, she notes a certain hypocrisy and disingenuity among Iranians, asexemplified, for instance, in their "veneration" of the American educational system (3), as mentioned earlier.

It is not only Mahmoody who upholds the moral and cultural "superiority" of Americans above Iranians. According to Mahmoody, even Iranians themselves recognize the "truth" that any Westerner is cleaner than an Iranian. The real estate agent who is helping Betty find a house is "delighted to learn that an American couple was looking for housing" and shows them several "western style" apartments owned either by investors living abroad or by "cultured Iranians who wished to keep them in good condition." These investors, according to Mahmoody, seem to acknowledge that "the easiest way to accomplish that was to refuse to rent them to Iranians" (268). On another occasion, she reminisces about a time she had no other choice but to forsake her "American" standards and adjust herself to the dramatically "inferior" and "backward" Iranian lifestyle and stoop so low as to be "ecstatic" to be provided with the rare opportunity of eating clean food:

> Together we spent hours meticulously cleaning the bugs out of the rice before we cooked it. How strange it was to be ecstatic over the opportunity to remove vermin from my food! In two months my priorities had changed dramatically. I realized how the American lifestyle had pampered me into fretting about minor concerns. Here, everything was different. Already I had learned that I must not allow the details of daily existence to impinge upon larger tasks. If there were bugs in the rice, you cleaned them out. If the baby pooped on the Persian carpet, you wiped up the mess. If your husband wanted to leave the park early, you left. (79)

As was mentioned before, *negation* results in exclusion, marginalization, and erasure of the Iranian Other (Walker 24). In all of the aforementioned excerpts both *negation* and *affirmation* occur conjunctively. Iran is assigned as the locus of the animalistic, the uncivilized, the abject, while the United States is extolled as the embodiment of civilization, culture, sophistication, and propriety. Also conspicuous in the aforementioned examples is the act of the Other's negation of their native culture and affirming the Westerner's superiority by assuming the "privileged" position of being Westernized. Not only are Westernized Iranians depicted as complicit in the debasement of everything related to their country, they are also distinguished from un-Westernized Iranians and exempted from the purported turpitude that characterizes them. More significantly, they are credited by the Western writer with the power to recognize and bear witness to the vices of their native ways—a gesture that earns them the status of pseudo-Westerners.

Mobs, Masses, Multitudes

One of the most familiar and dominant leitmotifs of colonial discourse—especially when white women's "entrapment" is concerned—is the image of mobs and the ochlophobic sensation "foreign" crowds evoke in the Western subject. De Hart has argued that intrinsic to captivity narratives and Orientalist accounts is "the recurring description of large crowds of people that threaten the Western individual just by being there, because they all look the same, speak foreign languages and smell terrible" (56). Such descriptions reinforce the image of the Western woman as stranded in the land of the "enemy" among the "alien," "minacious," and "unpredictable" forces of a nation, or a religion for that matter, which can apparently turn against her at any given moment and for no particular reason.

Analyzing representations of the 1979 Islamic Revolution and the ensuing Hostage Crisis in his *Covering Islam* (1981), Edward Said demonstrates how Iranians are almost always depicted as an "anonymous," "deindividualized," and "dehumanized" mob (6, 35, 43, 48, 86, 87, 95, 101). Such images of multitudes and mobs also run through Mahmoody's narrative. Upon her arrival in Tehran, Betty finds herself surrounded by Moody's "innumerable multitude of young male relatives" (7). In the streets of Tehran she cannot but think of herself as a foreign woman entrapped "in a city of fourteen million sometimes hostile and often unpredictable people" (274).[28] As Spurr has argued, the people of the "Third World" "are both reduced and magnified into the equivalent of natural disaster: influx, epidemic, inundation, the flooding of border" (91). In the aforementioned example, the sheer (erroneous) number of the people of Tehran resembles the force of an unpredictable and impending natural catastrophe, such as might be associated with a hurricane, a tsunami, or an earthquake. Images of huge masses of people recur throughout the narrative, and words like "multitude" (6, 32, 33, 68, 273) are often used to connote the "intimidating" mass identity of Iranians and to obliterate their individual differences, which also stand in stark contrast to Protestant ideas of individualism and one's individual relationship with God.

Walker has discussed the "appearance of swarming people" as an image frequently found within colonial discourse (67). Similarly, Spurr observes how Western reporting on and photography of the so-called Third World tends to favor images of crowds, depicting "the people, often as chaotic, irrational mobs," while stories from the Western world depict images of "well-groomed individuals, leaders identified by name, and portrayed as rational even in crisis" (165). Also, in his discussion of images of filth and defilement in the so-called Third World countries, Spurr demonstrates how "the crowded populations of the Third World take on the teeming, spawning character of disease itself" (88).

As a modern captivity narrative, *NWMD* is fraught with the image of multitudes, which are made all the more ominous and frightening when coupled with incarceration imagery. Throughout the narrative, Mahmoody describes the masses of people in a derogatory vocabulary, going as far as asserting that to her the country "seemed populated almost totally with villains" (334). The fact that she is "trapped" in such a land makes the fear of the "mobs" even more prominent. Thus, stripped of any sense of individuality, Iranians are represented as no more than masses that arouse an engulfing ochlophobia in the Western subject—a feeling that is made all the more baleful and inexorable by the painful knowledge that there is no escape from the land of the "villains."

Linguistic Sovereignty: A Bunch of Babblers

Language is one of the most crucial touchstones of any culture. In fact, so fundamental to human civilization has language been that such philosophers as Rousseau have expressed uncertainty as to whether the provenance of language lies within organized human society or vice versa. From ancient times, the notion of civilization has been contingent upon the idea of language, so much so that the word barbarian (in Greek *barbaros*) originally meant "one who babbled, who did not speak the language of civilized humanity" (Spurr 102). Similarly, Aristotle's grounds for his idea of the racial supremacy of Greeks were primarily based on their capability to "boast a superior, articulate medium, while the barbarians had but incoherent, inarticulate languages" (Acheraïou 56). A language is evaluated based on its "richness and complexity, its refinement from mere cry and gesture, its capacity to make distinctions, its multiplicity of names, its range from particularity to abstraction and its organization of time and space" (Spurr 102). In the domain of colonial discourse, language holds such an authoritative position that "the negation of civilized language as a faculty of the Other leads, through a series of related negations, to a conclusion which upholds the justice of colonial rule" (Spurr 103).

One can find references to language in the earliest figurations of the Other. There is a long-standing history of denying the non-Western subject the power of language and assigning them such features as muteness and incoherence. As Spurr has argued, the Other is "denied a voice in the ordinary idiomatic sense—not permitted to speak—and in a more radical sense—not recognized as capable of speech" (104)—an idea that also underlies the trope of infantilization in the discourse of Orientalism. Furthermore, similar to the trope of debasement—where the Other's physical appearance and surroundings signify their moral failure and depravity—"the degraded or inadequate condition of language signifies a corresponding degradation in the political and social order of the other" (Spurr 104).

Against this backdrop, therefore, it is unsurprising that Persian/Farsi language, which is one of the cornerstones of Iranian/Persian culture, is subject to Mahmoody's persistent vilification in her narrative. In *NWMD*, language is a prominent racial pointer on which the author capitalizes to further elaborate the alleged inferiority and primitivism of Iranian culture. As is the case with many modern examples of colonialist writing, the unintelligibility and incoherence of the language of the Other resurface throughout the text, thus "reaffirming language as a primary site of the effort to divide cultural presence from its opposite, which is to say clarity from confusion, articulation from silence" (Spurr 104).

Throughout *NWMD*, the language of the Iranian people is described as discordant, incomprehensible, and violent. For instance, Mahmoody describes family conversations as "the never-ending chatter of imponderable tongues" (18). Knowing that not many Westerners have been exposed to the "discordance" of Persian, she takes it upon herself to familiarize them with the language: "To a westerner a normal Iranian conversation appears to be a heated argument filled with shrill chatter and expansive gestures . . . The noise level is astounding" (18). Almost all "unappetizing scenes" of hungry Iranians "attacking" the food are "accompanied by a cacophony of Farsi" (15), and when Moody's relatives come to visit them, Mahmoody recounts how "the now-familiar din of chattering relatives assailed our ears" (33). Even though Mahmoody confesses to her ignorance of Persian language, which is also manifest in numerous cases of mistransliteration of Farsi words, she claims that the school teachers at Mahtob's school spent "most of their time in chatter that, although I could not understand the content, was obviously idle gossip" (115)—a statement reminiscent of Said's observation in his *Orientalism* (2003) that "Orientalists know things by definition that Orientals cannot know on their own" (300). This is a prevalent attitude that professor

Fatemeh Keshavarz has also criticized in her discussion of the so-called Iran "experts" who appear regularly on various TV programs in the West: "With regard to Europe, you are not a specialist on the whole region. You are a scholar of French art, German politics, or Italian social movements. But with the East, you know everything about them" (qtd. in Ghasemi Tari 243).

Characteristically, not only does the American writer negate the language of the Other, but also in so doing she also widens the seemingly unbridgeable gap between the two cultures, while simultaneously feeding the xenophobia that pervades the narrative by revealing another "menacing" feature of the Other's culture. Hence, Mahmoody manages to construct an image of the non-Western language, which "signifies its inherent unintelligibility, and thus its reduction to a cultural zero degree" (Spurr 104). Similar to every other aspect of Iranian culture, Persian language is not only contrasted with English but is also used to judge the character of its interlocutors. The Westernized Chamsey, for instance, who is reported to spend ten months of each year in the United States, speaks to Betty "kindly in impeccable English" (270). Describing Moody's relatives, Mahmoody observes that "[t]he other half [of the clan] seemed a bit more westernized, more open to variation, more cultured and friendly, and definitely more hygienic. They were more likely to speak English and were far more courteous to Mahtob and me" (32). The quote is particularly telling in that it proffers a prime example of how all the aforementioned attributes—ethics, culture, hygiene, and language—merge to construct two essentially different images of the Western(ized) subject and their Other. Moreover, as Acheraïou observes, "the whole colonial differentiating practice finally boils down to a self-mirroring strategy whereby the valorized native becomes a pale copy of the European self" (46). Therefore, throughout the text, anyone who has a better command of English is more likely to possess "American" values and is portrayed in a more positive light. For instance, Amahl, who reportedly arranges for Mahmoody to be smuggled out of Iran and pays for it, too, is portrayed as a selfless gentleman who, unsurprisingly, speaks "perfect accented English" (284)

Similar to the fundamental role that language plays in the development of societies and cultures, it also plays a significant role in Mahmoody's description of her husband's allegedly "overnight" transformation from a gracious, professional "American" doctor into an Iranian "brute":

> I noticed a strange new style to Moody's speech. At home he would have said, "You didn't . . ." Now he avoided the contraction, speaking in the more formal style often used by those to whom English is a second tongue. Long ago Moody had Americanized his language. Why the change? I wondered silently. Had he reverted to thinking in Farsi, translating into English before he spoke? (21).

As the excerpt suggests, Moody's alleged "reverting" to Farsi is represented as part of his greater "backsliding" into his Iranian ways, and serves to mark the two Moodys off from one another.

The question of language also figures prominently in the movie adaptation of the story. This appears not only in the shrill, high-pitched conversations in

Farsi (almost always by non-Iranian actors), but more importantly in the total absence of subtitles in the film, given that Betty (played by Sally Field) is the only main character who speaks only English and a rather considerable proportion of the dialogues are exchanged in Farsi. This cinematic stratagem reinforces the foreignness of the Iranian Other and magnifies the sense of alienation and apprehension of the protagonist, as well as the audience. In his review of the film, Roger Ebert raises significant questions about the lack of subtitles in the film, which merit quoting in full:

> It is one of the hallmarks of this film's style that no foreign speech is ever translated with subtitles. All of the "good" people in the film speak English. Everybody else speaks--usually in shrill, angry tones--in a tongue we cannot understand, and which is never subtitled. It must have been a deliberate decision to leave out the subtitles. Surely we would benefit by knowing the content of key conversations? Surely it would be interesting to hear the Muslim point of view articulated, whether or not we agree with it. Surely there must be one person in Iran who does not scream with spite and hostility? Yes, but then the Muslims in the film would be somewhat humanized, and the film is at pains to make them alien ciphers. Racism works by denying a people its specific humanity, and turning it into a stereotyped collection of negative attributes.

Along the same lines, Parinaz Eleish, an Iranian-born Boston filmmaker, has observed: "The main actors are not Iranian, and the background actors who are Iranian have no lines at all or scream the whole time or talk without subtitles so they look like screaming lunatics" (qtd. in Stocker). One could argue that, perhaps in an ironic way, the lack of subtitles and the unintelligibility of Iranian conversations are an apt indication of how, through such representations, Iranian people have been perpetually silenced and negated by the dominant Western Orientalist discourse.

The Mad Muslim Man

In a 2002 Finnish documentary, *Without My Daughter*, Dr. Sayed Bozorg Mahmoody, Betty's former husband, thus begins his version of the events: "I am a beast and a criminal in the eyes of the world. I have been portrayed as a liar, a woman-beater, and a kidnapper" (Tervo and Kouros). The statement, however, is more than a summing-up of how Dr. Mahmoody is perceived in the eyes of the world. It is a fragment of the vast array of dehumanizing adjectives that are attributed to the Oriental Muslim man in Western media and literature, and which are complicit in his dehumanization and demonization. In other words, it is within the framework of the jailer–prisoner, oppressor–oppressed interrelationship that the Oriental male and female are portrayed and perceived. In this Orientalist dichotomy, each pole imparts meaning to and reinforces the other while justifying its existence. In addition to their mutual interdependence, it is the amalgamation of Oriental male and female, the intercourse of the "Oriental brute" with the "Oriental sex object" that delivers, for the Western audience, the expected perception of the Orient. In the words of Ziauddin Sardar, "symbolically, the violent and the barbaric Muslim male and the sensual passive female, come together to represent the perfect Orient of Western perception" (48).

Betty Mahmoody's Orientalized Iran is no exception. It is a "crazy" (191), "bizarre" (389), and "horrid" (103) land, inhabited by violent Muslim male chauvinists who batter their wives to death, incarcerate them, and torture them on a whim. The book is packed with passages where Moody humiliates his American wife whenever he has the chance and subjects her to both physical and mental torments in cold blood (200). Nevertheless, it is not only Moody who commits such heinous acts of violence; one can find evidence of masculine oppression and brutality almost throughout the narrative. Recounting the story of Ellen, another American woman married to an Iranian doctor, Mahmoody tells her readers the same manner in which Hormoz treated her wife: "Once in Tehran, Ellen found herself hostage just as I was. Hormoz decreed that she was never going home. She was an Iranian citizen subject to the laws of the country and to his will. He locked her up for a time and beat her" (148).

In a passage where Moody is described as slamming Betty down, punching her, and screaming that he is going to kill her (102), Mahmoody informs her readers, quoting an "insider," Nasserine, the wife of one of Moody's "innumerable legion of nephews," how all Iranian men are the same: "It is ok. All men are like this. Mammal does the same thing to me. Reza does the same thing to Essey. All men are like this" (103). These "insider" confessions serve to corroborate Mahmoody's depictions of the country's misogynistic culture and the pervasiveness of the brutality of Muslim manhood.

In a scene in the movie we see Ellen, Betty's American friend whom she has met in a Quran class, beaten black and blue by her Iranian husband, with her lower lip torn and bruised, apparently because she has revealed Betty's secret escape plan to her husband. "It is your duty as a wife," Ellen's husband, Hormoz, yells at Betty, "to tell your husband everything. You cannot have secrets." The event, which Ellen denies ever happened in an interview in the documentary *Without His Daughter*, does not exist in the book and seems tagged on to the film—just like many other fictitious events—only to reinforce the omnipresence of domestic violence and masculine brutality, especially toward Westerners, in Iran.

In *For the Love of a Child*, Mahmoody provides her readers with a follow-up on Ellen's situation: the torture is still being inflicted, with the difference being that Ellen's Iranian husband has apparently grown more professional and "brags about being able to beat us up without leaving any marks" (248). Mahmoody's second book is almost entirely devoted to similar sensationalized accounts substantiating how irrational and perilous an adventure marrying non-Americans is. The book offers no room whatsoever for intercultural complexities, cultural diversity, social heterogeneity, and cross-cultural dialogue and, much like *NWMD*, rehashes the long-established narrative of "innocent" American women trapped in the clutches of "brutal" foreign men.

It is also important to note that it is not only Betty who allegedly falls prey to Moody's vicious and mercurial fits of rage. The innocent five-year-old Mahtob seems to have her fair share of her father's aggression, too: "In blind anger, he backhanded her sharply across the face. Blood spurted from a cut on her upper right lip, spattering into the dust" (68). It is no wonder, then, that when, in her second book, we hear Mahmoody recounting to Mahtob the news of "a plane crash" in Iran, Mahtob replies "with no hesitation": "Good! I hope my dad was on it!" (28). Like much else in the book, the incident, however, is grossly misrepresented. By the "plane crash" Mahmoody seems to be referring to the shooting down of a civilian jet airliner on July 3, 1989, flying from Tehran to Dubai, by a US cruiser in the Persian Gulf. The event, often referred to as "Flight 655", in which all 290 passengers died, marked a watershed in Iran–US relationship and significantly reinforced anti-American government sentiments in Iran. Far from acknowledging any wrongdoing, the United States has refused to formally apologize to Iran to this date. In fact, on August 2, 1988, the then–US vice president—George H. W. Bush—proclaimed that "I will never apologize for the United States, ever. I don't care what the facts are . . . I'm not an apologize-for-America kind of guy" (qtd. in Kinsley). None of this information, however, appears in the book, and the incident is merely recounted to serve as an example of how deeply the seven-year-old Mahtob loathed her father.

The demonization of Iranian manhood in the narrative does not stop at the description of their alleged violence and aggression. Iranian men, we are reminded throughout the book, are not just misogynists of the first order, barbaric woman- and child-beaters, foul-smelling, and cacophonous. The alleged molestation of Mahmoody by the "foul-smelling" driver mentioned earlier is further used to feed into the narrative's xenophobia when Mahmoody quotes Essey as saying that such acts are only performed on "foreign women" (266), thereby arousing even greater loathing and horror in the Western audience.

Any discussion of Muslim Oriental masculinity would be insufficient without recognizing its interdependence with that of Oriental femininity. It is in relation to the Oriental woman that the picture of Oriental manhood can be best understood. Similar to the Oriental/Muslim woman, the characteristics often attributed to the Oriental Muslim male—his "barbarism," "brutality," "irrationality," and "perversion"—are triggered and manifested mostly vis-à-vis women. Therefore, to gain a better understanding of this interrelationship and the bigger picture, one needs to examine the Oriental man and woman in relation to one another.

Going Native: From American Gentleman to Iranian Brute

The "difference" between Iranian men and their American counterparts is nowhere better exemplified than in Mahmoody's constant juxtaposition of the two Moodys, that is to say, how the Americanized Moody seems to have lapsed back into his former Iranian self. In the narrative's discourse on Iranian Muslim men, what stands out conspicuously is how Moody is depicted as metamorphosing from a polished American gentleman into an Iranian brute upon returning to Iran.

The ubiquitous idea in the narrative that Iranians are a "backward" nation—one of Mahmoody's favorite terms—falls perfectly in line with the proclivity of the Orientalist discourse for assigning "the Islamic Orient to an essentially ancient time and the West to modernity" (Said, *Orientalism* 271). Mahmoody seems to maintain that Moody had had enough of his homeland and had, therefore, chosen to leave it for good to reside in the United States, where "he found a world far different from his childhood, one that offered affluence, culture and basic human dignity that surpassed anything available in Iranian society." This, in turn, leads her to conclude that "Moody truly wanted to be a westerner" (49). Now back in Iran, Betty cannot but wonder why he has stooped so low from being "an osteopathic anesthesiologist, a respected professional with an annual income approaching one hundred thousand dollars" in the United States into being "merely Ameh Bozorg's [his elder sister] little boy once again" (9).

In this context, marriage seems to serve as a site where the "real" nature of the Oriental man is revealed and "the savage in the Oriental prince emerges" (De Hart 55). As Betty De Hart argues, the mysterious, "exotic" part, which initially constituted part of the courtship appeal, becomes increasingly more menacing, so much so that over time the Westernized Oriental prince transmogrifies into a monster. This itself both taps into the idea of the unreliability of the Other, while at the same time feeding back into it as well. In other words, no matter how "civilized" (i.e., Westernized) the Oriental man might initially look, there is always a frightening and untrustworthy facet to his character that he has somehow managed to keep under the façade of his seeming civility: "His beautiful dark eyes become dangerously sparkling. His strength and decisiveness turn into dominance and authoritarian behavior. His protectiveness and courtesy become jealousy and possessiveness that obstruct the woman's freedom" (De Hart 55).

The alleged transformation in the nature of the Oriental man is often characterized by a sense of immediacy and unpredictability. Mahmoody recounts how in the United States Moody had always been the perfect gentleman, an ardent suitor from the very start, "courting her in style," showering her with compliments and gifts, and always admiring her motherly care for her children: "My life was filled with roses," Mahmoody nostalgically reminisces (51). When she is obsessed with the thought that "once Moody brought Mahtob and me to Iran, he would try to keep us there forever," her fellow-American friends assure her that her obsession is irrational and that "Moody would never do that" as he was "thoroughly Americanized" and, thus, was no longer untrustworthy (3). In the movie adaptation, Moody reinforces the same mentality, reassuring his daughter that he is "as American as apple pie." Betty, nevertheless, has "ample ground" to think ill of Moody's intentions: "his renewed devotion to Islamic rituals" (Mahmoody and Dunchock 44). In the United States, Moody had been a successful doctor and "a loving husband and father," which qualified him as a real American family man who had managed to achieve the American Dream. Nevertheless, he appears to degenerate, as soon as he sets foot on Iranian turf, into a tyrannical husband and father intent on incarcerating and beating his wife and daughter into submission. This degeneration happens due to "the influence of the Iranian, Islamic culture and family that changes him from the prince into a monster"—a change that manifests itself in Moody's "backsliding into his own culture and tradition" (De Hart 55). Such gross stereotyping leaves many turns and twists of the plot ambiguous and, at times, engenders a *deus ex machina* effect. For instance, some critics have questioned the abrupt transformation of Moody from a doting husband and professional doctor into a monster. Nayereh Tohidi, an Iranian-American professor of Gender & Women Studies at California State University, points to the movie's failure "to explain how and why Betty's Iranian husband goes through such an apparently abrupt change from decent father and loving husband to fiend once he is home again. Such an unreal and simplistic portrayal of the main character indicates the filmmakers' lack of knowledge and understanding of Iranian culture and the Iranian psyche" (Tohidi).

The change, however, does not seem to have occurred only to Moody's temperament. Every other aspect of his character appears to have undergone some sort of negative transmutation. This transmutation gradually reveals itself in such other forms as Moody's language (as demonstrated in the above discussion of "linguistic sovereignty"), even though he had "long ago Americanized his language" (21). Moody's apparently rekindled devotion to his native religion, Islam, is another marked change which, according to Mahmoody, seems to have had far-reaching repercussions for Betty, Mahtob, and Moody himself. We are told that Moody did not practice "the extreme form of Islam under which he had been raised" (even though it is not clear at all what the statement really means), "enjoyed his glass of liquor," and overall could not be considered an observant Muslim (47). Nevertheless, he seems to have regained his faith with rekindled passion once back in his country. This fresh interest, however, is far from innocent and stretches far beyond a nostalgic reunion with faith.

Although the perfectly Americanized Moody is cast as an ideal husband and father, he is not without his innate Oriental faults and one can still see the collision of his Eastern and Western selves through Mahmoody's descriptions, which serve to reaffirm Betty's Western supremacist outlook. Describing Moody's "paradoxical personality" early in the story, Betty paints her husband in a chiaroscuro: "His mind was a blend of brilliance and dark confusion. Culturally he was a mixture of east and west" (4). The "brilliance," indeed, is the result of his years of Americanization and the "dark confusion" is rooted in Oriental mysteriousness, exoticism, and bewilderment.

In Mahmoody's second book, it becomes evident that it is not only Moody who has undergone the alleged metamorphosis. Mahmoody claims that the process of metamorphosis during which the husbands are de-Americanized and revert to their "primitive" native roots is bound to befall every non-American husband (and occasionally wife, too) whose stories she recounts in *For the Love of a Child*, once again reinforcing the notion of the untrustworthiness and mutability of the foreign Other. Mahmoody's sequel to *NWMD* is fraught with similar stories of Iraqi, Pakistani, Algerian, Iranian, and Yemeni fathers (never a Westerner) who, she claims, have abducted their children and undergone the same transmogrification as Moody has. All these people are similarly described in culturally degrading terms, thereby reducing the complexities of child abduction cases to stereotypically villainous fathers and victimized mothers, or, vice versa if the father is either an American or a "naturalized U.S. citizen" (110).

"Veiled Humanity": The Oriental Accomplice

"Would she [Mahtob] become a woman like Nasserine, or Essey, cloaking her beauty, her spirit, her soul, in the chador? Would Moody marry her off to a cousin who would beat her and impregnate her with vacant-eyed, deformed babies?" (103). Almost the whole gamut of stereotypes exploited to describe the Oriental Muslim woman appears in Mahmoody's narrative. One could argue that Flaubert's assertion that "the Oriental woman is no more than a machine: she makes no distinction between one man and another man" (qtd. in Said, *Orientalism* 187) is particularly relevant to Mahmoody's portrayal of Iranian women. All one would need to do is to divert the Orientalist gaze from the Oriental woman's sexual submissiveness to a more general conception of her passivity and subservience. As Said argues, chief among the repository of Oriental women's characteristics is that they ooze with "unlimited sensuality, they are more or less stupid, and above all they are willing" (*Orientalism* 207).

The very "willingness" that allowed the white male European colonizers/travelers of the last few centuries like Flaubert to enjoy the luxury of licentious "Oriental" sex, here earns the Iranian woman Mahmoody's undisguised contempt. From the very beginning of the narrative, it is almost impossible to overlook "how Iranian women are slaves to their husbands" and "how their religion as well as their government coerced them at every turn, the practice exemplified by their haughty insistence upon an antiquated and even unhealthy dress code" (35). The image of the veiled and "submissive Iranian woman" (102) pervades *NWMD*. Almost all references to Muslim women are accompanied by Mahmoody's utter and open contempt for the veil. Characteristically, the historical, social, political, and particularly religious significances of the veil are conveniently overlooked in the text. Instead, the dress code is always rejected wholesale, while at the same time the superiority of its Western counterpart is affirmed.

Like much else in the narrative, Mahmoody's representations of Muslim women are not exempt from the inconsistency that characterizes many Orientalist narratives. In fact, her representations of the alleged submissiveness of Iranian women are contradicted by her repeated references to the matriarchal position of Moody's elder sister who, according to Mahmoody, runs the whole "clan" (147): "Moody's sister . . . was the matriarch of the family, whom everyone addressed with a title of deep respect, Ameh Bozorg, 'Great-aunt'" (5). In fact, as Homa Hoodfar, an Iranian-Canadian sociologist, has pointed out in her analysis of the colonial images of Muslim women, even though Iranian/Muslim women are always depicted as willing, oppressed, and passive, they usually hold more power in their domestic spheres than their Western counterparts—a fact that many Western travelers and commentators have simply dismissed as exceptional (7). Along the same lines, Pershang Vaziri has remarked that "[e]ven though women have more freedom here [in the United States] legally, they don't enjoy as much power. Because family structure is stronger in Iran, and women rule the family, socially they have more power there" (qtd. in Stocker). Nevertheless, in Mahmoody's narrative women are stripped of all facets of their humanity and reduced to compliant, veiled automata who must only perform what they are commanded or programmed to do. Furthermore, oppression is not represented as every Iranian woman's lot only; foreign women who are married to Iranians seem to suffer the same fate. In other words, any encounter between the Oriental and Western subjects seems to afflict and contaminate the latter, thereby making them suffer what Spurr has dubbed "the demoralizing crisis of going native" (84). This, in fact, is a persistent fear in Western traditions, especially in the heyday of colonial era. Francis Bacon, for instance, warned against the influence of traveling to foreign lands in the *Of Travel* section of his *Essays* (1597): "Let it appear that he [the traveler] doth not change his country manners, for those of foreign parts" (Bacon).

Even Ellen, Betty's American friend in Tehran, is accused of betraying Betty and divulging her secret to her own husband, Hormoz. He, in turn, coerces Ellen into telling Moody about Betty's plan to run away: "He [Hormoz] told me that I have to tell Moody because it is my Islamic duty. If I don't tell him and something happens to you and Mahtob, then it is my sin, just like I killed you. I have to tell him" (182). Even though, as Walker believes, Ellen's betrayal of Betty's confidence is sure to outrage the American audience (86), it is far from unexpected. Ellen has already committed a double betrayal: her marriage to an Iranian is cast as a betrayal of her nationality and patriotism, but more significantly her conversion to Islam is presented as a betrayal of her faith, and even her soul. For Mahmoody, this is another sign of Ellen's irremediable transgression and her having become too Muslim, too Iranian and, therefore, too untrustworthy.

Mahmoody's account of Iranian women is informed by an inexplicable lacuna regarding the significant role of Iranian women who actively partook in the 1979 Islamic Revolution and during the Iraqi-imposed war to which Mahmoody makes many references. Once again, the powerful social, political, and religious agency and subjectivity of Iranian women are negated, eliminated, denied, or distorted. This omission becomes more marked when judged against Mahmoody's claim that when in the United States, she has been closely following, along with her husband, the news of the Islamic Revolution and how it unfolded. As the numerous photos and footage of Iranian women participating in demonstrations against the shah, most of which are easily accessible online, would prove, it was mostly women like the ones described in Mahmoody's account (and not the Westernized, upper-class elite) who participated in the revolution and later in the defense against the Iraqi aggression.

Willing Convicts vs. Western Rebels

As evident in the foregoing discussions of different characteristics of Iranians represented in *NWMD*, Mahmoody's descriptions are informed by the establishment of an essentially different Western counterpart posited against its Iranian Other. Hence, characteristically, her representations of Iranian women are interspersed with those of herself and other white or Westernized women. In her pioneering study on the role of perceptions about white women in the history of racism, *Beyond the Pale: White Women, Racism and History* (1992), Vron Ware identifies the three recurring categories of "the Good," "the Bad," and "the Foolhardy" under which white female characters in Orientalist and colonialist texts can be subsumed (232). The Good white woman emblematizes a moral opposition and resistance to any kind of tyranny and injustice. Like similar decent and virtuous characters in literature, especially female characters, a predictably unfortunate destiny of suffering awaits the morally upright woman, as she finds it beyond her powers to change the society in which she lives. Eventually, injustice prevails and the Good woman is subsequently subjugated by it.

The second type of white woman, the Bad, can, in a manner of speaking, be compared to what Malcolm X termed "the House Negro"—the Black slave who worked in the house and, therefore, enjoyed a higher quality of life than "the field Negro", who worked on the plantation (Mamdani 657). The House Negro, thus, was potentially more likely to uphold the apartheid power structures constructed upon ubiquitous racism and discrimination against his fellow people of color. The Bad white woman can be the exact opposite of the Good in that her codes of morality are rooted in self-interest and opportunism, rather than in moral integrity and ethical principles. She may detest the climate and the people surrounding her, but she makes the most of the privileged position she enjoys through her marriage to a colored man who, in turn, facilitates her access to the trappings of power, wealth, position, and class.

The third kind of white woman recurring in Oriental/colonial discourses is what Ware describes as the Foolhardy. In the context of this discussion, they often start as hapless victims of abusive husbands who batter and betray them. However, as De Hart has argued, this victimhood is a corollary of the women's earlier self-victimization through their misjudgment, since they "dabbled in marriage with an oriental man" (thus breaking the taboo of their own society) and, after all, "married this man voluntarily," disregarding the fact that "since western and eastern cultures do not mix, problems are unavoidable" (57).

The Foolhardy are, nevertheless, beyond mere unwitting victims. Victimized as they might be through both their own indiscretion and recklessness as well as their husbands' viciousness, they do not often linger in their predicament and move on to evince the heroism that distinguishes them from both other Western women and "servile" Oriental Muslim women. They are portrayed as proactive, resilient, tenacious, imbued with a spirit of resistance, survival, and hope, and they tend to create opportunities out of the most improbable and precarious situations. The Foolhardy woman is a non-conformist, if not a rebel, who displays staunch feminist proclivities. She is adamant in breaking the taboos of both Western and Oriental societies wherein she lives or is "trapped." This iconoclasm turns out to either have disastrous consequences for her—as her conduct "threatens to upset the whole system" (Ware 232)—or miraculously to save her from her predicament. Therefore, apart from "God's grace," it is the Foolhardy woman's bravery, intrepidity, and tenacity that guarantee her salvation after she has undergone the plight imposed on her by the Oriental brute. Moreover, the Foolhardy is the ideal figure through whom the cornerstones of American identity—perseverance, independence, self-reliance, and individuality—can be best represented.

In this light, one could argue that Mahmoody, and the kindred "heros/heroines" in similar narratives presented in her second book, exemplify Ware's category of the Foolhardy. They are "victims" both of their own decisions and a man often cast as a deranged husband. These victim-turned-heroines, however, manage to evoke the readers' sympathy almost immediately.[29] This is because the "victims" are often presented as plunged headlong into their predicaments with no prior warning about the trials and tribulations of intermarriage—especially when the cultures are presented as the extreme opposites—and could thus be forgiven for their "mistake." Even if they *were* cautioned against such courtships, they could not be expected to act any more judiciously, blinded as they often were by an exotic love, "lost in his dark, piercing eyes" (De Hart 57). If the Foolhardy's miscalculation calls for her punishment, it is through the same punishment, which often manifests itself in the form of captivity, child custody battle in parental abduction narratives, or a combination of both, that the Foolhardy woman displays her unwavering steadfastness and dedication. It is the same perseverance and loyalty that distinguishes the Western Foolhardy from the docility and inaction of her Oriental/Muslim counterparts.

Milani maintains that women like Betty in *NWMD* portray themselves in a totally different light than their Oriental peers: "Far from being willing convicts, passive victims in need of special and persistent deprogramming from abroad, they succeed in tearing down walls, pushing against the boundaries that contain them, making frontiers vanish, bearing witness to the hitherto unspoken, sprouting wings, flying through their texts" ("On Women's Captivity" 42). Iranian women, on the other hand, appear to be nothing but objects of what Said has called "a male power-fantasy" (*Orientalism* 208), playthings at the hands of tyrannical males, lifeless puppets manipulated by the puppeteer.

In *NWMD*, Iranian women never react to their own, or to each other's, brutalization; nor do they take any measures to change or prevent it. There are many passages in the book in which Iranian women relate how their husbands beat them. In all cases, these women are portrayed as completely defenseless and incapable of doing anything to prevent or mollify their husbands. In the passage where Betty is allegedly beaten by Moody in their daughter's school in front of all the teachers and staff, the women are depicted as standing idly by, only watching and doing nothing to defuse the situation: "All of these women were powerless against the wrath of a single invading man" (168), Mahmoody reports. The passage, thus, serves as a site wherein the fate of Iranian women and that of the "captive"

Western woman intersect: both are oppressed and can do nothing but submit to the tyranny of the brutal, misogynistic Iranian/Muslim male.

However, while both women may initially seem to share the same fate, Betty eventually turns out to be radically different. She fights back, defies Moody at every turn, and does everything in her power to find a way out of such impasses. She is represented as a proactive woman who devises plans, cultivates relationships, seizes every opportunity that arises, and is constantly seeking ways to break the chains that shackle her. When allegedly incarcerated within the confines of her house, or that of her husband's relatives, she persistently attempts every possible strategy for breaking out of the house. When she fails to break free, she tries communicating with the people outside, to ask for their help, or to notify them of her situation. In contrast to the Foolhardy Betty stands Ellen, the Bad white woman. Ellen, who has apparently been afflicted with the malaise of "going native," seems to be irremediably immersed into the fabric of Iranian culture and, as discussed earlier, has committed multiple betrayals, the last of which is her betrayal of Betty's secret. In the eyes of Mahmoody, Ellen's assimilation is no different from her betrayal of "American" values.

In *NWMD*, it is not only the adults who are subjected to such Orientalist binaries; even Iranian children uninitiated into the adult world, and not yet consciously identifying with any particular faith or value system, are portrayed in condescending and denigrating language with strong racist and white supremacist overtones. For example, Mahtob, the "American" child, is just a chip off the old block. She is depicted as exuding extraordinary tenacity, resilience, and bravery, and her precocious understanding and discretion are way beyond a five-year-old girl. Mahmoody makes sure no one misidentifies "her" daughter with Iranian children of her age just because she happens to have an Iranian father. As much as Mahtob's Iranian peers are sickly looking, "vacant-eyed," "deformed" (103), boisterous, dirty, and ill-behaved, she is gorgeous, vibrant, wise, and unyielding; she is, in one word, "American." Her "level of understanding" never ceases to "amaze" Betty when she tells her mother that she definitely wants to go back to America (365). Also, just like Betty, Moody has failed to shatter Mahtob's resistance and hope: "Moody had not beaten Mahtob into submission. Her spirit was bent, but not broken. She was not a dutiful Iranian child. She was my resolute American daughter" (361).

In an interview with Mahmoody, the notable German magazine *Der Spiegel* ("Wir Haben") summarized what hitherto has been discussed regarding the juxtaposition of the white Western man, woman, and child respectively with their Oriental counterparts. The people juxtaposed stand for entire cultures, religions, nations, and even such enormously controversial entities as West and East. The West is represented as standing for wisdom, courage, and sagacity while the East is couched in all-too-familiar stereotypes of mystery, threat, and the fear of the unknown: "She [Betty] is the pure West. She is brave, wise at the right time, crying at the humiliation and cold-blooded only when necessary. Her husband is the dark mystery, whose change from American into Iranian resembles the change from Dr. Jekyll into Mr. Hyde" (52).

The "Villain" Writes Back

In 2002, a much-belated documentary *Without My Daughter* was produced by the Finnish director Alexis Kouros, who set out to uncover the truth behind Mahmoody's narrative and to give voice to Betty Mahmoody's former husband's version of the story. The aim of the ninety-minute documentary, according to Kouros, was to reveal the mendacity in the American film and to present the real story behind what turned into an acrimonious custody battle for Mahtob Mahmoody. The documentary transcends the emotional yearning of a father seeking to revisit his daughter and probes the wider political and global contexts that complicate the case. In order to paint a fuller picture and counterpoise the sensationalism of *NWMD*, Kouros claims he accumulated evidence in both Iran and the United States. Nevertheless, he complains that Betty Mahmoody was uncooperative and that she prevented attempts at establishing contact with Mahtob.

The documentary is significant in many ways. First, it provides a new lens into Betty Mahmoody's much-publicized story, which raises significant questions about the authenticity of many of Mahmoody's allegations. Interviews with some of Mahmoody's friends in Iran, as well as Betty Mahmoody's refusal to clarify major inconsistencies in the narrative, raise serious doubts about the veracity of her account. For instance, Alice Sharif, an American friend of Betty's living with her Iranian husband in Tehran, has refuted many of Betty's accusations against both Iranian people and American women living in Iran at the time:

> We were friends but she did write several lies about me here in this book. And not just about me but many of the American women or the foreign women that live here. They were very upset with Betty for writing such a book. If my country and Iran have more than twenty years of no relations, her book and her film serve to only make the situation worse instead of to help the situation.

Alice Sharif further rejects Mahmoody's claims of being incarcerated in her house and remembers that Betty was "free to go out any time that I called her on the phone." She also disputes Mahmoody's claim that she managed to escape Iran through the mountains to Turkey. Similarly, Malek Sharif, a family friend of the Mahmoodys', while refuting many of Mahmoody's claims, highlights the effect of sensationalization as a selling point in the publishing industry: "If you wanna write a book and if you wanna make money in the States you have to sensationalize it and that sells." However, the most significant and revealing interview in the documentary is the one with the judge involved with the child custody case. Patrick Reed Joslyn, Circuit Court Judge, does admit that Dr. Mahmoody "didn't even know he was divorced until it was over and done with." When questioned if Mahmoody's treatment would have been different had he been the citizen of a different country, such as Canada, the judge responds: "As far as the court is concerned, oh no, never. Not in my court. I would never allow any kind of, as we might say, xenophobia, fear, or prejudice, or bias. Mr. Mahmoody would have received the red-carpet treatment in my courtroom."

Despite the judge's claim, however, what is extraordinary and, indeed, very revealing about Dr. Mahmoody's treatment in the US judicial system is the judge's subsequent statements about the case, when he vents his true feelings about both Mahmoody and Iranians:

> Then the next question is where is he in the spectrum? Is he one of these rabid fundamentalists that hates Americans? You remember the ones that took control of the Embassy? They abused American citizens. Now it's interesting from an American standpoint. I was in the military. If I were in control of this country there'd be a lot of dead Iranians. And it's not civilized and it's a terrible way of conducting business, but that seems to be the only way you can deal with these irrational folks. They don't believe in the law, international law. They believe in this terrible violence that you see. I have a bad picture painted of jihad and Hezbollah and maybe it's fashioned by our own media because we do have a lot of Jews in the media and controlling the information that comes to the United States.

The quotation highlights not only the judge's racism and anti-Semitism, but his ignorance, too, such as when he mentions Hezbollah, a Lebanese, not Iranian, organization, and jihad, a concept that is totally irrelevant to the divorce and custody case in question. Also, the claim that he would have given Dr. Mahmoody the "red-carpet treatment" is both quite ironic and disingenuous, given that Dr. Mahmoody lost not only all his property in the United States but also his daughter in a one-sided trial. Furthermore, the quote highlights the contamination of what was a merely judicial decision about a private, familial case with emotionally induced politics and the jingoism prevalent at the time of the court's ruling. The judge's statements are significant from various perspectives. They exemplify how indelible the effect of the Hostage Crisis remains to this date for many Americans and how it has come to shape both the policies of the United States and the public opinion toward Iran. It also signifies the underlying American exceptionalism in the US collective identity, as exemplified both in the judge's "[t]hey abused American citizens" as well as his disregard and apathy both for the hostile US policies against Iranians, in general, and the injustice done to Dr. Mahmoody, in particular. Furthermore, it illustrates the extent to which Orientalism can shape the "civilized world's" perception of its Other. Finally, the quotation highlights, as the judge confesses, the power of the US media, and its rather monolithic structure, in demonizing countries or religions deemed antagonistic to the United States.

In December 2013 *Lost without My Daughter* by Sayed Mahmoody (Betty's ex-husband) was published posthumously (Mahmoody passed away in 2009) by a London-based publisher, "Thistle Publishing." The back cover of *Lost without My Daughter* describes the book as "the last-ditch attempt of a father desperate to reach his daughter, to let her know that he is not the monster he has been portrayed to be." That the book has been published some twenty-six years after *Not without My Daughter*, could perhaps be attributed to the reluctance of Western publishers (as well as Western readership) to invest in the unpromising account of a Muslim Iranian man demonized beyond redemption. Unsurprisingly, Sayed Mahmoody's account has incurred the outrage of incredulous Western readers[30]—convinced of Sayed Mahmoody's mendacity and ruthlessness. Except for the few fulminating reader reviews on Amazon,[31] it seems that the book has never been critically studied or reviewed. Most surprisingly, the book's title does not even appear on the list of books published by its publisher. While establishing the truth value of Betty Mahmoody's memoir (not to be confused with its myriad historico-political inaccuracies) and the response to it is an exercise in futility, the comparison of the two books' receptions is a telling indicator of the hegemony not only of Orientalist narratives that best satisfy readers' expectations, but also the corporate media that has the power to propagate one account and stifle another.

At the end, no matter how superficial or propagandistic, cross-cultural narratives often speak volumes about the mindset, traditions, and the power structures that make their production, propagation, and reception possible. Although they often go to extremes to paint a monolithic picture of the Other, more often than not they end up problematizing the very reductivist modus operandi through which they operate, thereby destabilizing the dichotomous constructions upon which they are founded. As Colley has argued, "consciously or not, they almost always make clear by some incident, or passage, or giveaway line, that difference is not absolute, and that identities are invariably insecure" (206). In capitalizing on what Mahmoody sees as Iranian religious fanaticism, she also brings to light the religious chauvinism that informs her narrative. In a similar fashion, Mahmoody's vituperations against Iran's legislative and judicial systems are undermined by her experience of, and disappointment with, the American judicial system, when seeking custody of their daughter (Mahmoody and Dunchock 44), not to mention by the judge's unabashed racism and xenophobia demonstrated earlier.

Cross-cultural narratives can provide excellent grounds for cross-fertilization, mutual understanding, and reimagining the deeply entrenched Others. They are, alas, hardly ever employed to that end. With the US need for constructing new enemies, captivity narratives have gathered tremendous momentum, reappearing and being widely propagated, often in times of political tension. Hence, it should come as no surprise that at a time when tensions were high between Iran and the United States, a three-decade-old story of captivity—the Hostage Crisis—appears afresh in a Hollywood disguise in the film *Argo* (2012), and wins the Oscar Award, reiterating much of what *NWMD* epitomizes. Also, perhaps the fact that the Oscar was awarded by Michelle Obama from the White House speaks volumes about the relationship between power and the discourse of Orientalism. This is yet another testament to the protean nature of Orientalism and to the fact that, like the power that enables it and is reinforced by it, Orientalism as a discourse never perishes—neither do captivity narratives; they are only reincarnated when the time is ripe.

Chapter 3

READING LOLITA IN TEHRAN

MANUFACTURING MUSLIM LOLITAS FOR THE WEST

> If Edward Said dismantled the edifice of Orientalism, Azar Nafisi is recruited to re-accredit it.
>
> Professor Hamid Dabashi, *Native Informers and the Making of American Empire*

In the preceding chapter, *Not without My Daughter* was analyzed as "the mother of neo-Orientalist best-sellers"—a designation that, more than anything else, signifies the influential role that Mahmoody's book played in rejuvenating Orientalist narratives of white women's "captivity" in foreign lands. When in March 2003 Azar Nafisi's *Reading Lolita in Tehran*[1] was published to international plaudits, and was received with an éclat unprecedented for any Iranian-American writer to date, it was as though *Not without My Daughter* had not only made a comeback but had also finally given birth to its rightful heiress, as it were, some sixteen years after its initial publication. On the one hand, *RLT* belongs to the category of the memoirs and captivity narratives on Iran revivified in earnest by the success of Mahmoody's book. On the other, it can be regarded as the epitome of twenty-first-century neo-Orientalist autobiographical narratives published in the post-9/11 climate, as it instigated the dramatic upsurge in neo-Orientalist memoirs by expatriate Iranian-American women[2] (Marandi 179) and remains the iconic Iranian-American memoir hitherto (Whitlock, "From Tehran" 8). With this in mind, then, it is little wonder that *RLT* bears striking thematic and representational similarities to *Not without My Daughter*, which is indicative of the internal consistency of (neo-)Orientalist discursive practices underlying such narratives.

A twofold distinction, however, differentiates *RLT* from Mahmoody's memoir. The first distinction pertains to the role of the authorial self in the narration of the story. Even though both authors enjoy the "privilege" of access to the "Oriental" world of their Iranian/Muslim Others, Nafisi's account is distinguished by a native/insider element that reinforces the authenticity and the truth value of her narration for her Western audience.[3] The other difference concerns both the content and stylistics of the narratives, which are informed by the two authors' very different socio-educational backgrounds. While *Not without My Daughter* can, at best, be described as a work of hack writing co-written by Betty Mahmoody and her pulp-fiction ghost writer, *RLT* is the artifact of a university professor well versed in Western literature, literary narrative, and rhetorical strategies. Hence, while Mahmoody's book deals largely with the mundane details of everyday life in starkly black-and-white pictures, *RLT* capitalizes on the "higher," and more controversial, questions of politics, religion, gender roles, arts, and literature.

Synopsis

Before any discussion of the representational modus operandi of *RLT*, it is indispensable to provide a succinct synopsis of the memoir. Unlike *Not without My Daughter*, *RLT* does not follow a linear, unfolding story line. Essentially, the book chronicles Azar Nafisi's time in Tehran, Iran's capital, in the post–Islamic Revolution era, from 1979 to 1997. The book interlaces significant historical junctures in post-revolution Iran, such as the trajectory of the revolution, the Iran–Iraq War,[4] and the Hostage Crisis, with the author's recollections of teaching Western literature to Iranian students, her alleged expulsion, her resignation, and her eventual move to the United States. It is, however, her descriptions of the lived experiences of Iranian women under the new political system that lie at the heart of the narrative. The overarching narrative framework of the text is a private English literature class that Nafisi claims was held clandestinely with seven of "her best and most committed students" (1). From the fall of 1995— after resigning from her last academic position—to 1997, Nafisi met with her students in her own apartment to discuss what she describes as "forbidden" classic Western literature. The class, therefore, serves as a microcosm and the centerpiece of the memoir and is meant to provide a lens through which the reader is invited to peer into the inner workings of Iranian society, culture, politics, and religion. In the course of the class, personal narratives of Nafisi's "girls"[5]—as she affectionately calls them in her memoir—are interlaced with the journeys and fates of characters in the works of such canonical authors as Vladimir Nabokov, F. Scott Fitzgerald, Henry James, and Jane Austen. It is principally through the medium of this weekly class that Nafisi's responses to and reflections on the events in Iran are articulated.

Reception and Reader Responses

The phenomenal success of Nafisi's memoir must be understood in the context of a variety of political, temporal, literary, and cultural factors and, hence, reducing its runaway success to a singular cause risks oversimplification. Any thorough discussion of Nafisi's memoir and its reception also requires familiarity with the geopolitical and the cultural context of its production and the wave of Iranian-American memoirs penned in the last two decades. While the earlier, pre-9/11 Iranian-American memoirs and their reception were chiefly driven by a public inquisitiveness in the West about the 1979 Islamic Revolution, interest in the recent genre of female memoirs has been principally aroused by the public's growing appetite for and curiosity about the perceived threat of "Islamic fundamentalism" in the post-9/11 milieu. Against this backdrop, Amy Malek has attributed the popularity of the genre to the Western public's "seek[ing] insight into a country and a people that have been deemed 'evil' and an imminent threat to Western society" (362).

It was both in the post-9/11 atmosphere and against the backdrop of the 2003 US invasion of Iraq[6] that *RLT* was released and soon became the number one paperback bestseller on *The New York Times* bestseller list for more than 117 weeks. According to Nafisi's website, the book has been translated into thirty-two languages and has won numerous literary awards, including "the 2004 Non-fiction Book of the Year Award from Booksense, the Frederic W. Ness Book Award, the 2004 Latifeh Yarshater Book Award, an achievement award from the American Immigration Law Foundation, as well as being a finalist for the 2004 PEN/Martha Albrand Award for Memoir" ("Azar Nafisi Website"). Also, in 2006 Nafisi was awarded a Persian Golden Lioness Award for literature, presented by the World Academy of Arts, Literature, and Media. In the *Chronicle of Higher Education*, *RLT* was cited as the second most read book on American college campuses after *The Da Vinci Code* (2003) by April 2004 ("What They're Reading") and by September of the same year it ranked fifth on the list of the most borrowed nonfiction books across the United States ("Lj Bestsellers"). Before long the memoir became "a classic work, anthologized in the second edition of the popular college textbook *The New Humanities Reader*" (Rowe 257). The tremendous success of the book was followed by "universal rave reviews from even the most feared of book critics" (DePaul, "Re-Reading" 74) for more than a year after the publication of the book, offering overwhelmingly enthusiastic appraisals of the book's form and content (Mailloux 25).

At first glance, *RLT* is more than anything else a story about women and reading, or rather the story of women reading. It is, therefore, only too justified that the success of Nafisi's memoir is often attributed to the two major leitmotifs of the narrative, that is, the representation of women and (reading canonical Western) literature. In her memoir, Nafisi promotes a kind of universalist liberal-humanist approach to literature, exemplified in her "knack for dramatizing literature's transcendent values," which, as Richard Byrne has argued, "brought robust sales for her memoir" ("A Collision" 9). Furthermore, the narration of life narratives of women, especially when presented as both exotic and victimized, appeals to many Western readers. Like her literary ideology, Nafisi's version of feminism is equally informed by a universalism that naively overlooks the complexities, heterogeneities, and differences of sociohistorical circumstances of women in the non-Western world. This latter question (of women) itself owes much to the truth claim about the alleged oppression of the Iranian/Muslim Other propagated in the memoir and reinforced by scores of enthusiastic Western reviewers. As John Carlos Rowe has duly observed, "the book's popularity in the West has much to do with readers' desires to understand the authenticity of Iranian women" (260).

From a rather similar vantage point, *RLT* can be perceived as a narrative revolving around a women's book club. As such, understanding its success is contingent upon the awareness of the fact that the release of the memoir was concurrent with the phenomenon of female book clubs and reading groups starting in earnest in the 1990s, largely instigated by such factors as Oprah Winfrey's nationwide book club launched in 1996 (DePaul, "Re-Reading" 73; Malek 365). In a study published contemporaneously with *RLT*, *Book Clubs: Women and the Uses of Reading in Everyday Life* (2003), Elizabeth Long estimates that in the United States alone, there are between five and ten million female book club members (1). The proliferation of book clubs led to the publication of Reader's Guides by almost all major publishers as well as the promotion of authors through providing their biographies, and at times interviews, on their websites and by connecting the readers and authors by setting up conference calls (DePaul, "Re-Reading" 73). On the website of the publisher of *RLT*[7]—Random House—as well as on Nafisi's personal website,[8] the author's biography appears next to extensive accolades for the book and the Reader's Guide, which includes discussion questions, suggestions by the author herself, and an extensive Teachers' Guide or Note to Teachers. In this light, one could argue that the memoir seems to be preceded by its own heuristic apparatus, that is to say, the book is already "read" for the reader. With this in mind, it should not come as a surprise, then, that a memoir about the liberating power of literature with an all-female book club as its narrative centerpiece should be so enthusiastically received in the United States, especially as word-of-mouth recommendations by readers, book store owners, and book clubs alike have "exponentially amplif[ied] the buzz" surrounding it (Abbott).

Besides the rise of the book club phenomenon in the West, *RLT* also owes its success to the popularity of the memoir as a literary genre, especially when it is an essentially female memoir (Donadey and Ahmed-Ghosh 623; DePaul, "Re-Reading" 74). In conjunction with this reason is the narrative's apparent championing of feminist values and support for the women's cause (Bahramitash, "The War on Terror" 230). Furthermore, as critics have pointed out, the memoir's elicitation of reader empathy for the characters—reinforced through its highly selective and arguably manipulated portrayal of Iranian women's lives—has also contributed to its public reception (Donadey and Ahmed-Ghosh 624). In keeping with the book's treatment of the "woman question" in Iran, critics have argued that the book's affirmation of established preconceptions and the (Orientalist) ideological perspective that Western audiences have come to expect from women in Muslim countries has played a major role in the popularity of *RLT* (Keshavarz, *Jasmine and Stars* 112; Donadey and Ahmed-Ghosh 624; Bahramitash, "The War on Terror" 221). As a text emphasizing the role and ascendancy of Western literature, some critics have partially attributed its success to its literary merits (Malek 365; Donadey and Ahmed-Ghosh 624) and to "a nonfiction storyline that works off beloved literary classics"[9] (DePaul, "Re-Reading" 74). Being well versed in American and English literatures, Nafisi capitalizes on various narrative techniques. Throughout the memoir, the author creates and maintains suspense and often addresses the reader directly for effect and more empathetic engagement.

In one passage early in the book, Nafisi invites the reader to "imagine" the characters' "plight":

> I need you, the reader, to imagine us, for we won't really exist if you don't. Against the tyranny of time and politics, imagine us the way we sometimes didn't dare to imagine ourselves: in our most private and secret moments, in the most extraordinarily ordinary instances of life, listening to music, falling in love, walking down the shady streets or reading Lolita in Tehran. And then imagine us again with all this confiscated, driven underground, taken away from us. (6)

The excerpt serves several simultaneous functions: it emphasizes that the story is written for the intended Western readership, thus demanding their personal engagement with the narrative; it reaffirms that it is a story of women's "most private and secret moments," thus arousing the readers' curiosity, if not Orientalized fantasy, about the Oriental Other; and it confirms the mainstream Western discourse on Iran as an undemocratic, fundamentalist, and fanatical state that usurps its denizens' "most extraordinarily ordinary instances of life."

Undoubtedly, one of the most significant factors in the reception of any work of art is the historico-political moment out of which it emerges. As far as *RLT* is concerned, it is not by mere coincidence that the memoir was published in March 2003, when the traumatic memory of 9/11 was still fresh in the minds of the American public and, perhaps more importantly, while the United States was waging yet another war against Iraq (Koegeler 33; Donadey and Ahmed-Ghosh 623; Grogan 54). In the aftermath of 9/11 and the US invasion of Iraq, *RLT* catered to the mass curiosity about the Muslim Other—more than ever propagated in the public and official discourse as the United States' principal foe—and the status of women inhabiting Muslim countries (Keshavarz, *Jasmine and Stars* 112; Malek 365). Besides the foregoing reasons for the book's success and appeal, one can also refer to such other factors as the overwhelming number of rave reviews published in American journals and newspapers, as well as Nafisi's active participation in numerous talks and interviews to promote her memoir (DePaul, "Re-Reading" 74).

Reading Lolita in Tehran was not popular only in the immediate time and context of its publication. A quick survey of online book clubs, forums, bookstores, and book databases would confirm the fact that *RLT* still continues to enjoy overwhelming popularity with the Western readers.[10] Investigating reader responses to *RLT* reveals the extent to which the neo-Orientalism embedded in the narrative has been successful in shaping Western, and particularly US, readers' perceptions of the Iranian/Muslim Other. In her analysis of online reviews based on book club discussions and personal reading experiences discussed in literary forums, Martina Koegeler concludes that the predominant trends across the blogs in question are a testament to the fact that "exotic qualities sell and they are in turn what fuels neoliberal multiculturalism" (35). Succinctly put, neoliberal multiculturalism refers to the ideology of neoliberal political economic reforms (via a laissez-faire economic liberalism promoting free trade and privatization) with an appreciation of a multiculturality deemed indispensable for the globalizing endeavors inherent to free-market expansion. Nevertheless, while neoliberal multiculturalism purports to be a diversity-oriented ideology, it only authorizes a "superficial 'integration' of certain kinds of diversity without deconstructing present ethnic and cultural hierarchies" (Koegeler 35). Milton Fisk has best explained that the "paradox" of neoliberal multiculturalism lies in the fact that while

> [t]here is a growing recognition of different cultures . . . at the same time, there is a clear affirmation of the limits on that recognition; so, the state will not allow recognition to spill over into an effort to have equality of a form that would run counter to the economic norms the regime is expected in the global context to protect. (22)

Thus, while the publication and reception of such books as *RLT* might be accounted for as part of the growing multicultural zeitgeist of the time, this alleged multiculturality is welcomed and promoted principally because it both confirms the Orientalist assumptions of Western readers about their Iranian Others and is also in line with the official policies of the United States—especially those of the neoconservatives—vis-à-vis Iran. The reception and performance of *RLT* within the context of neoliberal multiculturalism are further explored in my discussion of Nafisi's representations of Iranian women, her implicit juxtaposition of Iran and the West, and, most importantly, her association with neoconservative politics both in her personal affiliations and in the content of *RLT*.

One of the major themes analyzed in the discussion forums is the memoir's "enlightening" nature and its mind-opening quality, especially for Americans, which in turn necessitates for American readers further appreciation of "American freedom" as opposed to their "oppressed" Iranian counterparts. According to Koegeler, not only do readers' responses to the memoir reinforce the Orientalism embedded in the text, the reader often "co-produces the neo-orientalism enabled through the memoir" (35), which often leads to the affirmation of the imperial and colonial implications of the book. This co-production is enabled where the memoir conforms to certain Western assumptions about the Oriental Other, particularly apropos Iranian women. The prevalent Orientalism in readers' reviews is exemplified in such reviewer comments as "[either these women tell their stories to America now, or they may not be able to tell them at all," which Koegeler regards as an instance of "the most blunt orientalist appropriation of the memoir to bolster US imperial perception of needing to save Muslim women" (36). Although there is occasionally a caveat in the reviews indicating that the author does not represent all Iranian women, the "enlightening" and "inspiring" values of the memoir apparently far outweigh such references.

In the analysis of reader responses, one conclusion drawn by one of the book clubs that Koegeler investigates is particularly illuminating. Nordeen Morello writes of the discussion of the memoir in the "Book-'Em" book club that the memoir "portrays a life, especially for women, that is almost beyond our comprehension. We thank both the author, Azar Nafisi, and our cultural interpreter, Farnaz Shemirani, for allowing us the opportunity to walk in someone else's shoes" (Morello). Morello's statement exemplifies how Nafisi's memoir has apparently made possible the paradox of representing, on the one hand, Iranian/Muslim women as incomprehensible, outlandish Others, while simultaneously providing American readers with the opportunity to "walk in their shoes." In other words, they readers are offered the experience of what E. Ann Kaplan has called "vicarious trauma" (87) from within the sanctuary of their homes and from a safe, "su[e]perior" position. Koegeler concludes that as long as auto-Orientalism is capable of creating and maintaining this paradox, "Nafisi buys her elite cosmopolitan status and gratitude of American readership by selling empathy under the imperial guise of Muslim women's inferiority" (38).

Contrary to the popular reception of *Not without My Daughter*, the academic response to *RLT* has been far from uncontested. In fact, even though the majority of initial reviews and critiques after the publication of the book in 2003 were predominantly acclamatory, and quite uncritically so, subsequent scholarly studies of the text were of a more critical nature. On the one hand, the extraordinary success of *RLT* in the United States, and the Western literary market at large, has often been regarded as one of the primary reasons for the burgeoning of memoirs penned by female members of the Iranian diaspora (Marandi 179) and has, *ipso facto*, contributed to the visibility of the Iranian-American community, especially in the US literary arena. On the other hand, and *a fortiori*, the text has played a major role in the propagation of the dominant Irano-Islamophobic rhetoric in the United States against Iran by advocating an Orientalist perception of the country and catering to the xenophobic zeitgeist of the time. Hence, reading the text as the pioneer of the new Orientalist wave of memoirs on Iran in the new millennium is far from an overstatement. In other words, even though the book—as well as the celebrity status it earned its author—played a remarkable role in the publication of many more Iranian-American memoirs and contributed to their authors' visibility, on a much larger scale, it fed into the prevalent demonization of Iran and Islam, particularly rampant in the post-9/11 era. In the United States, the book generated a contentious debate among American Muslim communities. Nevertheless, nowhere was the debate more vigorous than among the US-based Iranian-American intelligentsia, where many scholars voiced their disapprobation of the book, contending that by engaging in such grotesque distortions of the post-revolution Iranian landscape *RLT* both renders Iranians "subhuman" and hampers intellectual give-and-take and intercultural entente (Keshavarz, *Jasmine and Stars* 6). The controversy over the book peaked with the publication of Professor Hamid Dabashi's[11] *Native Informers and the Making of American Empire* in 2006, which will be discussed in the subsequent sections.

Orientalism Reconfigured: Neo-Orientalism and Auto-Orientalism

The remarkable thematic and representational affinities between *Not without My Daughter* and *RLT*, products of two different historico-political junctures, attest to the dominance of hegemonic, time-honored, and deeply entrenched Orientalist regimes of representation and knowledge production about the construction of the Iranian/Muslim Other. Nevertheless, it would be naïve to presume that Orientalism exists and operates as a monolithic, homogeneous discourse, as this would mean falling into the trap of Orientalist reductionism. Rather, it attests to the existence of certain Orientalist strategies that interlace form and content together and produce familiar and similar effects, images, and concepts.

The post-9/11 era witnessed a spate of memoirs about life in Middle Eastern countries authored predominantly by Western-based, diasporic authors. Even though female memoir writing is by now a well-established tradition in Western literature, the emergence of a significant number of memoirs by women of Middle Eastern origin in a relatively short span is little short of a literary phenomenon. Paramount in this phenomenon, however, is the emergence of a cluster of memoirs penned by Iranian-American women (and to a much smaller extent, men). What binds the majority of such memoirs together is an Orientalist underpinning that informs the overall thematic and representational dynamics of such autobiographical narratives. Therefore, to distinguish the earlier Orientalist narratives from the more recent ones, which proliferated especially in the post-9/11 landscape, some scholars have designated the latter category as "New/Neo-Orientalist."[12] Professor Fatemeh Keshavarz[13] has averred that the "New Orientalist" mode of writing on Middle Eastern societies, epitomized by *RLT*, encourages the same reductionism and oversimplification of older narratives by forging a binary perception of the world which, consequently, renders it "as silencing as its predecessor authored by the nineteenth-century European Orientalists" (*Jasmine and Stars* 2).

Despite their many essential similarities, there are several characteristics of neo-Orientalist narratives that distinguish them from both their classical predecessors and such more recent narratives as *Not without My Daughter*.[14] Chief among these features is the authorial perspective, or the "eyewitness," "testimonial" nature of such narratives, which, in turn, raises significant questions of authority and authenticity: while texts such as *Not without My Daughter* are produced by a Western "outsider"—even though the authors often posit themselves as insiders privy to the peculiarities of the Other's culture—the recent narratives are mostly written from the "insider" perspective of authors who, at least partially, belong to the country, culture, and religion they describe.[15]

In their discussion of the neo-Orientalism underlying the post-9/11 Middle Eastern memoir trend, Ali Behdad and Juliet Williams contend that "not only do Middle Eastern writers, scholars, and so-called experts participate in it, but they play an active and significant role in propagating it," especially as their "self-proclaimed authenticity sanctions and authorizes their discourses" (284). Such representations, therefore, are expected to impart more authenticity, originality, and firsthand knowledge of the allegedly omniscient author, as such narratives often demonstrate "awareness of the power of personal voice, nostalgia in exilic literature, the assurance that comes with insider knowledge and the certainty of eyewitness accounts" (Keshavarz, *Jasmine and Stars* 4).[16] In other words, not only do the authors of neo-Orientalist narratives engage in the systematic Othering of things Oriental, they also inscribe their authorial selves into the text, thereby partaking in and directing the discursive trajectory of their narratives more effectively.

To highlight the "eyewitness" feature of the new wave of Orientalist narratives, some scholars have described such works "auto-Orientalist." Auto-Orientalism (otherwise known as "self-Orientalism") can, therefore, be considered a key component of neo-Orientalism, and one of the major distinctions between neo-Orientalism and its classic counterpart. A rather recently developed notion (compared to the age-old legacy of Orientalism), auto-Orientalism has remained relatively undertheorized. Be that as it may, several scholars have set out to sketch the concept within the frameworks of their own scholarly spheres. Lamont Lindstrom has most aphoristically defined auto-Orientalism as "self-discourse among orientals" (36). In her influential study of *Argentine Orientalism and Arab Immigrants*, Christina Civantos has articulated auto-Orientalism as "the essentialization of the self based on preexisting archetypes" (22).

Similarly, in his study of "Japanese uniqueness," John Lie discusses the proliferation of post-war Japanese auto-Orientalist writings as "Orientalist writings by Japanese about themselves," the preponderance of which "described various pitfalls of Japanese culture and society in the immediate postwar years" (5). Also, in his discussion of psycholinguistic Orientalism in Maxine Hong Kingston's *Woman Warrior* (1976) and Joy Kogawa's *Obasan* (1981), Tomo Hattori argues that, contrary to Said's major contention, the Orientalist controversy over the foregoing texts is "not about how the writer represents the other but how the writer represents herself and her cultural identity" (120). In other words, the hyphenated female authors of the two texts (Chinese-American and Japanese-Canadian, respectively) engage in a "unique case here of auto-Orientalism" that "necessitates an approach that can examine the relationship between the subject and her own linguistic construction of herself as a Chinese American female subject" (Hattori 120). Taking the context of Lie's definition of auto-Orientalism as a case in point (the postwar Japan), one can argue that as a mode of representation, auto-Orientalism has been particularly current in the discursive practices of post-crisis societies or the ones emerging out of grand social paradigm shifts. This can, in large part, be attributed to both the ideological resistance to such massive social transformations, and the disillusionment with the immediate post-crisis/revolution status quo.

Building on the existing formulations of the concept, Edmund Burke and David Prochaska have also employed the definition of auto-Orientalism to frame Western representations of the West, arguing that along with Orientalist representations of the Other, the West

> was quite as active in developing representations of itself, as of others. Indeed, we can say that Western civilization is the form of auto-Orientalism by which the West represented itself to itself, a form of self-blinding quite as destructive ultimately as any Orientalist representation of a non-Western society. (49)

As evident in all of the foregoing conceptualizations of the term, the authorial/ representational "self," signified by the prefix "auto," distinguishes this later species of Orientalism from its forebears. It seems fitting, however, to point out that notwithstanding the authorial self's engagement in the Orientalization of the native people/ society of her origin, she is careful not to implicate her own self as an exotic or primitive Other. In fact, representing herself as belonging to, or at least being sufficiently *au courant* with the Other's culture and, *ipso facto*, securing the authenticity of her voice, the author inscribes herself into the narrative and her towering presence pervades the story's entire structure. Yet, almost always, through self-exempting discursive strategies (paramount among which is association with or, more accurately, assimilation into the Western culture) she manages to maintain her distance and to exonerate herself from the Oriental "maladies" imputed to the Others she represents, while simultaneously identifying herself with and within the Western context with which she is affiliated. In *RLT*, Nafisi manages to create this critical distance between herself and the "victimized" Iranian women by making repeated references to her associations with the Western world. This is primarily achieved by her references to her life and education in the West, particularly in the United States (82). The narrative also contains many instances of the author's self-referentiality which, more than anything else, highlight her association and ideological affinities with Western culture. During the war years when Tehran was heavily bombarded by an Iraqi air force fully supported by Western powers, Nafisi sought solace in Western novels (186), films, and "Vishnovka, a homemade cherry vodka" (232). In one significant passage describing one of her "girls," Yassi, Nafisi quotes her as saying, "[w]hat seems natural to someone like you . . . is so strange and unfamiliar to me." Nafisi then speculates: "Could she ever live the life of someone like me, live on her own, take long walks holding hands with someone she loved, even have a little dog perhaps?" (32). Another noteworthy reference to Nafisi's difference from the "oppressed" Iranian women is her adamant refusal to wear the veil (152), which not only distinguishes her from those who did observe the practice but also immediately identifies her with "free" Western women. Thus, Nafisi sets herself off from the "black-scarved, timid faces in the city" through what "became a way of life" for her, that is, "insubordination" (45). Such instances of self-demarcation are reminiscent of Vron Ware's categorization of white women appearing in Orientalist and captivity narratives into "the Good," "the Bad," and "the Foolhardy," as discussed in the "Western Rebels vs. Willing Convicts" in the preceding chapter.

Quite similar to Mahmoody's references to herself as the embodiment of "proper," American womanhood, as well as her favorable representation of Westernized Iranians, not only does Nafisi draw a line of demarcation between herself and "oppressed" Iranian women, she never misses an opportunity to create the same critical distance for Iranians who favor the West. Throughout the narrative, the author's Westernized friends are portrayed as the only worthy people she can associate with. Prominent among this elitist coterie are a man she cryptically calls her "magician," who uses "his British training" (281) when reasoning with her, and her "sophisticated French-educated friend, Leyly" (265).

According to McAlister, "the particular logic of Orientalism," and by extension its derivatives neo- and auto-Orientalism, is contingent upon the triumvirate of being "binary, feminized, and citational" (12). These principal characteristics neither exist in isolation nor can function separately; rather, they form a complex nexus of figurations and associations that work collaboratively and serve to reinforce one another so as to manufacture the ultimate Orientalist product. In effect, one could argue that the aforementioned features cannot exist and perform except symbiotically and reciprocally. That is to say, deploying the citational feature of Orientalism is only possible within the context of the West vs. East, superior vs. inferior binary which, in turn, reinforces the feminizing nature of Orientalism. In other words, citationality, that is, the citation of established Orientalist tropes such as the veil as the symbol of Muslim women's "backwardness" and "oppression," is predicated on an absolutist binarism often verging on Manicheanism (for instance the "free" Western woman vs. the "oppressed" Muslim one), within the paradigm of which Orientalist tropes can be exploited as a representational strategy. Furthermore, the employment of citationality leads, in turn, to the construction of a (sexist) feminized image of the Other (i.e., weak, submissive, oppressed, sexually exotic, and the like), while simultaneously underpinning the binary context in which it functions.

The essence of the aforesaid features is transferred almost verbatim from antecedent classic Orientalist discourses to the more recent types of neo-Orientalism, even though the texts, contexts, and styles within which they are exploited remain dynamic and fluid. Thus, the same Orientalist representational strategies of citation, feminization, and binarism that characterize nineteenth-century Orientalist accounts, or captivity narratives, can be seen extensively at work in *RLT*. In other words, neo-/auto-Orientalism is best understood as an ancillary to classic Orientalism, rather than a *sui generis* entity. As Behdad and Williams have argued, "[a]lthough the term 'neo-Orientalism' designates a shift in the discourse of Orientalism, that represents a distinct, and in ways novel formation, it nonetheless entails certain discursive repetitions of and conceptual continuities with its precursor" (284).

As far as acceptance, reception, and marketing logistics are concerned, the hyphenated author can gain the privilege of entrance into Western literary markets and, consequently, halls of fame by availing herself of the potential embedded in the auto-Orientalism that underlies such works as *RLT*. This, as Koegeler contends, is made possible more than anything else via the "citation of orientalist tropes," which opens the door for the active participation of the minority author in the dominant discursive practices concerning Islam, Muslim womanhood, and Americanness and grants her "access to publication by way of its mutual legibility by majority discourses and minority writers" (iii). In the following exegesis of *RLT*, I will elaborate how the author, through a sustained recycling of the most familiar and enduring Orientalist tropes, portrays a phantasmagoric picture of post-revolutionary Iran. She does this through employing a neo-Orientalist discourse, which is as "monolithic, totalizing, reliant on a binary logic, and based on an assumption of moral and cultural superiority over the Oriental other" as classic Orientalist narratives (Behdad and Williams 284).

In her discussion of post-9/11 Arab-American writing, Koegeler argues that the citationality of Orientalist tropes generates two types of auto-Orientalist discourses, namely, essentialist and strategic auto-Orientalism. It is, however, upon the essentialist brand of auto-Orientalism—that is the deployment of established Orientalist tropes to represent the Other—that the thematic structure of *RLT* has been constructed. Through calculated exploitation of essentialist auto-Orientalism, Nafisi performs a purely eastward gaze, rather than a simultaneously eastward and westward gaze,[17] which only testifies to and solidifies American stereotypes of Muslim womanhood, among other things, rather than questioning them (Koegeler 31).

Uncovering the Front Cover: Cropping Iranian Womanhood

In order to better appreciate the production, reception, and consumption of any work of art or literature, it is indispensable to examine its paratextual characteristics. In his influential *Paratexts: Thresholds of Interpretation* (1997), the renowned French literary theorist, Gérard Genette, defines paratexts as "those liminal devices and conventions, both within the book (*peritext*) and outside it (*epitext*), that mediate the book to the reader: titles and subtitles, pseudonyms, forewords, dedications, epigraphs, prefaces, intertitles, notes, epilogues, and afterwords" (xviii). The paratextual features of a text are often conditioned by the sociocultural and political atmosphere of the time of their production. Insomuch as Iranian-American memoirs are concerned, perhaps the paramount feature of their peritexts (i.e., whatever appears on and between the front and back covers of a book) is "the outermost peritext": the front cover (15).

The front covers of Middle Eastern memoirs predominantly portray images of exotic(ized) Middle Eastern women shrouded, to varying degrees, in black veils. Such images readily resonate with Western readers' expectations of Muslim women as veiled, oppressed, and in need of being "liberated." Some Iranian-American memoirs that purport to be stories of female resistance, perseverance, and insubordination portray a more "defiant" practice of veiling (i.e., in bright colors or scantily veiled), while still depicting an exotic—often dark-haired, dark-eyed—Oriental woman. Among this trend, the cover photo of *RLT* is an exception of sorts that complicates this almost established pattern, thereby foreshadowing not only the narrative maneuvers and representational stratagems of the text, but also its highly controversial critical reception. Against this backdrop, Richard Byrne has stressed that the cover photo of *RLT* serves as a "battleground" that encapsulates "the complexities and competing claims" of the memoir and Professor Hamid Dabashi's analysis and trenchant criticism of it ("Peeking under the Cover"). All versions of the front cover of *RLT* depict two teenage girls in their black headscarves standing shoulder to shoulder with their heads bent slightly downward apparently immersed in perusing something the knowledge of which is withheld from the reader. However, as right above the image (and in one edition below the girl's faces) the words "Reading Lolita in Tehran" appear in big typeface, the immediate implication is that they are immersed in reading Vladimir Nabokov's *Lolita*, in a charming manner which "solicits sympathy, and even evokes complicity" (Dabashi "Native Informers"). The cover of *RLT*, therefore, symbolizes the two overarching themes of the text: women and reading (Western literature).

The cover image thus becomes a site of hermeneutic contestation, prefiguring the multifaceted nexus of associations and insinuations that underpin the text. The image of the two black-veiled young girls is consistent with the Orientalist conceptions of the oppression, passivity, and even submissiveness of Oriental/ Muslim women. Ostensibly, what the cover image denotes is that the two young girls in the image—who, with hindsight, evoke Nafisi's "girls"—are reading Nabokov's *Lolita* in the city of Tehran. This impression is further reinforced by the title that appears above the image. The connotations of such a combination of image and title, however, are not as innocuous as what the image seems to initially denote, infused as it is with Orientalist innuendo and insinuation. For one thing, the cover photo is strongly, and perhaps nostalgically, too, reminiscent of the genre of the colonial postcards of exotic Oriental girls manufactured by and for the consumption of colonial officers and, by extension, of imperial metropolitan centers' populace.[18]

There is, however, much more to the cover photo of *RLT* than meets the eye at first sight. In what Dabashi has dubbed a case of "iconic burglary" ("Native Informers"), the image of the teenagers apparently reading *Lolita* is, in actual fact, excised from a news report belonging to an entirely different context—the 2000 parliamentary election in Iran. Far from being oppressed Iranian Lolitas, the girls in the original image are reading not Nabokov's *Lolita* but the latest election updates from the leading reformist newspaper of the time, *Moshaarekat* (meaning "participation") on what appears to be a college campus. In its manipulated format, which appears on the cover of *RLT*, the image is cropped so the reader cannot see what the two young women are in fact reading, convinced by the title that they are indeed reading *Lolita*. Through decontextualizing the image, by way of cropping not only what the girls are reading, but other female students behind the two teenagers, and most importantly a poster of the progressive then-president Seyed Mohammad Khatami—the embodiment of the reformist movement in Iran to date—Nafisi, or her publisher for that matter, has chosen to divest the girls of their individuality as well as "their moral intelligence and their participation in the democratic aspirations of their homeland, ushering them into a colonial harem" (Dabashi "Native Informers"). In response to Dabashi's observation, Nafisi has dismissed the criticism against the choice of the cover photo as outlandish, arguing that the girls simply "seem to be reading" and that the choice of the final cover is at the discretion of the publisher, not the author. However, even if one is tempted to accept Nafisi's justification, one cannot concur more with Dabashi that "the cropping of Iranian culture that is done inside is even more insidious, and that is her writing" (qtd. in Byrne, "Peeking under the Cover").

Cover photos of neo-Orientalist memoirs have significant marketing implications. In an interview Nafisi has claimed that she has advised the publisher of her memoir, Random House, against choosing an "exotic" cover photo and has rejected such suggestions as "to have a woman with Lolita glasses with a chador" (Byrne, "Peeking under the Cover"). However, the image, which is effectively doctored—even though it may not seem overtly exotic at first glance—not only fulfills the demands of marketing strategies, but in fact achieves much more than the clichéd images of women in black chadors or burkas do. It serves to pique the readers' curiosity, engages their attention, and promises a narrative that simultaneously corroborates their Orientalist perceptions of the Iranian Other, while purporting to be intellectually rewarding for its alleged literary merits. Furthermore, as far as attracting the readers' attention and meeting marketing demands are concerned, the title of the book tallies well with its cover image in signification. Rarely has the title of any neo-Orientalist memoir been so reflective of the narrative content, and so controversial, too.[19] To a significant extent, the choice of the title owes to the author's literary background and her linguistic expertise, contrary to the preponderance of neo-Orientalist memoirs, which are produced either by amateur writers or by ghost authors and literary aides.

Concordant with the cover photo, the other outermost peritext of *RLT*, its title, signifies several concepts simultaneously. For one thing, one might ask the question if Western classics are as tenably universal as Nafisi and reviewers like Heather Hewett purport, what renders reading Nabokov's *Lolita* in the city of Tehran so extraordinary? As Professor Keshavarz has observed, the title of the book bears a conspicuous "undertone of Otherness to it" that renders the very act of reading Nabokov's novel in Tehran a curious and unlikely possibility (*Jasmine and Stars* 22). Consistent with the polarizing proclivity of (neo-)Orientalist narratives, the title insinuates an Orientalist binarism from the very outset, thereby juxtaposing the "free," "liberal" West signified by *Lolita* with Islamic "fundamentalism" and the Western, Orientalist trope of the oppressed Muslim woman symbolized by the word Tehran. From another perspective, Christine Grogan has argued that *Lolita* serves as a "model text for exposing solipsists who deny their subjects humanity" (53). In this light, by conjuring up Lolita's narrative and, ineluctably, her relationship with Humbert Humbert, Nafisi is inviting her readers to draw an analogy between the dynamics of the relationship between the Islamic Republic of Iran (or its then-leader, Ayatollah Khomeini) and the people of Iran (Papan-Matin 31; Rowe 268). Against this backdrop, the concept of reading conjoins the gap—unbridgeable though it turns out to be from the story—between the two signifiers for both Nafisi's "girls," who are shown engaged in reading Western classics in the memoir, as well as the readership of *RLT*. Furthermore, as Donadey maintains, "[t]he use of Lolita as an intertext sensationalizes Iranian women's situation; the title is shocking in an Iranian context and tantalizing in a western one" (632). Thus, together, the title and the cover image exert a dramatic effect: while the titular Lolita becomes a signifier conjuring up illicit sex with underage girls, the image of the scarf-donning Iranian teenagers evokes Orientalist fantasies, thus attaching a "tantalising addition of an Oriental twist to the most notorious case of pedophilia in modern literary imagination" (Dabashi "Native Informers"). This, in turn, contributes to "the slick and predictable marketing package by catering to a western audience's expectations" (Abbott 106) of seeing either oppressed-looking, or "exotic" Muslim/Oriental women on the covers of Middle Eastern narratives.

Damsels in Distress: Reading Muslim "Lolitas" in the West

They [Persian women] are adopting our dress, they will get our education in a measure, perhaps our freedom to a certain extent. Shall they have our Christ?

Annie Woodman Stocking, *The New Woman in Persia*

No one can study the tragic story of women under the Muslim faith without an earnest longing and prayer that something may be done by the united Church of Christ to meet this need. We think with pity and sorrow of the veiled women of Islam.

Zwemer & Zwemer, *Muslim Women*

Since Azar Nafisi is both geographically and ideologically positioned in the West—especially in a country that deems itself under attack from "Islamic fundamentalism"—and because she is writing primarily for a Western, and in particular American, audience, it is necessary to consider her geopolitical situatedness and the context in which the debates over the Muslim Other are taking place. One overarching concept at the heart of the debates surrounding Islam is the question of women in Muslim countries. The overriding theme in discussions on Muslim women, who are almost always treated monolithically by the mainstream discourse in the West, is their alleged suppression and victimization by a chauvinistic, patriarchal religious dogma (Bahramitash, "The War on Terror" 221).

In her discussion of post-revolutionary Iran, Nafisi focuses more than anything else on the Iranian "woman question." In zooming in on the sociopolitical status of women after the revolution, Nafisi's main claim is that the Islamic Republic has been oppressive toward women and has "confiscated" (6) their personal freedoms and private lives. Unsurprisingly, paramount in Nafisi's portrayal of Iranian women is her fixation with the veil—an *idée fixe* that she shares with the Orientalist/Western discourse on Muslim women. Even though Nafisi's accounts of the "oppression" of women are decontextualized, dehistoricized, and far too exaggerated, it is an incontrovertible fact that women's dress code, especially with the enforcement of veiling, and opposite-sex relationships became more restricted after the revolution. However, in critiquing Nafisi's work, the real issue at stake is not as much whether or not women's freedoms were restricted following the revolution; rather, it is the insidious manner in which she represents the status of Iranian women and how such mode of representation can, in turn, become appropriated by the United States to serve its imperial/colonial aspirations toward Muslim/Middle Eastern countries, as the role of self-narratives in advocating US invasions of Iraq and Afghanistan vividly demonstrates. Nafisi's narrative also suffers from a most conspicuous lacuna: the absence of as little as a single reference to the dramatic improvements in the lives of Iranian women after the revolution. Instead, she prefers to portray their situation as static and passive in a manner that ignores their sociopolitical agency, participation, ambitions, and achievements. Such (under)representation paves the way for the exploitation of the cause of women's rights and implies the need for Iranian women's "liberation."

As a point of departure, it is crucial to demonstrate how Nafisi's discussion of the Iranian "woman question," and particularly the veil, in Iran is framed by a convergence of "feminist Orientalism" and "Orientalist feminism." Narrating her experience of teaching Middle Eastern memoirs to her students in the United States, Lisa Eck concludes that the predominant ideological barrier that students face in the current academic milieu in the United States is feminist Orientalism: "the urge to read sexist traditions as an inevitable part of the Other's otherness, and liberated femininity as a cultural and political fait accompli in the West" (13). Orientalist feminism, according to Roxana Bahramitash, is a "modern project and a type of feminism that advocates and supports particular foreign policies toward the Middle East" ("The War on Terror" 221). As will be later demonstrated, although the recent genre of neo-Orientalist narratives, epitomized by *RLT*, purports to defend women's rights and causes, it is heavily infused with classic Orientalist stereotypes that only serve to further marginalize, silence, and oppress women.

Building on Edward Said's theorization of Orientalism, Parvin Paidar's important study, *Women and the Political Process in Twentieth Century Iran* (1995), dissects the triple interconnected lineaments of Orientalist feminism. First, Orientalist feminism assumes an "oppositional dichotomy" of the West as a progressive and dynamic locus for women versus the East as a site where women are dominated by "traditionalism," defined as "a static and indigenous condition" (7). This dichotomy insinuates that Muslim women are "doomed to an unchanging condition in the absence of a Western challenge to Islam" (7). Therefore, the "essential difference" between the Oriental/Muslim woman and her Western counterpart constitutes a site of "political and cultural contestations" and serves as the central "metaphor for demarcating the self and the other" (Tavakoli-Targhi 74). Challenging the "simplistic" notions of "progress" and "development" in this reductionist dichotomy, Laura Nader has also referred to the "widespread belief" that Western women are "better off vis-à-vis their menfolk than their sisters in societies that are not 'developed'" (323). She further argues that such "misleading cultural comparisons" promote simplistic contentions of "positional superiority which divert attention from the processes which are controlling women in both worlds" (323).

Second, Orientalist feminism is characterized by the denial of any agency and subjectivity to Oriental/Muslim women, thereby reducing them to mere "victims and not . . . agents of social transformation" (Bahramitash, "The War on Terror" 222). Hence, Oriental/Muslim women's resistance against restrictive or discriminatory sociocultural structures imposed on them, and their endeavors toward self-empowerment and self-determination, are conspicuously absent in this discourse. Bereft of any agential potentiality, Muslim women desperately need "saviors" who are none other than their "Western sisters" (Bahramitash, "The War on Terror" 222).[20] This particular feature of Orientalist feminism derives from one of the principal assumptions of Orientalism that deems Orientals unsuited for self-governance (Said *Orientalism* 109, 230) and, hence, in need of being "redeemed" and "civilized." The idea is perhaps most succinctly expressed in the epigraph hat Edward Said has borrowed from Karl Marx's essay *The Eighteenth Brumaire of Louis Bonaparte*: "They cannot represent themselves; they must be represented" (*Orientalism* xiii). Crucial in this "civilizing" scheme was the condition of Oriental women, which continues to be, invoked as an indicator of the Muslim world's "primitivism."[21] This, in turn, made the "civilizing mission" even more of a *sine qua non* and consequently led to the colonization of what is now called the Middle East as well as North Africa (Bahramitash, "The War on Terror" 222).

The third characteristic of Orientalist feminism is what Paidar has termed the "essentialisation and reification of women's history" (7). This final characteristic ascribes a unified singularity, homogeneity, and monolithicity to all Oriental, and in particular Muslim, women, thereby robbing them of their diversity, multiplicity, and heterogeneity, purporting that all Oriental societies are essentially alike, and all their Muslim female inhabitants live under the same (deplorable) conditions. The following passage from Paidar's book encapsulates the three defining features of Orientalist feminism:

> While the history of women in the West was regarded as the product of complex economic and social development, Middle Eastern women's history was considered to be the product of the "traditional Muslim view" seen "as an inherited given" (Tucker, 1983). As a result, the process of historical change was often bypassed by Orientalist observers and countless essays on "women in Islam" did little to explain the development of women's positions in various

Middle Eastern societies and the differences which existed in Muslim women's histories within the region. (7)

Put concisely, Paidar asserts that "the Orientalist approach to the question of women and political change suffered from endemic essentialisation, ethnocentrism and stereotyping" (8).

Formulating a Gramscian-Foucauldian framework, Bahramitash has argued that the "hegemonic knowledge" produced about Oriental and Muslim women constructs a frame of reference that not only represents "the interests of the dominant class that manages to universalize its own beliefs and value systems to subordinate classes" but is also "restrictive and exclusive of alternative conceptions of reality" ("The War on Terror" 223). The dominant (neo-)Orientalist discourse on Oriental/Muslim women, then, is not only formed over time through its proliferation by such institutions as the mainstream Western media, it is also exclusive of concepts that can offer a different understanding of how various modes of power can function. In this light, well-worn, negative clichés about Muslim women have become such an integral part of the dominant discourse that it is almost impossible to disregard them.

More subtle in, but vital to, the construction of a hegemonic discourse is the successful engagement of "the opposition" toward serving hegemonic power structures and the discursive practices they propagate. As far as Orientalist feminism is concerned, the selfsame feminism that is allegedly opposed to indigenous tyranny turns into a tool, a plaything, at the disposal of the globalized hegemonic machine. In the post-9/11 landscape, Orientalist feminists have actively (even if unwittingly) contributed to the interventionist US foreign policies by perpetuating stereotypes of the oppressed, victimized Muslim womanhood and advocating for the need to "liberate" them. On the other hand, as Bahramitash contends, (works of) Orientalist feminists, here epitomized by Nafisi, make the task of defending both their citizen and gender rights for Muslim women much more difficult ("The War on Terror" 222). This is because foreign intervention only serves to further compound their condition in societies most of which have paid a heavy price to break free from the trammels either of foreign colonization or native despotic rule. The connection between Orientalist feminism and imperial/colonial hegemony will be further elaborated in the discussion of Nafisi's connection with US neoconservatism in the following sections.

Behind the Veil: The Topos Obligé of Feminist Orientalism

Throughout her narrative, Nafisi thoroughly exploits the gamut of shopworn Orientalist stereotypes associated with Oriental women that are most familiar to Western readers: obsession with virginity (19, 30, 57, 60, 73, 212), sexual abuse (273), underage marriage (27, 43, 60, 61, 257), polygamy (335), and, most persistently, the veil.[22] Most such tropes are constructed around the character of Humbert, to whom the author persistently likens Iranian men. The following passage offers a telling example of how Nafisi exploits every opportunity, even in the midst of her literary analyses, to link the moral corruption and perversion that permeates the world of *Lolita* to the post-revolutionary Iran, in general, and Iranian men, in particular:

> You do see how Nabokov's prose provides trapdoors for the unsuspecting reader: the credibility of every one of Humbert's assertions is simultaneously challenged and exposed by the hidden truth implied by his descriptions. Thus another Lolita emerges that reaches beyond the caricature of the vulgar insensitive minx, although she is that, too. A hurt, lonely girl, deprived of her childhood, orphaned and with no refuge. Humbert's rare insights give glimpses into Lolita's character, her vulnerability and aloneness. Were he to paint the murals in the Enchanted Hunters, the motel where he first raped her, he tells us, he would have painted a lake, an arbor in flames and finally there would have been "a fire opal dissolving within a ripple-ringed pool, a last throb, a last dab of color, stinging red, smarting pink, a sigh, a wincing child." (Child, please remember, ladies and gentlemen of the jury, although this child, had she lived in the Islamic Republic, would have been long ripe for marriage to men older than Humbert.) (43)

Interestingly, much like Nabokov's prose, Nafisi's "provides trapdoors for the unsuspecting reader" into the Orientalist world of the narrative. The passage, in particular the parenthetical addition, which sounds oddly tagged-on and reads like a last-minute afterthought imposed on the original quote from *Lolita*, "gives glimpses" into how the author manipulates sophisticated-sounding literary discussions to offer her "rare insights" into life in post-revolutionary Iran.

In a similar vein, the chapter on Austen opens with a parody of one of Austen's most famous quotes: "It is a truth universally acknowledged that a Muslim man, regardless of his fortune, must be in want of a nine-year-old virgin wife" (257). In a single statement, Nafisi yokes together the Orientalist tropes of Muslim men's licentiousness, obsession with virginity, and child marriage, to say nothing of the "universality" of such Orientalist conceptions. Such "facts" are presented as intrinsic components of Iranian/Muslim culture throughout the narrative, which apparently make Iran "a man's paradise" (335).

More than any other Orientalist topos, however, Nafisi draws on the most familiar of all established (neo-)Orientalist topoi—the veil. As many scholars have argued, the veil has turned into the most persistent Orientalist preoccupation (Asha 48), or what Behdad and Williams have dubbed the *topos obligé* of neo-Orientalist discourses (293). As far as the Oriental/Muslim woman is concerned, no other feature has generated as much obsessive fixation as the veil. So evident is the neo-Orientalist obsession with the veil that the concept appears in titles, subtitles, or cover photos of almost all neo-Orientalist memoirs, Iranian-American or otherwise, which display images of "submissive" Muslim women clad, typically, in black veils. The veil, therefore, becomes an all-embracing signifier encapsulating the alleged backwardness, oppression, docility, and submissiveness of the Muslim woman all at once (Asha 49). More than ever before, post-9/11 Middle Eastern memoirs adopted the veil as the quintessential symbol of Muslim women's repression and the urgent need for their liberation. In the dominant (neo-) Orientalist feminist discourse surrounding Muslim women's self-determination, the veil is often framed as an impediment to their visibility and social mobility. Chandra Mohanty has remarked that "colonization almost invariably implies . . . a discursive or political suppression of the heterogeneity of the subject(s) in question" (293). Characteristically, Orientalist and colonial discourses treat the veil as a homogeneous and monolithic entity and, as such, efface not only the diversity and multiplicity of its practices—both across Muslim countries and within particular cultures—but also its social, cultural, religious, and political contexts, histories, and significations.

This is particularly significant since various veiling practices, which are rooted much more in cultural praxis than merely in religious ones, lead to different levels of what the Orientalist discourse deems to be Muslim women's invisibility and immobility. On a much broader plane, yet, the veil has not only come to represent the disadvantaged social status of Muslim women but is constantly utilized as "one of the most popular Western ways of representing the 'problems of Islam'" (Watson 153), or, as Douglas J. Loveless has pointed out, "all that is perceived to be wrong with a Muslim world linked to suppression, abuse, and terror" (1). As the iconic post-9/11 neo-Orientalist female life narrative, *RLT* shares the Western, Orientalist obsession with the veil, not only by rehashing hackneyed stereotypes but also by building on and expanding them in novel ways. Being one of the most recurrent themes in Nafisi's narrative, the politics of the veil, therefore, deserves special attention not only as a running leitmotif but also since, like much else in the text, it is perpetually dehistoricized, decontextualized, oversimplified, and even debased.

In presenting the image of the veil and Muslim women, Nafisi's account carries the impress of (neo-)Orientalist discourses representing the veil as a primitive and restrictive practice, and an "unnatural encumbrance" (Asha 49). In a significant passage, Nafisi recounts her self-professed fixation with the veil, which leads her to literally act out being made invisible by the veil:

> My constant obsession with the veil had made me buy a very wide black robe that covered me down to my ankles, with kimonolike sleeves, wide and long. I had gotten into the habit of withdrawing my hands into the sleeves and pretending that I had no hands. Gradually, I pretended that when I wore the robe, my whole body disappeared: my arms, breasts, stomach and legs melted and disappeared and what was left was a piece of cloth the shape of my body that moved here and there, guided by some invisible force. (167)

What is striking in the aforementioned passage is not only that Nafisi's description lends credence to the Orientalist motif of the veil as a signifier of Muslim women's invisibility; her enactment of the alleged invisibility further reifies the concept, thereby transposing it from the theoretical realm of Orientalist, white feminism to the level of theatrical performance and pragmatism. Similarly, the "pretense" of having "no hands" is an equally important signification, as it insinuates the immobility supposedly caused by the veil, while also evoking the notion of Muslim women's alleged powerlessness and their lack of social and political agency in their own destiny. This, consequently, indicates their need to be "saved" and "liberated" from the oppressive "patriarchalism" of their religion, culture, and society, which has "veiled" and "subjugated" them. Furthermore, it also suggests that Iranian women's lives are controlled and "guided" by the "invisible force" which appears to be the state.

Nafisi does not dissimulate her revulsion at the practice, which, for her, goes far beyond covering the body and masks the identity and subjectivity of those who observe it, too. In this light, the narrative represents the veil as dehumanizing and Nafisi's "girls" are, as if miraculously, revealed as human only when they have shed their veils. The author's desire to see the "girls" unveiled is highly reminiscent of the colonial desire "to catch a glimpse of Eastern women unveiled" (Hoglund 2). However, the colonial fantasy of unveiling the Muslim woman transcends the boundaries of obsessive voyeurism and sexual exoticism. It is, instead, part of the larger project of "liberating" and "civilizing" the Orient as a whole. As Meyda Yeğenoğlu has argued, there is a "metonymic association" between the Orient and its women whereby Oriental women are perceived as "the essence of the Orient," which, *ipso facto*, lends more urgency to lifting the veil, for "unveiling and thereby modernizing the woman of the Orient signifie[s] the transformation of the Orient itself" (84). The first step, as the massive repository of colonial and Orientalist literature suggests, on the path to the liberation of the "suppressed" Muslim/Oriental woman is to strip her of her veil. Along the same line, in his seminal *Black Skin, White Masks* (1991), Franz Fanon has demonstrated how unveiling was employed as part of the French colonizers' civilizing modus operandi in Algeria: "Here and there it thus happened that a woman was 'saved' and symbolically 'unveiled'" (42). The idea is most pithily articulated in Gayatri Spivak's *locus classicus*, "white men saving brown women from brown men," which she enunciated in her analysis of the British campaign against the sati in her influential "Can the Subaltern Speak?" to illustrate the colonial "civilizing mission" (48).

In "Liberation Under Siege: U.S. Military Occupation and Japanese Women's Enfranchisement," Lisa Yoneyama discusses the long history of US wars against, and military intervention in, sovereign countries under the pretext of "feminist emancipation," as was the case with the US occupation of Japan (1945–52) (889). In a similar vein, in his important study *To the Halls of the Montezumas: The Mexican War in the American Imagination* (1985), Robert Walter Johannsen dissects the nexus between cultural work and US foreign policy during the Mexican–American War (1846-8), and investigates "the visions of romance and chivalry in which U.S. forces 'saved' Mexican women from barbarous Mexican men" (Rowe 260).

With this in perspective, it is little surprise, then, that a crucial part of Reza Shah's "modernizing" venture was the highly controversial forced unveiling of Iranian women in 1936, the justification of which was predicated on the colonialist assumption of the veil being a hindrance to Muslim women's contribution to and participation in society (Paidar 104). As Bahramitash has argued, Reza Shah's "liberation" project was completely in keeping with the project of enforcing a

Western lifestyle "that replicated the economic and political interests of the West" ("The War on Terror" 225).

In a significant passage in *RLT*, Nafisi describes her reaction to her "girls" removing their veils, thus asserting that her students' unveiling constituted taking off "more than their scarves and robes," implying that their true subjectivities and identities were fully revealed only when their veils were shed:

> When my students came into that room [Nafisi's living room], they took off more than their scarves and robes. Gradually, each one gained an outline and a shape, becoming her own inimitable self. Our world in that living room with its window framing my beloved Elburz Mountains became our sanctuary, our self-contained universe, mocking the reality of blackscarved, timid faces in the city that sprawled below. (6)

The aforementioned excerpt is misleading in a Western context, as it suggests that the veil could not be shed in other contexts and Nafisi's living room provides a unique sanctuary wherein the girls had the unusual liberty of not wearing it. In actual fact, however, the veil need not be observed in any private homosocial spaces—and in many heterosocial ones, too—and Nafisi's living room offers only one of many such private spaces. Since the average non-Muslim Western reader is not usually conversant with the Iranian/Islamic context, Nafisi takes liberties with her descriptions of the veiling practice and the contexts of its observance. More significantly, the excerpt suggests that the students' realization of their "inimitable self" seems to be contingent solely upon the removal of their veils. In other words, the students' identity and their perceptions of themselves, or, to borrow from Jungian terminology, their individuation, are reduced to a simplistic form of body politics in which they are judged by the measure to which they observe the veil. This becomes more evident in the author's homogenizing representation of veil-observing Muslim girls and women as ugly, fanatical, backward, and brainwashed, vis-à-vis the beautiful, enlightened, intellectual, and autonomous non-observants. Furthermore, Nafisi's provision of a "liberating" space for her girls both to "unveil" and to study "forbidden" Western literature tallies well with what Minoo Moallem has dubbed "feminist imperialism" in Western women's desire "to enlighten third world women to the civilizing project of the West, wherein first world women become the norm and third world women get constructed as a singular, non-Western other" (Elkholy).

In a similar vein, many Western reviewers have echoed Nafisi's description of "the mundane activity of women's taking off their outerwear, something women in Iran do regularly" as a "process of individualization" (Rastegar 113). In these reviews, as in *RLT*, the veil is portrayed as an impediment to women's sense of individuality and agency and symbolizes drab uniformity and intellectual retardation. Mitra Rastegar has pointed out the discursive alignment apropos veiling between *RLT* and these reviews where unveiling is presented as a process "whereby the women 'emerge as individuals' (Azar Nafisi, 2004), revealing 'vivid personalities' (Hook 2003), and shedding 'their inhibitions, speaking openly' (Sismondo 2003)" (113).

The aforementioned unveiling scene is also significant from another perspective. One of the defining characteristics of the Orientalist discourse pertains to its intended audience, that is, how it "Orientalizes the Orient for the purpose of Occidental consumption" (Bahramitash, "The War on Terror" 226). Hence, in describing the unveiling of her "girls" in the alleged enclosed privacy of her living room, Nafisi strikes a familiar chord with her Western audience: by divulging to her readers the physical and personal characteristics of her students, she assumes the position of "the agent who 'reveals', offering Westerners a view into Iranian women's lives and, more significantly, humanizing the previously 'anonymous veiled figures'" (Rastegar 113).

Nafisi's intermediary, authorial role, however, is far from unprecedented. Her comprador positionality, in fact, is reminiscent of white Western women who had the "privilege" of accessing Oriental harems and whose accounts of the harem could gratify the Orientalist/masculine desire to have access to this "hidden space." One example is Lady Mary Wortley-Montagu's account, the *Turkish Embassy Letters* (1763), possibly the most famous and inaugural of these sorts of accounts, which goes beyond simply reporting what the author sees. Her comparisons are quite pragmatic, particular, and sensitive. Far from being merely a viewer, Lady Mary participates as much as she can, though ironically, her tightly laced corset does not allow her to shed her own "veil."

In *Colonial Fantasies: Towards a Feminist Reading of Orientalism* (1998), Meyda Yeğenoğlu argues that the Western subject, "frustrated by the closure of the space of the Oriental woman," and determined to have access to the "hidden" interiority of the harem, can only resort to Western women's accounts of the harem life:

> It is thus only through the assistance of the Western woman (for she is the only "foreigner" allowed to enter into the "forbidden zone") that the mysteries of this inaccessible "inner space" and the "essence" of the Orient secluded in it could be unconcealed; it is she who can remedy the longlasting lack of the Western subject. The inability to see and have access to the interiority of the other and to the space of woman reminds men of their limit, their lack. (75)

In this light, it could be argued that Nafisi's living room functions as an Oriental harem into which she offers her Western readers a glimpse to see "behind the veil." Like the "privileged" Western women who could access the interior space of the harem, Nafisi's simultaneously insider-outsider position enables her to offer "rare" descriptions of unveiled girls and the details of their everyday lives without implicating herself as exotic, mysterious, victimized, and submissive.[23] Significantly, subordinating her girls in the name of displaying her own subjectivity does, in fact, raise important ethical questions around such issues as exploitation.

Besides the manner in which Nafisi's depictions of the veil echo Orientalist clichés and cater to the Western fantasy of unveiling the Oriental woman, they are also characterized by an egregious elimination of many significant historico-political contexts that have to be allowed for in any discussion of Iranian women, their rights, and the veil. Such instances of omission (or arguably, ignorance) and selective historicity will be further elaborated in the following sections. Nevertheless, as far as the question of veiling is concerned, the following extract from *RLT* best exemplifies the problematic juxtaposition of post-revolutionary mandatory veiling with the forced unveiling decreed by Reza Shah:

> From the beginning of the revolution there had been many aborted attempts to impose the veil on women; these attempts failed because of persistent and militant resistance put up mainly by Iranian women. In many important ways the veil had gained a symbolic significance for the regime. Its reimposition would signify the complete victory of the Islamic aspect of the revolution, which in those first years was not a foregone conclusion. The unveiling of women mandated by Reza Shah in 1936 had been a controversial symbol of modernization, a powerful sign of the reduction of the clergy's power. It was important for the ruling clerics to reassert that power. (112)

Even though the aforementioned passage appropriates the veil trope as the most powerful and recurrent symbol of (mis)representing Muslim women, the quasi-historical space within which it is situated in the memoir is almost completely devoid of any meaningful religious, historical, or sociopolitical context. Even the author's presentation of the mandatory unveiling by Reza Shah is at best misinformed, reducing the forced unveiling project and the brutal force employed in implementing it merely to a "symbol of modernization, a sign of the reduction of the clergy's power."

It is important to stress that the imposition of a dress code on Iranian women started well before the 1979 revolution, when in 1936, under Reza Shah Pahlavi, Iran became the first Muslim country to ban the veil, forcibly unveiling women who resisted the decree (DePaul, "Re-Reading" 85). However, not as little as a single passing reference is made in the narrative to the atrocities perpetrated against Iranian women in the forced execution of Reza Shah's "modernization" project. The mandatory unveiling of Iranian women, instigated by Reza Shah's visit to Turkey, where Kemal Atatürk's secular regime had introduced a series of clothing regulations, had grave ramifications for the greater majority of Iranian women, who were practicing Muslims. Quite ironically, the edict, which was meant to enhance Iranian women's social visibility, mobility, and participation, banned them from the heterosocial public sphere and confined the larger portion of the female population to the interior of the domestic space, as they found appearing unveiled in public averse to their religious and cultural ethics and sentiments. Also, the ban caused greater dependency for Iranian women by making them even more reliant on male members of their households to run the errands that required exposure to the public eye, *ipso facto* reinforcing the patriarchal structures of a profoundly traditional society.

Women's refusal to enter the public arena unveiled—predicated upon both religious doctrines and the traditional association of the veil with feminine virtue and modesty—was met with severe repression, whereby the police aggressively unveiled women and searched private houses for veils (Paidar 107). Ironically, such violent measures were not taken by Atatürk's regime, whose model Reza Shah sought to emulate. The imposed unveiling, therefore, made educational access for the religious and traditional families, which formed the vast majority of the population, virtually impossible and contributed significantly to the perpetuation of illiteracy among them. The "imposed absence" of the veil led to women's state-sanctioned social immobility and their outright elimination from the public landscape (Balasescu 744). Behdad and Williams have argued that Reza Shah's forceful unveiling project not only met with strong resistance from Iranian women "whose access to education and socialization was ironically curtailed . . ., but it also maligned independent socialists, liberal nationalists, and feminists who were fighting for women's rights at the time as puppets of the tyrannical regime" (290), thereby leading to the oppression of both the religious and secular social agency of Iranian women.

Apropos the post-revolutionary imposition of the veil, scholars have observed that, as controversial as both projects have been, both the democratic and social impacts of the imposed unveiling and veiling projects are by no means comparable. On the one hand, in the constitutional referendum held in Iran on 2 and 3 December 1979, 99.5 percent of the voters voted for an Islamic constitution based on the principles and laws of the religion of Islam. On the other hand, while the forced unveiling of women made a large part of the female population invisible, and literally eliminated them from the heterosocial public arena, the post-revolutionary mandatory veiling—while admittedly encroaching upon some women's freedom of choice—did not preclude them from the public space. In contrast, as Ramazani has demonstrated, the revolution provided the greater majority of the female population with unprecedented social, educational, and professional opportunities that were once almost exclusive to the privileged upper echelons of the society ("Persepolis" 280). In the sphere of education, for instance, Mitra Shavarini has remarked that it has been under the Islamic Republic that the highest number of Iranian women has been most successful in entering and graduating from institutions of higher education (1979).[24] In other words, while the boundaries of individual body politics were redemarcated after the Islamic Revolution, which was seen as restrictive of personal freedoms by a minority of women, yet at a much larger scale "mobility increased for women who had previously been deprived of the opportunity to be present in socially meaningful spaces" (Balasescu 764).

Behdad and Williams have similarly argued that Nafisi's discussion of the imposition of the veil insinuates that the veil was imposed "from above," disavowing the fact that the unveiling edict was eventually abrogated by Reza Shah's son, Mohammad Reza, when "he had to lift the compulsory unveiling soon after his inauguration as king in 1941 due to strong public opposition" (290). It bears noting that during the reign of the last shah, with the exception of a minority of women in the capital, Tehran, and a few other major cities, Iranian women wore the chador, "a garment whose origin dates back to the pre-Islamic Achaemenid rulers who imposed it to protect their wives and concubines from the public gaze" (Behdad and Williams 290). Furthermore, Nafisi's ahistoricized and decontextualized description of the respective veiling and unveiling laws also overlooks the fact that what made the veiling mandate possible after the Iranian Revolution was the existence of "profound cultural and religious notions of modesty and piety among Iranian women, without whose consensus mandatory veiling would have been difficult, if not impossible" (Behdad and Williams 290). Also, Amy DePaul has highlighted the fact that even though some Iranian women felt uncomfortable with the new dress code, most women "welcomed it and, inadvertently, were liberated by it" ("Re-Reading" 83).

Nafisi's account also suffers from numerous lacunae, which account for the gross exaggeration and flagrant underrepresentation of the question of Iranian women, both pre- and post-revolution. According to Nafisi, prior to the revolution Iranian women could "walk the streets freely, enjoy the company of the opposite sex, join the police force, become pilots, live under laws that were among the most progressive in the world regarding women" (27). Nevertheless, Nafisi's curtailed account of Iranian women suffers from a simultaneous romanticization of women's pre-revolution status and an oversimplification of their condition after the revolution. Nesta Ramazani, another US-based Iranian-American memoirist, who is born of an English Christian mother and an Iranian Zoroastrian father, maintains that in placing the blame squarely on the Islamic Republic for whatever she disapproves of, Nafisi betrays her ignorance of the fact that many of the challenges she and her students encountered "were products of a deeply traditional, patriarchal society coming abruptly face-to-face with modernity and all that it implies" ("Persepolis" 280). She has further challenged Nafisi's idealization of the pre-revolutionary status of Iranian women, arguing that family law (except for minor modifications) as well as "laws governing divorce, alimony, child custody, payment of 'blood money,' testimony in a court of law, and other issues were all governed by Shari'a then as they are now" (280). She then proceeds to further elaborate how in her discussions of the Iranian woman question, Nafisi either disregards or is ignorant of many social and historical facts:

> Nafisi similarly overlooks the fact that in pre-revolutionary days the women who enjoyed the benefits of pursuing educations and professions were a relatively small number of women, mostly from the elite, upper and middle-classes. One would never guess from reading this book that Iranian women's educational opportunities have expanded, that they today enjoy an exceptionally high rate of literacy, are the beneficiaries of one of the most successful family planning programs in the world, and constitute sixty-three per cent of university entrants and roughly fifteen per cent of university faculty members. Nor would one guess that Iran has a female vice-president, a female advisor to the president and thirteen female members of parliament, and that women are at the forefront of a nascent, widespread democratic movement in Iran. ("Persepolis" 280)[25]

Similarly, other critics, notable among them Ansia Khaz Ali, the former president of one of Iran's leading—and its major all-female—universities, have pointed out that the overall condition of Iranian women has improved tremendously after the Iranian Revolution, judging by such factors as the literacy rate, higher education, social, political, and economic participation, lower infant mortality rate, and higher life expectancy, as indices of that improvement (Khaz Ali 6–20; Koegeler 34; Bahramitash, "The War on Terror").

Other critics, such as S. Asha, have yet drawn attention to the fact that "to Nafisi's credit ... she does not condemn the veil outright" (49) and that in the narrative, Nafisi has openly expressed her stance on the veil by stressing that the issue for her is not "as much the veil itself as the freedom of choice" (*Reading Lolita* 152). Nonetheless, similar to Nafisi's misleading, or naïve, reference to Reza Shah's forceful unveiling project, her assertion is hardly convincing. Even though the author attempts on occasions to frame her revulsion against the practice as a feminist and intellectual opposition to mandatory veiling (rather than to the veil per se), her highly unflattering characterization and caricaturing of Muslim women who observe the practice prove the contrary. Throughout the narrative, Iranian women, especially students, who had chosen to observe the veil, are all too frequently denigrated and depicted as driven by sheer revolutionary zeal, religious fanaticism, or submission to a patriarchal tradition, rather than out of personal principle, choice, and conviction.

One such student is Nassrin, who happens to be the only chador-wearing student who is ever allowed a voice in the narrative, regardless of how authentic her voice is, given that the author has self-admittedly "chang[ed] and interchange[ed] facets of [the students'] lives." However, both her brief life story and her participation in Nafisi's classes reveal that apparently the only reason she is given a voice is that through her—significantly, an apparently devout Muslim girl—the reader is invited to witness both the "brutality" of the Islamic government and the sanctimonious, sexually perverse religious patriarchy that is presented in the narrative as integral to Muslim beliefs. Nafisi's description of her first encounter with Nassrin after seven years, in which, to Nafisi's utter surprise, she is wearing a chador is quite telling:

> The last time I had seen her she was wearing a navy scarf and a flowing robe, but now she was dressed in a thick black chador from head to foot. She looked even smaller in the chador, her whole body hidden behind the bulk of the dark, shapeless cloth. Another transformation was her posture: she used to sit bolt upright on the edge of the chair, as if prepared to run at a moment's notice; now she slumped almost lethargically, looking dreamy and absentminded, writing in slow motion. (191)

Not only does the chador seem to have shrunk Nassrin's physical body, it has also "transformed" her posture, transmogrifying her from a confident and vivacious young lady to a "lethargic," "dreamy," and "absent-minded" girl. In other words, the chador seems to be the chief culprit in Nassrin's alleged physical and temperamental metamorphosis. Nafisi adds, however, that "some of her old familiar gestures were still with her, like the restless movement of her hands and her constant shifting from one foot to the other" (191). In other words, the garment seems to have bereft Nassrin of her buoyancy and ambitiousness and left her only her less flattering attributes of disconcertion and restlessness.

In Nafisi's class, to the right of Nassrin sit "the two members of the Muslim Students' Association," whose names Nafisi has, unsurprisingly, forgotten,[26] so she names them Miss Hatef and Miss Ruhi. This is how Nafisi characterizes the two students: "They are all negative attention. Every once in a while, from beneath their black chadors, which reveal no more than a sharp nose on one and a small, upturned one on the other, they whisper; sometimes they even smile" (192). Similar to a whole tradition of characters in colonial and Orientalist narratives, the two "Muslim" students are represented as nameless, shapeless, and faceless subhumans in such a dehumanizing manner that Nafisi feels compelled to add an emphatic "even" to stress that smiling was not something the two "Muslim" students were normally capable of. Nafisi then goes on to share her impression of the veil—that is, the chador—that the two students are wearing, lamenting the transformation of what she deems to be its meaning:

> There is something peculiar about the way they wear their chadors. I have noticed it in many other women, especially the younger ones. For there is in them, in their gestures and movements, none of the shy withdrawal of my grandmother, whose every gesture begged and commanded the beholder to ignore her, to bypass her and leave her alone. All through my childhood and early youth, my grandmother's chador had a special meaning to me. It was a shelter, a world apart from the rest of the world. I remember the way she wrapped her chador around her body and the way she walked around her yard when the pomegranates were in bloom. Now the chador was forever marred by the political significance it had gained. It had become cold and menacing, worn by women like Miss Hatef and Miss Ruhi with defiance. (192)

Not only does the aforementioned passage demonstrate Nafisi's total lack of sympathy for, and appreciation of, the complexities of the veiling practice, it is also quite ironic in the way it romanticizes her grandmother's practice—which reminds her of "pomegranates in bloom"—and denigrates that of the others. Furthermore, the irony of the manner in which Nafisi represents the chador lies in the fact that, earlier in the narrative, she makes a reference to her grandmother's refusal "to leave the house for three months when she was forced to unveil" (152). As discussed earlier, the refusal to appear unveiled in public and to rather stay within the interiority of the domestic space was an overtly political gesture in defiance of the government-mandated prohibition of veiling in public. However, such a gesture of political "defiance," as well as her grandmother's act of "withdrawal" and "defiance," which "commanded the beholder to ignore her, to bypass her and leave her alone," is made to sound valid, even praiseworthy, whereas the same act of "defiance" in her "Muslim" students is labeled "cold," "menacing," and driven by blind religious fanaticism. Thus, one could argue that

Nafisi's facile and reductionist treatment of the veil as romanticized nostalgia bereft of its sociopolitical significations reveals a blind spot in her thinking about and reading of the veil, which ignores its significance in the majority of Iranian and Muslim women's lives.

Characters like Miss Ruhi, who are also prevalent among Nafisi's male students, are not only disparaged for their observance of their religious beliefs but are without exception portrayed as philistine and lacking intellectual depth and sophistication. Discussing Henry James's *Daisy Miller* in her university class, Nafisi informs her students that "Winterbourne was not the only one to feel relief on discovering the answer to Daisy's riddle," stressing that his view was shared by students like Miss Ruhi:

> Miss Ruhi asked why the novel did not end with Daisy's death. Did that not seem the best place to stop? Daisy's death seemed like a nice ending for all parties concerned. Mr. Ghomi could gloat over the fact that she had paid for her sins with her life, and most others in the class could now sympathize with her without any feeling of guilt. (197)

While Nafisi sardonically gives Miss Ruhi credit for "describing the plot" of the assigned works, "which at least demonstrated that she had read the books" and that "she even, in some cases, had ... read about them" (199), she adds that "she seldom expressed her own opinions." Such an ostensibly innocuous statement, however, insinuates that Nafisi's "Muslim" student was incapable of forming independent judgment or having opinions of her own, thereby reducing her to an automaton only capable of memorization and rote learning. Even when Miss Ruhi does voice her views, she only evinces her literary philistinism and dogmatism. She objects to "Wuthering Heights's immorality," writes that "Daisy was not merely immoral, she was 'unreasonable,'" "lament[s] the fact that the right-thinking Mrs. Costello or Mrs. Walker was cast in such a negative light," and contends that "[a] writer like James ... was like Satan: he had infinite powers, but he used them to do evil, to create sympathy for a sinner like Daisy and distaste for more virtuous people like Mrs. Walker" (197). Nafisi's accounts of her literary discussions in her university classes are interspersed with such aforementioned oversimplistic and reductivist comments by her "Muslim" and "fundamentalist" students (regardless of how authentic they are in the first place and how accurately the author remembers them, some two decades after her teaching). Such statements further reinforce the implication that those students who did not entirely agree with Nafisi's interpretation of the Western classics were intellectually inferior to her and, as such, deserved nothing more than derision. She thus clinches the paragraph describing Miss Ruhi, declaring that "Miss Ruhi had imbibed the same dregs as Mr. Nyazi[27] [another "fundamentalist" student] and so many others" (197).

To complement the binary characterization of "Muslim" vs. "non-Muslim" girls in her university class, immediately after descriptions of the dour, chador-donning students, Nafisi turns to a student who does not wear the chador and is both attractive and intelligent: "The beautiful girl with the too-sweet face in the fourth row" is Mitra, "who always gets the highest grades" (192). The immediate effect is a classic neo-Orientalist binary predicated on the colonial strategies of affirmation and negation:[28] the philistine, aesthetically unflattering, fundamentalist Muslim girls vis-à-vis their attractive, intellectual, secular counterparts. Interestingly, later on Nafisi describes her encounter with Miss Ruhi, this time without her chador, and finds out, to her surprise, that she was not, in fact, as "plain" as she had thought her to be:

> She was dressed in black, but not in a chador, and had curled a long black scarf around her neck, fastened with a silvery pin that seemed to quiver like a spider's web against the black cloth. Her makeup was pale, and a few strands of dark brown hair showed from under the scarf. I kept remembering her other face, the austere one, so withdrawn that her lips seemed constantly pursed. I noticed now that she was not plain, as I had believed her to be. (331)

In other words, not until Miss Ruhi sheds her veil is she given the dignity of being humanized in the woefully black-and-white world of the narrative.

It is imperative to add that the criticism of Nafisi's representation of Iranian women and the veil should by no means be mistaken for a repudiation of the existence of patriarchal social structures in Iranian society or an affirmation of the post-revolution enactment of compulsory veiling. Rather, what renders Nafisi's account profoundly problematic is her almost total elimination of the social, historical, and political contexts within which discussions of Iranian women and the veil must be understood. Moreover, still even more problematic is the fact that the narrative does not offer as little as a single reference to the strong and popular advocacy of Iranian women both inside and outside the country for women's rights and their significant participation in the social and political affairs of their country.[29]

In caricaturing Iranian Muslim women and advocating an image of the "free" Western woman as the ideal to aspire to, Nafisi also evinces an ignorance characteristic of white Western Orientalist feminist discourses, which are only too often blind to the unfortunate situation of minority women. This (willful) ignorance, in turn, contributes to the perpetuation and preservation of the deplorable binarism into which dominant Western discourses on the Orient bifurcate the world. Such a polarization is one of the by-products of avoiding any meaningful criticism of the treatment of women of color, immigrants, indigenous populations, and other underprivileged communities. Along these lines, Bahramitash has drawn attention to the popularization of Orientalist feminism and the "boom industry" it has generated through literature and cinema, particularly in the post-9/11 milieu. She has also cautioned against the far-reaching, pernicious effect it continues to have on Muslim women's lives by inciting racist, anti-Muslim, and xenophobic sentiments across the Western world ("The War on Terror" 227)—a fact that has become clearer since the presidency of Donald Trump and the dominance of white supremacy in Europe, when xenophobia and Islamophobia have reached unprecedented levels. Against this backdrop, Bahramitash argues that the writings of such (neo-)Orientalist feminists as Nafisi are all too frequently appropriated as the most effective propaganda in the West's "War on Terror" against Muslim nations, as the personal experiences of such "self-proclaimed feminists" with the status of women in Muslim countries "impart an aura of authenticity to their portrayals of the primitive and misogynist nature of the religion [of Islam]" ("The War on Terror" 227).

In a similar fashion, Leela Gandhi has argued in her analysis of liberal feminist imperialism that "feminist opportunists seem to speak to the third world through a shared vocabulary" (86). In the case of *RLT*, this communal jargon is evidenced by the endorsement of the book and its author by a coterie of like-minded, often white Western feminists. Geraldine Brooks, for instance, who has also written a highly problematic account of the lives of Muslim women, which shows extensive ignorance, misinformation, and selectivity (Bahramitash, "The War on Terror" 229), has praised Nafisi in her endorsement of *RLT* as "one of the heroes of the Islamic Republic"—a "heroism" that, as Bahramitash has also observed, consists of "her experience in teaching English literature in post-revolutionary Iran and then leaving university to teach eight women at home about the glories of English literature" ("The War on Terror" 230).

Bridging the "Oriental Harem" to the "Free World"

I have previously demonstrated that one of the common denominators of both Orientalist feminism and feminist Orientalism is the belief in the need to "liberate" and "save" Muslim women. I have also illustrated that, historically, unveiling the Muslim woman has perhaps been the most significant colonial/Orientalist ambition on the path to this "liberation"—a concept that also figures prominently in *RLT*. The "liberating mission," however, operates on a more profound level in Nafisi's narrative. As will be later elaborated, Nafisi's medium for liberating her "girls" and resisting what she sees as the tyranny of the post-revolutionary Iranian government is teaching Western literature—a practice that Nafisi, quite disingenuously, insists on portraying as a herculean feat and a very dangerous venture in post-revolutionary Iran. In the private weekly sessions she holds in her apartment in the affluent north Tehran, she uses Western literary classics to discuss contemporary issues surrounding the lives of Iranian women, as (mis) represented by her and her coterie of students. Whitlock has remarked that Nafisi creates in her private class "a cell of resistance for a small group of bright young women, who cast off the chador at her door and enter a space of enchantment and empathy created by Austen, Fitzgerald, and Nabokov" ("From Tehran" 11). Even if we take Whitlock's remark—that there is "enchantment" in the works of the mentioned authors—at face value, the idea that this "enchantment and empathy" are really "liberating" is, to say the least, highly questionable.

The appropriation of Western literary classics as a liberating medium in the post-revolutionary Iran of the 1980s is, as critics have suggested, a very problematic concept from different aspects. Nevertheless, before discussing Nafisi's pedagogical politics, it is necessary to first examine the space within which the private literature class is held. "The living room," as it is frequently referred to in the memoir, is the most significant *mise-en-scène* in the narrative and functions as the narrative's spatial/physical centerpiece. As such, it is persistently presented as an alternative world, a "protective cocoon" (26), a "sanctuary," and a "self-contained universe" (6) into which its temporary inhabitants can escape what is deemed the cruelty of the oppressive world outside. In a passage juxtaposing two photographs of her students, one inside a university class and the other in her living room, Nafisi remarks:

> The second photograph belonged to the world inside the living room. But outside, underneath the window that deceptively showcased only the mountains and the tree outside our house, was the other world, where the bad witches and furies were waiting to transform us into the hooded creatures of the first. (24)

For the Western reader, Nafisi's private class is made to represent, in microcosm, the goings-on of Iranian society, running the whole gamut of Iranian culture, religion, politics, education, gender issues, and sex. Nafisi and her "girls," therefore, become the embodiments of resistance to "tyranny" through whom the reader is invited to observe the tangled web of social, religious, and political "ills" of Iranian society. The full scope of the world inside the living room is revealed only when juxtaposed with the outside world. Comparing the worlds within and without the living room, Nafisi states that "[w]e tried to live in the open spaces, in the chinks created between that room, which had become our protective cocoon, and the censor's world of witches and goblins outside" (26). The binary enforced upon the two worlds could hardly be more Orientalist in nature: the living room is "blessed" with Western novels, sophisticated literary discussions, Western delicacies, and unveiled, colorful girls; the world outside, on the other hand, is dominated by fanatics, masses, "the black-scarved, timid faces" (6), and "witches" (24, 26), "furies" (24), and "goblins" (26). Judging by Nafisi's dehumanizing choice of diction and her tone in representing the non-Western world outside the living room, one cannot but be tempted to infer that the author views those outside her literary coterie as devoid of any humanity. Unsurprisingly, such a mode of characterization, or rather demonization, bears an uncanny resemblance to Betty Mahmoody's view of Iran as "a country ... populated almost totally with villains" (334) and her animalization of the average Iranian, as discussed at length in the chapter on Mahmoody's narrative.

The aforementioned quotes are also noteworthy for the infantilism embedded in the author's choice of diction, which likens the world outside Nafisi's living room to a fairy-tale world dominated by "bad witches" and "furies." This infantilism informs some of Nafisi's other descriptions, too. Describing the changes she observes on her arrival in the Tehran airport, Nafisi remarks that "[i]t seemed as if a bad witch with her broomstick had flown over the building and in one sweep had taken away the restaurants, the children and the women in colorful clothes that I remembered" (82). Similarly, listening to the stories of her girls, Nafisi thus expresses her emotional response: "I had a feeling that we were living a series of fairy tales in which all the good fairies had gone on strike, leaving us stranded in the middle of a forest not far from the wicked witch's candy house" (241).

This simultaneous romanticization of pre-revolutionary Iran and demonization of the post-revolution era is a common leitmotif of the memoirs and travelogues written on Iran. What makes such romanticization especially bizarre is the fact that the authors of some of these narratives, such as V. S. Naipaul in his two "Islamic" travelogues, had never visited the country prior to the 1979 revolution; furthermore, the knowledge of some others such as Nafisi does not go beyond childhood or adolescence nostalgia and distant memories.

The material space afforded by the living room is characterized by a paradoxical dual signification. On the one hand, it can be regarded as a haremesque space wherein Nafisi's young "girls" are shown unveiling and divulging their private lives and secrets. In this light, it can be argued that Nafisi's narrative offers her Western readers a rare opportunity for voyeurism—a "privilege" that is not normally accessible to the Western masculine gaze. In this Oriental harem, Nafisi assumes the role of a Scheherazade whose Oriental tales not only provide her curious Western readers with a peephole through which to penetrate the interiority of this exclusively feminine space but also go a long way toward "saving" the girls through Western literature, as eventually most of them reportedly seek refuge in the West. On the other hand, however, Nafisi's "subversive" book club constitutes a simulacrum of the "Free World"—a deliberately all-female space to which its denizens are encouraged to bring "their secrets, their pains and their gifts" (58). In this women's shelter, as it were, Nafisi's "girls" read and discuss "forbidden" Western literature, savor their coffees and Western delicacies, engage in enthusiastic discussions about gender issues and women's rights, and broach such "taboos" as sex. For Western readers the space, then, turns into a familiar sight, which DePaul has dubbed a "literary 'Sex and the City' (except the city is Tehran)" ("Re-Reading" 73). "In the magical space of my living room" (58), Nafisi remarks, she assumes the role of the mentor, the illuminator, the savior, and even the mother (exemplified by her repeated references to her students as her "girls"), while her students come "in a disembodied state of suspension" (58) only to be made whole again through the "liberating" medium of Western literature. She presides over her class in her living room, introducing her students to the "enchantment" of the world of Western classics:

> In a world unknown and presumably unknowable to Nabokov, in a forlorn living room with windows looking out towards distant white-capped mountains, time and again I would stand witness to the unlikeliest of readers as they lost themselves in a madness of hair-ruffling. (22)

Thus, having opened the door to, and therefore liberated, her students by teaching them Nabokov's *Lolita* and other classics, Nafisi posits herself in the position of the savior who "stands witness" to her "girls" who have apparently been charmed by their newly earned freedom and bliss. That the girls are described as "the unlikeliest of readers" of Nabokov's novels only serves to reinforce Nafisi's fraudulent assertions both about "forbidden" Western classics and the purported philistinism of Iranian culture (which will be discussed later in the chapter). It is within the same space that Nafisi's students have their moments of epiphany:

> There, in that living room, we rediscovered that we were also living, breathing human beings; and no matter how repressive the state became, no matter how intimidated and frightened we were, like Lolita we tried to escape and to create our own little pockets of freedom. (26)

In keeping with the view of the living room as a microcosmic replica of "the free West," Melamed has argued that the living room "is an unspoken and unspeakably bourgeois space, where western cultural and political supremacy are taken for granted, and home is part of a moral and affective code that legitimates a politics of privatization" ("Reading Tehran in Lolita: Making Racialized" 82). The living room, therefore, constitutes a very complex site characterized by an intersecting nexus of associations: it offers a "Western" space where Nafisi's young "girls" are shown shedding their veils and, thus, becoming "free" from the "oppression" of the outside world, but are simultaneously subjected to a Western, Orientalizing gaze that cannot but see them as Oriental Lolitas, but also perhaps feel proud of the "freedom" bestowed upon them by the West.

The Ominous Alliance: From Neo-Orientalism to Neoconservatism

As demonstrated earlier, Orientalist feminism has a history of complicity in interventionist politics, appropriated as it continues to be by Western far-right, (neo-)conservative, and supremacist ideologies toward the demonization of non-Western others and the justification of foreign interventionism and occupation, as seen in the US invasions of Iraq and Afghanistan. In this light, it is little surprise that *RLT*, as the epitome of Orientalist-feminist narratives, enjoyed such an enthusiastic reception in one of the most belligerent periods of contemporary US history, which saw two devastating wars against two Muslim nations. Some critics, therefore, were quick to draw attention to how Nafisi's "memoir" can go a long way toward serving Western hegemonic and imperialistic agendas. Such complicity seems all the more valid in light of the author's affiliation with the US neoconservative coterie and her propagation, wittingly or otherwise, of their foreign policy vis-à-vis the Middle East through the demonization of yet another Muslim nation already the target of some of the most severe US-imposed sanctions in the world. Such complicity is also one of the main reasons for which Nafisi's work has come under criticism even by some of the staunchest critics of the Islamic Republic, such as professor Hamid Dabashi.

The dynamics of the reception, promotion, and association of the book and its author can be read within the framework of Genette's paratextuality as part of the elements intertwined with the politics of the book, in the form of both peritexts (as shown in the case of the front cover of *RLT*) and epitexts (i.e., beyond the print copy). Rowe has argued that US neoconservatives have varied the pattern for the promotion of "Anglo-Saxonism" or "Western supremacism"—formerly conducted by a clique of white male politicians, intellectuals, and writers—by "supporting women and ethnic minorities who share their views and thus give legitimacy to the cultural diversity of their presumed meritocracy" (253). In a similar vein, Melamed has observed that since her immigration to the United States, Nafisi has been inducted "as a new immigrant intellectual into centrist and neo-conservative policy and academic circles" ("Reading Tehran in Lolita: Making Racialized" 81).

Critics have also cited the many instances of circumstantial evidence corroborating Nafisi's neoconservative political and intellectual affiliations. Nafisi herself has mentioned in *RLT* that after leaving Iran in 1997, she found an "academic and intellectual home" at the Paul H. Nitze School for Advanced International Studies (SAIS) at Johns Hopkins University, where she was able to complete her "memoir" and "pursue [her] projects at SAIS" with a "generous grant from the Smith Richardson Foundation" (346–7). According to Phil Wilayto, "SAIS has long been a bastion of Cold War thinking" ("An Open Letter") and the Foundation, as Rowe has noted, "provides significant support to conservative think-tanks across the country" and its board "includes some of the most influential neo-conservatives from government, the military, and higher education" (255). Wilayto also describes the Foundation as "one of the 15 or so major right-wing foundations in the U.S. and one that has a special focus of demonizing Iran." He then proceeds to reveal that "[f]rom 1998 to 2004, according to its annual reports, the foundation gave Nafisi six grants totaling \$675,500." Most significantly, yet, is the fact that, as Wilayto reveals "In 1996, Nafisi also received \$25,000 from the Lynde and Harry Bradley Foundation 'to support a series of workshops in Tehran, Iran, under the direction of Dr. Azar Nafisi.' (Bradley annual report, 1996) That 'series of workshops' was the private book discussion club that formed the basis of 'Reading Lolita.'" ("An Open Letter").

At SAIS Nafisi was also the director of the Dialogue Project. The project is introduced on its website as "a multi-year initiative designed to promote—in a primarily cultural context—the development of democracy and human rights in the Muslim world" and engages with issues "that have been the main targets of Islamists and, as a result, are the most significant impediments to the creation of open and pluralistic societies in the Muslim world, including culture and the myth of Western culture [sic] imperialism, women's issues, and human rights, among others."[30]

Interestingly, the aforementioned description bears an uncanny resemblance to the content of *RLT,* so much so that the reader can be forgiven for mistaking it for a passage excerpted from the book. Perhaps even more telling is the description of the project on the website of the Foreign Policy Institute at SAIS, which reports that the Project "included discussions on perspectives of the general populace in Iran, Iraq, and Afghanistan; human rights in Iran; the influence of Western culture around the world; and literature as it relates to international affairs."[31] It would be naïve to assume that it is only coincidental that of the three countries that are "discussed" in the project, one was already invaded by the United States in 2001, one would soon be invaded in 2003, and the other has been constantly threatened with wars by different US administrations. The project, thus, can be encapsulated as such: saving Muslim women from Muslim men (to borrow from Gayatri Spivak) by initiating them into the glorious world of Western culture and literature, reminding them of their human rights as prescribed by their savior, the United States, and removing the stigma of Western imperialism by simply dismissing it as a "myth."

Even though a few critics have dismissed discussions of Nafisi's neoconservative political affiliations as irrelevant, many others have argued that the connection is, indeed, quite crucial for a better appreciation of the politics of the production and reception of *RLT* in the United States. In the aftermath of 9/11, when the United States was at the peak of its "War on Terror," and Iran was branded by the then–US president as a member of an "axis of evil" and an "outpost of tyranny," such cultural productions served to "reinforce what many North Americans want to believe about the 'oppression' of Iranian women" and were utilized to "raise support for the neoconservative agenda to stir anti-Muslim sentiment in North America as well as to promote the war on terror" (Bahramitash "The War on Terror" 221). It is little surprise, then, that an article titled *To Bomb or Not to Bomb, That Is the Iran Question*, published in the neoconservative *Weekly Standard*, actually cites *RLT* to argue for a first-strike against Iran:

> Although some Western female journalists have tried to depict Iranian women as liberated under their headscarves and veils, these sentiments have an uneasy time with other reporting that shows Iranian women, however strong-willed and independent, being severely abused by the regime's Islamic-law system. The phenomenal global success of Azar Nafisi's *Reading Lolita in Tehran* has also made it more difficult to view the Islamic Republic's internal ethics, particularly regarding women, benignly. (Gerecht)

As the quote demonstrates, the complicity between neo-Orientalist literature produced by US-based native informers and a belligerent, interventionist foreign policy, or in the rather innocuous-sounding phrasing of the Dialogue Project, "literature as it relates to international affairs," can hardly be overemphasized. In a similar vein, professor Hamid Dabashi, one of the most outspoken critics of the Islamic Republic of Iran, has explained how the memoir has helped further the Bush administration's foreign policy agendas:

> One can now clearly see and suggest that this book is partially responsible for cultivating the U.S. (and by extension the global) public opinion against Iran,

having already done a great deal by being a key propaganda tool at the disposal of the Bush administration during its prolonged wars in such Muslim countries as Afghanistan (since 2001) and Iraq (since 2003). ("Native Informers")

Paramount in Nafisi's political and intellectual association is, first, her affiliation with the renowned veteran Orientalist Bernard Lewis—a relationship that DePaul has dubbed Nafisi's "most damning association" with US neoconservatives ("Re-Reading" 78). Lewis is known for his (in)famous "clash of civilizations" mindset, as proposed in his 1990 *Atlantic Monthly* essay, titled "The Roots of Muslim Rage", which postulates an ineluctable "clash" between the West and Islam. This clash, in turn, has been adopted as a point of departure by top US neoconservative policymakers. Therefore, when Donald Trump told CNN's Anderson Cooper that "I think Islam hates us" when asked whether the religion was "at war with the West," he was, in fact, echoing the Islamophobic mindset long propagated by Bernard Lewis and such neoconservative think tanks as Nafisi is associated with. The "clash of civilizations" theory has been since then widely criticized, particularly by the late Edward Said, who remarked that Lewis's "ideological colors are manifest in [the] title [of his article]" ("The Clash of Ignorance").

Nafisi's association with Bernard Lewis is of particular significance, given his controversial theorization of the civilizational "degeneration" in the Islamic world, while his own bestseller, *What Went Wrong?* (2002), still continues to serve as one of the crucial "ahistorical scaffolding[s] upon which the neo-conservative hard core . . . hang their policy prescriptions" (Mottahedeh). In a similar vein, Lewis's stance on the Iraq War—he has been designated as "the most significant intellectual influence behind the invasion of Iraq" (Weisberg; Hirsch)—as well as the Iranian "nuclear issue" provides a significant context in which Nafisi's memoir can be better understood. Equally important is Nafisi's association with Fouad Ajami, one of her major supporters, as well as her "neo-conservative mentor [and] her boss at the School of Advanced International Studies in Washington" (Bahramitash "The War on Terror" 230), who was also another staunch advocate of the 2003 US invasion of Iraq (Ajami xii).

Quite similar to the shared language through which, according to Gandhi, Orientalist-feminists speak of the Muslim world (86), is the reciprocal affirmation of neoconservative ideologues. Such affirmations figure in such peritexts of Nafisi's memoir as the blurbs and the book's Acknowledgment. In the blurb Bernard Lewis has written for Nafisi's memoir, he has commended *RLT* as "a masterpiece" offering "profound and fascinating insights" into both Western literature and post-revolutionary Iran. Nafisi, in turn, has reciprocated by cryptically thanking Bernard Lewis as the one "who opened the door" in her Acknowledgment (346)—a gesture of gratitude that has generated much criticism and raised questions about her consorting with political and intellectual neoconservative circles in the United States. As several scholars have noted (Bahramitash, "The War on Terror" 230; Dabashi "Native Informers"; Donadey and Ahmed-Ghosh 636; Mottahedeh), this connection serves to shed light on the production, promotion, and reception of Nafisi's "memoir" and helps elucidate her position with regard to matters both Iranian and American.

The significance of this association in the publication and reception of *RLT* is better understood if one puts into perspective the fact that both prior to and after the publication of her book, Nafisi was promoted by Benador Associates, a public relations corporation that promotes neoconservative luminaries and public speakers advocating US foreign policy in the Middle East, which is also well known for its hawkish, especially its Irano-Islamophobic, stance. As a case in point, in May 2006, Canada's *National Post* published a sensational piece entitled "A Colour Code for Iran's 'Infidels'" by Benador Associates and Amir Taheri, a prominent Iranian-born US neoconservative, claiming that the Iranian Parliament had passed a sumptuary law requiring its Jewish citizens to wear a yellow insignia—reminiscent of the policies of Nazi Germany (Taheri). The story, as it turned out, was a scandalous hoax, entirely a figment of Taheri's Islamophobic imagination, which was quickly discredited and Benador Associates admitted to planting the piece (Kelly).

What should also be taken into consideration about the promotion of Nafisi and her work by Benador Associates is that the firm played an active role in the propagation of the "liberating Muslim women" agenda, the US invasion of Iraq, and other interventionist policies of the Bush administration. Negar Mottahedeh refers to an article by the firm's founder, Eleana Benador, in which, contemplating the participation of an Afghan and an Iraqi woman in the 2004 Athens Olympics, she comments: "We are winning! . . . We have rescued from the hands of those extremists these women who have regained their status as human beings, and who are learning now what it is to be treated with respect and dignity."

Perhaps the most telling indicator of Nafisi's controversial collaboration with US neoconservatives is her induction into the School of Advanced International Studies at Johns Hopkins University, where she was hired while Paul Wolfowitz, himself a staunch disciple of Bernard Lewis, was dean before he became a key advocate of the US invasion of Iraq as deputy secretary of defense from 2001 to 2005 under George W. Bush. As Rowe has suggested, for someone with a PhD in English literature "to hold her appointment in SAIS, a school for the training of diplomats, certainly does pose a set of intriguing questions" (256). Even if one dismisses the naiveté of conspiracy theories apropos Nafisi's collaboration with US neoconservatives, one could still effectively argue that her induction and promotion is based on shared political sensibilities. There is little discord among critics concerning the implications of Nafisi's association with US political and intellectual neoconservative circles for the promotion and reception of her memoir. Nevertheless, such neoconservatism is not exclusive to Nafisi's politics. Rather, it permeates the narrative itself and is especially embedded in Nafisi's descriptions of Iranian women and her discussions of particular Western classics.

One of the most significant ways in which the text promotes the neoconservative political ideology is rendering a perverse formulation of Islam as tantamount to Marxism and Communism in "its totalitarian intent, methods, and effects" (DePaul, "Re-Reading" 77). In her discussion of the political milieu that dominated the immediate post-revolution sociopolitical landscape in Iran, Nafisi's memoir exhibits a tendency to equate the predominant Islamic movement of the time with those of the Marxist and Communist parties. While it is true that the Islamic, Marxist, and Communist groups formed the major opposition to the monarchy, there were radical differences that distinguished them from one another in both ideology and modus operandi. However, as is characteristic of (neo-)Orientalist discourses, this heterogeneity is effaced in *RLT* in favor of a simplistic rendition of them all as "anti-American."

In the chapter on *Gatsby*, Nafisi repeatedly interlaces Marxist terminology with her descriptions of what she sees as Islamism, concluding that *Gatsby* offended the sensibilities of both her Muslim and Marxist students for its immorality and materialism (DePaul, "Re-Reading" 77). In an important passage, not only does Nafisi conflate Islam with Marxism, but characteristically dehumanizes her "political" students by denying them such primordial human emotions as love and passion and demarcating their individuality only within the confines of frenzied politics:

> My students were slightly baffled by Gatsby. The story of an idealistic guy, so much in love with this beautiful rich girl who betrays him, could not be satisfying to those for whom sacrifice was defined by words such as masses, revolution and Islam. Passion and betrayal were for them political emotions, and love far removed from the stirrings of Jay Gatsby for Mrs. Tom Buchanan. (108)

Nafisi further equates the two ideologies when juxtaposing Mike Gold, a proletarian author, with Fitzgerald, claiming that "the revolution Gold desired was a Marxist one and ours was Islamic, but they had a great deal in common, in that they were both ideological and totalitarian" (109). Speaking of the "revolutionary" mottos allegedly used by some of her students, she lampoons them, stating sardonically that "[o]ne had a feeling ... that they spoke from a script, playing characters from an Islamized version of a Soviet novel" (165), thereby constructing an odd affinity between the Islamic Iran and the Communist Soviet. DePaul has argued that Nafisi is "at her most neoconservative" in her conflation of Islam and Marxism and her invocation of "Soviet totalitarianism" to describe Islam, since "portraying Islamism glibly as an equivalent to Marxism invokes a particularly troubling paradigm for global conflict, the Cold War" and exerts "a powerful effect on many American readers, suggesting an imperative to confront an ideologically opposed enemy that is armed (or soon to be) and extremely dangerous" ("Re-Reading" 80). DePaul's observation serves to shed further light on the signification of "literature as it relates to international affairs," or, in other words, the nexus between literature, neoconservatism, and neo-Orientalism.

Another instance in which the Islam vis-à-vis Marxism comparison is invoked is in Nafisi's discussion of Nabokov's novels, especially *Lolita*. Nafisi approaches *Lolita* both as an artistic expression of female victimization by patriarchal authority and as a story that is essentially anti-totalitarian (DePaul, "Re-Reading" 80). In discussing the works of Nabokov, Nafisi constantly stresses what she deems to be a strain of resistance against totalitarianism and oppression as essential in the appreciation of Nabokov's novels. In her discussion of Nabokov's *Invitation to a Beheading*, she likens the arbitrary authorities with Russian names, who have imprisoned and want to execute the protagonist, Cincinnatus, to Muslim authorities, remarking that "here was not much difference between our jailers and Cincinnatus's executioners. They invaded all private spaces and tried to shape every gesture, to force us to become one of them, and that in itself was another form of execution" (77). In a similar vein, Iranian authorities are constantly likened to Humbert Humbert, Lolita's rapist (who blames Lolita's tantalizing nature) for viewing women as capable of the sexual provocation of the opposite sex (DePaul, "Re-Reading" 80). Thus, not only does *RLT* juxtapose post-revolutionary Iran with the world of Nabokov's novels wherein the themes of resistance and female victimization figure prominently, in so doing it invokes the menace of communist authoritarianism by associating post-revolutionary Iran with the Soviet Union, "thus hinting at a threat of global magnitude that conceivably contributed to American readers' fears" (DePaul, "Re-Reading" 81).

Nafisi's neoconservative leanings are also manifest in the ill-informed rendition of pre-revolutionary Iran as a benign and democratic golden age compared to the post-revolution era in *RLT*. This is particularly evident in the references to the highly exaggerated condition of Iranian women prior to the revolution, a neoconservative line of thinking made famous by Jeane J. Kirkpatrick (DePaul, "Re-Reading" 81).[32] In her 1979 *Dictatorships and Double Standards*, Kirkpatrick thus expresses her underlying thesis:

> Only intellectual fashion and the tyranny of Right/Left thinking prevent intelligent men of good will from perceiving the facts that traditional authoritarian governments are less repressive than revolutionary autocracies, that they are more susceptible of liberalization, and that they are more compatible with U.S. interests. (72)

Kirkpatrick further criticizes the Carter administration's foreign policy for being "unrealistic" and for having failed to prevent "the replacement of moderate autocrats friendly to American interests with less friendly autocrats of extremist persuasion" (61). *Reading Lolita in Tehran* does echo this latter neoconservative strain manifestly in exaggerating and romanticizing the pre-revolutionary "freedoms" that Iranian people allegedly enjoyed, while turning a blind eye both to the numerous atrocities perpetrated by the last monarchial regime[33] and to the significant improvements in the social life of Iranian people, especially women, as noted earlier. Hence, according to DePaul, "in tacitly excusing bad dictators rather than focusing on the superpowers that propped them up," Nafisi invokes, while ironically trying to efface, one of the saddest chapters in the contemporary Iranian historico-political collective consciousness, that is, the role of the United States and Britain in the coup d'état that overthrew Iran's, and the Middle East's, first democratically elected prime minister and anti-colonialist, Dr. Mohammad Mosaddeq (82).

From the Western Canon to the West's Cannons

One of the most contentious aspects of Nafisi's memoir is her pedagogical modus operandi, which is entirely reliant on the canonical Western literature she teaches to her "girls" in her clandestine weekly sessions. Before discussing Nafisi's literary pedagogy, however, it is necessary to point out that Nafisi's primary assertion that the works of the authors she discusses in her secret class were "forbidden" in post-revolutionary Iran is disingenuous. As Seyed Mohammad Marandi, professor of English literature at the University of Tehran, has noted, not only were Western classics not banned, in the same time span that Nafisi has written about there were "students at the University of Tehran who even wrote their theses on Nabokov, after checking out his novels from the university library" (182). As such, while the promotion of Western culture and literature remains a controversial issue to this date in Iran, there has never been an official ban on the teaching of Western classics and, in fact, such works of literature continued to be taught at different universities throughout the country even during the 1980s when the revolutionary zeal was at its peak.

Like almost all other leitmotifs underlying the narrative, the discussion of Western literary classics in *RLT* has engendered plenty of critical controversy. *Reading Lolita in Tehran* has earned much of its acclaim by dint of Nafisi's corroboration of the power of imagination and literature. Many Western reviewers and critics have lauded *RLT* for demonstrating the "limitless," "transformative," "illuminating," and "democratic" power of Western literature and fiction (Atwood; Grogan 69; Flint; Hewett; Kakutani; Kamran; Yardley). The first four pages of the book acclaim it as a literary "masterpiece" and a remarkable testament to the power and significance of Western literature. Kate Flint, for instance, has summarized the reason the book has been so enthusiastically welcomed in the West: its eye-opening quality, its appreciation of the taken-for-granted and liberating potential of Western literature, and its resistance against oppression. Flint has further built upon Nafisi's argument about the connection between reading Western literature, democratic ethics, and Western liberalism, averring that

> *Reading Lolita in Tehran* is remarkable for the ways it lends new eyes to those of us who take the reading privileges of a Western democracy more or less for granted. Reading—presented, to be sure, by someone whose experience has made her a fervent advocate of Western liberalism—becomes simultaneously an escape from oppression, especially gender oppression; an intellectual transgression; and a promise that life might and can be otherwise. Reading provides liberation through the imagination. (512)

Nafisi's idea of teaching Western literature as a liberating, democratic medium is also echoed in the reviews of her work. Writing in the *Middle East Journal*—the official journal of The Middle East Institute, a Washington DC think tank generously funded by such Arab countries as the UAE[34]—Cameron Kamran reiterated Nafisi's universalist, Western liberal-humanist position on literature, remarking that for Nafisi Western literature "is a universal language that bridges cultures and instills a form of democracy by teaching us empathy for the complexities of the human condition" (512). Ironically, however, not only does Nafisi's exploitation of Western literature not contribute to "bridging cultures," it does, in fact, go a long way toward creating a chasm between the "civilized" West and the "backward" post-revolutionary Iran by idolizing the former and demonizing the latter. Similarly, if there is one thing *RLT* does not teach, it is "empathy for the complexities of the human condition." In fact, rather than highlighting the multilayered complexities of life in a nascent Islamic Republic that, having just emerged out of a revolution found itself at an all-out eight-year war fully supported by the West, Nafisi's narrative flattens and oversimplifies the complex realities of life in post-revolutionary Iran by representing anyone whose ideology differs from her as intellectually inferior and by subjecting them to her barely concealed vitriol.

The views shared by Nafisi, her neoconservative mentors, and a number of like-minded reviewers about the alleged liberating potential of classical Western literature are enmeshed in their own problematics. Some of the most significant grounds that render Nafisi's literary pedagogy highly contentious include the intrinsic connection between teaching Western literature to Iranian girls and the promulgation of American cultural and political hegemony, the colonial implications of much of the literature she teaches and preaches, and, finally, her almost total disregard for, or arguably ignorance of, a very rich and diversified Persian/Iranian literary heritage.

Nafisi's selection of literary texts consists of some of the most famous canonical novels arranged in a reverse-chronological sequence, beginning with Nabokov's *Lolita* (1955 in Paris; 1958 in the United States) and followed in order by F. Scott Fitzgerald's *The Great Gatsby* (1925), Henry James's *Daisy Miller* and *Washington Square* (1878 and 1881), and Jane Austen's *Pride and Prejudice* and *Mansfield Park* (1813 and 1814). Even though Nafisi's account "devotes an inordinate number of pages to literary analysis of the Western works she and her students studied" (Ramazani, "Persepolis" 279), critics have drawn attention to the conspicuous absence in her analyses of the manner in which the hermeneutics of Nabokov, Fitzgerald, James, and Austen have mutated in the past few decades under the influences of such critical paradigms as deconstruction, feminism, New Historicism, postcolonial studies, and cultural studies. Moreover, if there is any reference to critical theory in her narrative, Nafisi follows the neoconservative predisposition to disregard various competing critical perspectives as "postmodernist" or "relativist" (Rowe 263). This is best exemplified in Nafisi's reference to Edward Said's influential *Culture and Imperialism*, which illustrates both her ignorance of and dismissive attitude toward any alternative readings of canonical Western literature:

> One day after class, Mr. Nahvi followed me to my office. He tried to tell me that Austen was not only anti-Islamic but that she was guilty of another sin: she

was a colonial writer. I was surprised to hear this from the mouth of someone who until then had mainly quoted and misquoted the Koran. He told me that *Mansfield Park* was a book that condoned slavery, that even in the West they had now seen the error of their ways. What confounded me was that I was almost certain Mr. Nahvi had not read *Mansfield Park*.

It was only later, on a trip to the States, that I found out where Mr. Nahvi was getting his ideas from when I bought a copy of Edward Said's *Culture and Imperialism*. It was ironic that a Muslim fundamentalist should quote Said against Austen. It was just as ironic that the most reactionary elements in Iran had come to identify with and co-opt the work and theories of those considered revolutionary in the West. (290)

The excerpt, which Donadey and Ahmed-Ghosh have described as "one of the most ironic moments of the memoir" (637), is quite significant not only in shedding light on Nafisi's literary pedagogy but also in highlighting the manner in which Nafisi represents "Muslim" students. In line with Nafisi's characteristic representation of "Muslim" students as philistine, Mr. Nahvi—in whom Nafisi is "unable to find a single redeeming quality" (290)—is portrayed as someone who can "quote and misquote Koran," but is not expected to be conversant with Western critical theories, and thus his reading and quoting Said is treated as something of an aberration. Similarly troubling is Nafisi's accusation that Mr. Nahvi had not even read *Mansfield Park*—an assertion that is reminiscent of Said's contention that Orientalists simply "knew" what the Orientals were like. The double "irony" that Nafisi is quick to point out is, ironically, overridden by a triple irony that undermines Nafisi's own reading of the event. First, it is the "fundamentalist" student, rather than the secular, US-trained English professor, who is conversant with the most recent literary criticism in the West. Second, as the bulk of postcolonial critiques of Austen's corpus demonstrates, Said's reading of Austen's *Mansfield Park* as implicated in the British colonial enterprise is warranted and, as such, its inclusion in the debates surrounding the work is entirely justified. Finally, and perhaps the greatest irony, is that Nafisi's own memoir is "as easily appropriated as Said's work, this time by westerners seeking a justification to vilify Islam wholesale" (Donadey and Ahmed-Ghosh 637) as well as by fellow neo-Orientalists, Orientalist feminists, and neoconservatives across the globe.

Paramount in the perusal and construal of any work of literature, and by extension of art, is the locus in which the work is both constructed and consumed. The significance of a writer's, and consequently of the readership's, sociopolitical and geographical situatedness in the appreciation of any given work of literature cannot be overstated. Cheryl Miller, for instance, has pointed out how "the act of reading is always colored by our place in the world" (93). Similarly, Rowe argues that the popularity of *RLT* is, significantly germane to the manner in which the meaning of literary productions is contingent upon the location where they are perused. He further argues that, penned by a US-educated and US-based Iranian immigrant and "published only in English for Anglophone readers, *Reading*

Lolita in Tehran relies primarily on its location within the United States" (258). Throughout her narrative Nafisi demonstrates her awareness of "the place one's social location may play in the reading life" (T. Bush "Bookish Lives" 32). The significance of time and place in appreciation of works of literature is manifest, more than anywhere else, in the title of the book and thus accounts for *Reading Lolita "in Tehran"* as opposed to simply *Reading Lolita* (DePaul, "Re-Reading" 75). Significantly, in the opening pages of the memoir Nafisi delineates how the setting in which a work of literature is perused can shape the meaning of the text:

> It is of *Lolita* that I want to write, but right now there is no way I can write about that novel without also writing about Tehran. This, then, is the story of *Lolita* in Tehran, how *Lolita* gave a different color to Tehran and how Tehran helped redefine Nabokov's novel, turning it into this *Lolita*, our *Lolita*. (6)

Nabokov's *Lolita*, then, is turned into a fertile ground for the English literature professor to manufacture her own Iranian Lolitas through whose (self-admittedly manipulated) life narratives she seeks to write her account of, or rather political tract on, post-revolutionary Iranian. Along the same lines, Rowe has argued that one of the strong appeals of Nafisi's exploitation of canonical Western literature is the fact that "they do new political work in the radically different cultural context" of the Islamic Republic of Iran (263). It is on the same grounds that *The Great Gatsby*, hardly a subject of controversy in Western colleges, allegedly turns out to be the most contentious work on Nafisi's syllabus for a class she teaches in Tehran in the thick of a fledgling revolution fiercely claimed by stalwart adherents of the antithetical ideologies of Marxism and Islam. According to Nafisi, student adherents of both parties took issue with Fitzgerald's work respectively for the unwarranted materialism and "idealized portrayal of Gatsby's aristocratic pretensions and corrupt accumulation of wealth" and the moral degeneracy of its antagonist exemplified in "romanticizing the adulterous relationship between Gatsby and Daisy Buchanan" (Rowe 263). By the same token, just as reading Nabokov's *Lolita* in Tehran infuses the very act of reading with an almost totally distinct set of semantic significations, the manner in which *RLT* is perused and perceived in the West is also bound to be tellingly discrete from the way it is construed in the East, not least in the Muslim East.

In addition to the aforementioned question of Iranian/Muslim women and the colonial, neo-Orientalist venture of "liberating" them, promoting the moral supremacy and universal ascendancy of Western values epitomized by the Western literary canon, and presenting them "as being both necessary and sufficient," is another major way through which *RLT* buttresses the US neoconservative ideology (Donadey and Ahmed-Ghosh 637).[35] The reinvigoration of the white, bourgeois, and predominantly androcentric Western canon from the pen of a female expatriate Iranian writer can be, as indeed has been, appropriated as "fodder in the U.S. culture wars" by the US neoconservatives disregarding the contributions made by feminism, postcolonialism, and ethnic studies and, as such, goes a long way toward reinforcing a Western supremacist and exclusionist approach to multicultural perspectives (Donadey and Ahmed-Ghosh 637–9). On the same grounds, Rowe has argued that *RLT* offers a perfect example of the manner in which the rhetoric of neoliberalism is now being exploited by neoconservatives and the special importance they have attached to the cultural arena (253).

Inspected from the vantage point of the nexus between culture, particularly literature, and imperialism, as spelled out in Edward Said's seminal *Culture and Imperialism* (1993), narratives such as *RLT* engage concurrently in a double mode of performance. This duality consists of the affirmation of the white, Americo-European cultures and civilizations as well as the negation of the civilizations and cultures of their non-white, predominantly Muslim Others. Such hegemonic discourses, as Said argues, are underpinned by a persistent and influential rhetoric of "American specialness, altruism, and opportunity" so much so that the very concept of imperialism is almost rendered anachronistic in mainstream discussions of such works. In this light, Nafisi's memoir could be said to epitomize such a frame of reference by depicting America so much as a utopic state as Iran is rendered dystopic. As Said has averred,

> American attitudes to American "greatness," to hierarchies of race, to the perils of other revolutions (the American revolution being considered unique and somehow unrepeatable anywhere else in the world) have remained constant, have dictated, have obscured, the realities of empire, while apologists for overseas American interests have insisted on American innocence, doing good, fighting for freedom. (*Culture and Imperialism* 8)

One of the most direct instances of such a binary opposition can be observed in Nafisi's naïve, and equally supercilious, proclamation that "[w]e in ancient countries have our past—we obsess over the past. They, the Americans, have a dream: they feel nostalgia about the promise of the future" (109). Nafisi's juxtaposition of Iran and the United States is in keeping not only with the Orientalist assumption of the essential difference between the West and its Other, but also with the dichotomy of an irremediably primitive, passive, and frozen-in-the-past Orient versus a dynamic, progressive, and ever-improving West. In a similar vein, Nafisi's repeated references to "life, liberty, and the pursuit of happiness" (42, 47, 281, 341)—one of the key phrases in the United States Declaration of Independence—and her depictions of Iran as its very antithesis serve to reinforce such a simplistic binarism, which is perpetuated, more than anything else, through characters either from or associated with both countries.

Throughout the narrative, non-Westernized Iranian men are likened to Humbert in what the author persistently frames as their "confiscation" (one of Nafisi's favorite terms) of personal freedoms, their intimidating omnipresence, and their pedophilic sexual perversion. Discussing "the hypocrisy of some officials and activists in various Muslim associations" with Nassrin, one of her "girls," Nafisi claims that Nassrin's youngest uncle, "a very pious man, had sexually abused her when she was barely eleven years old" (48). Nassrin's suitor seems to be no less of a pervert: he "stare[s] at women in the way . . . in the way my uncle touched me" (323). Sanaz's life is similarly "dominated" by "two very important men," one of whom is her "spoiled" nineteen-year-old brother whose "one obsession in life was Sanaz," and who "had taken to proving his masculinity by spying on her, listening to her phone conversations, driving her car around and monitoring her actions" (16). Yassi, another one of Nafisi's students, was "shielded" all her life, and "was never let out of sight; she never had a private corner in which to think, to feel, to dream, to write" (32). In stark contrast to Nassrin's pedophilic "Muslim" uncle is Yassi's "favorite" uncle who lives in the United States and pays occasional visits to Iran. Nafisi's description of Yassi's uncle is significant in its own right:

> He was patient, attentive, encouraging and at the same time a bit critical, pointing out this little flaw, that weakness. Yassi was elated whenever he came for visits, or on the rare occasions he wrote home or called from the States and asked specifically to talk to her. He was the only one who was allowed to put ideas into Yassi's head without any reproach. And he did put ideas into her head. First, he had encouraged her to continue her musical practices; then he had said, Why not go to the university in Tehran? Now he advised her to continue her studies in America. Everything he told Yassi about life in America—events that seemed routine to him—gained a magical glow in her greedy eyes. (270)

One cannot but have the immediate impression that the reported sophistication and moral influence of Yassi's uncle is due, more than anything else, to his connection to the United States. It remains for Yassi's US-based uncle—she has another uncle with "fanatical religious leanings" with whom she partly lives—to come and "put ideas into her head" and to eventually lead her to the United States. Toward the end of the memoir, we hear about Yassi's uncle again:

> Every time her uncle visited Iran—and it was not often—he provoked doubts and questions in Yassi, who would be plagued for weeks with vague and uneasy longings that made her yearn, without exactly knowing what for. She knew now that she must go to America, as she had known when she was twelve that she must play the forbidden musical instrument. (285)

"Going to America," therefore, seems to be the final stage in the liberation and intellectual development and refinement of the young and enterprising Yassi, as well as her classmates. In the same vein, when another one of Nafisi's students, Sanaz, tells the class about her suitors, Manna responds by issuing a caution: "If I were you, I'd get out of this country while I can . . . Don't stay here and don't marry anyone who'll have to stay here. You'll only rot" (286). If in the world of *RLT*, practicing "forbidden" music (the ban, indeed, being entirely fictitious) and discussing "forbidden" works of literature—among other "Western" values—are both modes of political protest and means of intellectual development, yet the ultimate solution, as implied by Nafisi's own emigration to the United States, can only be heading West—the only alternative to "rotting." The circle of liberation, therefore, becomes complete only when the "girls," like their mentor, venture to make the final move and leave the country for the "safety" of the West:

> Nassrin, I know, arrived safely in England. I do not know what happened to her after that. Mitra left for Canada a few months after we moved to the U.S. She used to write me e-mails or call me regularly, but I have not heard from her for a long time. Yassi tells me that she enrolled in college and now has a son. I heard from Sanaz, too, when I first came to the States. She called me from Europe to inform me that she was now married and intended to enroll at the university. But Azin tells me she dropped that plan and is keeping house, as the saying goes. (342)

In keeping with Nafisi's representations of things Iranian and their juxtaposition with the United States are her many references to the 1979 revolution, which, unlike its "exceptional" American counterpart, is depicted as an anachronistic phenomenon driven solely by blind religious fervor. In reading Nafisi's account of post-revolutionary Iran, as Keshavarz has aptly pointed out, one has to bear in mind the fact that "[i]n general, revolutions do not present their perspectives politely and peacefully. They throw them at you. Where peaceful means have not failed, a revolution does not take place. In Iran of the 1970s, peaceful means had failed" (*Jasmine and Stars* 10). In fact, as is often the case with all revolutions, the 1979 revolution was the final episode in a long series of peaceful protests, to which the Pahlavi regime often responded by massacring protestors, as in the Black Friday massacre (September 8, 1978), and the June 5, 1963 uprising (known as 15 Khordad), to name but a few.

As is characteristic of the neo-Orientalist rhetoric, the revolution and the succeeding governments are portrayed as a unified and homogeneous entity, rather than as the outcome of the complex sociopolitical and religious dynamics of a traditional society undergoing a sea change and a political paradigm shift, not to mention its confrontation with Western modernity. Nafisi uses the terms "the Revolution," "the Islamic Republic," "the Revolutionary Committee," and "the Revolutionary Guards" haphazardly, all of which are often anthropomorphized (though never humanized) in the figures of Ayatollah Khomeini, the "blind censor," and such other characters as her "fanatic" Muslim students. The revolution and the individuals and institutions associated with it are always treated monolithically; that is, they are often depicted as having a singular ideology, intention, task, and agenda. Thus the narrative is riddled with such assertions as "the Revolution imposed the scarf on others" (13), it "had come in the name of our collective past and had wrecked our lives in the name of a dream" (144), and its "first task had been to blur the lines and boundaries between the personal and the political, thereby destroying both" (173).

Never does Nafisi make even a single reference to the fact that from the very outset, "the Revolution" was so radically diversely interpreted by its key figures—including different prime ministers, presidents, and clerical leaders—and that they had very different, and quite often conflicting, views about such major issues as relations with the West, the War, the Hostage Crisis, and even the new dress code laws. Instead, "The Islamic Republic" is depicted as a cataclysmic monolithic force preying upon people's lives and bent on their destruction. Manna claims, for instance, that "[a]bout a year after the revolution, my father died of a heart attack, and then the government confiscated our house and our garden and we moved into an apartment" (12), thus insinuating that since her family was in a weaker position after the passing of her father, the government saw it fit to confiscate their property. No reason is ever provided by Manna, or by Nafisi for that matter, in other similar instances, either. While it is true that such acts of confiscation did occur in post-revolutionary Iran, and at times on grounds that were perhaps biased or without due judicial procedures, insinuating that the government confiscated "weak" people's properties for no apparent reason is simply absurd.

"The Revolution" and its "founders" are also represented as having a morbid obsession with death. Nafisi deems, for instance, the public funeral services for the founders of the revolution—which were attended, on occasions, by millions of people[36]—not as signs of their respect for the deceased person and their support for the ideals of the Islamic Republic, but as "a symptom of the symbiosis between the revolution's founders and death" (90), or what she alternatively calls "the death wish of the regime" (209). More than being an indication of the sociopolitical dynamics of post-revolutionary Iran, such bizarre observations reveal more about Nafisi's state of mind and the warped lens through which she interpreted the state of affairs in the country.

However, in the absurd world that Nafisi constructs in *RLT*, such occasions as funerals are not merely manifestations of the "regime's" thanatophilia; they also provide "the one place where people mingled and touched bodies and shared emotions without restraint or guilt. There was a wild, sexually flavored frenzy in the air" (90). Once again, seeing a public mourning as a site of unbridled sexuality, and funerals as an outlet for Iranians' pent-up sexual desire, is more an indication of Nafisi's perverted mind than the funeral attendants'. Also, quite ironically, such statements shed light on Nafisi's claim that "our culture shunned sex because it was too involved with it" (304), thereby making the claims evidently, though inadvertently, self-reflexive. After all, it was Nafisi who had for "the first time . . . experienced the desperate, orgiastic pleasure of this form of public mourning" (90).[37] No less preposterous is Nafisi's comment on the funeral of Ayatollah Khomeini. When the millions of funeral participants were sprayed "at intervals with water to cool them off" because of the extreme heat, Nafisi sees the effect as making the scene "oddly sexual" (244).

Nafisi's Orientalist representations of the revolution are extended to her views on the war that Iraq and its Western allies perpetrated against Iran. Among such views is the claim that Iran was the "perpetrator" of the war (209)—a fabrication that was shared perhaps only by Saddam Hussein, and refuted by the United Nations Iran–Iraq Military Observer Group (UNIIMOG). Characteristically, while Iran's defense against the Iraqi occupation is persistently criticized and misrepresented, US wars are treated in a very different light. Discussing the life of Henry James, whom Nafisi admires and regards as a hero, she describes how he was involved in writing "war propaganda from the fall of 1914 until December 1915," "appeal[ed] to America to join the war," and became "so actively involved in the war effort" (214). She then continues to explain the whys and wherefores of James's involvement with the war:

> One reason for his involvement was the carnage, the death of so many young men, and the dislocation and destruction. While he mourned the mutilation of existence, he had endless admiration for the simple courage he encountered, both in the many young men who went to war and in those they left behind. (214)

While James's warmongering efforts are rendered as patriotic and heroic, throughout the narrative Nafisi describes Iranian soldiers fighting in the war imposed on their country as brainwashed, deluded, and driven by religious fanaticism. James's two younger brothers, for instance, are described as heroes who "fought with courage and honor" in the war, apparently not influenced by any form of propaganda and merely fighting out of their commitment to the noble principles of justice and freedom (213). In her many references to the Iran–Iraq war, Nafisi unquestioningly propagates some of the most hackneyed myths surrounding it. She claims, for instance, that on the Iranian front "any and all methods" were utilized to achieve their goals, including

> what became known as "human wave" attacks, where thousands of Iranian soldiers, mainly very young boys ranging in age from ten to sixteen and middle-aged and old men, cleared the minefields by walking over them. The very young were caught up in the government propaganda that offered them a heroic and adventurous life at the front and encouraged them to join the militia, even against their parents' wishes. (208)

Another notorious myth perpetuated in the narrative has to do with the young soldiers "who had been mobilized by the excitement of carrying real guns and the promise of keys to a heaven where they could finally enjoy all the pleasures from which they had abstained in life" (209). Professor Seyed Mohammad Marandi, himself a veteran of that war, has called Nafisi's claims "ludicrous," as such keys never existed in reality, adding that the "absurdity of such claims" is characteristic of the Iranian native Orientalist discourse (184).

Indeed, Nafisi's glorification of the United States has a particular currency in the post-9/11 milieu in which the "nearly hysterical patriotism" of the United States "has taken on a peculiarly isolationist aura that is at the same time compounded by a deep investment in its own international deployment" as well as a "rhetorical emphasis on the United States as the democratic model for the rest of the world" (Rowe 253). This "mythology" has precedents in such ideologies as nineteenth-century "Manifest Destiny" and the late-nineteenth-century "March of the Anglo-Saxon" insomuch as they are contingent upon "a U.S. democratic utopianism built upon the heritage of Western Civilization" (Rowe 253).

Rowe has observed that "the tendency to transform personal memoirs, however idiosyncratic, into ethnographies of foreign peoples has long been recognized as integral to cultural imperialism, especially in the history of the literature of exploration and travel" (260). As demonstrated in the analysis of some of Nafisi's representations of things Iranian, the observations of travel writers reveal as much, if not more, about the observer than the observed. American reviewers such as Heather Hewett, for instance, have lauded the book, citing *RLT* as a testament to the universality of Western values: "Nafisi's memoir makes a good case for reading the classics of western literature no matter where you are . . . 'Reading Lolita in Tehran' provides a stirring testament to the power of Western literature to cultivate democratic change and open-mindedness" . It is, in fact, this particular perusal of the text that Donadey and Ahmed-Ghosh have dubbed "a danger of conservative appropriation" by American reviewers, critics, politicians, and think tanks alike (637). It is not surprising that not even a single one of the many rave reviews has alluded to the implications of the book both for the neoconservative administration of the time and for Iranian and other Muslim communities or, in general, for hyphenated Iranians and Muslims living in the West. As Said argues, traditionally and historically, major critics and scholars have tended to ignore or bypass critical discussions of colonialism and imperialism (*Culture and Imperialism* 65).

The most significant criticism of the appropriation of *RLT* by, and its collusion with, belligerent US neoconservatism has been voiced by professor Hamid Dabashi in his influential and astringent essay, "Native Informers and the Making of the American Empire" (2006).[38] Dabashi's critique of *RLT* merits special attention for two major reasons. First, like Nafisi, Dabashi is an Iranian immigrant based in the United States—and in fact one of the most prominent Iranian-American exilic intellectuals—and a professor of Comparative Literature and Iranian Studies.[39] Second, his essay on *RLT* is the most critical and the most frequently cited article on the memoir thus far. In his important essay, Dabashi argues that even though the cluster of post-9/11 neo-Orientalist memoirs epitomized by *RLT* point to some legitimate concerns, "yet [they] put that predicament squarely at the service of the US ideological psy-op, militarily stipulated in the US global warmongering." Concurrent with the US belligerency and militarism reaching its apex in recent history, and with the prospect of yet another US war against Iran looming large (S. Hersh), *RLT* has tremendously cultivated the US, and by extension the Western, public opinion against both Iran and Islam ("Native Informers"). Also, Rowe has argued that even though he does not advocate the contention that "there is a direct relationship between Nafisi's work and US plans for military action in Iran," he does believe that *RLT* "represents the larger effort of neo-conservatives to build the cultural and political case against diplomatic negotiations" with the country (254). Similarly, Fitzpatrick has pointed out the interconnection between *RLT* and advancing the hegemonic and militarist policies of the United States, averring that

> This portrayal of the Muslim world as holding values completely antithetical to what are seen as American values helps to explain why Americans come to see the overthrow of regimes such as Saddam Hussein's or Mahmoud Ahmedinjad's as a moral obligation, and not just one that they see to be in their own country's

interest. The idea that in invading and occupying another country we are 'freeing people' plays well, and becomes itself the focus of American preoccupation with violent regime change. Readers can point to Nafisi's book as justification for invasion: "you see, they are brutally oppressive there . . . I read about it in this book." (247)

The legitimacy of resistance against any form of tyranny, or of struggles for a more democratic society and more expansive civil rights, can hardly be overemphasized. The struggles and aspirations of women of diverse ideological and political convictions are not only legitimate but also an exigent imperative; nonetheless, in the context of the current discussion, what is pernicious and counterproductive is "when these perfectly legitimate critiques mutate into entirely illegitimate formulations at the service of facilitating the US global domination" (Dabashi "Lolita and Beyond").

Paul Berman, a well-known American political and cultural critic, who also advocated the invasion of Iraq ("Why Germany") and justified it on the pretext of the seemingly benign ideology of "liberal interventionism" and the fight against "Islamic authoritarianism," actually utilizes *RLT* in his book as an exemplar of resisting autochthonous tyranny (*Power and the Idealists* 152–71). Placed in the broader framework of his discussion and his former advocacy of the invasion of Iraq, Berman's invocation of Nafisi's memoir and his endorsement of the liberal ideals represented by the Western authors whom Nafisi discusses are suggestive of another military intervention under the pretext of saving Iraqis from their own plight and promoting liberal and democratic values. Berman also employs Nafisi's narrative as a notable example of the transmutation of people with formerly leftist leanings to (neo-)conservative persuasions, a coming-of-age narrative as it were. In doing so, Berman perpetuates, in quite an unquestioning manner, some of the most absurd myths propagated by *RLT*, claiming, for instance, that "the Islamists established the practice of suicide bombings as early as 1979, the year of their triumph" or writes of young Iranian soldiers marching into Iraqi minefields "with keys dangling from their necks to symbolize the opening of the gates of heaven" (*Power and the Idealists* 160).

In his famously uninhibited critique of *RLT*, Dabashi enunciates how Nafisi's memoir, in tandem with her collaboration with American cultural and political neoconservative circles, has turned her into a latter-day embodiment of colonial native informers "facilitating public consent to imperial hubris" ("Native Informers"). According to Dabashi, as the epitome of "native informers turned comprador intellectuals," Nafisi has achieved three simultaneous objectives "with one stroke":

(1) systematically and unfailingly denigrating an entire culture of revolutionary resistance to a history of savage colonialism; (2) doing so by blatantly advancing the presumed cultural foregrounding of a predatory empire; and (3) while at the very same time catering to the most retrograde and reactionary forces within the United States, waging an all out war against a pride of place by

various immigrant communities and racialised minorities seeking curricular recognition on university campuses and in the American society at large.

As the "*locus classicus* of the ideological foregrounding of the US imperial domination at home and abroad," *RLT* has achieved the aforementioned objectives through three simultaneous moves: by relying on the "collective amnesia" of the history of US imperial hegemony; by systematically appropriating what are essentially legitimate causes for illegitimate ends; and by "seeking to provoke the darkest corners of the Euro-American Oriental fantasies" through the modus operandi of English literature, facilitated by deliberate positioning of the authorial voice as a latter-day Scheherazade (Dabashi "Native Informers"). Fitzpatrick has argued that the power that "native" authorial voice and personal testimony accounts exert is quite significant in native informers' accounts as it lends credibility to such works and "underscores the idea that regime change is not only in the strategic interest of the USA, but is also our moral obligation (as the more civilized power) toward the citizens suffering under these regimes" (246).

Issued from one of the most prominent exilic intellectuals in the United States, Dabashi's critique of *RLT* bears particular significance as it unravels the political implications of a text that serves to undermine the aspirations and struggles of minority writers who seek inclusion and recognition in the American literary market and on university curricula. Along these lines, Dabashi has argued that part of the "complicity" of *RLT* in promoting Western hegemony is its advocacy of the ascendancy of Western classics as arbiters of universal values at a juncture when, at long last, decades of struggles by postcolonial, Black, and "Third World" scholars and feminists, as well as racialized minorities, have come to fruition with the introduction of "a modicum of attention to world literatures" ("Native Informers"). Nafisi's advocacy of the Western literary tradition,[40] "especially in the Euroamerican examples she uses to organize her book, appeals powerfully to liberal cultural values in ways specifically geared to attract intellectuals disaffected by the so-called culture wars of the late 1980s and early 1990s" (Rowe 253). If one concurs with Said's maxim that "[n]ations themselves *are* narrations," then one can also acknowledge the manner in which "the power to narrate, or to block other narratives from forming and emerging" (*Culture and Imperialism* xiii) is inextricably linked to the idea of imperialism and the destiny of disenfranchised minorities, as a microcosm of the non-Western world.

For Dabashi, the achievement of the three foregoing objectives, particularly the undermining of the struggles of postcolonial and minority writers for curricular recognition and inclusion, seems even more untenable—a fact that he considers "quite a feat for an ex-professor of English literature with not a single credible book or scholarly credential to her name other than *Reading Lolita in Tehran*" ("Native Informers"). However, in tandem with the denigration of Iranian and Islamic cultures, another equally significant implication of *RLT* is its implicit dismissal and denigration of nonwhite, immigrant cultures, racialized minorities, and disenfranchised communities. Given the unprecedented support for and the promotion of Nafisi by neoconservative US think tanks, this conclusion sounds tenable.

Paramount in the analysis of works like Nafisi's is the pivotal function of US-based expatriate "intellectuals" in promoting the ideological foregrounding of American and, by extension, Western hegemony, given the globalized and transcultural nature of the empire-building enterprise. The prevalent mode of "Third World" comprador intellectualism facilitates the transmission of the so-called native knowledge, as well as the transmutation of legitimate social causes—especially apropos the question of women's rights—into fodders the main function of which is promoting the ideological and cultural supremacy of an essentially imperialistic agenda. In the aftermath of 9/11, the recruitment of native comprador intellectuals accelerated significantly, owing both to the Western preoccupation with Islam and the Middle East reaching its acme, and such interventionist US foreign policies as the "war on terror." In this context, the comprador intellectuals who "feign[ed] authority, authenticity, and native knowledge" to inform the Western audience of the "deplorable" state of their countries of provenance played an instrumental role in justifying the hegemonic interests of the United States under the pretext of humanitarian intervention and benign liberation of Middle Eastern nations from their own "evil" (Dabashi, "Native Informers").

The problematics posed by Nafisi's work, therefore, are not particularly exclusive to the substance of her narrative or the whys and wherefores of her vitriol against certain aspects of Iranian and Muslim life and culture. After all, as Said has aptly argued in *Culture and Imperialism*, authors are not simply mechanically shaped by their ideological, class, or economic persuasions, but are rather "very much in the history of their societies, shaping and shaped by that history and their social experience in different measure" (xxii) and their works derive, to various degrees, from their historical experience.

Inasmuch as the authenticity of comprador intellectuals' accounts is concerned, Dabashi asserts that like all forms of "propaganda and disinformation," *RLT* is predicated on "an element of truth" ("Native Informers"). Native informer accounts such as Nafisi's, then, package that element of truth, either wittingly or otherwise, in the manner that best serves the interests of the empire "in the disguise of a legitimate critic of localised tyranny facilitating the operation of a far more insidious global domination—effectively perpetuating (indeed aggravating) the domestic terror they purport to expose" ("Native Informers"). Mitra Rategar has observed that "[d]espite ambivalence about Nafisi's own 'authenticity' as a 'representative' Iranian woman, her representation of other women and their interests and desires is read [by reviewers] as 'authentic,' as is her account of the appropriate solutions" (111). Several critics have also pointed out the significance of Nafisi's own social background in both the extent of the authenticity of her narrative and her stance on the array of issues she discusses in her memoir.

Nafisi belongs to an echelon of the Iranian society with which very few Iranians would identify. She comes from a highly privileged family background: her father, Ahmad Nafisi, was the mayor of Tehran under the shah (and was imprisoned on charges of embezzlement) (*Reading Lolita* 45); her mother had been a Member of Parliament during the shah's reign (261), and her family's affluence enabled her to pursue her education in Switzerland, England, and the United States (82). Indeed,

Nafisi is not alone in her privileged background. Many other Iranian-American memoirists belonged to the highest echelons of the Iranian society before the revolution. For instance, in her *Out of Iran: One Woman's Escape from the Ayatollahs* (1987), Sousan Azadi writes that "[w]e were the rich of Iran, the ruling elite, the nation's leaders" (1). A similar sentiment is voiced by Cherry Mosteshar in her *Unveiled: One Woman's Nightmare in Iran* (1995): "There was a day, before the revolution of 1979, when I had been one of the richest young women on our street in wealthy North Tehran" (6). Or this is how Azadeh Moaveni, the author of another famous neo-Orientalist memoir, *Lipstick Jihad: A Memoir of Growing Up Iranian in America and American in Iran* (2005), described her family background:

> My mother's family fell somewhere in the area between middle and upper-middle, which meant that they were landowners, and able to send four children to the West for university. Most strands of my father's family were wealthy, and belonged to that upper class that the revolutionaries of 1979 were bent on unseating. (6)

The significance of Nafisi's family background is twofold. On the one hand, her family background, especially her family's affiliation with the second Pahlavi regime, is more than a matter of family history. It goes a long way toward explaining, at least partially, her romanticization of the pre-revolution era as well as her advocacy of regime change in Iran—another reason for her popularity among like-minded neoconservatives who also have "a close alliance . . . [with] the exile monarchists in Iranian diaspora community in the United States" (Bahramitash, "The War on Terror" 230). On the other hand, her highly privileged background can account for her almost total lack of concern, shared by the majority of Iranian population, especially the female population, regarding such issues as the religious sensibilities of the Iranian society, access to free education, and much higher social mobility and visibility for Muslim women, as elaborated previously. Rowe has argued that even though Nafisi's memoir is far from representative of the lives of average Iranian women, "by stressing the diverse personalities of the women students in her private reading group, she offers the reader a deceptive synecdoche for Iranian women" (260). Rastegar has equally noted that while Nafisi and her girls are quite committed to the aesthetic merits of the Anglo-American canonical texts they peruse, "views of female students who actively supported the revolution are never described" (117). Such conspicuous lacuna, indeed, is far from surprising and is, in fact, quite consistent with the Orientalist/colonial tropes of affirmation and negation, as expounded in the discussion of colonial rhetoric in *NWMD*.

In critiquing such works as *RLT*, the main bone of contention is not whether the author is justified in criticizing her native country or not. Rather, as Fitzpatrick argues, the main concern is "the extent to which such works contribute to the normalization of the Islamic world as violent and irrational and of all Muslim women as oppressed by Muslim men and Muslim governments" (247). In other words, while criticizing the Islamic Republic of Iran, or any other country for that matter, is a perfectly legitimate given, works such as *RLT* voice this criticism "so simplistically that the conclusion readers reach is that forceful regime change and belligerence is the correct response, indeed the only acceptable response" (Fitzpatrick 253). Nevertheless, the foregoing argument should not be confused with falling into the trap of conspiracy theories. Rather, one can detect an uncanny alignment of interests between US global hegemony and the comprador intellectuals, especially in the post-9/11 era.

Curricular and Minority Questions

As a work addressed at a primarily Western audience, Nafisi's systematic distortion and denigration of things Iranian and Islamic is only one manifestation of another major problematic of her work—that is "how utterly ignorant (indifferent or dismissive) [she is] of the massive debates of a counter-culture movement in the US academy, briefly code-named *multiculturalism*" (Dabashi, "Native Informers"). As a comprador intellectual, Nafisi has joined forces with some of the most conservative figures opposing curricular (and, by extension, sociopolitical) changes by exclusively putting the Anglo-European literary imagination on a pedestal while concurrently placing "yet another non-European culture outside the fold of the literary—of the sublime and the beautiful" (Dabashi, "Native Informers").

The controversy surrounding curricular, cultural, and sociopolitical inclusion is particularly significant in the US context. In fact, it forms one of the principal discussions of Said's theorization of the nexus between culture and imperialism. As Said has pointed out, there is a prevalent perception in the United States that upholds the Eurocentrality of literary imagination and defines cultural and humanistic study as "the recovery of the Judeo-Christian or Western heritage, free from native American culture (which the Judeo-Christian tradition in its early American embodiments set about to massacre) and from that tradition's adventures in the non-Western world" (*Culture and Imperialism* 320). Paramount in this politics of cultural identity is the role of literature or, more specifically, "the contest over what books and authorities constitute 'our' tradition" (*Culture and Imperialism* xxv)—an exercise which Said deems "most debilitating." In this light, the neoconservative refutation of what it regards as alien to American cultural identity is predicated upon the presumption that in admitting multiculturality and such disciplines as Marxism, structuralism, feminism, postcolonialism, "Third World" Studies, and non-Western, non-mainstream literature into the curriculum, "the American university sabotaged the basis of its supposed authority and is now ruled by a Blanquist cabal of intolerant ideologues who 'control' it" (*Culture and Imperialism* 321).

In 1989, Bernard Lewis, the senior American Orientalist luminary, wrote a column for *The Wall Street Journal*, titled "Western Culture Must Go", in the way of contribution to the debate surrounding the modification of the Western canon. He addressed students and professors at Stanford and other American universities who had voted in favor of revising the curriculum with a view to including more writing by non-Anglo-European and women writers. Speaking as an omniscient Orientalist authority, Lewis cautions his addressees that the modification of university curricula is tantamount to the demise of Western culture, which, in turn, means nothing less than the restoration of such "non-Western" institutions as "slavery," "the harem," "child marriage," and "widow burning". Lewis closes his article by reiterating his essentially fallacious premise that "if Western culture goes," with it go both its unique "curiosity" about other cultures and "our chance of learning about and learning from other cultures".

One cannot but be astounded by the supreme irony of arguing against the inclusion of multicultural perspectives in order not to lose the chance of learning about other cultures. Lewis's argument, as Said remarks, is quite symptomatic of an Orientalist mindset and is, in fact, "an indication not only of a highly inflated sense of Western exclusivity in cultural accomplishment, but also of a tremendously limited, almost hysterically antagonistic view of the rest of the world" (*Culture and Imperialism* 37).

Building on Lewis's argument, Nafisi reiterates Bernard Lewis's caveat in a significant passage in *RLT*, where she thus describes her "girls":

> They had a genuine curiosity, a real thirst for the works of great writers, those condemned to obscure shadows by both the regime and the revolutionary intellectuals, most of their books banned and forbidden. Unlike in pre-revolutionary times, now the "non-Revolutionary writers," the bearers of the canon, were the ones celebrated by the young: James, Nabokov, Woolf, Bellow, Austen and Joyce were revered names, emissaries of that forbidden world which we would turn into something more pure and golden than it ever was or will be. (39)

The passage interweaves several methods used by Nafisi in her representations of the country. It reiterates one of the text's underlying themes: the fallacious claim that "works of great writers" were forbidden in Iran. It naively contrasts the pre- and post-revolution times by their literary zeitgeists. After all, one could argue that the "non-Revolutionary writers" were favored by Nafisi and perhaps her select students and, if anything, the challenge posed by "Muslim" students—which Nafisi simply attributes to their lack of literary sensibilities—indicates that Nafisi's choices of texts were not as unanimously welcomed by her students as she seems to suggest. Also, while Nafisi reserves this "genuine curiosity" for her "girls," she persistently describes her "Muslim" students as philistine, which renders them even more analogous to Humbert who "was a villain because he lacked curiosity about other people and their lives" (48). Furthermore, by celebrating the "revered names" in the Western canon, Nafisi seems to be cautioning her American readers, à la Lewis, that taking their "great writers" and the "bearers of the canon" for granted by the proponents of multicultural ethics and a more inclusive canon may well bring about an authoritarianism in the United States similar to the one Nafisi seems to observe in Iran (Rowe 267). In sum, perhaps the uncanny literary and ideological alignment between Nafisi's selection of literary works and that of the proponents of a conservative, white, Anglo-American cannon, coupled with her ignorance and dismissal of non-mainstream literature, is a telling indication not only of where she stands in the curricular debate but also of the implications of her narrative for her Western audience.

The West as Novel, the Novel as West

In her review of *RLT* published in *The Christian Science Monitor*, Heather Hewett remarks that

> Azar Nafisi's memoir makes a good case for reading the classics of western literature no matter where you are . . . 'Reading Lolita in Tehran' provides a stirring testament to the power of Western literature to cultivate democratic change and open-mindedness.

While Hewett's observation is in keeping with Nafisi's glamorization of Western literature, it is exactly such a conclusion that highlights the problematic embedded in Nafisi's stance. As Mailloux has demonstrated, a "very different lesson might in fact be taken from Fitzgerald's novel, its reception in Nafisi's memoir, and the reception of that memoir: Where you are does matter in reading Western classics, indeed, in reading anything" (26). Significantly, Hewett's assertion reverberates with Nafisi's discussions of the alleged supremacy and universality of the values expressed in Western classics. During the terror-inducing nights of the bombardment of Tehran by Iraqi warplanes, Nafisi seeks solace in the works of Western fiction, pondering and framing her ideas about the novel in particular:

> Over the next decade and a half, more than anything else, I thought, wrote about and taught fiction. These readings made me curious about the origins of the novel and what I came to understand as its basically democratic structure. And I became curious as to why the realistic novel was never truly successful in our country. (187)

By associating Western novels with democratic ethics, *RLT* commends Western literature and civilization, promoting it as democratic and liberating for Iranians (DePaul "Re-Reading" 86). Also, by casting Western literature as a refuge for herself and other "progressive" Iranians, the memoir engages in "political work" by "posing the Western literary canon as the savior of Iranian women" (Balaghi and Toensing). This view is reinforced when one takes into consideration the fact that beside framing Western literature as a haven and a liberating medium, Nafisi also represents the very act of teaching it in Iran as a daunting feat or, as Keshavarz has put it, "something on the order of taming the savages" (*Jasmine and Stars* 19).

In fact, Nafisi goes as far as insinuating that "talking about Nabokov, Bellow and Fielding" was dangerous, when she remarks that she discussed such works "at all costs to myself and them" (68). The nature of such imaginary "danger," however, remains unclear, which makes the claim even more ludicrous, as the authors and works that Nafisi deems "dangerous" have been, and continue to be, taught across universities in the country—a fact corroborated, among other things, by the significant number of theses written on the "forbidden" authors whom Nafisi admires.

Through the instrumentality of the novel genre, Nafisi reinforces the Orientalist binary of the superior, democratic West versus the inferior, totalitarian Orient. What, however, is absent in Nafisi's juxtaposition is the rootedness of the novel form in a colonial provenance, much more than in democratic aspirations. As Said argues in *Culture and Imperialism*, the genre saw its inauguration in England by Daniel Defoe's *Robinson Crusoe* (1719), "a work whose protagonist is the founder of a new world, which he rules and reclaims for Christianity and England" (70). Said also effectively delineates the convergence between the patterns of narrative authority that form the novelistic tradition and "a complex ideological configuration underlying the tendency to imperialism" (69). He infers, for example, that it is far from coincidental that by the mid-1800s when the novel had emerged as "*the* aesthetic form," the British Empire had reached its apex, so much so that toward the end of the nineteenth century the novel was the centerpiece of the British literary tradition. Thus, Said argues that since the novel assumed such immense significance in "the condition of England" question, it can also be observed as partaking in the country's overseas imperial enterprises as well as in the formation of a paradigm of "imperial attitudes, references, and experiences" (71–2). The great European realist novel, for instance, achieved one of its fundamental objectives: "almost unnoticeably sustaining the society's consent in overseas expansion, a consent that, in J. A. Hobson's words, 'the selfish forces which direct Imperialism should utilize the protective colours of . . . disinterested movements' such as philanthropy, religion, science and art" (*Culture and Imperialism* 19). For Said the novel—a cultural production of a bourgeois society—and imperialism are so closely intertwined as to render one inconceivable without the other:

> Of all the major literary forms, the novel is the most recent, its emergence the most datable, its occurrence the most Western, its normative pattern of social authority the most structured; imperialism and the novel fortified each other to such a degree that it is impossible, I would argue, to read one without in some way dealing with the other. (*Culture and Imperialism* 70)

A sustained body of scholarship corroborates how the teaching of English literature to colonial subjects has been definitive to the British and American imperial adventures. In her *Masks of Conquest: Literary Study and British Rule in India* (1990), Gauri Viswanathan cogently demonstrates how the study of English literature played an instrumental role in the British colonization of India through educating a generation of Indians who, in the words of Thomas Babington Macaulay, were "Indian in blood and colour, but English in taste, in opinions, words and intellect" (qtd. in Dabashi, "Native Informers").

As demonstrated earlier, *RLT* is located at the same strategic confluence of literature and hegemony as its classic predecessors. Hence, one can observe that the literary pride of place enjoyed by the novel in the second half of the nineteenth century has found a ready equivalent in the post-9/11 Middle Eastern memoir in the United States in terms of its instrumentality in manufacturing imperial consent.

The foregoing critique of the nexus between *RLT* and US neoconservatism, as well as Said's emphasis on the symbiotic interconnection between literary artifacts and hegemony, is by no means suggestive of analyzing a work of literature reductively and oversimplifying it to its author's sociopolitical affiliations or interpreting it merely within the context of the politics of its time. Such an oversimplification would fall into the trap of believing that reductive interpretations can be made substitutes for a very complex phenomenon. The critique, rather, is intended to elucidate the relationship between literature—or, in a broader sense, culture—and the idea of Empire, not to reduce novels, or any other literary form for that matter, to "subsidiary forms of class, ideology, or interest" (Said, *Culture and Imperialism* 73). Far from reducing the literary to the political, the idea is to posit a political interlocutor next to the literary work "by way of a hermeneutic provocation of meaning and significance" (Dabashi, "Native Informers"). Nor does acknowledging the connection between the literary and the political diminish the value of works of art and, in this case, novels. Conversely, as Said points out, "because of their *worldliness*, because of their complex affiliations with their real setting" the artifacts studied in this light are "*more* interesting and *more* valuable as works of art" (*Culture and Imperialism* 13). In a similar vein, critiquing the Western canon is not tantamount to dismissing its literary or cultural merits. Rather, canonical texts must be perused and examined with a view to highlighting and giving voice to the aesthetically and ideologically marginalized, underrepresented, and negated.

Ahistorical Historicism and Learned Amnesia

Like most other neo-Orientalist narratives, *RLT* is characterized by a selective historicity and informed elimination of important sociohistorical, political, religious, and cultural contexts and facts. Such characteristic eliminations signify a misinformed, at best, and mendacious, at worst, mode of knowledge production on the part of the author, one upshot of which is a travesty of the facts and a highly deformed picture of the social, political, and literary fabric of both pre- and post-revolutionary Iran. In this light, several critics have delineated how Nafisi plays fast and loose with Iranian/Islamic realities and, in so doing, offers an image of the Iranian society that is profoundly misleading (Bahramitash "The War on Terror"; Dabashi "Lolita and Beyond"; Keshavarz *Jasmine and Stars;* Koegeler). In Fitzpatrick's words, "the problem with these atomized, isolated elements of truth (particularly when they are presented as the only moment we must attend) is that they offer us only atomized, isolated elements of solution" (254). This becomes even more problematic when Nafisi predicates the "truth" of her Orientalist narrative on her arrogation to herself of academic excellence, asserting in *RLT* that "I am too much of an academic: I have written too many papers and articles to turn my experiences and ideas into narratives without pontificating" (266). Such a claim to academic expertise and prolificacy, however, could hardly be more disingenuous. Before *RLT*, Nafisi's only other scholarly contribution had been a book on Nabokov written in Persian and published by the Iranian Ministry of Culture and Islamic Guidance—a supreme irony, indeed, given Nafisi's pertinacious insistence that discussions of Nabokov and other canonical Western authors were "dangerous" and that their works were banned in Iran. Even though Nafisi often credits herself with being the author of *Anti-Terra: A Critical Study of Vladimir Nabokov's Novels*, the book has never been translated into English or published in the West and the gesture smacks of self-promotion to posit the author as a Nabokov expert.

The selective historicity of Nafisi's memoir includes both the elimination of broader historico-political frameworks indispensable for understanding her narrative, and more specific instances of distortion or negation of events in the particular period spanning her narrative. In an interview with Foaad Khosmood, Dabashi has pointed out some of the major acts of dehistoricization and decontextualization in *RLT*:

> Nafisi not once refers to the historical trauma of all Iranians following the CIA sponsored coup of 1953 which toppled the democratically elected government of prime minister Mohammad Mussaddeq, not once to the subsequent mutation of Iran into a military base for the US involvement in Vietnam, not once about the fact that at the very time that these poor Iranians were screaming at the gates of the US embassy, there were in fact US plans for a possible military coup against the revolution.

The concepts of selective memory and collective amnesia are also closely tied to the notions of empire and hegemony. In this light, Dabashi has argued that "dismantling the very notion of history and the fabrication of instant stories to fill its vacuum is one way of sustaining the imperial momentum." This, in turn, accounts for the dearth of reliable historical narratives and the unprecedented and inordinate proliferation of personal memoirs "which remains at a very superficial and entirely self-indulgent level" (Dabashi, "Lolita and Beyond").

In her discussion of Nabokov's *Lolita*, Nafisi frames Lolita as a double victim both because of the confiscation of her childhood life by her pedophilic stepfather, Humbert, and because she is denied self-representation—the chance to author her life story. Hence, Nafisi and her students reportedly develop a kind of sensitivity to the absences and omissions that Lolita suffers, arguing that they do not know much about her except for what Humbert chooses to divulge about her. This observation, in turn, leads them to the conclusion that the absences can, in fact, be more significant than the presences. Grogan, however, has demonstrated that contrary to Nafisi's assertion, "Nabokov makes it easier to sympathize with Humbert, whom we know so much about, than with Lolita, who is virtually unknown to the reader, and the little bit of information he does share of her, reveals her to be 'a most exasperating brat'" (59). Reflecting on the two photographs of her "girls"—one with the girls observing *hijab* and the other one without—and those who are absent in them, Nafisi draws a parallel between the world of *Lolita* and post-revolutionary Iran, remarking that "[t]heir absences persist, like an acute pain that seems to have no physical source. This is Tehran for me: its absences were more real than its presences" (5).

According to Nafisi, a good novel is "democratic" in that it "shows the complexity of individuals, and creates enough space for all these characters to have a voice" (132). Quite ironically though, but indeed characteristically, Nafisi commits the same omission apropos almost all the characters with whom she disagrees ideologically or politically and for some of whom she reserves nothing more than a self-confessed "eternal contempt" (288). This makes the world of *RLT* one in which absences predominate, much more than presences. If Nafisi "reads the omissions as strategic moves on Nabokov's part to expose the dangers of solipsism" (Grogan 58), a reading deemed quite unconvincing by some critics, there are no legitimate grounds for the blatant omission and silencing of ideologically different characters in *RLT*, except the author's penchant for squeezing them into a black-and-white Orientalist binary. Therefore, a contrapuntal reading of the narrative would reveal that even though Nafisi likens the Islamic Republic of Iran and its then-leader, the late Ayatollah Khomeini, to Humbert Humbert in terms of their imposition of their dreams on other people's lives, one could observe that, most ironically, Nafisi turns out to be the Humbert of her own story by depriving many characters of their voices, identities, and even names, not to mention her utter contempt for them.

The many absences and lacunae in *RLT* are manifestations of one of the principal denominators of almost all Orientalist and neo-Orientalist discourses: the simultaneous double function of affirmation (of the superior/colonial/Western) and negation (of its fabricated Other). Thus far, it has been demonstrated how *RLT* corroborates the alleged supremacy of Western cultural and democratic values, as epitomized by what it deems to be the universalism of the Western literary canon as well as its facilitation of US imperial enterprises and manufacturing consent. In tandem with this affirmation, however, *RLT* engages in an act of almost total negation via historical erasure, narrow preferential selectivity, and informed elimination of the "lesser" end of the (neo-)Orientalist dichotomy. This omission bears particular interpretive significance in the overall scheme of the narrative and has crucial epistemological implications. As Keshavarz has remarked:

> Narratives achieve their sense of closure through an inherent claim to completeness. Whether they specify that or not, by virtue of telling a story, they take responsibility for giving their readers the whole truth. If they adopt a strategy of selective narration they should underline the fictive nature of their

presentation or risk becoming a tool for erasure, a kind of silencing medium. (*Jasmine and Stars* 19)

In her narrative, Nafisi exploits almost every opportunity to foreground and criticize the idea of censorship in post-revolution Iran, making repeated disparaging references, for instance, to one of the many particular figures for whom she reserves a special loathing: the "blind censor" (24, 25, 38, 44, 74, 273, 315). In a claim that defies reason and seems more intended to ridicule than to inform, she claims early in her memoir that "the chief film censor in Iran, up until 1994, was blind. Well, nearly blind" (24) and proceeds to remark that the world in which she and her students lived "was shaped by the colorless lenses of the blind censor" (25). According to Nafisi, this censorship, which was in keeping with, and meant to promote, the state ideology, encroached upon people's individual freedoms and deprived them of any real sense of agency and self-determination in their lives. What, however, is striking—besides the falsity and absurdity of Nafisi's initial statement—is the fact that Nafisi chooses to do the selfsame act by engaging in a much more substantial censorship of the histories and narratives presented in her memoir.[41] It is, therefore, indispensable to peruse and analyze any given work of literature or art with a view not only to what it puts forth but also what it leaves out.

Nafisi's memoir is characterized by the lack of a sense of wholeness and integrity. What the reader is presented with is little more than disembodied, decontextualized fragments instead of an organic whole; black-and-white reductionism in place of kaleidoscopic diversity; and sweeping generalization, pernicious exaggeration, and vulgar oversimplification in lieu of genuine analysis and meaningful contextualization. While Nafisi fulminates against the authorities who, she claims, "censored the colors and tones of reality to suit their black-and-white world" (277), the landscape she presents of the post-revolution Iran, as well as of Islam, could hardly be more monochromatic. Paramount in the negation strategy underlying *RLT* is the erasure of Iranian and Muslim women's sociopolitical agency, the elimination of an extremely rich Persian literary heritage and its ever-increasing dynamism, and numerous instances of ignorant or malicious disinformation and falsification. Following Nafisi's unequivocal affirmation and glamorization of the Western literary canon, it is apropos to examine her treatment of Iranian/Persian literature in *RLT*.

The intellectual rewards of teaching and studying arts and literature hardly need to be emphasized. What, however, remains conspicuous in *RLT* is not the teaching of literature per se as a "liberating" medium; rather, the rub lies in placing canonical Western authors on the pedestal as arbiters of universal truths, while concurrently overlooking a native literature that has produced such literary world giants as Rumi and Khayyam, to name only two of the best known and most translated in the West. In his discussion of English literature in *Culture and Imperialism*, Said argues that the alleged universalism of Western classics is so "Eurocentric in the extreme, as if other literatures and societies had either an inferior or a transcended value" (44). Ironically, Nafisi makes a passing reference to "the tales of our own lady of fiction, Scheherazade, from *A Thousand and One Nights*" (6) as an instance of subversive storytelling; nonetheless, her pedagogics include works only by Vladimir Nabokov, F. Scott Fitzgerald, Henry James, and Jane Austen—figures after whom, or whose works, the book chapters are also named. Such double act of simultaneous affirmation (of the Western canon) and negation (of Persian literature) "obscures any agency and sources of empowerment from within the Muslim literary traditions and politics even while Nafisi creates herself as a supposedly subversive storytelling Scheherazade" (Koegeler 32), thus further reinforcing the Orientalist binary of the "civilized," "superior" West vis-à-vis the "uncivilized," "inferior" Orient.

One of the features of the (neo-)Orientalist discourse is the attribution of what is too impressive to be simply discredited as inferior to a glorious, yet distant and discontinued past. This is exactly the vein in which an extraordinarily rich tradition of Persian literature extending more than a millennium is treated in *RLT*. Investigating the repository of both classical and recent Orientalist texts makes it clear that almost all (neo-)Orientalist discourses seek to efface any trace of cultural, artistic, or literary accomplishments and dynamism in non-Western cultures. On the very rare occasions when such accomplishments are broached, they are almost always ascribed to a bygone past, hence treated as irrelevant. This is particularly true of Iranian history and culture, especially literature. In the preponderance of Iranian-American memoirs, any discussion of history, arts, literature, or culture is attributed to either a "glorious" ancient past—often the era of the Persian Empire—or on occasions to the more recent, highly romanticized pre-revolution era. As Keshavarz has argued, such literary productions

> carry a powerful damaging subtext, a testimony to a fundamental corruption in the culture. In this narration, all good things in the Muslim Middle East belong to the past. For in their current state these societies have been disembodied of their treasures, which have been replaced with unrelenting religious fanaticism. (*Jasmine and Stars* 70)

In *RLT*, this is true both of Iranian culture and history in the broader sense and of Persian literature, in particular. Ramazani, for instance, has observed that, reading *RLT*,

> a reader unfamiliar with Persian literature will reach the last page of this book without any inkling that there exist many contemporary works written by Iranian women the reading of which could have been an equally subversive act as reading Nabokov ... Nafisi thus seems to make the reading of Western literature the necessary requisite for redemption and liberation of the mind. ("Persepolis" 279)

Describing her participation in a literary coterie in Tehran, where classical Persian literature was discussed, Nafisi thus concludes her ruminations about Persian literary masterpieces:

We would take turns reading passages aloud, and words literally rose up in the air and descended upon us like a fine mist, touching all five senses. There was such a teasing, playful quality to their words, such joy in the power of language to delight and astonish. I kept wondering: when did we lose that quality, that ability to tease and make light of life through our poetry? At what precise moment was this lost? (172)

As the excerpt illustrates, the power and joy of reading Persian literature is treated as something, a prerogative, as it were, belonging to the past. It is reduced to an anachronism in contemporary Iranian literary landscape and seems to have vanished all at once at a particular juncture which, as it turns out from the narrative, is the advent of the Islamic Revolution in Iran. Besides being a common denominator of neo-Orientalist discourses, some critics have also imputed such a dismissive and denigrating attitude to the author's ignorance of Persian literature and her fixation with its Western counterpart (Keshavarz, *Jasmine and Stars* 93). In keeping with the essentializing and polarizing proclivity of neo-Orientalist discourses, *RLT* persistently suppresses the multiplicity, polyphony, and variegated tapestry of the literary landscape in Iran, presenting it, instead, as dormant, dogmatic, and insipid. Keshavarz has pointed out that notwithstanding the discussion in *RLT* of a wide range of classic English literature, it "shows no awareness whatsoever of the lively and controversial literature created in Iran itself in the years prior to, and after the revolution. In fact, it suggests a total absence of interest in literature by local culture" (*Jasmine and Stars* 7). Whether such omission is committed by virtue of the author's ignorance of the Persian/Iranian literary tradition or is simply consistent with her demonization and negation of Iranian realities does not really matter. What does, however, matter is how such a blatant obliteration serves to reinforce the author's Orientalist binary as well as her dystopian depiction of the country of her origin.

Not only is the multifarious Iranian literary tapestry totally absent in *RLT*, its absence is imputed to what the author deems to be the alleged philistinism characteristic of the Iranian culture. Thus, Nafisi asserts that "[w]e lived in a culture that denied any merit to literary works, considering them important only when they were handmaidens to something seemingly more urgent—namely ideology" (25). Keshavarz, herself a professor of Persian and Comparative literature in the United States, has called Nafisi's accusation "shocking," adding that "[w]e did more than value the world of literature, we lived in it" (*Jasmine and Stars* 30). There are probably very few cultures in which poetry, for instance, is as popular and revered as in Iranian culture, where lines of poetry appear on the walls of every other home or shop or on public spaces and even many bumper stickers. As far as the place of books, in general, and literature, in particular, and their popular reception in the country is concerned, suffice it to say that Iran's annual popular and international book fair, which has been dubbed "the world's biggest book labyrinth," "attracts half a million visitors a day ... more than the number of people who visit Frankfurt Book Fair, which claims to be the biggest in the world, over its duration" (Kamali Dehghan).

In *Jasmine and Stars*, Keshavarz instantiates in meticulous detail the liveliness and diversity of the literary arena in Iran, thus responding to Nafisi's commentary on Persian literature:

> I had lived, studied, and worked on three continents, and if there was a culture in which people expressed their enthusiasm for literature more publicly than in Iran, I could not think of one. It would be difficult to live in Iran and not see that this enthusiasm was not limited to the educated elite either. How many a baker, shopkeeper, or taxi driver had I heard whispering Omar Khayyam under his breath. Now this book, which meant to celebrate the power of literature, denied and erased this most prevalent cultural behavior in the society I knew so well. (17)

In a similar fashion, Nafisi's formulations of the novel genre in the Iranian literary landscape are problematic and questionable. I previously discussed that Nafisi imputes what she deems to be the failure of the novel in Iran to the genre's "basically democratic structure" (187). In other words, what she sees as the undemocratic sociopolitical condition of Iranian society has precluded the genre from flourishing in Iran. Dabashi and Keshavarz, among others, have strongly disputed Nafisi's conclusion apropos the reception of novels in Iran. As Keshavarz argues, Nafisi's idea of the novel is predicated upon Mikhail Bakhtin's theorization of the polyphonic nature of novel as a quintessentially Western genre, "a result of the democratization of social structure" (*Jasmine and Stars* 92), which, deems non-Western cultures incapable of making any meaningful contributions to the genre. She further argues that "[t]he New Orientalist narrative continues to perpetuate the outmoded Eurocentric approach to the novel" (92) and, in doing so, *RLT* "uses the same simplistic method of literary analysis for which it criticizes the Muslim activist bad guys: confusing fiction with real life" (*s* 92). While Nafisi ridicules, and in fact loathes, Muslim activist students for their alleged lack of sophistication in reducing the literary to the political—as exemplified by some of her students' objections to Gatsby's "decadence—she "judges the current state of the Persian novel (which it does not examine) to be poor and considers the condition to be the literary implication of reality in Persian society" (Keshavarz *Jasmine and Stars* 93).

Both Dabashi and Keshavarz have enunciated in detail how the post-revolution Iranian literary and cultural landscape has been as animated, dynamic, and varied as ever before and is all but wanting in modern counterparts of its ancient literary giants. Also, Nafisi's attack on the Iranian cinema and censorship is contradicted by the many global accomplishments of Iranian cinema almost all achieved after the Islamic Revolution.[42]

It goes without saying that cultural analysis and commentary are contingent upon specificity, historicization, and contextualization. One cannot concur more with the truism that censorship is an undesirable phenomenon in all its manners. However, even though none of the Western novels Nafisi discusses in *RLT* were forbidden (at least in their English versions) in Iran in the first place, as Keshavarz has shrewdly observed, "what is surprising is the speed with which the revolution opened its doors on Nabokov again by allowing a government-funded agency to publish, in 1994, a book by the author of *RLT* about the controversial Russian writer" (*Jasmine and Stars* 37).⁴³ Characteristically, Nafisi remains silent on the far more serious censorship that existed in her romanticized pre-revolutionary Iran. Azar Mahloujian has explained that the publication or possession of forbidden books under the shah was "dangerous for all concerned—writers, readers, booksellers and publishers—so those who are not political activists will seldom risk reading them." She goes on to add that the possession of Maxim Gorki's *Mother*, for instance, could "lead to a three-year jail sentence" (Mahloujian).

Finally, it should be stressed that to criticize Nafisi for the many learned omissions, literary and otherwise, is not to fall into the trap of what Said has dubbed a "politics/rhetoric of blame."⁴⁴ On the contrary, it is to contextualize and shed light on the many significant aspects surrounding the production of the memoir which, being known, can lead to a very different reading of the book. Similarly, as much as reflecting on the shortcomings of the Islamic Republic and appreciating the struggles and aspirations of a nation for more democratic change and reform is not only legitimate but urgently indispensable, colluding with US neoconservative politics is counterproductive and detrimental to the indigenous struggles of Iranians. While the former involves restoration of hope to a nation and a committed appreciation of its democratic aspirations and resistance to authoritarianism, the latter divests it of its hope, dignity, and self-determination (Dabashi "Native Informers").

As Said has asserted, "[w]e live of course in a world not only of commodities but also of representation, and representations—their production, circulation, history, and interpretation—are the very element of culture" (*Culture and Imperialism* 56). Against this backdrop, it would be apt to return to the link established at the beginning of this chapter between *RLT* and *Not without My Daughter*, by the following juxtaposition of the two books by Dabashi to help illuminate the connection between the two:

> So far as its unfailing hatred of everything Iranian—from its literary masterpieces to its ordinary people—is concerned, not since Betty Mahmoody's notorious book *Not Without My Daughter* (1984) has a text exuded so systematic a visceral hatred of everything Iranian. ("Native Informers")

If anything, the unprecedented reception of Nafisi's memoir in the West, and particularly in the United States, by both the reading public and Western reviewers is a testament to the appeal of Orientalism as an ideology, the Western obsession with the Orient, especially its women, and the belief in the universal superiority of Western norms and values. Furthermore, the much-less enthusiastic reception of Nafisi's next memoir, *Things I Have Been Silent About* (2008)—a far more personal and far less "political" and "exotic" narrative about her mother's life and Nafisi's troubled relationship with her—is an additional proof of the power that Orientalism in all its shapes, forms, and manners exerts over both the general

Western readership's understanding of its Other and the reception of the literary and cultural products about them. Finally, it is worth reiterating that *RLT* is a book about Iranian women and reading. It is equally about the liberating power of Western literature for Iranian women. Nafisi's memoir is Western—in language, locus, and its frame of reference—and the numerous rave reviews and ratings promote it as a "literary masterpiece." The question that lingers after reading *RLT* is how liberated would Iranian women feel after reading *Reading Lolita in Tehran*?

Chapter 4

SIGHTING PERSIAN STARS IN THE WESTERN SKY

THE DAWN OF A DISCOURSE OF RESISTANCE IN *JASMINE AND STARS*

The Persians have been called "the French of Asia", and their superior intelligence, their esteem for men of learning, tepgheir welcome to Western travelers, and their tolerance of Christian sects in their territory ... would seem to derive from the rich culture of this choir of great poets, perpetually reinforced through five hundred years, which again and again has enabled the Persians to refine and civilize their conquerors, and to preserve a national identity.

Ralph Waldo Emerson, *Preface* to translation of Saadi's *Rose Garden*

As exemplified in the two previous chapters, the mainstream Western discourse on Iran is essentially predicated on an Orientalist paradigm. Nevertheless, in recent years a body of knowledge and art has started to germinate, which proffers an alternative discourse on Iran and Islam. This discourse is characterized by a comparatively less stereotypical, less bipolar, and more informed and balanced representation of the complexities of the country and the variegated tapestry of its cultures, religions, politics, and peoples. Indeed, this rather novel discourse pales in comparison to the dominance and authority of the prevailing Western regimes of knowledge production on Iran and Islam. Nevertheless, it is indispensable to engage with works of a resistant strain in any discussion of Orientalism—and especially its more recent offshoots, neo- and auto-Orientalism—not only to avoid the folly of Orientalist exclusionism but also to examine the manner in which such works serve to subvert mainstream Orientalist discourses and construct alternative lenses. As professor Fatemeh Keshavarz has proposed, the recognition of these resistant narratives and the "multiplicity of voices will empower us to resist all totalizing and silencing efforts" of Orientalist and colonial discourses (*Jasmine and Stars* 16).

What I wish to centralize here as crucial to the discussion at hand is the profound significance of discursive and narrative resistance to Orientalist regimes of representation, themselves being direct corollaries of imperial and hegemonic power. In *Culture and Imperialism* (1993), Said initiates a series of new conceptualizations that he had left out of his seminal *Orientalism*. These discussions that inform Said's theorizations on the nexus between culture and imperialism include both a global pattern of Western imperial culture and the response to Western dominance, hegemony, and colonization, which, in turn, led to decolonizing movements throughout the colonized world. In conjunction with the armed resistance of colonized peoples, Said maintains, "went considerable efforts in cultural resistance almost everywhere, the assertions of nationalist identities, and, in the political realm, the creation of associations and parties whose common goal was self-determination and national independence" (*Culture and Imperialism* xii). What I will be calling a "resistant discourse" in this chapter is an example of the cultural resistance to the power of hegemonic Orientalist discourses that are inextricably intertwined with issues of national identity and self-determination. Far from trivializing, overlooking, or outright obliterating significant historico-political, religious, and cultural contexts—as (neo-)Orientalist narratives characteristically do—these alternative discourses engage with such contexts both as essential narrative components and as a way of contextualizing representations, thereby lending a much-needed balance to discourses on Iran and Islam.

Investigating the repertoire of the mentioned alternative discourses is indispensable for a variety of reasons. First, it brings to light the numerous voices, perspectives, and contexts left out in the dominant narratives constructed about the Other. This can be achieved "by extending our reading of the texts to include what was once forcibly excluded" (Said, *Culture and Imperialism* 66). Second, by the same token that any discussion of Western imperialism and colonization is incomplete without attending to the resistances against and oppositions to them, any discussion of (neo-)Orientalist narratives would be similarly incomplete and insufficient without cultural forms that deviate from dominant Western discourses. In fact, Said regards such counternarratives not as sui generis discursive entities but rather as inextricable from narratives of Western imperialism. In other words, to leave out such narratives would be tantamount to acknowledging— in the same exclusionist Orientalist vein best exemplified in the rhetorical strategy of negation—that they do not actually exist. Such acknowledgment helps intensify the marginalization and often ill-fated receptions of such narratives, thereby further solidifying the power that the dominant narratives exert on representations of the Other. Finally, positioning narratives of resistance at the fore of the discussions of (neo-)Orientalism would provide them with a space wherein they can be observed, studied, and investigated. This, in turn, contribute to propelling them out of the marginality and obscurity zone to which they are currently destined.

The significance of the voices that resist or challenge dominant narratives of the Oriental Other should not be underestimated. Narratives play such a pivotal role in the self-determination of colonized and marginalized societies that Edward Said asserts, in his seminal *Culture and Imperialism*, that "[n]ations themselves are narrations." He then proceeds to elaborate on the nexus between the notions of narration, resistance, and emancipation:

The power to narrate, or to block other narratives from forming and emerging, is very important to culture and imperialism, and constitutes one of the main connections between them. Most important, the grand narratives of emancipation and enlightenment mobilized people in the colonial world to rise up and throw off imperial subjection; in the process, many Europeans and Americans were also stirred by these stories and their protagonists, and they too fought for new narratives of equality and human community.[1] (xii)

Said's point about Orientalist exclusionism and blocking other narratives has been touched upon in previous chapters in discussions of negation, learned elimination, dehistoricization, and decontextualization in the works of Mahmoody and Nafisi, wherein the conspicuous absence of significant historico-political contexts in these accounts was elaborated. What in this chapter is referred to as "resistant narratives", however, not only does not obliterate or negate these contexts as much as neo-Orientalist narratives do, but rather tries to engage with them both as essential constituents of the narrative and as a way of contextualization and balancing of the discourse.

In this chapter, I will explicate how this alternative discourse operates predominantly through the modus operandi of what has been termed "*strategic* (auto-)Orientalism," as opposed to its *essentialist* counterpart. Essentialist (auto-) Orientalism, as evident from its appellation, is the kind of Orientalism—basically the same as classical Orientalism—that is characterized by a binary opposition between the perceived "essences" of the West and its Other. The concept is adopted from Gayatri Chakravorty Spivak's theorization of "strategic" utilization of "essentialism" (183). Strategic (auto-)Orientalism encompasses the strategic deployment of the fluid nature of what are perceived as particular essences— expressed in the form of Orientalist tropes such as the veil—which are "necessary to express and intervene in discursive negotiations about representation," without necessarily rehashing or consolidating them (Koegeler 19). In a similar vein, Homi Bhabha has articulated such "essences" in "the concept of 'fixity' in the ideological construction of otherness" ("The Other Question" 66). Fixity, according to Bhabha, is the major discursive strategy and "the sign of cultural/historical/racial difference in the discourse of colonialism," which can be defined as "a form of knowledge and identification that vacillates between what is always 'in place', already known, and something that must be anxiously repeated" (66).

Such "essences" function as the fulcrum of Orientalist frames of reference, and their strategic employment serves only to demystify and contextualize them by way of drawing attention to the complexities, nuances, and diversified contexts that characterize them, aiming to eventually undermine or subvert them. Thus, Spivak cautions that strategic essentialism should not be misconstrued as either "perpetuating ethnicities" or constructing superior interlocutory positions. In other words, she deems indispensable the existence of a "minimalizable essence" in communicating "difference" (30). In this light, as a discursive strategy, strategic (auto)Orientalism can be adopted as a potentially empowering representational medium via which hyphenated minority writers, can represent themselves and their native cultures. It is worth mentioning that the auto-Orientalism involved in strategic auto-Orientalism is based on the broader definition of the concept—also presented in the previous chapter—as "self-discourse among orientals" (Carrier 36), which stresses the eyewitness quality and the "native or seminative insider tone" of the narrator (Keshavarz, *Jasmine and Stars* 3).

Insofar as auto-Orientalist self-representation is concerned, both strategic and essentialist modes of Orientalism share two major denominators. First, they both rely predominantly on citationality—that is, the citation of established Orientalist topoi. As Koegeler has argued, this contributes to enabling minority authors to achieve

> access to the U.S. literary market via citation of orientalist tropes and thus [to] actively participate in the majority discourses surrounding Islam, Muslim women and Americanness. Citation of established orientalist tropes provides access to publication by way of its mutual legibility by majority discourses and minority writers. (iii)

While employing citationality may lead to further solidification of the existing stereotypes, it can also serve as a space for interlocution, contestation, intervention, and eventually subversion of Orientalist binary oppositions. In other words, while the citation of certain Orientalist tropes enables the minority writer to gain access to the American literary market, she can employ that access to proactively and subversively modify these "essences" while keeping them fluid and malleable. Thus, a strategically auto-Orientalist formulation can help construct a counterhegemonic discursive intervention in the monolithic Orientalist images of Iranian/Muslim societies, and particularly their women's subjectivities, and lay their representations bare, "thus reveal[ing] these images to be empty signifiers detached from actual practices" (Koegeler 30). In both modes of Orientalism, according to Koegeler, "access depends on the referent being mutually recognizable" both by a majority Western readership and by the hyphenated American audience (6).

This discursive intervention is facilitated by another denominator of auto-Orientalism, that is, the authorial dual-situatedness, which reflects the intermediary, compradorial position of the author and serves two distinct purposes in each mode of representation. Dual rootedness imparts a certain measure of authenticity, credibility, and power to the personal voice of the minority author and can open up a discursive space for the in-between subjectivities of minority women who employ it strategically "as cultural mediators that defy East/West binaries and thus destabilize a clear cut notion of a stable U.S. culture based on normativity and escape a neoliberal logic of validating only certain kinds of diversity" (Koegeler iii).

Nevertheless, contrary to essentialist Orientalism, which presents the culture of the Other as fundamentally inferior to and distinct from the Western—especially American—culture, strategic Orientalism posits the same culturewithin and as an inherent part of the melting pot of cultures in the United States. Thus, while strategic utilization of Orientalist signifiers contributes to the empowerment of the minority writer to access the American literary market, she can take advantage of her access and double-situatedness to destabilize Orientalist tropes and forge new sites for minority women's self-expression. This new space, and the strategic uses of "essences," can also be understood in the context of what Homi K. Bhabha has termed the "Third Space", "which constitutes the discursive conditions of enunciation that ensure that the meaning and symbols of culture have no primordial unity or fixity; that even the same signs can be appropriated, translated, rehistoricized and read anew" (*The Location of Culture* 37).

It should be added that the employment of strategic Orientalism through citationality is only one form of subverting and challenging Orientalist stereotypes in both fictional and nonfictional narratives. Even though fictional narratives are typically perceived as lending themselves more readily to the manipulation and exploitation of fictional and literary stratagems required for the strategic employment of Orientalist representations, one could argue that nonfiction forms borrow as much from other literary traditions as fiction proper. In fact, as pointed out in the two previous chapters, the distinction between fiction and nonfiction is particularly problematic with Orientalist texts, as almost all (neo-)Orientalist narratives are characterized by a constant blurring of the boundaries between fact and fiction. Thus, in as much as any text is constructed, the "fictions" of Orientalism may just become more naturalized in a nonfiction text.

Similarly, fiction authors are often deemed to have more normative control over their representations, since the questions of authenticity and truth value are not nearly as determining and challenging in fiction as they are in such "nonfiction" genres as memoir and autobiography. Nevertheless, one could argue that apropos such literary forms as historical fiction, for instance, or fiction that seems to rely on specific cultural contexts, fiction writers can also be challenged for liberties taken.[2]

While the boundary between fact and fiction remains obfuscated, it is not difficult to observe that as far as direct and explicit instances of Orientalist tropes are concerned, they are mostly to be found in texts that are labeled as fiction. Even though autobiographical accounts are as much subject to construction (through the processes of selection and deletion), rhetoric, allusion, and emplotment as a work of fiction is, the readers commonly regard a memoir to be a true account, by virtue of the supposed firsthand, eyewitness nature of the genre. Therefore, as far as autobiographical narratives are concerned, it is predominantly the same "native" knowledge purported by the narrator and the power of unmediated observation fortified by the author's immersion in Western language and culture that enables her to offer an alternative account . It has to be stressed that these are only a few of the genre's features that follow audience expectation, but not the only claims to authority and authenticity in self-writing. Also, features of native knowledge and direct observation and experience are not limited to this literary form and may appear in such other forms as the historical novel.

To investigate the representations of Iran both in the public sphere and in literary discourses is to be struck by the power and prevalence of Orientalist discourses that seek to define and represent the country, as typified by Mahmoody's and Nafisi's works. Narratives of a resistant character are so few and far between that they form only a minute portion of the repertoire of literary knowledge production on Iran. The majority of such divergent representations perhaps belong to the documentaries that do not expressly deal with Iran's political landscape, often produced by Westerners who have visited the country and have found themselves astounded by the disparity between media representations of the country and the realities on the ground. Even so, these documentaries are neither significant in number nor do they go unchallenged by the scores of political and propagandistic documentaries burgeoning most specifically in the context of Iran's so-called nuclear issue.[3]

In the literary sphere, with very few exceptions, it has only been recently that such narratives have started to emerge in earnest in the canon of Iranian-American memoirs. Significantly, and ironically perhaps, some of these narratives are influenced by Azar Nafisi's *Reading Lolita in Tehran*. In other words, in the same manner that the success of Nafisi's memoir instigated a new wave of neo-Orientalist Iranian-American memoirs, one could argue that it has also triggered, both directly and indirectly, the emergence of alternative voices among the female Iranian-American exilic writers and scholars, especially those in the academia.

Narratives of resistance share a few denominators. Predominantly, such narratives are accounts of in-betweenness, dual marginalization, and identity crisis, which often recount the author's quest for her true self or native roots, sometimes in the form of a homecoming narrative. Furthermore, there is a glaring discrepancy between their reception, which is often at best lukewarm, and the enthusiastic reception of their neo-Orientalist counterparts both by the Western reading public and reviewers. Ironically though, such narratives provide much richer ethnographic details as well as historical, social, political, and religious contexts. S. Asha has lamented the fact that "[w]hat is most unfortunate is that such books [neo-Orientalist narratives] get published at the cost of other books, that give a fuller, authentic account of the Middle Eastern woman" (48). This contextualization paves the way for more nuanced discussions of such controversial and complex events as the Iranian Revolution, the Hostage Crisis, the Iraqi-imposed war, the question of women and veil, and the pre-revolution era, which frequently appear in Iranian-American life writing and thus help the Western reader arrive at a more nuanced and more realistic understanding of the country.

Jasmine and Stars: *Cracking the Orientalist Monolith*

By far the foremost "resistant" memoir on Iran, Fatemeh Keshavarz's[4] *Jasmine and Stars: Reading More Than Lolita in Tehran*[5] (henceforth abbreviated as

J&S) is particularly significant for several reasons. First, as the memoir title clearly demonstrates, *J&S* is produced in direct response to Nafisi's *RLT* as the epitome of neo-Orientalist Middle Eastern memoirs. As such, it sets out to challenge Nafisi's representations of things Iranian and Islamic and to furnish an alternative lens through which she hopes to familiarize her Western readers with the variegated tapestry of Iranian and Islamic cultures. In this light, one could argue that Keshavarz's counter-discursive strategies are well aligned with Helen Tiffin's observation that "counter-discursive strategies involve a mapping of the dominant discourse, a reading and exposing of its underlying assumptions, and the dis/mantling of these assumptions from the cross-cultural standpoint of the imperially subjectified 'local'" (98). It is for the provision of such counter-discursive insights that David Pitt has recommended *J&S* as "an excellent counterpoint for book-group discussions of Nafisi's book" (53). Professor Keshavarz herself has described one of the motivations for writing her narrative, which testifies to her consciousness of the discursive paradigm within which her book was meant to be published and received, especially in the context of US academia:

> In terms of classroom use, what convinced me to write *Jasmine and Stars* is that I did a web search and realized that *Reading Lolita in Tehran* is on over 500 syllabi across the country. It blew my mind (particularly that some of the courses where on totally unrelated topics such as Islamic Studies, or as you say International Relations). That is also why I kept the subtitle "Reading More Than Lolita in Tehran" because I wanted those who search the web to be able to find my response to her book and I think that has been a successful strategy. So many people email me and tell me "I used to teach *Reading Lolita in Tehran*, now I know about your response and I have added yours to my syllabus." (qtd. in Ghasemi Tari, 243)

Furthermore, *J&S* is perhaps the only other Iranian-American memoir, besides *RLT*, whose author is not only quite well versed in Western literatures but also draws extensively on her native (that is, Persian) literature to represent her country of origin. Contrary to Nafisi, however, Keshavarz displays a profound familiarity with both the classic and contemporary Persian/Iranian literary traditions. Along these lines, Keshavarz has remarked that:

> *RLT* benefits from reading a range of good Western literature to understand the cultural exchange taking place in the early decades of the 1979 Iranian Revolution. However, it shows no awareness whatsoever of the lively and controversial literature created in Iran itself in the years prior to, and after the revolution. In fact, it suggests a total absence of interest in literature by local culture. (*Jasmine and Stars* 7)

Moreover, like Nafisi's memoir, the content of *J&S* is divided between autobiography and critical analyses of literary works, except that here the works are predominantly Persian fiction and poetry. Keshavarz's introduction and analysis of some towering figures of both classical and contemporary Persian literary traditions is one of the major strengths of the narrative, making it distinct from similar works by Iranian-American women. As Elisheva Machlis has observed, "The novelty of *Jasmine and Stars* lies less in its discourse on Orientalism and more in its attempt to forge through its lavish Persian literature a new understanding of Iran for a non-specialist Western readership, in a personal account of Iranian culture" (103).

Both the choice of memoir as the genre in which Keshavarz endeavors to write back to *RLT* and the main themes underlying *J&S* are significant for two interrelated reasons. On the one hand, one of Keshavarz's main reasons for writing *J&S*—as demonstrated in the titular "Reading More Than *Lolita* in Tehran"—is a counterhegemonic response to *RLT*. Therefore, it is only apt to write back within the boundaries of the same narrative and thematic structure in which *RLT* is framed; hence, not only the formal choice of memoir, but also the interspersed analyses of contemporary Persian literature in *J&S*. In this light, Amy Motlagh has observed that Keshavarz has "to meet the claims of the memoirists on their own ground, penning a memoir that explicitly engages some of the assertions leveled by *Reading Lolita in Tehran*" ("Towards a Theory" 32).

On the other hand, in choosing to write a memoir addressing issues, such as the question of Iranian women and representations of Islam, which have gained renewed currency in the aftermath of 9/11, Keshavarz demonstrates an accurate understanding of the expectations of the American publishing market and also her intended Western readership.

Keshavarz herself has termed her contribution to the representations of Iran and Islam "a literary and cultural analysis long in the making" (7); yet, in presenting her social and cultural analysis, she "keep[s] [her] personal voice in the foreground," emphasizing that "[everything in the book is centered on my own personal stories, even when I reach out to classical Sufi masters to illustrate a point" (7). Such a description of the narrative strategies of *J&S* corresponds with Keshavarz's characterization of the dominant features of the formalistic and representational strategies of "New Orientalist" narratives (Keshavarz's terminology) and is evidence of the existence of a structural and thematic pattern in Iranian-American self-writing, which Keshavarz herself has both identified and deployed effectively:

> They often have an informal tone and a hybrid nature that make for an accessible read. Most of them blend travel writing, personal memoir, journalistic reporting, and social commentary. They show awareness of the power of personal voice, nostalgia in exilic literature, the assurance that comes with insider knowledge, and the certainty of eyewitness accounts. (7)

In other words, in laying out the denominators of what Keshavarz has designated as the "New Orientalist" discourse, she displays a considerable measure of self-referentiality, although her memoir stands in stark contrast to such narratives. *Jasmine and Stars* employs a tone that is at times much more informal than many other Iranian-American memoirs, such as when the autobiographical Keshavarz directly addresses her audience: "There are so many other stories I could have told you. But this is how I want you to meet my maternal uncle the painter, in his elegant military uniform, completely unimpressed with corrupt power" (59); or "Let me tell you why I loved to have tea with Rumi so much" (161). Keshavarz also enunciates her own hybridity through an unreserved demarcation of her subjectivity as an Iranian-American woman:

> Before everything else, I am an Iranian American woman . . . I have lived and worked in the United States since 1987. I visit Iran every year and stay for anywhere from weeks to months at a time. When I am there, I see relatives, catch up with high school and university friends, buy books, visit universities and other institutions of learning, and connect with Iranian poets and scholars. Iran and America are both my home. Both make me delighted and furious at short and frequent intervals. (8)

Similarly, Keshavarz blends "travel writing, personal memoir, journalistic reporting, and social commentary", if not more, then just as much as most Iranian-American memoirs. She describes, for instance, her frequent travels to Iran, as well as other parts of the world, draws heavily on personal reminiscences and the power of nostalgia, and her commentary runs the gamut of issues ranging from representations of Muslims in the West to learned discussions of both classical and contemporary Persian literature. Some of these themes will be elaborated in the ensuing discussions of Keshavarz's memoir.

Similar to other Iranian-American memoirs, Keshavarz's narrative also evinces consciousness of the power of unmediated observation and engagement (7). Written in the autobiographical first person, Keshavarz establishes herself as an Iranian woman—hence, an "insider"—born, raised, and partly educated in Iran: "I grew up in the historic city of Shiraz in southwest Iran, where I went to school and university" (8). Personal narratives and childhood nostalgia, along with her constant trips to Iran and the close connection she has maintained over the years with different echelons of Iranian society and its intelligentsia, are meant to qualify her as a narrator empowered by the privilege of firsthand observation and insider knowledge.

In fact, Keshavarz's personal reminiscences and experience of Iran, which she has romantically dubbed her "jasmine and stars," are among the most powerful passages of her memoir. Lynne Dahmen has argued that "[t]he strength of Keshavarz's work lies in her passionate descriptions of her childhood, family members, and various people and poets who have greatly impacted her" (202). Apart from the vicarious joy, sorrow, and nostalgia that such personal anecdotes impart to readers, they contribute to the humanization of a nation that has been subject to constant demonization and dehumanization in the West since the 1979 revolution, with an added momentum after 9/11. The appeal of Keshavarz's personal narratives of home, childhood, and Persian literature also lies in the fact that even though she sets out to challenge and subvert dominant stereotypes about Iran and Islam, she does not engage in a romanticized portrayal of her native country. Rather, she treats her subjects in their everyday ordinariness, their human frailties and strengths, and thus avoids the (neo-)Orientalist polarization of characters into Nafisi's world of "witches" and "fairies." In this context, one could also observe that in constructing authority, privileging first-person narration, selectivity, and familiarity with the literary discussions presented Keshavarz's strategy is similar to Nafisi's politics of the personal, although, as it will be illustrated, she uses such strategies toward a totally different purpose.

Throughout her narrative, Keshavarz engages in an extensive critique of what she describes as the "Islamization of wickedness" (118) and the "Westernization of goodness" (119) in recent narratives on the Middle East, exemplified by *RLT*:

> I view this narration of the Middle East as exaggerated and oversimplified at best and fully distorted at worst. In particular, I critique the silencing nature of the narrative reflected in its selective remembering, lack of sensitivity to traditional cultures, and basic contempt for religious practice. My personal stories and analysis are meant to counter the New Orientalist narrative's tendency to amplify fear and mistrust by ignoring similarity and highlighting difference. (110)

In an elaborate attempt to subvert the Orientalist connotations of the manipulated cover photo of *RLT*, the image on the front cover of *J&S* displays two effervescent, smiling young Iranian women attending a demonstration outside the University of Tehran in 2005 (Keshavarz, "An Interview"). In the image the young women are posited against a backdrop of jasmine flowers, and are wearing sunglasses, lipsticks, nail polish, and colorful shawls (as their "veils") with most of their hair showing from underneath their scarves. Adding to the significance of the multihued portrayal of the two young women are the posters they are holding in their hands, which have feminist slogans printed on them, declaring "We women demand equal rights with men" and "Injustice to women = Injustice to the entire human society." The image, therefore, not only stands in marked contrast to that of *RLT* and subverts its monochromatic representation, it also presents an alternative picture of Iranian women, or rather of a different and sizeable portion of their considerable population, defined both by their different grooming practices and by their active social agency in identifying with domestic feminist causes. The vibrant and cheerful countenance of the two young women also poses a telling counterpoint to the often desperate and distressed images of women in black veils, as if calling for liberation, which appear on the covers of the majority of (neo-)Orientalist narratives. Placed against the backdrop of jasmine flowers (which symbolize beauty and fragrance), the image of the smiling and defiant young women foreshadows a narrative about the untold beauties of the culture and its women's resilience and social agency.

Rumi: The Muslim Persian Bard

Jasmine and Stars opens with a chapter titled after one of the most famous Persian allegories, "the elephant in the room," quoted from Rumi's magnum opus, *Masnavi*.[6] Keshavarz's discussion of Rumi's allegory at the beginning of her narrative to caution against "the dangers of partial or distorted vision" (1) could hardly have been more appropriate and serves several simultaneous functions. For one thing, it testifies to the author's knowledge of canonical Persian literature and especially poetry, subjects in which Keshavarz has established herself as a well-versed academic as evidenced by her publications.[7] As another significant peritextual element of the book, it is worth noting that *J&S* is published by an academic press (the University of North Carolina Press), which further distinguishes the work from *RLT* (published by Random House) and almost all other Iranian-American memoirs.

Keshavarz's reference to Rumi is also quite significant in the way it sets up and signals the author's subsequent discussions of Persian literature and her subversion of a supremacist reading of canonical Western literature in *RLT*. Keshavarz's focus on Persian literary traditions stands in stark contrast to Nafisi's glorification of Western literature. In *RLT*, Nafisi mentions Rumi, as well as other Persian literary giants, adding that "[t]here was such a teasing, playful quality to their words, such joy in the power of language to delight and astonish" (172). Nevertheless, while Keshavarz demonstrates a lively culture "that did more than value the world of literature; it 'lived it' through the ups and downs of life" (Tourage 102), for Nafisi such Persian literary classics belong to an inaccessibly distant past and seem to have no currency in contemporary times. Thus, Nafisi proceeds to declare extinct a whole tradition of Persian literature and the aesthetic, moral, and humanistic values associated with it:

> I kept wondering: when did we lose that quality, that ability to tease and make light of life through our poetry? At what precise moment was this lost? What we had now, this saccharine rhetoric, putrid and deceptive hyperbole, reeked of too much cheap rosewater. (172)

In this light, one could argue that Nafisi's view of the Persian literary tradition is reminiscent of the "fatal impact" trope used by Westerners to seemingly celebrate the cultures they were destroying—a position that, as elaborated in the discussion of *RLT*, suggests Nafisi's evident allegiance to the Western perspective.

Keshavarz's choice of Rumi is a calculated subversive narrative technique, not only because it challenges Nafisi's aforementioned assertion about classical Persian literature, but also because Rumi remains the bestselling poet in the United States and, in fact, the most widely read poet from this tradition in the world (Ciabattari). As such, opening the memoir with Rumi's anecdote would strike a ready chord with the intended Western audience of the book. Finally, the reference to Rumi's allegory emphasizes the potentiality of Persian literature conspicuously absent in *RLT* and other neo-Orientalist Iranian-American memoirs and initiates the author's discussions of Iran and Islam, before the chapters devoted to the liberating and subversive potential of Persian literature.

Re-orienting Orientalism

From the very outset, Keshavarz makes it clear that her memoir sets out to investigate the regime of representation through which the Oriental/Muslim Other is packaged for Western consumption, particularly in the United States. Thus, she declares in her introduction that

> Since 9/11, knowing about the Muslim Middle East is not a luxury, it is a matter of life and death. We need to know if "they" and their many constellations of cultures out there are really the media-packaged, neat rows of prayer driven by faith, emotion, and instinct. We hear that some blow themselves up just so someone else might die in the process. It feels so unnatural, so wrong. Didn't these same people write delightful poetry at one time? Didn't they carve exquisite calligraphy on their window panes and even doorknobs? Didn't they welcome an exiled Jewish community fleeing Spain in the late fifteenth century? What happened? Something says we must find a candle, for there has to be more to the elephant. (2)

Keshavarz's professed intention in penning her memoir and elaboration on her subject distinguishes her narrative from its neo-Orientalist counterparts where the underlying Orientalism, or sometimes the author's intention, is not often expressly stated and gradually emerges during the course of the narrative.[8] In addition, Keshavarz's reference to the past of the Orientalized Muslim community serves to provide a historical context that challenges hackneyed Orientalist representations by humanizing the subjects of representation through not only their artistic practices but also their religious tolerance—a clear antithesis to "people blowing themselves up."

Keshavarz's awareness of the challenges and obstacles posed by the Western grand narratives of Othering, dictating how to view the Other, further distinguishes her narrative:

> The prevailing perceptions make it very hard for me to give you my gifts [of jasmine and stars]. It is as if a voice in the background, a master narrative has told us how to imagine each other. The narrative has seeped into the fabric of our daily thought and the simplest of our interactions. To empower both of us to break out of that narrative is my challenge. (16)

Quite cognizant of such impediments, Keshavarz attempts to avoid Orientalist dichotomies and monochromatic portrayals that characterize neo-Orientalist narratives. In doing so, she evinces awareness of the Orientalist traps of generalization, oversimplification, exaggeration, and negation that might undermine her own account. Hence, besides presenting her titular "jasmines" and "stars"—which stand for what comprises the rich diversity of Iranian society and culture—she also presents her readers with the less flattering aspects of the same society and culture—the occasional "grasshoppers" that invaded the sky of her childhood (15).

Well aware of the power invested in personal voice, as well as in her association with US academia, Keshavarz uses her dual situatedness as a self-professed Iranian-American effectively to drive her messages home and to offer as much a comprehensive view of the profound complexity and diversity of her representational subjects as possible. In other words, Keshavarz's representational strategy capitalizes more on her authorial positionality than direct citation of Orientalist tropes. Contrary to Nafisi, when she does cite the established tropes directly it is not intended to resonate with her Western readers and to recapitulate what they have come to expect from Western accounts of the Middle East; rather, it is to contextualize them and investigate their truth value. Additionally, Keshavarz attempts to interrupt the exotic image of the oppressed female in seclusion not only by showing that many women do, in fact, choose to wear the veil, but also by averring that "these women seem to have a stronger, more articulate voice than quite a few of their unveiled counterparts elsewhere in the world" (50). Also, drawing on the power of self-referentiality and firsthand experience she informs her readers that "When I go to Iran for a visit, I wear the head scarf that is now mandated by the constitution. I do not wear the scarf while outside Iran, and in principle, I like people to be able to choose what they wear" (8).

Keshavarz's narrative self-reflexivity is especially significant since she has already set herself up as a highly educated academic and a feminist living in the West and, as such, her practice of wearing the veil is unlikely to be construed as a sign of oppression, invisibility, and immobility. In fact, if anything, it undermines Nafisi's rehashing of the Orientalist trope of the irreconcilability of the Islamic faith with feminist principles.

Keshavarz's prefatory remarks and her positioning of herself are quite significant both in the appreciation of her work an in the manner in which she aspires to present her alternative account of Iranian culture and literature. The explicit reference to her hyphenated identity as an Iranian-American (8) conveys her sense of belonging to and familiarity with both sides of the Orientalist binary of the West versus the East, thereby creating a network of significations and associations with both locales for her intended audience.

Keshavarz's double situatedness is also manifest in the way she posits herself as a professor of "Persian/comparative literature and Islamic cultures"—disciplines that she teaches and researches at the University of Maryland. Such an academic affiliation serves to make her sound qualified as a commentator on and analyst of both the country of her origin and Islam (7). In her own words, "[i]n *Jasmine and Stars*, I carefully and painstakingly weave a multihued tapestry of human voice and experience. I turn my narrating voice into a vehicle for the rainbow of the faces and words that filled my childhood and youth in Iran" (5). In other words, unlike Nafisi who used her dual situatedness to reinforce Orientalist stereotypes about Iran and Islam, Keshavarz—quite consciously, indeed—uses the same position strategically to subvert the same stereotypes and offer an alternative mode of viewing the Iranian Other. Despite the ostensible similarity between Nafisi and Keshavarz in terms of their dual positionality and the fact that they are both affiliated with US academia, Keshavarz's position allows her to import Islam and Persian culture and literature into the West, whereas Nafisi seems to be framing Islam and Persian culture by a misplaced juxtaposition of the West as the norm in Tehran.

Following the reference to her birthplace in Iran and her British doctorate in Near Eastern Studies from London University, Keshavarz thus continues her introduction of herself: "I am a Muslim, a feminist, a literary scholar, and a poet, though not always in that order" (8). The fact that she clearly posits herself as a Muslim and a feminist bears particular significance in understanding her narrative. On the one hand, she is positing herself in stark contrast to Nafisi and her version of Western feminism, which deems being a Muslim and a feminist incompatible or, as she has called it in *RLT,* "the myth of Islamic feminism—a contradictory notion, attempting to reconcile the concept of women's rights with the tenets of Islam" (262). In this light, it is quite significant that Keshavarz not only articulates her religious identification confidently, but the fact that she identifies as a "Muslim" living in the West is noteworthy. In doing so, however, while she is subjecting herself to the Orientalist tropes apropos Muslim women,[9] she employs such an association with the religion strategically to impart greater authenticity and credibility to her authorial voice, while her Western situatedness, especially her education and academic position, also facilitate this reception for her intended American readership. Therefore, by identifying as a Muslim and a feminist, Keshavarz is questioning Nafisi's Western brand of feminism (which denies the recognition of Islamic feminism) while simultaneously casting herself as a Muslim woman committed to the principles of gender equality and social activism.

Rewriting the Revolution and the War

Keshavarz uses her Iranian rootedness as well as her Western education to subvert some of the most (re)current myths surrounding Iran and Islam, which also appear in *RLT.* One such myth has to do with the 1979 Revolution, which figures throughout the entire narrative in *RLT.* While the conspicuously reductionist and simplistic treatment of the Revolution in *RLT* reduces the manifold sociopolitical causes of the Revolution to Islamic "fanaticism" and "fundamentalism," the occasional analysis that *J&S* offers on the Revolution is vivid and takes note of historical, political, and social causes underlying the Revolution. Keshavarz begins her take on the Revolution with an apt general observation that

> In general, revolutions do not present their perspectives politely and peacefully. They throw them at you. Where peaceful means have not failed, a revolution does not take place. In Iran of the 1970s, peaceful means had failed. A look at the writings of major Iranian writers of the 1960s, not all particularly sympathetic to Islam, shows that they predicted the explosion as early as those years. (10)

Rebutting the dominant view of the Revolution as simply a result of "absolutist Islam" or a dislike for "freedom and modernization" (19), Keshavarz points to centuries of "unresolved issues" and "local problems," asserting that

> the part that powerful nations of the world have played in sustaining—and at times exploiting—the mess is by no means negligible. These range from the outright colonization of territories and reckless pursuit of short-term economic goals to cultural illiteracy and disrespect. (10)

The latter, that is the crucial role of foreign interventionism—especially that of the United States—in pre-revolutionary Iran is a fact either neglected or denied by almost all Orientalist accounts of contemporary Iran. Keshavarz also points out to "the corruption of the pre-revolutionary system and the absence of civil liberties" as main reasons behind the sweeping uprisings of the late 1970s in Iran, which eventually led to the 1979 Revolution (21). This latter cause is quite significant, since it poses a sharp contrast to the often highly romanticized portrayal of pre-revolutionary Iran as a benign and democratic golden age in other Iranian-American memoirs.

The same argument holds true for Keshavarz's discussions of the war imposed on Iran by Saddam Hussein. Nafisi makes quite a few references to Iraq's bombardment of Iranian cities. Nevertheless, she makes no mention of who the perpetrator of the war was and if there is any condemnation of the war at all, it is, most oddly, leveled against the Iranian government (209). Furthermore, the war is principally portrayed in *RLT* as driven by religious fanaticism and the young Iranian volunteers going to the war are presented as brainwashed by governmenr propaganda (108).

As discussed in the preceding chapter, contrary to "fanatic" and "gullible" Iranian volunteers, Nafisi glorifies Henry James, who was "so actively involved in the war effort" (214) and refers to his two brothers as having "fought with courage and honor" (213). Keshavarz, on the other hand, makes it very clear that "[a]fter all, Iranians were not the aggressors, they were the ones attacked" (132)—a fact that is never mentioned in *RLT* and hardly acknowledged in other kindred memoirs. Keshavarz further contextualizes the war in her discussion of the factual errors in *RLT*:

> The records of that terrible war are not classified information. Saddam Hussein took a few cities, used his weapons against Iraqi Kurds and Iranians, fired his missiles as far as they could reach into Iran, lost control over the parts of the

country that he had occupied, and finally retreated back into Iraqi territory. (138)

By providing the irrefutable facts about the war, Keshavarz puts into perspective the information that both she and Nafisi provide in their respective accounts about the war.

Like similar occasions in *J&S* for contextualization, comparison, and subversion, Keshavarz engages with the issue of the Iran–Iraq War only to juxtapose it with its counterparts in US history. First, she draws attention to Nafisi's contradictory attitude toward the question of the war when fought by Iran and the United States. Such a double standard as Nafisi employs proves, more than anything else, not only her strong political and ideological allegiance with the United States and the many wars it has waged in contemporary history, but also her "eternal contempt" for those who defended their country in a war waged by Saddam Hussein and fully backed by Western powers. Second, Keshavarz broaches the 2003 US occupation of Iraq and hints at the full American support for Saddam Hussein:

> As much as many of us loathe war—and as much as we wished at the time that the Iran-Iraq war would end quickly—it is distressing to see the struggle so badly misrepresented. The official line of argument out of Iran at the time, not mentioned in *RLT*, was that it was not enough to recapture the city of Khorramshahr from the Iraqis. The aggressor must be made to pay for his action or he will resume his attacks the instant he has regrouped. Saddam was a criminal who used chemical weapons against innocent people, and he must not be allowed to get away with his invasion. Does this line of argument ring a bell with regard to the current American war? Or has Saddam Hussein changed nature as a result of walking out of American grace and friendship? (132–3)

Keshavarz further criticizes the American invasion of Iraq in which the United States "dragg[ed] the largest army of the world halfway across the globe to fight imaginary weapons of mass destruction" (113). To further undermine Nafisi's apathy toward and disregard for those involved in the war—which Nafisi portrays in *RLT* not as her own peculiarity but as an extension of the alleged public disillusionment with the war—Keshavarz turns to personal reminiscence and testimony to humanize those disparaged by Nafisi:

> I will never forget one morning in the summer of 1987 when I was traveling on a bus in north Tehran to visit a friend. I overheard two young men who had apparently been to the war front talking . . . One of the voices said: "Fighting at night was the worst. I just did not want to be hit in the dark, you see. You wouldn't even know exactly which part of you was hit for a while." The other responded, "I know, but it was more frightening when those things they fired above our heads lighted up the sky. You could suddenly see everything." I did not look at them, not even when I got off. I would not have known what to do if one had had an arm or a leg missing. I can tell you for sure that neither of them

had enjoyed the war, or had looked for heroism, and yet neither had run away—which is why that country is still intact. (134)

Keshavarz proceeds to further dispute Nafisi's claim about the unpopularity of the war among Iranians by testifying to the high esteem in which the majority of Iranians hold the war veterans who "literally stopped Saddam Hussein from landing one morning at the Tehran airport" (134). Once again, highlighting the historical Western antagonism toward Iran, she asks: "Had he [Saddam] done so, would the armies of the democratic and peace-loving parts of the world have come to the rescue of the Iranians?" (134). Keshavarz's rhetorical question further highlights "the double standards that many of us in the democratic world live with comfortably" (135).

There are other occasions when Keshavarz directly challenges descriptions or claims made in RLT that she deems to be either highly exaggerated or founded on a Western supremacist frame of reference. In one noteworthy instance, she compares a concert in Tehran—which Nafisi turns into an object of ridicule and which she leaves early lest she gets "trampled by the mob" (301)—with a Speaker Series event held in Washington University. Coincidentally, because Keshavarz taught at Washington University at the time) she is assigned to introduce the speaker. The speaker happens to be no one else than Nafisi and the subject of her talk is, indeed, RLT. Juxtaposing the two situations, Keshavarz observes that if the language of RLT in describing Iranian audiences attending a concert were to be adopted, "one could say people 'were stuffed into the hall'" (20). She also refers to Nafisi's framing of the concert attendants as the "mob" and adds:

> But this eager American audience would not be the "mob." RLT reserved such pejorative terms as the "mob" and "mediocre" for performances in Iran and even suggested that the word concert be placed in quotation marks so that "such cultural affairs" would not be mistaken for "the real thing" (RLT, 299). (20)

Keshavarz's descriptive strategy is at once subversive and effective. While analyzing Nafisi's representational discourse for its "pejorative" use of the language, she juxtaposes the two situations, implying that the same diction could potentially be used to describe the event in which Nafisi herself was the guest speaker. However, by hinting at, but refraining from employing, the disparaging language of Nafisi's description, she contextualizes the event at Washington University by recognizing its complexity while criticizing Nafisi's denigration and ridiculing of the Iranian concert. Also, by suspending the use of "pejoratives" herself, she demonstrates restraint and another level of metafictional self-referential awareness above Nafisi's.

In the same analytical vein, Keshavarz engages with such complex and sensitive issues as the status of women in Iran. The fact that she has earlier posited herself as a feminist and a Muslim is quite significant in her response to the representations of Iranian/Muslim women in Orientalist narratives. Once again, by drawing on some restrictions that some women face in different Muslim societies, indeed to very different degrees, she strategically utilizes established Orientalist tropes only to subvert the mainstream perceptions of Iranian women in the West:

> It is true that a traditionalist wave in Iran has promoted (and continues to promote) the cult of domesticity and motherhood in the aftermath of the revolution. Legal reform in areas related to gender is needed, as is also the case regarding the rights of religious minorities and election laws. But the traditional articulations of women's role are not unanimously endorsed, not even among Islamist movements. Secondly, this perception does not correspond to the reality of women's public participation in postrevolutionary Iran. Women are everywhere, including in the legislative body. Iranian men and women have engaged in reform-oriented activism since the revolution. Shirin Ebadi, the recipient of the 2003 Nobel Peace Prize, is one such activist. (115)

As a professor of Comparative Literature, Keshavarz does find something to praise in *RLT*: "its attention to the rich tapestry of world literature" and its "attempt to understand the human experience that transcends religious, social, and cultural boundaries" (22). Keshavarz's recognition of the merits of *RLT* allows her to avoid the black-and-white Orientalist binarism that dominates the world of Nafisi's memoir. However, even though Keshavarz's acknowledgment of the attention paid in *RLT* to world literature and the transcendental human experience reflected in literature is significant in its own right, it is her analyses and discussions of both classical and contemporary Persian literature that serve to distinguish her narrative from its Orientalist predecessors and contemporaries.

Writing the Rebel: "The Eternal Forough"

Keshavarz's engagement with modern Persian literature is quite noteworthy since it refutes the Orientalist assertion that if there is any "great" Persian literature, it belongs to a long-bygone past. It also challenges Nafisi's exclusionist approach that completely disregards Iranian women writers and thus silences both their literary and social contributions and aspirations. Thus, in the second chapter of *J&S*, "The Eternal Forough: The Voice of Our Earthly Rebellion," in a counterhegemonic attempt to subvert the view of Iranian women as docile and oppressed Keshavarz turns to Forough Farrokhzad (1935–67), one of the most renowned and arguably one of the most influential modern Iranian female poets. In so doing, she also offers an example of the rich tapestry of modern Persian poetry and fiction and their enlightening and emancipatory potential. Significantly, Farrokhzad is also one of the very few contemporary Iranian poets whose life and poetry have been the topic of academic investigation in the West.

Keshavarz describes Farrokhzad as "bold, imaginative, curious, full of the urge to live, and certainly not afraid of death" in real life as in her poetry (33). She credits her with "revitaliz[ing] Persian poetry by opening up its thematic horizons" attending both to such ordinary topics "as simple as smoking a cigarette and walking home with a basket of fruit, or as complicated as the horrors of intellectual inertia and the intricacies of womanhood" (34). Keshavarz's choice of Farrokhzad is also significant from another respect. As Sanaz Fotouhi has argued, Farrokhzad is often considered the first Iranian woman to "write about her very personal life openly while she was still alive," as reflected in her "autobiographical poems that reflected her unconventional life" (103).

Keshavarz's introduction of Farrokhzad as a source of active agency and empowerment through her poetry and personal life counterpoints neo-Orientalist representations of Iranian women as submissive and oppressed. Interwoven with Keshavarz's narrative of the life and poetry of Farrokhzad and her own reminiscences about the poet are counterhegemonic accounts of the status of women in Iran. In this light, her discussion of Farrokhzad opens up a discursive space wherein the often-unheard-of facts about the active agency of Iranian women in shaping their destiny come to the fore. To further substantiate her account of the status of Iranian women, Keshavarz offers factual and statistical evidence about their active agency in shaping their destiny, thus counterpoising their Orientalist depiction as oppressed victims of Islamic patriarchy:

> Iranian women make up 65 to 70 percent of university students, work in all public offices, and play a vital role in the artistic and intellectual life of the country. It would take an entire book to name and briefly describe the women who have made their mark on Persian poetry and fiction, painting, cinema, photography, hiking, biking, car racing, horse riding, music, scholarship, and more. Yes, women would like to reform electoral law and various other legal codes in Iran to get better representation, and, yes, they are still involved in various struggles to improve their lot. (52)

By referring to Iranian women's "struggles" toward social reformation and greater representation, Keshavarz not only acknowledges the need for reform and improvement but also highlights the active presence of Iranian women in the sociopolitical life of their society.

Focusing on the controversial life, character, and poetry of Farrokhzad, Keshavarz seeks to challenge the neo-Orientalist narratives that negate the fact that "a voice as feminine, strong, and articulate as that of Farrokhzad ever existed in Iran" (36). She refers to Farrokhzad's "passionate love affair with Ibrahim Gulestan, a man to whom she was not married" (34)—an affair that sent shock waves through the society—and discusses how "Farrokhzad celebrated the fullness of her personhood, sexuality included" (34). In so doing, Keshavarz not only offers a fuller picture of Farrokhzad, but also challenges the dominant perception of Oriental/Muslim women as docile sex objects, indicating that they can choose to be as deviant as their Western counterparts.

In the figure of Farrokhzad, Keshavarz sees an iconoclast who not only broke out of the societal and conventional bounds but, more daringly, defied authority and "refused to swallow the national rhetoric of self-worship" (40). When the last shah of Iran decided to revive the "glory" of the ancient Persian Empire, Farrokhzad castigated the pompous and extravagant design via her sarcastic poetry. In her "The Bejeweled Land," she thus wrote:

> O, how comfortable I am
> In the loving arms of the motherland!
> The pacifier of the glorious historical past
> The lullaby of civilization and culture
> And the rattling noise of the ratchet of law
> O, how comfortable I am! (40)

The reference to Farrokhzad's defiance of authoritarianism, in fact, highlights a strong tradition of Iranian women's active political agency, which has continued to date with ever-increasing vigor.

In quoting Farrokhzad, Keshavarz also taps into the repertoire of modern Persian literature, and especially poetry, that defied and challenged both the conventional societal norms as well as authority much more explicitly and daringly than the Western examples offered by Nafisi. So far as Farrokhzad's bold challenging of authority is concerned, it is worth mentioning that contemporaneous with her times, the shah's notorious intelligence agency, SAVAK, was implicated in the death of a number of prominent Iranian intellectuals and artists, which at the time aroused suspicions that the poet's death might also have been a planned murder.

Keshavarz's celebration of Farrokhzad for her novelty of subject and diction, as well as her defiant iconoclasm, is warranted. Her reference to Farrokhzad's rebellion against the monarchy through her poetry serves to undermine both the "golden" image of the pre-revolutionary Iran and the obsession among certain diasporic Iranians with their "glorious" past often perpetuated by the neo-Orientalist narratives.

Apropos Farrokhzad's social iconoclasm, she is often considered the first modern Iranian female poet who has celebrated human corporeality via writing about sexuality, passion, lovemaking, and nudity:

> I sinned a sin full of pleasure,
> In an embrace which was warm and fiery.
> I sinned surrounded by arms
> That were hot and avenging and iron.
> In that dark and silent seclusion
> I looked into his secret-full eyes.
> My heart impatiently shook in my breast
> In response to the request of his needful eyes.[10]

That Farrokhzad still remains one of the most popular female poets in Iran is indubitable. So is also the fact that she has been one of the most outspoken iconoclasts in contemporary Persian poetry and has influenced later generations of poets in Iran. What, however, seems to be absent in Keshavarz's account of Farrokhzad and her appraisal of her poetry is the fact that, especially in the early stages of her career, Farrokhzad owes much of her popularity to the unprecedented physicality of her diction as well as her tragic death at a young age, rather than necessarily to the quality of her poetry. Also, as much as the poet's insistence on the corporeal popularized her, it led to her ostracism as well. In this light, one could argue that—Farrokhzad's novelty, daring, and iconoclasm notwithstanding—she is hardly representative of the sensibilities of Iranian womanhood. In fact, while her audaciousness in divesting herself from accepted literary and social conventions and her treatment of taboo subjects may have appealed to a certain class of readers, they, along with her affair, appalled the more traditionalist, conservative, and religious segments of the society—fact to which, to some measure, Farrokhzad's quick temperament has been attributed (Behbahani). In this light, Simin Behbahani, another prominent contemporary Iranian female poet, recalls how Farrokhzad offended the sensibilities of some "people [who] did not want their daughters to read Forough's poetry" (Behbahani). Significantly, decades after the poet's death, the same sentiments prevail among certain classes of Iranian society and that is one of the reasons Farrokhzad's life and poetry remain both popular and intensely controversial in Iran to date.

From a different perspective yet, Keshavarz can be said to engage in her own mode of social and literary "rebellion" by casting a highly controversial figure as a powerful instance of Iranian women's social and political agency. The gesture is also audacious in that it deems Farrokhzad's poetry as, if not more, significant and "liberating" as her Western counterparts, thus undermining Nafisi's glorification of such English authors as Jane Austen.

My Uncle the Painter: Repainting Iranian Masculinity

Porochista Khakpour, a young Iranian-American novelist, has asserted that in the United States, "there's nothing more sinister or threatening than a Middle Eastern man right now" (qtd.in Pandey). Ergo, after her discussion of Iranian female iconoclasm reflected in a rich and lively contemporary literary tradition in the poetry of Farrokhzad, Keshavarz proceeds to challenge the monolithic construction of Iranian/Muslim masculinity in Orientalist discourses as fanatical, philistine, hypocritical, and sexually depraved, by offering her own counterdiscourse. To this end, she analyzes a subcategory of characters she aptly dubs "The Faceless":

> The Faceless comprise a subcategory of the ugly Muslim men. In a sense, they are the most unfairly treated because they do not have a voice. We do not know their names, nor do we hear them quoted, even indirectly. They are male and are somehow related to one of the girls we have met in the group. We know that these men are cruel and heartless to their female relatives, which has something to do with their religious convictions. (117)

It is because of the descriptions of such "faceless" characters that, in the third chapter of *J&S*, titled "My Uncle the Painter," Keshavarz introduces her maternal uncle to furnish her "brief counter-Orientalist narration of decent Iranian manhood" (65). The uncle is a former army officer whom she describes as incorruptible, delicate, artistic, suave, and intellectually sensitive. The third chapter is packed with narratives of the author's uncle's humility and humanity, as well as his artistic passion reflected in his virtuoso watercolor painting. She describes her uncle in all his human ordinariness, which manifests itself in her reminiscences, such as the times when her uncle "teased us by putting us on his shoulders and simply walking around" (61). Once again, Keshavarz's intention in telling the story of her uncle is to subvert the neo-Orientalist depictions of Iranian/Muslim men as male chauvinists, oppressors, and sexual predators, and to paint a picture that portrays them in their most ordinary circumstances and as normal human beings capable of all the emotions and sensibilities attributed to their Western counterparts. Hence, Keshavarz remarks:

> In the New Orientalist narration of the Middle East, men like my uncle are almost entirely absent . . . [the New Orientalist narrative] presents fathers, brothers, and uncles primarily as a menacing group of people. No doubt Iran has its fair share of cruel, unimaginative, sick, or fanatical people. If that were not the case, it would be an unreal country, an invented place, a fantasy. But when you read about the grasshoppers that darken the sky, you should be given a chance to imagine the stars as well. My uncle is a man from that culture, and a permanent star in my sky. (61)

In the neo-Orientalist accounts of Muslim men, they are most often denied any detailed physical/behavioral description, except that they are menacing, cruel, oppressive, and they remain "a vague, brute force" throughout (63). Keshavarz, however, seeks to subvert such tropes by reflecting on the physical description of her uncle coupled with his sensitivity, humor, humanity, artistry, and affection for his fellow human beings.

Such descriptions of the author's uncle defy those of Muslim men in neo-Orientalist narratives in almost every sense. Nonetheless, she attaches a particular significance to what she thinks may come as a shock to her Western readers, that is, her uncle's devout religiousness (63). Since "New Orientalist" narratives trace almost all the "evils" and "vices" imputed to Muslim men mainly to their religion, Keshavarz takes great pains to illuminate her uncle's religious faith and the role it played in shaping and influencing almost all aspects of his life:

> I can easily describe my often-smiling uncle, and many other fantastic people I know from my life in Iran, as religious. My uncle will tell you himself that his greatest, most fundamental, and most enduring gift is not his talent for painting. It is his love for God. This is a version of love that includes all life. And yes, it is rooted unambiguously in religion. (63)

While Keshavarz describes her uncle as very much a practicing Muslim who "would not miss a single daily prayer at the age of eighty five" (63), she makes it clear that her uncle's religiosity transcends the boundaries of strict ritual observance and is, in fact, rooted in his love for God and, by extension, His creation. For example, Keshavarz demonstrates that his uncle's vision and perception of the religion of Islam was all-embracing enough to hold "Laurel and Hardy, who are neither Muslim nor Iranian" in high esteem and deem them as being "bound to be good people" since "[b]eing able to make others laugh is a gift from God" (66–7).

Keshavarz elaborates that in his "openness, his ability to empathize with those whose beliefs and practices differ from his own," his uncle was "standing on the shoulder of giants" such as Attar of Nishabur[11] and Rumi (67). She thus highlights the fact that her uncle is far from an exception, as some readers might be tempted to believe, and situates him within a long tradition of religious tolerance as promoted by classical Persian poets, many of whom were also renowned religious figures. She recounts how at the time when the Crusaders were "burning young boys at the stake," Attar preached tolerance and an all-encompassing love for all humanity. Through presenting Attar as a symbol of tolerance and unconditional love for all human beings, Keshavarz elucidates the provenance of her uncle's all-embracing religious philosophy. Furthermore, she challenges the dominant Western perception of Islam as a religion driven by intolerance, fanaticism, and violence. This is especially significant since in the aftermath of 9/11 and the ensuing "War on Terror," there was a concerted effort in mainstream Western media to present such terrorist groups as Al-Qaeda and Taliban, and more recently ISIS and Boko Haram, as the "true" embodiments of Islam. Also, in citing the horrors of the Crusades, while stressing that "Christ had never preached war in his life" (67), she is reminding her Western readers of the truism that no religion should be judged by the actions of a few radicals and, therefore, further questions the rampant Islamophobia in the aftermath of 9/11, which has led to further marginalization, demonization, and Othering of Muslims. Keshavarz's commentary on religion is especially pertinent in an era of renewed Islamophobia initiated by Donald Trump, when the then-president of the United States falsely accused US Muslims of "celebrating 9/11"[12] (Kressler) and had no qualms about asserting that "Islam hates us," not to mention many similar inflammatory statements against Islam and Muslims (Johnson and Hauslohner), thereby effectively casting more than 1.8 billion Muslims as the enemy.

In order to contextualize her uncle's emphasis on staying "connected" to God rather than overplaying ritual practice and strict religious propriety, Keshavarz invokes one of the most famous anecdotes from Rumi's *Masnavi*, "Moses and the Shepherd."[13] In this narrative, Moses, overhearing the prayer of a shepherd, reproves him for what he deems to be his inappropriate way of conversing with the Lord, treating Him "as if the Almighty were another shepherd visiting his house" (68). The Almighty, however, seems to disagree with Moses, thus admonishing him for being too obsessed with the aesthetics of relating to God, reminding His Prophet that "[y]ou have come (as a Prophet) in order to connect, not to sever." Besides illuminating the religious tradition—as reflected in classical Persian literature—that has nurtured her uncle's all-inclusive religiosity, through the citation of this well-known anecdote Keshavarz seeks to undermine the portrayal of Islam as an exclusionist, intolerant creed, obsessed with outward appearance and strict ritual observance. Furthermore, Keshavarz is also implicitly criticizing the Western double standard of the pride of place attributed to Rumi as the bestselling poet in the United States, while erasing his Islamic identity and treating him as irrelevant to the Islamic faith and the tolerance and inclusivity that it preaches. This is whereas, as Jawid Mojadeddi has noted, "the universality that many revere in Rumi today comes from his Muslim context" (qtd. in Ali).

With a narrative embedded with stories of religious tolerance and openness, Keshavarz characteristically proceeds, unlike Nafisi, to balance her portrayals of "giant" Muslim classical men both of letters and of the robe:

> Obviously not all Iranians or Muslims share the openness and clarity of vision that Attar and Rumi display. Cultures do not produce giants only. But it is true that many like Attar and Rumi existed, and continue to exist, in the religious culture that these two thinkers represent. This is why the vision of these masters has been cherished and carried forth to our times. How else would my uncle learn to stand on their shoulders and allow his God to grow bigger than his personal closet? (69)

It is such tempering practices that distinguish Keshavarz's memoir from that of Nafisi. In the aforementioned quote, not only does Keshavarz balance her descriptions of major Muslim figures by acknowledging the existence of the inverse, but in so doing, she also acknowledges that such figures "continue to exist" and their legacy has shaped and influenced the lives of many like her uncle. Furthermore, she uses the occasion strategically to embark on her criticism both of the Western "habit" of "not seeing giants like him [Attar] but focus[ing] instead on runts" (69). She also highlights the larger problem of understanding knowledge "almost exclusively in terms of scientific discoveries," which has led to the normalization of ignorance regarding the significance of the issues to which she attempts to draw her readers' attention.

Keshavarz's descriptions of her uncle, therefore, stand in stark contrast to the hypocritical, oppressive, and sexually abusive Muslim men that dominate such narratives as *RLT*. In stressing the religious character of her uncle, Keshavarz challenges the "New Orientalist" tendency to impute and reduce personal vices and wrongdoings to the single cause of one's religion. Furthermore, she not only refutes religious sentiments as the root cause of "evil" behavior among Muslim men in such narratives, but also argues that much in her uncle's amiable character owes to his religious faith:

> My uncle is very much a Muslim. He believes in the human ability to make direct contact with God and in looking for the inner meanings of things rather than obsessing with their thin surface. Acts of worship are therefore a means for getting somewhere. They are not ends in themselves. (63)

Keshavarz's subversion of the "Islamization of wickedness" begins not with the introduction of her uncle, but in fact much earlier on in her narrative.

Explicating the titular "jasmine" in the first chapter of her book, Keshavarz associates the fragrant flower not only with the Muslim faith and prayers, but also with a broader human affection—beauty—and the intimacy with which she was cherished as a young girl in her hometown of Shiraz. She thus reminisces how her grandmother

> would not go back to bed after the dawn prayer. She would walk around the yard, quietly water the plants, and pick little, white jasmine blossoms from the tree ... My grandmother somehow associated these flowers with prayer and collected fresh jasmine to keep inside her prayer rug until the next morning. But she always collected a few extra flowers for us children and left them on our respective pillows right under our sleepy noses. I would wake up first to their scent, then to their white smiles, and finally to the softness of their petals. They were not just jasmines. They were inseparable from grandma and her prayer rug. (15)

As far as depictions of Iranian manhood are concerned, DePaul contends that Keshavarz's descriptions of her uncle, and later her father, do not displace those of Nafisi's "villainous" characters and argues that "Nafisi's dislikable Islamist characters are misunderstood as depictions of Iranian manhood, since her true target is totalitarian ideological extremists of any political party" ("Reviews" 185). Nevertheless, as previously demonstrated in the critique of *RLT*, Nafisi's monochromatic depictions of "villainous" Iranian men are extended to almost all the male characters in her memoir, whether "Islamist" or otherwise, except those who are in various measures associated with the West—ranging from her father to her "magician"—and for whom Nafisi reserves a special liking. What is more, through the medium of her personal and often quite ordinary narratives, Keshavarz illustrates that her uncle's character was not an exception, "but rather the continuation of a norm extending far back into Iran's literary and cultural history," as demonstrated in the cases of Attar and Rumi (Tourage 103).

Shahrnush Parsipur: The Latter-Day Persian Scheherazade

In her review of *Jasmine and Stars*, Amy DePaul has argued that Keshavarz's narrative is at its best when it explicates

> the verse and fiction, respectively, of poet Forough Farrokhzad and novelist Shahrnush Parsipur. The portrait that emerges of these two exciting writers and their work goes a long way toward proving Keshavarz's contention that more than *Lolita* is being read in Tehran, if there was ever any doubt. ("Reviews" 185)

While discussions of Farrokhzad and Parsipur are meant to exemplify and highlight Iranian women's social, political, and literary agency and dynamism, they each have a unique literary significance which might have been overshadowed had Keshavarz decided to introduce them in a single chapter. Moreover, the difference in the genre in which the two women wrote may also serve to explain the decision to discuss each figure separately.

In the fourth chapter of *J&S*, Keshavarz turns to literary analysis of what she considers a "phenomenon in contemporary Persian fiction," namely *Women without Men* (1989), a novella by Shahrnush Parsipur, another influential contemporary Iranian female author. Keshavarz's taxonomic approach in naming the chapter—and the chapter on Farrokhzad, too—is reminiscent of Nafisi's practice in naming the chapters of *RLT* after Western classics or their authors; a fact that makes Keshavarz's narrative partly "a memoir in books," as the subtitle of *RLT* reads. Furthermore, Keshavarz begins her subversion both of the myopic representations and of the larger Orientalist assumptions underlying *RLT* from the titles of her chapters. In the chapter on Farrokhzad, the phrase "The Voice of our Earthly Rebellion" that follows the name of the poet foreshadows not only the "rebellious" nature of the poet and her poetry, but also the possessive pronoun "our" signifies that her "rebelliousness" was, and continues to be, shared by a larger population of Iranian women. Similarly, the phrase "Fireworks of the Imagination" that comes after the title of Parsipur's novella, *Women without Men*, serves to posit the narrative as one characterized by literary novelty, ingenuity, and an imaginative turn of mind. A close reading of the novella corroborates the associations and connotations implied by the phrase in the chapter title, as the power of imagination in Iranian women's personal lives (as well as in their literature) appears as a major leitmotif throughout the narrative.

Keshavarz's meticulous analysis of *Women without Men* serves a threefold purpose. On the one hand, by devoting an entire chapter to the analysis of the work of a contemporary Iranian woman writer, Keshavarz is unsettling the Orientalist assumption of the absence of any significant contemporary literary tradition in Iran. In this light, Keshavarz's introduction of the author is particularly noteworthy:

> Parsipur is a star brightening the way for men and women privileged to read her writings in Persian or in any language into which they have been translated. She is one of the Iranian women writers who wrote before, during, and after the Iranian Revolution of 1979 and lived in Iran until the 1990s. The silence in the New Orientalist narrative about Parsipur and others like her needs to be remedied. Hence my close reading of *Women without Men*, a simple affirmation of her towering presence in contemporary Iranian literature. (106)

Also, through her analysis of *Women without Men*, a novella with Iranian women's resilience and self-empowerment as its narrative centerpiece, Keshavarz is refuting Nafisi's conception of the novel as an essentially Western genre which has failed to flourish in the Eastern hemisphere due to a lack of democratic social and political structures and aspirations. In fact, as Keshavarz remarks, Parsipur's novel remains popular in Iran; it has been translated into English twice,[14] along with some of Parsipur's other major works, and into other languages as well. Finally, through her critique of Parsipur's novel, Keshavarz strikes a balance between her previous discussions of classical Persian literary giants, which, without any contemporary counterpart, may only confirm the Orientalist notion of a rupture in the Persian literary tradition and the lack of any meaningful contribution to Persian literature by contemporary writers, especially by women.

Women without Men is a story of self-discovery, resilience, and imagination pivoting on the lives of several suffering women. Although the women may be initially viewed as beset by conservative and traditionalist social patriarchy, they are by no means identical to Nafisi's hapless victims. Rather, they eventually break out of the social boundaries that constrain them, and forge a new space for themselves—a woman's refuge, as it were—in a garden in the city of Karaj near Tehran, and are all eventually redeemed from their plights in one way or another.

Besides the narrative content that asserts the power of imagination and engages with a wide variety of feminist issues, the novella is significant for the timing of its production and publication. As Keshavarz has pointed out, "this colorful tale of self discovery was written during the same time period highlighted in *RLT*" (105), that is, the first decade after the 1979 revolution, when the new political order, and perhaps the popular literary taste, preferred stories of revolution, sacrifice, and devotion to stories with a strong feminist underpinning.

Reflecting on the concept of imagination, Nafisi thus writes in *RLT* that:

> I have a recurring fantasy that one more article has been added to the Bill of Rights: the right to free access to imagination. I have come to believe that genuine democracy cannot exist without the freedom to imagine and the right to use imaginative works without any restrictions. (338)

Disputing Nafisi's claims of "lack of imagination" in Iran, Keshavarz describes Parsipur's fiction as "brightly imaginative," asserting that Parsipur

> has *personally* given herself the "right to free access to imagination," the article that Nafisi wants to add to the Bill of Rights in her "recurring fantasy" in *Reading Lolita in Tehran* (*RLT*, 338). No, Parsipur's imagination is not a fantasy. It is real. And it is a phenomenon in contemporary Persian fiction. (85)

Keshavarz's choice of Parsipur's work as a contemporary Iranian woman writer is an informed one. It is particularly pertinent since some of Parsipur's major works are colored by a strong element of magic realism which accredits the author as being a pioneer of the genre in Iranian contemporary literary landscape. For example, Munis, one of the main protagonists in *Women without Men*, dies twice and is resurrected each time to continue her journey of self-discovery. Another character, Mahdukht, plants herself in the garden as a tree and gives birth to flowers. The strain of magic realism in *Women without Men*, as well as some of Parsipur's other works, further debunks Nafisi's claims of lack of imagination both in the Iran of the time and in its literary tradition. Notwithstanding, it is important to note that the novella Keshavarz focuses on for the purposes of her counter-narrative, as well as some of Parsipur' other works, share some of the characteristics of neo-Orientalist narratives on Iran.

For instance, even though in its totality *Women without Men* is a far cry from Nafisi's *RLT* in terms of the Orientalist depiction of Iranian culture and Islam, Parsipur's treatment of Iranian masculinity at times suffers from similar oversimplification. A case in point is Amir, one of the major male characters and a seemingly devout young Muslim man, who is characterized by dishonesty, cowardice, and opportunism. He murders his sister for being on the streets by herself for a month, and desires to marry a neighbor's "pretty, soft, quiet, shy, kind, reserved" daughter (*Jasmine and Stars* 89). A second male character, Mr. Gulchehreh, is portrayed as an insensitive, petty man with a "bad temper and antisocial behavior" (*Jasmine and Stars* 98) who, despite his intense love for his wife, is terrified of expressing it to her, fearing that she might never take him seriously or might even leave him. Not only does Mr. Gulchehreh try to conceal his true emotions for his wife, he also teases her for the way she dresses, her appearance, and the fact that she is approaching menopause.

The other men one encounters in the narrative are a truck driver and his assistant, who rape two of the female protagonists—Munis and Faizeh—in a "cold-blooded encounter," as Keshavarz puts it, "made all the more horrible by the fact that the rapists treat it like a stop to get a cup of tea or smoke a cigarette" (*Jasmine and Stars* 96). Therefore, in a vein akin to the dominant neo-Orientalist discourse of Muslim-male chauvinism, *Women without Men* seems to portray a society suffocated by oppressive patriarchalism. Nevertheless, Parsipur departs from a total black-and-white characterization of Iranian masculinity through the introduction of the figure of the only truly "harmless" man in the story, "the good gardener," a "sweet and nurturing" man who "serves and entertains the women but is not a threat" (*Jasmine and Stars* 88). Also, unlike the male characters in *RLT*, the personal vices of Parsipur's characters are attributed to the capacity of human beings for wickedness and malevolence rather than simply to their religious beliefs, perhaps with the exception of Amir. Furthermore, contrary to their counterparts in neo-Orientalist narratives, the women protagonists in Parsipur's novella do not seem to remain eternally "victimized" and eventually manage to break out of the confines imposed upon them by the society. Even more significantly, they do not seek redemption and "liberation" beyond the borders of their country, but rather within themselves, and manage to survive their plights through a combination of their inner resilience, creativity, and empathy for fellow-sufferers.

Keshavarz has responded to the criticism about representations of men in *Women without Men*, arguing that Parsipur's work is "fiction" and, therefore, she is not "chronicling historical incident" (90). Furthermore, she argues, Parsipur's novel is about "human frailty and flaw," and it does not promote a binary and Orientalist perception of the world. Also, she has pointed out that the novella is written shortly after the 1979 revolution, which many predicted would promote patriarchal habits. As such, Parsipur's novel fictionalizes "potential agents or targets of patriarchy" (90).

As convincing as Keshavarz's explanation of what may be viewed as the vilification of men in *Women without Men* may sound, one could still observe a similar pattern running through some of Parsipur's other works. Her other major novel, *Touba and the Meaning of Night* (1987), a quasi-philosophical epic novel of magic realism that explores the changing fortunes of Iranian women, is also tinged by an Orientalist flavor that invests in some clichéd representations both of Iranian manhood and womanhood.

In a vein quite similar to Parsipur's novella, *Touba and the Meaning of Night* is replete with episodes including rape and murder of women by men. Setareh, one of the protagonists, is first raped by Cossack soldiers and then murdered and her body mutilated by her uncle in an act of honor killing. Significantly, the novel was first published in English in 2006 (during the upsurge in the wave of post-9/11 Iranian-American memoirs) by The Feminist Press in the United States and a blurb by Azar Nafisi thus commends the book and its author: "Like Parsipur herself, her protagonists are women whose rebellions are not merely political but existential, against a system that denies them their individual dignity and stunts their potentials for growth" ("Touba and the Meaning of Night"). Ironically, as Keshavarz has argued in *J&S*, Nafisi does all but acknowledge the existence of such imaginative and feminist works in contemporary Persian literary tradition in *RLT*, instead overemphasizing the "liberating" and "empowering" potential of their Western counterparts.

Even though none of Parsipur's fictional works are as nearly deeply entrenched in the discourse of neo-Orientalism as *RLT* and its likes, since their publications in English, they seem to have been co-opted by the dominant Western/native informer feminist discourses as testaments to the oppression of women In Iran. This is evident in some of the reviews on the English translation of *Women without Men*, also published by The Feminist Press in 2004, which are almost identical to the rave reviews written on neo-Orientalist narratives. A 2010 review published on Kirkus Reviews, for instance, proclaims that

> The oppression of women in Iran's male-dominated culture and the power inherent in female solidarity are the themes of Parsipur's ingenious "novel," which is composed of thirteen related stories depicting five abused women whose assertions of their independence take vivid symbolic forms. A girl terrified of sex, for example, becomes a tree in order to retain her virginity; a docile woman killed by her dictatorial brother is reborn, only to be victimized again by a man. ("Women without Men (Review)")

One final point about Keshavarz's commendation of Parsipur and her work warrants attention. Even though Parsipur has contributed to Iran's contemporary literary tradition—especially that of women writers—and has produced works of literary merit, novelty, ingenuity, and significance, the restrictions surrounding the publication of her works and her treatment of controversial taboo subjects in Iran of the 1990s led her to choose self-exile and to seek refuge in the United States, where she now resides (Bashi). Furthermore, like Farrokhzad, at least a part of her fiction has been, and continues to be, received with skepticism and reservation in contemporary Iranian society, for the same reasons mentioned earlier apropos the reception of Farrokhzad's poetry. Nevertheless, none of the criticism offered above confutes the impress Parsipur has left on contemporary Persian fiction, especially those by female authors, nor do they undermine the fact that her oeuvre is a testament to the power of imagination and the resilience of the female protagonists that do not merely survive, but eventually become masters of their own destinies.

The Good, the Missing, and the Faceless: Unmasking Lolita *in the West*

The fourth chapter of *J&S*, "*The Good, the Missing, and the Faceless*: What Is Wrong with *Reading Lolita in Tehran*," initiates an extensive discussion of *RLT* and what the author perceives to be some of its major thematic and representational problematics. Keshavarz reveals the factual inaccuracies of *RLT*, its misrepresentation of things Iranian and Islamic, as well as the total elimination of the native poetic and literary traditions which, according to Nassrin Rahimieh, is "more than equal to the masterpieces of English literature Nafisi posits as the sole source of nourishment for her students in Iran" (535).

One of Keshavarz's major criticisms against *RLT* is its characterization, or what she terms "typological problems" (113). According to Keshavarz, the world of *RLT* is one dominated by "the ugly" and "the faceless," and the peculiar absence of the "missing." Thus, to proffer a fuller picture of the country and counter such a myopic and unbalanced characterization, Keshavarz attempts to offer her own iteration of Iranian men and women—the titular "stars"—who stand in sharp contrast to the evil characters that permeate Nafisi's world, while also acknowledging that "the ugly" do exist in her native culture, as they do in any other culture.

DePaul has argued that while Keshavarz's dissection of *RLT* as "part of an emerging 'New Orientalist' school of writing is intriguing and could have been expanded," she "focuses a little too obsessively on *Reading Lolita*, and this preoccupation becomes grating, a burden on the writing" ("Reviews" 186). Along the same lines, Elisheva Machlis has remarked that:

> Keshavarz's critique is meticulous, and systematically demonstrates how Nafisi's book represents this new Orientalist approach. Nevertheless, this focus on a single publication somewhat undermines Keshavraz's [sic] attempt to deliver a broader message both on Orientalism and on the cultural significance of the Persian literary culture. (104)

While the aforementioned critics' observations are fairly valid, one could argue that the "preoccupation" seems warranted given that the phrase "Reading More Than Lolita in Tehran," as well as the author's expression of intent at the beginning of her book makes it perfectly clear from the very outset that the narrative is intended as a counterhegemonic response to *RLT*. Keshavarz engages with *RLT* precisely because of its unprecedented popularity in the West and its effect on subsequent Iranian-American memoirs and, in so doing, she sets out to address the same audience of readers. This is particularly significant for Keshavarz since she is writing back to a kind of neo-Orientalist "literacy" established, in part, by Nafisi. In other words, *RLT* has exerted such a considerable impact on Middle Eastern, and particularly Iranian-American, life writing that it is hardly an exaggeration to say that it established both the "standard" genre and leitmotifs within which subsequent Iranian-American memoirists had to formulate their works. This is clearly evidenced by the substantial number of Iranian-American memoirs that followed the publication of *RLT* and fairly closely match the narrative's underlying assumptions, representations, and motifs. Nonetheless, one could concur with Dahmen that "as Nafisi's own work is sometimes hampered by the weight of unfamiliar references for non-expert readers, Keshavarz's writing becomes disjointed by interjected comments about *RLT*" (203).

Even though Keshavarz's two self-professed goals in writing *J&S* are to offer her "jasmine and stars" and to point out the intellectual dangers of distorted and partial vision promoted by *RLT* and kindred narratives, her critique of the "New Orientalist" discourse is not solely confined to *RLT*. In fact, through the medium of her personal narratives and experiences in the West, Keshavarz does voice her criticism of an essentially Orientalist perception of the Western-constructed Other, and the ignorance and hatred that it has bred in the West apropos Muslim cultures . Drawing on such narratives, she sets out to critique the all-too-familiar representations of Muslim cultures and to counter Nafisi's characterization of Iranians as fanatical, ignorant, philistine, and sexually obsessed. Furthermore, through the medium of her personal narratives, she invites her Western readers to rethink their perceptions and receptions of such representations, in the same way that she invites them to view Iran through the alternative lens provided by her work.

To elucidate the dangers of the ignorance and the fear promoted by the neo-Orientalist discourse, early in her first chapter, Keshavarz recounts an incident involving her and an ordinary American woman in a local grocery store:

> She was more or less my age, very likely heading home from work, and had similar things in her shopping basket. Our eyes met for a second and we laughed. There was no need to say anything. We almost knew each other's thoughts: "You are tired, too . . . and glad to be heading home!" (16)

Nevertheless, at the mere mention of Keshavarz's Muslim-sounding married name (Karamustafa), the woman's smile gives way to "a mix of discomfort and suspicion" (16). Keshavarz recounts the story to illuminate the ways in which the "master narrative," the voice in the background dictates how the average Westerner should perceive their Oriental/Muslim Other. It can also serve as a counterpoint to Nafisi's depictions of "fanatic" (Muslim) Iranians who beheld things Western with a mixture of suspicion and loathing. Unlike Nafisi, however, Keshavarz does not offer the example of the woman in the supermarket as the quintessential

Westerner. In fact, one could say that as an individual, the woman herself is irrelevant to Keshavarz's argument. Neither does Keshavarz demonize nor ridicule her. Instead, she draws on the incident to raise awareness about the real, greater danger, that is, the dominant discourse that promulgates a particular understanding of the Muslim Other as a "threat" and dictates how to perceive and receive them. The shocking rise in Islamophobia under Donald Trump, not only in the United States but throughout much of the West, is a testament to the urgency and pertinence of Keshavarz's observation about the many perils of the demonizing Orientalist discourse, only one example of which is the massacre of Muslims at prayer in a New Zealand mosque on March 15, 2019.

On another occasion, Keshavarz offers an account of how she and her husband discontinued their decade-old subscription to a major national newspaper for the manner in which it persistently portrayed the situation in the war-torn Iraq. She thus describes how they were

> tired of finding destitute Iraqi peddler women wrapped in black chadors staring from the front page with angry eyes, clearly not pleased with the presence of the photographer. Or, on other days, it might be a toothless, turbaned old man contemplating a bottle of water as if it had dropped from heaven, or a bare Iraqi body laid on the table to be prepared for the "mysterious" Muslim burial ritual. In today's Iraq, one might ask, are there no young children to be found in a school yard, sitting on a bench chatting and laughing? Are there no young Iraqi men and women looking normal and walking in a park somewhere? (51)

By taking issue with representations of Iraq in Western press and posing a rhetorical question about alternative subjects of representation, Keshavarz both criticizes the prevailing clichés of the Muslim world, and draws attention to the role the West, especially the United States, has played in wreaking havoc through an all-destructive war against Iraq and other Muslim countries.

In another seemingly disjointed, but quite pertinent, episode, Keshavarz registers her American friends' shock at a program on NPR about "how in rich parts of the country, Iranian women buy very expensive underwear" (53). The message, according to Keshavarz, is clear: "Look at these hypocritical pious Muslims covering themselves in public. In reality, they are nothing but sex objects to their husbands. They buy the stuff to please men" (53). In this episode, Keshavarz censures the Western sensationalization and exoticization of Muslim women's sexuality, by corroborating her friend's observation that "we sometimes try to make the enemy sound like ourselves. It is our way of coming to terms with differences" (53). Also, she uses the occasion strategically to draw her Western readers' attention to the sexualization of women's bodies and what in this case is a fetishization of their wardrobe in the West. Additionally, her friend's observation is a testament to the Orientalist strategy of the Western projection of certain unpleasant attributes, here the sexualization of the female body, to a faraway Orient. Through the citation of this particular instance, and especially her friend's observation, Keshavarz is counterpoising Nafisi's assertions in *RLT* about Iranians' "obsession" with sexuality. This "obsession" is exemplified in her assertion, among many others, that "our culture shunned sex because it was too involved with it" (304)—a claim that, as previously shown in the discussion of *RLT*, reveals more about Nafisi's obsession with sexuality than the Iranians she chides.

Tea with My Father and the Saints: Re-Portraying the Persian Patriarch

In the final chapter of *J&S*, "Tea with My Father and the Saints," Keshavarz once again resorts to the power of personal narratives of her life in Iran and devotes most of the chapter to descriptions of her personal and intellectual dialogues with her father. It may initially seem that Keshavarz's arrangement of the chapters of *J&S* in her discontinued presentation of the female and male "stars" creates a kind of narrative rupture for the purposes of her memoir. Nevertheless, this discontinuity between the respective discussions of the female and male figures seems well devised and is in line with her intended narrative objectives. In fact, such an arrangement enables Keshavarz to treat each figure on their own merit and as distinct from the other, despite their obvious similarities, and to draws more attention to what makes each figure unique in their own way. While Farrokhzad and Parsipur are both meant to exemplify Iranian women's social, political, and literary agency and dynamism, they each have a unique literary significance that might have been overshadowed had Keshavarz opted for discussing them together in a single chapter. Similarly, while Keshavarz's uncle and father may both share similar human attributes, in giving each of them their own space she has managed to flesh out each character, thereby positing each as a counterexample to Nafisi's male characters.

More than any other chapter in *J&S*, the final chapter serves to humanize ordinary Iranians and Muslims. If Keshavarz represents Farrokhzad and Parsipur as phenomenal writers and iconoclasts, and her uncle as a "saint" and the epitome of "decent Iranian manhood" (66), she does not reserve such complements for her father. In fact, she makes it increasingly clear from the very outset that her father was anything but extraordinary. This is how Keshavarz opens the final chapter of *J&S*:

> I can easily compare my uncle the painter to a saint. In fact, I have a hard time imagining a saint in any other way. My father, by contrast, was not a saint by any stretch of the imagination. He was emotional, demanding, and easily offended. Our relationship, which grew closer in the latter years of his life, always remained stormy. (145)

This depiction of her father in all his ordinariness, in effect, invalidates the misplaced criticism that "no one in Keshavarz's family seems to have any flaws or shortcomings" (Mannani 324).

In depicting a real-life portrait of her father, with all his niceties and less-than-pleasant attributes, Keshavarz acts against the Orientalist penchant for zooming in on the dark side of characters and representing them in stereotypical black-and-white clichés. Her personal differences and disagreements with her father notwithstanding, Keshavarz makes a point of how her father was exceptionally "generous" and how poetry and literature served as an intellectual medium through which they bonded with one another (145). Refuting Nafisi's claims about the lack of literary interest among Iranians, Keshavarz declares that she "never encountered another person with such sensitivity to poetry" as her father (146). Furthermore, her literary dialogues with her father serve to illustrate the fact that literature, and especially poetry, in Iran, are not limited to the literati, and people as ordinary as Keshavarz's father draw on it to educate and bond with their children. Thus, it can be observed that much like Nafisi, Keshavarz capitalizes on the power both of personal narratives and literature to drive her message home. It could be safely argued that through her reminiscences and literary discussions, Keshavarz effectively demonstrates her firm belief in the transcendental, empowering, and nourishing potential of literature much more than Nafisi does in *RLT*, with the difference that the literature she promotes is indigenous and originates from a rich tapestry of Perso-Islamic culture. Additionally, while Nafisi capitalizes on Western classics and invokes such characters as Humbert Humbert to demonize Iranian men, Keshavarz taps into both classical and contemporary Persian literature to not only give voice to those rendered voiceless in Nafisi's narrative, but also to show that human vices and virtues are far from exclusive to particular cultures and civilizations, thus effectively dismissing the Orientalist binarism on which narratives such as *R LT* are founded.

Reading Beyond *Jasmine* and *Stars*

Due to its comparatively much less controversial narrative content, unlike *RLT*, Keshavarz's memoir has neither been put on a pedestal nor come under considerable criticism. The only exception, however, has been Manijeh Mannani's trenchant critique of *J&S*, in which she claims, among other things, that "'the true self' is disguised by the subject more in Keshavarz's memoir than by Nafisi in *RLT*", and that "Keshavarz's response to Nafisi is far from objective and realistic" (322). Mannani also accuses Keshavarz of having made the "boastful and naive claim to have written *J&S* with the aid of an unfailing memory" which "only undermines the sincerity and authenticity of her response to *RLT*" (322). Mannani's strident points of contention with Keshavarz smack of an ad hominem attack on both Keshavarz and her work and are at best largely misplaced and misconceived.

To begin with, Keshavarz does not even hint at the possession of an "unfailing memory" let alone "boast" of it, and Mannani fails to provide any quotes or references to back up her assertion. The question of authenticity, especially as regards narratives that rely on authorial memory, is a common, and indeed highly controversial, one. In her review of *J&S*, Amy DePaul has asked an apt question:

"How are one person's reminiscences to be judged more definitive than another's?" ("Reviews" 185). As far as Nafisi's representations in *RLT* are concerned, it was previously shown how many of the assertions made in *RLT* proved to be either historically unsound or too exaggerated, the authenticity of which were further undermined not only by the self-professed alterations the author has introduced in her narrative, but also by her dubious political affiliations, which at times make her work border on neo-conservative propaganda. Keshavarz, on the other hand, makes far less controversial assertions in her work, and her reminiscences are more of a personal and intimate nature, even when she discusses prominent contemporary figures in Persian literature. Regardless of the nature of the statements Nafisi and Keshavarz make in their works, accusing Keshavarz of claiming an infallible memory is simply inaccurate.

Equally unfounded is Mannani's criticism that in *J&S* "[o]n the one hand, there is the beautification of Iranian culture, and on the other, the demonization of anyone who criticizes it" (322). Once again, Mannani's contention remains at the level of unsubstantiated generality and misplaced allegation. One could argue that Keshavarz's focus on her more pleasant reminiscences as well as the more appealing facets of Iranian society and culture is anything but unjustified. In the introduction to *J&S*, Keshavarz very clearly states her belief that readers "deserve to partake of the peaceful and enriching gifts that Iran has to offer" (7) and expressly enunciates the reason behind the writing of her work:

> Too many good things fall through the cracks in many books written about the country of my birth and the people who nurtured me. So I have decided to write one that focuses on the good things, one that gives voice to what has previously been silenced and overlooked. (15-16)

Keshavarz further accounts for her approach to the representation of her native culture in an interview, remarking that "I do not add more villains to the picture for the simple reason that there is an abundance of them in view already" ("Jasmine and Stars: An Interview"). Even so, Mannani has taken the aforementioned quotation not as a clear expression of authorial intention to shed light on what the author deems to be overlooked, silenced, and marginalized about her home country, which sounds justified in light of the prevalent demonization of Iran and Islam, but rather as evidence that Keshavarz "ignorantly or even naively, admits her highly selective approach" (325). It is apt to stress here that like any other text that bears the title "memoir," the authors are always bound to make choices, consciously or otherwise, about what they set out to represent. Furthermore, one could observe in *J&S* that Keshavarz's "positive" views of her native country and Islam are still tempered and humanized (as, for example, seeing the faults in the character of her father) to minimize the risk of idealization and "beautification."

Even though Keshavarz's narrative is profoundly personal, it opens up new vistas to the culture, religion, and specifically literature of the country of her origin and even the country of her residence (the United States). It also serves as a significant reminder of how crucial it is to read various and contrasting narratives when trying to understand a place, particularly one as controversially differently portrayed as Iran (DePaul, "Reviews" 186). Thus, addressing her readers directly, Keshavarz benefits from her own gift of poetic voice and, perhaps reflecting Nafisi's narrative strategy, weaves intimately personal reminiscences into her discourse. She does this both to offer her gifts of jasmine and stars to her Western readers and to "legitimize her case against Nafisi" (Machlis 104). While both Nafisi and Keshavarz believe in what Nasrin Rahimieh has termed "the salutary function of the life of letters," contrary to Nafisi, Keshavarz adamantly illustrates that years of revolution and war have all but banished her Iranian compatriots from the realm of the letters (535).

Keshavarz's strategy in presenting her "stars" is consistently effective. Through weaving her narrative with those of the figures she presents, she grafts the voices of her "stars," especially the women authors she introduces, onto her own and thus not only advances her criticism of a "New Orientalist" discourse, but also provides a space for those figures to be seen and to make their impact on the intended Western audience. In other words, contrary to Nafisi's memoir which serves to silence the aspirations and achievements of Iranian women through a persistent negation strategy, *J&S* operates as a space within which the literary, social, and political dynamism of Iranian women are illustrated through Keshavarz's affirmation approach. The fact that the English translations of both Farrokhzad and Parsipur are finding a broader readership in the United States today is a testament to both the necessity and the significant impact of the space that such narratives as Keshavarz's provide.

Throughout her narrative Keshavarz manages to decouple the Orient (in this case both Iran and Islam) from the tragedy and crisis perpetually imputed to it in the West. She achieves this dissociation by offering her "jasmine and stars" and at times by counterpoising a similar human tragedy and crisis in the Western Hemisphere. In so doing, she elucidates the fact that not only are such calamities not exclusive to Muslim or Eastern countries, but they are, in actual fact, in many cases either precipitated or fully supported by Western powers. One can refer to the wars in Iraq and Afghanistan, and more recently in Syria and Yemen, where Western support for regional dictatorships such as Saudi Arabia, belligerent states such as the Israeli regime occupying Palestinian territories, or terrorist groups such as ISIS has led to the massacre of innocent civilians, annihilation of entire cities, and displacement of millions of their inhabitants.

In presenting Farrokhzad and Parsipur as powerful voices of native women's literature and agents of social activism, she effectively decouples Iranian women from the Orientalist notions of oppression, docility, victimhood, and the need for their liberation through Western intervention. In the humaneness of her uncle and the human ordinariness of her father, she manages to decouple Iranian men from the male-chauvinism, fanaticism, and violence attributed to them by the "master narrative" exemplified by *RLT*. Similarly, by choosing to focus on such Persian literary giants as Attar and Rumi and their all-embracing, openhearted religious philosophies, she seeks to dissociate Islam from the violence and intolerance by which it has come to be known in the West. That is why it is fair to say that *J&S* ultimately transcends a critique of *RLT* by presenting "its own rich and complex account of lives blended with religion and culture" (Tourage 103). Furthermore, apart from the literary giants Keshavarz discusses, she introduces to her readers such towering contemporary Iranian figures as Simin Behbahani (literature), Mohammad Reza Shafi'i-Kadkani (literature), Abdulkarim Soroush (philosophy), Shirin Ebadi (law; Nobel Laureate), Abbas Kiarostami (cinema), Tahmineh Milani (cinema), Rakhshan Bani Itemad (cinema), and Mohsen Makhmalbaf (cinema) (124–6)—figures some of whom are among the most outspoken critics of the Islamic Republic. Although these figures remain conspicuously absent in neo-Orientalist narratives on Iran, they are part and parcel of Iranian society and culture and their works and contributions to the Perso-Islamic culture of the country are powerful testaments to the vibrancy and dynamism of the Iranian cultural and political landscape.

It is apt to conclude Keshavarz's resistant narrative by returning to Said's discussion of resisting hegemony. In his *Culture and Imperialism*, Said thus asseverates that

> Never was it the case that the imperial encounter pitted an active Western intruder against a supine or inert non-Western native; there was always some form of active resistance, and in the overwhelming majority of cases, the resistance finally won out. (xii)

Jasmine and Stars has certainly not been as popular and enthusiastically received as *RLT*, since, among other things, it does not cater to the expectations of a mass market used to Orientalist tales of exoticism and female victimhood from the Middle East. Also, it lacks the timing and promotion factors that significantly kept *RLT* on top of the bestseller list in the United States. Nonetheless, if the reviews by both literary critics and readers are any indication, Keshavarz's narrative has been successful in its "invitation to see beyond fear." As a narrative of resistance against the prevalent Western Orientalist discourse, it remains a significant pioneering work in writing about Iran and Islam—a narrative that transcends and pierces the dark world of *RLT* and other neo-Orientalist tales and opens a window out to a multihued vista fragrant with jasmine and bright with stars.

Chapter 5

TOWARD AN AMBIVALENT FUTURE

Change does not roll in on the wheels of inevitability, but comes through continuous struggle. And so we must straighten our backs and work for our freedom. A man can't ride you unless your back is bent.
        Martin Luther King, Jr.; "The Death of Evil upon the Seashore"

This book aimed to offer a critique of the representations of contemporary Iran and Islam through the analysis of three paradigmatic texts written by contemporary female authors. Throughout the book, I demonstrated how the narratives in question were conditioned by such momentous historical junctures as the 1979 Islamic Revolution, the Iran–Iraq War, the Hostage Crisis, and 9/11. Such historical specificity goes a long way toward distinguishing these narratives from other hyphenated American memoirs published in the United States—narratives that mostly invest in the question of nostalgia, belonging, and homeland, and that their ideological and political implications are not as strong as those of what in this book I have been calling neo-Orientalist narratives. Investigating the representations of Iran, especially Iranian womanhood, in the first two texts revealed how such representations operate within the framework of an Orientalist episteme apropos Iran, and how they can be co-opted for promoting certain interventionist political agendas in the so-called Muslim World.

The critical perusal of Betty Mahmoody's *NWMD* as one of the bestselling, most translated, and earliest contemporary Orientalist memoirs on Iran revealed the manner in which the text extensively appropriates the deeply entrenched tradition of American captivity narratives to narrate the "true" story of a white American woman and "her" daughter entrapped in the land of the "savages," where "life was primitive under the best of conditions" (379). Mahmoody's eventual purported "escape" from Iran renders her saga as a captivity narrative of trauma, escape, and return to the "civilized world": this final phase of the narrative is melodramatically encapsulated in Mahtob's elation at seeing the stars and stripes: "'Mummy, look. Look!' She pointed to the American flag, waving freely in the wind" (416). Mahmoody's alleged escape and her return underpin the Orientalist-feminist binary of the free Western woman vis-à-vis her victimized Muslim counterparts who are apparently destined to remain haplessly, and endlessly, oppressed, if not liberated by the West or their "free" Western sisters. While Mahmoody returns to the sanctuary of the "free world," apparently through the benefaction of her Westernized Iranian friends, the many "oppressed" Iranian women seem to remain "captive" within a three-tier oppressive structure: "imprisoned" within the geographical boundaries of their country, ensnared in a social structure predicated upon male chauvinism, and, on a much deeper level, captives of an "authoritarian" religion that has subdued them apparently beyond any hope of redemption.

While Betty Mahmoody toured the world, promoting her tale, and increasingly earning more money and fame, Sayed Bozorg Mahmoody remained a man who was internationally defamed beyond redemption, separated from his daughter for the rest of his life, and eventually died on August 23, 2009, his side of the story never heard the way it should have been.

The striking thematic consanguinity between Azar Nafisi's *Reading Lolita in Tehran* and Mahmoody's memoir, despite the authors' extremely different backgrounds, is perhaps the best testament to one of the principal denominators of (neo-)Orientalist narratives, that is, their internal consistency. As Said maintains in his *Orientalism*:

> The phenomenon of Orientalism ... deals principally, not with a correspondence between Orientalism and Orient, but with the internal consistency of Orientalism and its ideas about the Orient ... despite or beyond any correspondence, or lack thereof, with a "real" Orient. (5)

Hence, Nafisi's memoir was shown to recycle the underlying topoi of Mahmoody's captivity narrative while transposing them into the context of a women's book club of sorts and the seemingly sophisticated modus operandi of English literature. The conspicuous kinship between representations of Iran/Islam by Nafisi and Mahmoody, the former's work the product of post-9/11 era and the latter's post–Islamic Revolution, attests not only to the protean and multifarious nature of Orientalism, but also to the pride of place it enjoys in all constructions of Otherness in mainstream social, political, and literary Western discourses.

In a similar fashion, like Mahmoody, whose alleged escape to the "civilized world" marked her eventual redemption, Nafisi—and by extension her "girls"—seems to become truly "liberated" only after she becomes a denizen of the United States and can narrate her story for the Western world. Nafisi's idea of the liberation of Iranian women, as demonstrated in Chapter 3, is well aligned with those of the neoconservative clique in the United States—a lucrative affiliation which both made possible the publication of *RLT* and was conducive to the vigorous promotion of the memoir and its author in the United States. Phil Wilayto's observation in this regard is worth quoting:

> It should come as no surprise that a secular, upper-class university professor, reared and educated in the West, might resent the dress codes imposed on her by a government she despises. That's an honest opposition.

But to take three-quarters-of-a-million dollars from right-wing, anti-working class, neocon foundations to paint a patently false picture of a society that is now under direct military threat by the most powerful country in the world – and to portray yourself as only concerned about women's rights when you know the real issue is who controls the vast oil wealth of the country – that's not honest. (*In Defense* 142)

Significantly, despite its deep investment in personal revelation (for an Iranian-American memoir, at least) and the author's international fame as the author of *RLT*, Nafisi's next book, *Things I've Been Silent About* (2008), which recounts the story of Nafisi's mother and the author's troubled relationship with her, has not been even remotely as successful or well-received in the West as *RLT*.[1] Not only does this further testify to the power of Orientalist discourse and the reader's expectations of a good Oriental(ist) tale, but it also proves the significance of the timing of production and the political zeitgeist of the time that catapulted both Mahmoody's and Nafisi's memoirs onto the bestseller list.

Writing within the framework of the established mainstream discourse not only on, but also *against*, Iran has brought both Mahmoody and Nafisi enormous fortune and publicity.[2] In fact, the statement made by Nafisi's "magician" in RLT that "[s]o many people have made their name through their opposition to the regime" (181) could not be more ironic. Nafisi's horror stories about the "Islamic Republic" keep resurfacing in her later works, despite their seeming contextual detachment from the politics of post-revolutionary Iran. Nafisi's latest work, *The Republic of Imagination: America in Three Books* (2014), an account, apparently, of the author's reflection "on her lifelong love for Western literature through an exhilarating exploration of three American classics" (as the praise on the *Oprah Magazine* has it), opens with yet another account of the arrest of one of Nafisi's fans, his imprisonment, and flogging in post-revolutionary Iran. Nafisi thus concludes the paragraph describing the alleged imprisonment: "There was no denying that a normal day in the life of a young Iranian is very different from that of most young Americans" (1). The use of the term "most" could not have been more judicious; certainly there are more than a few African-Americans, Muslim Americans, and immigrants who would have been slightly disappointed had Nafisi not hedged the claim.

Nafisi's (and Mahmoody's) memoir, as well as many kindred Iranian-American memoirs, tally well with Marandi and Pirnajmuddin's observation that "[i]n the market for such 'memoirs,' the tellers of these modern 'oriental tales' or 'memories' feel sure that anything sells—and the more sensational the stuff, the better it sells and the more 'popular' it gets" (41). In her *To See and See Again: A Life in Iran and America* (1999), Tara Bahrampour, the author of one of the few pre-9/11 Iranian-American memoirs, describes how her mother, who had written a fictional narrative about a woman whose innocent husband is executed in revolutionary Iran, was approached by an American publisher who wanted "to know if Mama will go on TV and say it's true" (143). As another instance, Anita Amirrezvani and M. Persis Karim have related a similar experience happening to one of the authors contributing to their co-edited 2013 anthology, *Tremors*:

> One of the writers in our anthology recently relayed that she'd had so much trouble getting a book contract because her novel portrays a mother-daughter relationship and an extremely loving Iranian father. She was asked by an interested publisher, via her agent, to change some of the characters so that they'd conform to a view of Iranian men as oppressive, domineering, and violent. She refused and said that that would not be her story. As a result, she had to shop the novel for an additional two years in order to find a publisher. This is just one of many examples in which publishers and agents have an expectation about how Iranian men, and narratives about Iran, in general, should reflect some of our own media stereotypes. (qtd. in Wilson)

Nafisi's "true" account is further underpinned by her misplaced arrogation to academic excellence: "I am too much of an academic: I have written too many papers and articles to turn my experiences and ideas into narratives without pontificating" (*Reading Lolita* 266). Professor Hamid Dabashi has rightly observed that prior to *RLT* Nafisi lacks the credit of "a single credible book or scholarly credential to her name other than *Reading Lolita in Tehran*" ("Native Informers") and that it has been her "career opportunism" that has "led her to [the] corridors of power" (Dabashi, "Lolita and Beyond").

As the only major narrative of resistance discussed in the book, Fatemeh Keshavarz's pioneering *Jasmine and Stars* manages to fulfill the promises it makes in its Introduction: it offers the Western readers much food for thought and an alternative vantage point through which they are invited to revisit the dominant Orientalist perceptions about various Others constructed by the West at different times for different purposes. By adopting the structural and thematic denominators of Iranian-American narratives, Keshavarz embarks on her counter-narrative. Ultimately transcending a mere critique of Nafisi's memoir, Keshavarz writes back to the dominant Western grand narratives on the Oriental Other both by laying bare their underlying flaws and assumptions and by crafting a space wherein her voice of resistance, along with those of the "stars" she introduces, begins to emerge. Unlike Nafisi's women, the women in Keshavarz's narrative seek no benevolent outside liberator, be it literary or military. Being quite cognizant of their social, political, and religious rootedness, they strive to break free from restrictive societal confines.

Even though changing the dominant perceptions of any nation is a Herculean task, if not impossible, Keshavarz seems to have raised some new measure of critical awareness by drawing attention to the complexities, nuances, and intricacies of cultures. In an interview about her book and its reception in the United States, Keshavarz related that

> Readers—exposed only to negative news on Iran—are amazed at how imaginative, vibrant, and articulate contemporary Iranians can be . . . This is most shocking in the case of women writers and artists. For example, I have a chapter dedicated to the writer Sharhnush Parsipour and the novel she wrote after the 1979 revolution, *Women Without Men* . . . I receive daily e-mails from

people who want to read more of Parsipour's writing. ("Jasmine and Stars: An Interview")

Keshavarz redoubles her efforts in presenting a more realistic picture of Iran by maintaining a blog, *Windows on Iran: Explorations of Persian Culture and Politics*,[3] in which she offers nuanced cultural and political commentary on mostly contemporary Iranian affairs, à la *Jasmine and Stars*.

The completion of the first iteration of this book coincided with the landmark accord, known as the Joint Comprehensive Plan of Action (JCPOA), between Iran and the P5+1 over Iran's nuclear program. Most interestingly, soon after the deal, images of Iran as a land ripe for Western commercial investment began to emerge in Western media and in the discourse of Western politicians, once again reminding one of Said's *locus classicus,* "the East as career" (*Orientalism* 5), which he borrowed from Benjamin Disraeli's *Tancred* (1847). Along the same lines, images of chic, young Iranian women celebrating the "historic" deal became more prevalent in popular media, temporarily replacing the images of "angry mobs," executions, and "mad mullahs." Alas, I wrote in the Conclusion to the first iteration of this book that

> Whether this recent political rapprochement would herald a change both in the relationship between Iran and the United States, as well as the broader representations of Iran, could only be a matter of wild speculation and wishful thinking for the present. If the deal and its myriad implications for both countries do influence the dominant perceptions of Iran, it would be a worthwhile suggestion for further research on representations of Iran.

On May 8, 2018, US president Donald Trump shredded the deal that was hardly ever fully implemented in any meaningful way under President Barack Obama. While there was really no change in the Orientalist images of Iran perpetuated through mainstream Western media, there was a rather significant change in how the West, particularly the United States, is viewed in Iran. Perhaps more than ever before, the terms "unreliable," "untrustworthy," "disingenuous", and "arrogant" came to be associated with the United States and its European allies. Perhaps the greatest irony of the US violation of the deal is that US officials in both Obama and Trump administrations had been going out of their way to frame the Iranian party as unreliable and given to deception, as reflected in the outrageous statement by Wendy Sherman, US undersecretary of state under President Obama, in a testimony to the US Senate Foreign Relations Committee, that "deception is part of the [Iranians'] DNA." Trump's withdrawal from the deal, along with his many other hostile, xenophobic, and Islamophobic actions and stands, also served to reinforce the trope of the United States as the "Great Satan" in Iranian popular and political discourse.

Since the deal was neither fully implemented nor lasted long enough, it is not possible to study whether the representations of Iran (and Islam) have undergone any meaningful change post-JCPOA and post-US withdrawal. There are, however, areas in Iranian-American self-narratives and life writing that still remain understudied. It is important, for example, to investigate the few memoirs produced in the aftermath of the controversial 2009 presidential elections in Iran,[4] to gauge any possible significant generic or thematic distinction or diversion from other post-9/11 Iranian-American memoirs. It would also be worthwhile to juxtapose memoirs written by Iranian men with the ones written by Iranian women to see if gender politics play any significant role in the manner of representation.

Insofar as mainstream representations of Iran and Islam, as critiqued in this book, are concerned, one cannot but concur that they are a woeful testament to both the hegemony and legacy of Orientalism and its progeny. However, such modes of representation also speak volumes about a mindset that makes such representations possible in the first place. It is, therefore, apt to conclude this book with Said's lament in his *Culture and Imperialism* that the power and predominance of such representations bear witness to the fact that "we face as a nation the deep, profoundly perturbed and perturbing question of our relationship to others—other cultures, states, histories, experiences, traditions, peoples, and destinies" (55).

NOTES

Chapter 1

1 The exonym Persia was the official name of Iran used in the Western world until 1935. In March 1935, Reza Shah Pahlavi, the penultimate shah of Persia, issued a decree asking foreign delegates to use the term "Iran" (meaning "the land of Aryans") in formal correspondence. Nowadays both terms are employed in different contexts in the West. While "Persia" and "Persian" are more commonly used in historical and cultural contexts, and to invoke the sense of the country's ancientness, "Iran" is used mostly in political and Islamic ones, or in relation to the country's contemporary history.
2 Even though such images of Persia/Iran have been supplanted by the stereotypes of Iranians as backward, fanatic, and violent, they have not vanished completely from view and have reappeared in new forms and contexts. One such context is the representations of wealthy Iranian-Americans, especially those living in Los Angeles. For example, Porochista Khakpour (2010) refers to the movie *Clueless* (1995) and observes how "pointing to a cloud of Cartier, Armani and Aqua Net," the main character, Cher, declares "And that's the Persian mafia. You can't hang with them unless you have a BMW."
3 The dominance of such representations of Persia in the Western discourse notwithstanding, they were at times interrupted by representations that were not as negatively stereotypical. For instance, we read in Sir John Malcolm's *Sketches of Persia* (1849) that Persians "are the most cheerful people in the world; and they delight in familiar conversation . . . Poets, historians, astrologers, wits, and reciters of stories and fables who have acquired eminence, are not only admitted into the first circles, but honoured" (66–7).
4 Morier's other works include his travelogues *A Journey through Iran, Armenia and Asia Minor to Constantinople in the years 1808 and 1809* (1812), and its sequel *A Second Journey through Iran to Constantinople between the years 1810 and 1816* (1818). His other literary works *The Adventures of Hajji Baba of Ispahan in England* (1828), followed by *Zohrab the Hostage* (1832), *Ayesha the Maid of Kars* (1834), and *The Mirza* (1841) all engage with Persia and its people in one way or another.
5 This Western interpretation of the Islamic Revolution overlooked the fact that Islam had always remained an essential part of the Iranian society and national identity, and is a further testament to the prevalent ignorance of the West regarding its Muslim Other.
6 The former travelogue purports to recount the author's travels to the four mentioned countries to observe the workings of Islam in the fabric of the society. The latter alleges to be an investigation on the theme of "conversion" in the four non-Arab Muslim countries.
7 Such representations by Naipaul are not limited to Muslim countries and also appear in his writings on Africa, India, and the West Indies, too.

8   Notable in this category are the works of Nahid Rachlin, one of the pioneers of Iranian-American literature. Most of Rachlin's works, such as *Foreigner* (1978), *Married to a Stranger* (1983), and *The Heart's Desire* (1995), were published prior to the post 9/11 wave of Iranian-American writing.

9   Later, Donald Trump drew on the September 11 attacks to propagate his own version of Islamophobia, falsely accusing US Muslims of celebrating 9/11.

10 These collections are *A World Between: Poems Short Stories and Essays by Iranian Americans* (1999), *Let Me Tell You Where I've Been: New Writing by Women of the Iranian Diaspora* (2006), and *Tremors: New Fiction by Iranian American Writers* (2013).

11 The first Iranian female autobiography is often credited to the Princess Tāj-al-Salṭana (1884–1936), the daughter of the Qajar king Nāṣer-al-Din Shah. The controversial *Khāterāt* (meaning, the memoirs), whose authenticity some scholars have questioned, was written in 1914 and was first partially published in 1969 in Persian and later translated into English in 1994.

12 Philippe Lejeune has also argued that the memoir does not share the "subject treated" element of the autobiography, which he defines as "individual life, story of a personality" (4).

13 Published in the United States under the title *Honor Lost*.

14 Among such writers are Tara Bahrampour (*To See and See Again*, 1999), Azaddeh Moaveni (*Lipstick Jihad*, 2005; *Honeymoon in Tehran*, 2009), Porochista Khakpour (*Sons and Other Flammable Objects*, 2007), Jasmine Darznik (*The Good Daughter*, 2011; *Song of a Captive Bird*, 2018; *The Bohemians*, 2021), Davar Ardalan (*My Name is Iran*, 2007), Ava Homa (*Echoes from the Other Land*, 2010), and Afschineh Latifi (*Even After All This Time*, 2005). There are many other senior Iranian-American writers, such as Azar Nafisi (*Reading Lolita in Tehran*, 2003; *Things I've Been Silent About*, 2008; *The Republic of Imagination: America in Three Books*, 2014), Fatemeh Keshavarz (*Jasmine and Stars: Reading More Than Lolita in Tehran*, 2007), Nahid Rachlin (*Jumping over Fire*, 2005; *Persian Girls*, 2006), Roya Hakkakian (*Journey From the Land of No*, 2004), and Nesta Ramazani (*Dance of the Rose and the Nightingale*, 2002) who published their first or major works after 9/11.

15 As famous instances of such television programs and series one can refer to "Sex and the City," "Dr. Phil," and the myriad "The Moment of Truth"-style game shows.

16 These articles are: *Islam, Orientalism, and the West: An Attack on Learned Ignorance*, published in "Times" (1979); *Islam Through Western Eyes*, published in "The Nation" (1980); *Iran and the Press: Whose Holy War?*, published in "Columbia Journalism Review" (1980); and *Inside Islam: How the Press Missed the Story in Iran*, published in "Harper's Magazine" (1981).

17 Evelyn Alsultany argues that in the aftermath of the Hostage Crisis the conflation of Iranians with Arabs was reinforced and "Iran came to stand for Arabs, the Middle East, Islam and terrorism, all of which terms came to be used interchangeably" (9).

18 Some notable studies in this category are, chronologically, Nilou Mostofi's *Who We Are: The Perplexity of Iranian-American Identity* (2003); Babak Elahi's *Translating the Self: Language and Identity in Iranian-American Women's Memoirs* (2006); Amy Malek's *Memoir as Iranian Exile Cultural Production: A Case Study of Marjane Satrapi's "Persepolis" Series* (2006); Jasmine Darznik's *The Perils and Seductions of Home: Return Narratives of the Iranian Diaspora* (2008); Liora Hendelman-Baavur's *Guardians of New Spaces: "Home" and "Exile" in Azar Nafisi's Reading Lolita in Tehran, Marjane Satrapi's Persepolis Series and Azadeh Moaveni's Lipstick Jihad* (2008);

Amy Motlagh's *Towards a Theory of Iranian American Life Writing* (2008); Gillian Whitlock's *From Tehran to Tehrangeles: The Generic Fix of Iranian Exilic Memoirs* (2008); Nima Naghibi's *Revolution, Trauma, and Nostalgia in Diasporic Iranian Women's Autobiographies* (2009); Amy Motlagh's *Autobiography and Authority in the Writings of the Iranian Diaspora* (2011); and Farzaneh Milani's *Iranian Women's Life Narratives* (2013).

19 Some of the major responses to Nafisi's *RLT* include, chronologically, Roksana Bahramitash's *The War on Terror, Feminist Orientalism and Orientalist Feminism: Case Studies of Two North American Bestsellers* (2005); Hamid Dabashi's *Lolita and Beyond* (2006); Mitra Rastegar's *Reading Nafisi in the West: Authenticity, Orientalism, and "Liberating" Iranian Women* (2006); Firoozeh Papan-Matin's *Reading (and Misreading) Lolita in Tehran* (2007); Catherine Burwell's *Reading Lolita in Times of War: Women's Book Clubs and the Politics of Reception* (2007); John Carlos Rowe's *Reading Reading Lolita in Tehran in Idaho* (2007); Catherine Burwell, Hilary E. Davis, and Lisa K. Taylor's *Reading Nafisi in the West: Feminist Reading Practices and Ethical Concerns* (2008); Amy DePaul's *Re-Reading Reading Lolita in Tehran* (2008); Anne Donadey and Huma Ahmed-Ghosh's *Why Americans Love Azar Nafisi's Reading Lolita in Tehran* (2008); Seyed Mohammed Marandi's *Reading Azar Nafisi in Tehran* (2008); and Asha S.'s *Reading Lolita in Tehran: Rehashing Orientalist Stereotypes* (2009).

20 From this category some noteworthy titles are Kate Flint's *Women and Reading* (2006); Simon Hay's *Why Read Reading Lolita? Teaching Critical Thinking in a Culture of Choice* (2008); Georgiana Banita's *Affect, Kitsch and Transnational Literature: Azar Nafisi's Portable Worlds* (2009); and Jodi Melamed's *Reading Tehran in Lolita: Seizing Literary Value for Neoliberal Multiculturalism* (2011).

21 In her thesis, Saljoughi positions her argument at the interface between representation, race, and immigration and investigates how "a discourse of racialized whiteness that is a feature and governing principle of Western immigration" can contribute to an "attempt to control and 'liberate' the Muslim migrant subject" (iii).

22 Through the examination of the works of Azar Nafisi and Ayaan Hirsi Ali, Zarei Toossi demonstrates "how a variety of Muslim narratives in English problematize the perception of religiosity as always being a result of the imposition of external forces that are invariably oppressive or politically charged."

23 Amiri's dissertation argues that "post-9/11 narratives by Iranian women represent Iran via similar frameworks of knowledge and a similar set of questions and that these questions and approaches are conditioned by a historical moment that has made the sudden appearance of these texts possible."

24 Ghasemi Tari's important study is the only dissertation that, besides offering a discourse analysis of certain Iranian-American memoirs, also engages with academic knowledge production on Iran through an in-depth examination of the journal *Iranian Studies*. In her study, Ghasemi investigates the interconnectedness of academic and popular texts on post-revolutionary Iran, elucidating the manner in which the two discourses converge "by reproducing, reaffirming and recycling the stereotypical image of post-revolutionary Iran."

25 Darznik claims that her study offers "the first full-length study of Iranian immigrant literature" (iii).

26 This dissertation has been published as *The Literature of the Iranian Diaspora: Meaning and Identity since the Islamic Revolution* (2015) and, like Darznik's study,

offers a broader survey of Iranian-American literary landscape, rather than focusing on individual works.

27 Even though Marjane Satrapi's *Persepolis* series (a *Bildungsroman* of sorts) has been a major bestselling title in Iranian memoirs written in the West, it has not been considered in this study for several reasons. First, Satrapi (and her "memoirs") does not belong to the category of Iranian-American literature. Persepolis was originally written in French in 2000 and translated into English in 2003. Also, *Persepolis* is a graphic memoir and, as such, does not share the formal characteristics of the works critiqued in this study. More importantly, Satrapi's memoir does not display the thematic and representational complexities of Nafisi's *Reading Lolita in Tehran* and, therefore, could not be selected as the iconic post-9/11 memoir.

28 A cinematic adaptation of the narrative by the same title ensued in 1991, directed by Brian Gilbert and starring Sally Field and Alfred Molina.

29 Since Orientalism, as a mode of Western knowledge production operating through the recycling of stereotypes, makes it possible to "know" the Orientals.

Chapter 2

1 In the interest of brevity, the title will be henceforth abbreviated as *NWMD*, except where it appears at the start of a sentence.

2 The war is commonly known as the Iran–Iraq War or the First Persian Gulf War. However, since Iraq was the perpetrator, in Iran it is often referred to as "The Imposed War" or "The Holy Defense."

3 There are no up-to-date statistics on the books' sales figures, and the statistics mentioned come from Mahmoody's second book, *For the Love of a Child*, published in 1992.

4 It is possible that the book's genre might explain the lack of attention paid to it by scholars or literary critics, as one could argue that the book does not qualify as what would normally be considered "Literature."

5 For instance, in her analysis of captivity narratives as "low literature," Linda Colley argues that captivity narratives were "exported to America, along with so much else, by 17th century English immigrants" and the insistence that such tales possess a "peculiar American quality" is rooted in "American exceptionalism" (201).

6 The full title is: *Mary Rowlandson, The Sovereignty and Goodness of God, Together With the Faithfulness of His Promises Displayed; Being a Narrative of the Captivity and Restauration of Mrs. Mary Rowlandson*.

7 "There is no compulsion in religion. The right way has become distinct from error." (2:256)

8 "And you will find the nearest in love to Muslims those who say: 'We are Christians.'" (5:82)

9 It might also be noteworthy to point out that the mentioned religious minorities are officially recognized in the Constitution of the Islamic Republic of Iran and are all represented in the Iranian Parliament. Also, it bears mentioning that despite the Western media's representations of Iranians an anti-Semitic, Iran is home to the largest number of Jews in the Middle East outside the Occupied Palestinian Territories.

10 There is not even a hint of the mentioned "denial" either in the book or the movie, which renders the claim even more bizarre.

11 This notion was elaborated in the discussion of scriptotherapy on page 12.
12 On the book's title page, Mahmoody declares that: "This is a true story. The characters are authentic, the events are real. But the names and identifying details of certain individuals have been disguised in order to protect them and their families against the possibility of arrest and execution by the government of the Islamic Republic of Iran."
13 There are numerous other instances of inaccuracy, over-exaggeration, and downright fabrication, a detailed discussion of which is simply beyond the scope of this study. However, one can refer to such instances as erroneous information on Iranian divorce laws (134), exaggeration of the population of Tehran at the time (26, 67, 154, 248), the nonexistent concept of "Islamic cooking" (52), false information about Shi'ite customs and practices (38, 60, 67, 234, 281), and many other exaggerations and fabrications (107, 109, 163, 253, 312, 385).
14 Stephen Kinzer reports that in the United States, "the television news program 'Nightline' emerged to give nightly updates on the crisis, with anchorman Ted Koppel beginning each report by announcing that it was now 'Day 53' or 'Day 318' of the crisis" (Kinzer).
15 Here is how Kinzer exemplifies the living memory of the crisis in one of his speeches on US intervention in Iran: "We just met a member of the congress today who said that I approached someone on the floor of the House to ask him if he would support a resolution for negotiating with Iran, and he looked at me and said: 'No, they took over our embassy and seized our diplomats.'" (Kinzer).
16 In so doing, he refers to the recollection of an episode by Bruce Laingen, a career diplomat who was chief of the US Embassy staff at the time of hostage-taking, and the highest-ranking hostage.

One day, after Laingen had spent more than a year as a hostage, one of his captors visited him in his solitary cell. Laingen exploded in rage, shouting at his jailer that this hostage-taking was immoral, illegal and "totally wrong." The jailer waited for him to finish, then replied without sympathy: "You have nothing to complain about," he told Laingen. "The United States took our whole country hostage in 1953" (Kinzer).
17 See pages 23, 24, 26, 42, 48, 54, 56, 61, 69, 91, 94, 119, 204, 324, 419.
18 These forms include *hejab* (the generic term used for both any kind of head covering and for Muslim women's dress code in general), *chador* (an optional full-length robe-like garment worn by some Muslim women, especially in Iran), *roosarie* (the Persian word for headscarf), and *manteau* (a full- or half-length coat), all of which, according to Mahmoody, have "drab" colors (11).
19 Given that Betty, too, is restrained by her own faith in an Orientalist ideology, one could argue that she is "trapped" in more than one way as she might at first seem.
20 Zaim Dervis and Aslihan Tokgöz have also elaborated, in their analyses of representations of Turkishness, how William Hoffer's book and the subsequent film engage in the crudest form of Orientalist essentialization and Othering of things Turkish (Tokgöz; Dervis).
21 Unsurprisingly, the film won two Oscars and six Golden Globes (Mutlu 475).
22 That Mahmoody uses "fundamentalists" as a synonym for ordinary Iranians reveals more about her fundamentalist tendencies than those of ordinary people in Iran.
23 A 2008 World Public Opinion poll on "Trends in Attitudes toward the United States, Americans, and Relations between Islam and the West" revealed that there is a substantial difference in Iranian people's views of the US government and their attitude toward American people ("Public Opinion in Iran").

24 Ironically, of course, high on the George W. Bush administration's dossier of justifications for the US invasion of Iraq in 2003 were Saddam Hussein's alleged stockpiling of chemical weapons, and nuclear and biological programs, which turned out to be fabricated and nonexistent (Ross).
25 The correct spelling would be *sofreh*. Such misspellings apply to almost every single Persian word that Mahmoody transliterates.
26 After all, in the manner of the scapegoat, Moody is within the family/America and must be driven out.
27 I will discuss later, drawing on the case of Dr. Mahmoody's treatment by the judiciary system of the United States, the irony of criticizing Iran's judiciary.
28 It seems that Mahmoody's insistence on the erroneous figure for the population of Tehran (26, 67, 154, 248) is meant to evoke in the reader a sense of alarm and apprehension. According to the *Atlas of Tehran Metropolis*, the city's population at the time was less than six million ("Population Increase").
29 One could argue that the success of the text for an American audience is guaranteed to the extent to which the text successfully repeats the narratives its readers *already know*. In this context, the colonial and Orientalist discourses are the mechanisms of this reiteration.
30 A short video of Dr. Mahmoody's final remarks about his daughter recorded four months before his death (available at https://www.youtube.com/watch?v=lrMf0Lfxbe8) and the Finnish documentary (https://www.youtube.com/watch?v=_W2SUn1ZNU0) have suffered a similar fate as that of Sayed Mahmoody's book.
31 Available at: http://www.amazon.com/Lost-Without-Daughter-Sayed-Mahmoody/dp/1909869791

Chapter 3

1 For the sake of brevity, the title *Reading Lolita in Tehran* will henceforth be abbreviated as *RLT*.
2 There are about forty memoirs about post-revolutionary Iran published in the past decade, most of which were, in various measures, influenced by the success of *Reading Lolita in Tehran*.
3 This is one of the most significant elements that distinguish neo-Orientalist narratives from their classical precedents, which will be further elaborated in this chapter.
4 Also known as the First Persian Gulf War (September 1980 to August 1988).
5 The fact that Nafisi refers to her students as her "girls," in fact, reinforces the idea that she sets herself up as a mother to her students. This becomes more significant in the context of the "feminizing" tendency of Orientalism and especially given the intermediary role of the narrator as a model/mother for her "girls."
6 *RLT* was released in March 2003 in the United States, a few months after the 2003 US invasion of Iraq on the pretext of Iraq's (nonexistent) stockpile of weapons of mass destruction.
7 Accessible at http://www.randomhouse.com/book/119522/reading-lolita-in-tehran-by-azar-nafisi
8 Accessible at http://azarnafisi.com/
9 It should, however, be noted that Nafisi's memoir is characterized by a problematic blurring of distinctions between fiction and nonfiction (i.e., the "real-life" significance

of fiction and the fictional casting of the real life, except that Nafisi's unilateral reading of the canonical texts is dubious and her own writing also manipulates "reality" to fit into stereotype devices and fictions).

10 If user ratings are anything to go by, the memoir enjoys an average rating of almost 4 out of 5 on such popular and widely used online communities of book enthusiasts as *goodreads, Google Books,* and *Amazon.*
11 Hamid Dabashi is an Iranian-American Professor of Iranian Studies and Comparative Literature at Columbia University in New York City.
12 Both "New Orientalist" and "neo-Orientalist" have been proposed by scholars to refer to the recent literary manifestations of Orientalism. However, to emphasize the continuity between contemporary and classical modes of Orientalism, following professor Ali Behd, the term "neo-Orientalism" would be used in this book.
13 Fatemeh Keshavarz is an Iranian-American Professor of Comparative Literature at the University of Maryland, the Roshan Chair of Persian Studies, and the director of the Roshan Institute for Persian Studies at University of Maryland.
14 These distinguishing features are discussed at length in the Introduction.
15 The ideas of "home," "belonging," and "identity" are relative and complex notions, especially in the postmodern era, the significance of which—particularly in the memoir genre—cannot be overemphasized, as they do exert a certain influence upon the text. However, since a more in-depth discussion of these ideas would diverge from the main discussion, the idea of belonging is used here in the literal sense of the word to denote the native origins of the author.
16 It should be added that a tradition of native informants and apologists figure in some classical Orientalist accounts, too. However, these figures are not in the forefront of Orientalist production and their roles were mediated and, therefore, far less direct and personal.
17 The idea is borrowed from Lisa Suhair Majaj's notion of a simultaneously East and Westward gaze in her study of Arab-American writing (Majaj).
18 Dabashi has gone as far as suggesting that the cover photo connotes an "overtly Orientalised pedophilia" that, combined with the title of the memoir, would conjure up one of the most pleasing Orientalist clichés, that is, the fantasy of illicit sex with Oriental Lolitas. While to some, Dabashi's observation may sound rather exaggerated, when considered in light of the highly controversial content of Nabakov's *Lolita,* it does not sound entirely irrelevant.
19 Interestingly, the title of many of the scholarly critiques written on *RLT* imitates the title of the memoir in one way or another. One can refer, for instance, to *Reading Nafisi in the West* (2006) by Mitra Rastegar; *Reading Lolita at Guantanamo* (2006) by Andrew Koppelman; *Jasmine and Stars: Reading More Than Lolita in Tehran* (2007) by Fatemeh Keshavarz; *Reading and Misreading Lolita in Tehran* (2007) by Firoozeh Papan-Matin; *Reading Reading Lolita in Tehran in Idaho* (2007) by John Carlos Rowe; *Reading Lolita in Times of War* (2007) by Catherine Burwell; *Why Americans Love Reading Lolita in Tehran* (2008) by Anne Donadey and Huma Ahmed-Ghosh; *Re-Reading Reading Lolita in Tehran* (2008) by Amy DePaul; *Reading Azar Nafisi in the West* (2008) by Seyyed Mohammad Marandi; *Why Read Reading Lolita?* (2008) by Simon Hay; and *Reading Tehran in Lolita* (2011) by Jodi Melamed.
20 To provide a contemporary case, Bahramitash cites the example of George W. Bush's speech on the need to save Afghan women ("The War on Terror" 222).
21 Bahramitash argues that while Muslim women were being constructed as backward and repressed, in the late nineteenth and early twentieth centuries, women in

Western countries had few legal rights and were not allowed to vote ("The War on Terror" 222). This is a further example of what Nader has dubbed "misleading cultural comparisons" between Western and Eastern women (323).

22   The word "veil" and its synonymous derivatives appear more than 160 times in the memoir and the narrative is packed with numerous descriptions of characters' veiling and unveiling routines, including the following pages (5, 12, 15, 26, 27, 28, 32, 46, 51, 53, 95, 97, 103, 105, 111, 112, 116, 134, 146, 151, 152, 153, 160, 163, 165, 167, 174, 176, 179, 181, 183, 184, 191, 192, 200, 203, 207, 217, 218, 222, 244, 253, 280, 296, 300, 327, 328, 331, 343, 351, 352).

23   A contemporary precedent is Geraldine Brooks, a white middle-class Australian woman, and the author of *Nine Parts of Desire: The Hidden World of Islamic Women* (1994), who used her position as a journalist in the Middle East and North Africa to enter the "private" world of Muslim women.

24   Incidentally, it is important to note that Paidar, Ramazani, and Shavarini are all women of Iranian origin, all of whom live in the United States and none of whom observe the practice of Islamic hijab.

25   Some of the figures in Ramazani's comment have changed since the publication of her review. However, the thrust of her discussion rings even truer today, with the ever-increasing participation of Iranian women in social, political, and academic spheres.

26   Notwithstanding the identities of "Muslim" and politically active students, the names of the students and other people with whom Nafisi sympathizes are never forgotten. Moreover, the names she assigns to these "nameless" characters have often negative connotations in Persian.

27   The surname given to him by Nafisi means "in need."

28   A thorough discussion of the strategies appears in the chapter on *Not without My Daughter*.

29   This alternative perspective is the subject of the next chapter, which deals with alternative discourses, especially as regards the question of Iranian women.

30   http://dialogueproject.sais-jhu.edu/anafisi.php

31   https://www.fpi.sais-jhu.edu/about

32   Jeane J. Kirkpatrick (1926–2006) was Ronald Reagan's first ambassador in the United Nations. She was best known for the "Kirkpatrick Doctrine," which advocated US support of anticommunist governments around the world, for which she was criticized by Noam Chomsky as the "Chief sadist-in-residence of the Reagan Administration" (*Turning the Tide* 8).

33   Marandi, for instance, has drawn attention to how "thousands of people taking part in demonstrations throughout the country in support of Ayatollah Khomeini were killed on the streets" during the premiership of Iran's last prime minister under the shah, whom Nafisi describes as "a very democratic-minded and farsighted" person (102).

34   https://theintercept.com/2017/08/09/gulf-government-gave-secret-20-million-gift-to-d-c-think-tank/

35   The relationship between neo-Orientalist memoirs and the question of women in Muslim societies is elaborated at some length in the section regarding the Iranian womanqQuestion.

36   Even Nafisi admits that "millions had come from all around the country" to participate in Ayatollah Khomeini's funeral (*Reading Lolita* 245).

37   Similar to Nafisi's sexual reading of the public funerals is her comment on the funeral of Ayatollah Khomeini. When the millions of funeral participants were sprayed "at

intervals with water to cool them off" because of the extreme heat, Nafisi sees the effect as making the scene "oddly sexual" (244).
38 The terms often utilized in postcolonial contexts to refer to native intellectuals imparting knowledge about their home countries is "native informant." However, as Dabashi's article is crucial in understanding Nafisi's memoir, his variation of the term, that is, "native informer," will be drawn upon in the current discussion.
39 Hamid Dabashi is currently the Hagop Kevorkian Professor of Iranian Studies and Comparative Literature at Columbia University, where he has taught for many years alongside the late Edward Said.
40 Or at least how she uses her literary choices, that is, more as tokens of "universal" Western cultural tropes (individualism, romance, freedom) than the complexities and criticism often embedded in these texts.
41 This censorship, in fact, begins from the cropped cover image of the memoir as previously discussed.
42 Best Foreign Language Film.
43 One of the significant omissions—and one of the greatest ironies, too—in *RLT* is how despite lengthy discussions of *Lolita*, Nafisi does not make as much as a passing reference to its publication history. Grogan has noted how "[a]fter being rejected by four American publishers, one of whom said that if he printed the book both he and Nabokov would go to jail, the novel was released in Paris in 1955 by Olympia Press, primarily a publisher of pornography. It would take another three years for Lolita to make its debut in the United States" (52).
44 This is particularly true of such omissions as the Iranian grievances against US intervention in their country, manifest in such events as the Iran–Iraq war imposed on Iran by the unstinting support of the United States.

Chapter 4

1 A prominent example of Said's argument is the case of the Black Jacobins, who radicalized aspects of the French Revolution. However, even with this example, there are limits to the extent to which such fights are incitements to further fights, or are subject to containment;hence, Said's point about "blocking" narratives.
2 For instance, one could refer to Salman Rushdie as an example of someone not effectively able to defer criticism of *The Satanic Verses* (1988) despite its "fictional" status.
3 This recent genre of political documentaries is epitomized by *Iranium*, a 2011 film by director Alex Traiman, which, in the US neoconservative vein, portrays Iran as no less than a threat to the entire world (Izadi et al.).
4 Professor Keshavarz is currently the director of the Roshan Institute for Persian Studies at the University of Maryland.
5 There are a number of other memoirs, which display both formal and thematic strains of resistant to the neo-Orientalist discourse. Firoozeh Dumas's *Funny in Farsi: A Memoir of Growing up Iranian in America* (2003), and *Laughing without an Accent: Adventures of a Global Citizen* (2008) are notable for their investment in the language of humor. Gelareh Asayesh's *Saffron Sky* (1999) and Nesta Ramazani's *The Dance of the Rose and the Nightingale* (2002) also depart from the prevalent Orientalist depictions of Iran through contextualization of historical events. Shirin Ebadi's *Iran Awakening* (2006)—even though invested in perpetuating some of the clichéd myths regarding the revolution and the Iran–Iraq war—is also noteworthy

for its representations of the social and political agency of Iranian women, its identification with the Islamic faith, its contextualization of historical events, and its criticism of American double standards. More recently, *The Good Daughter* (2011), by Jasmine Darznik, displays an awareness of the representational complexities of three Iranian women's lives and the need for specificity and contextualization.

6 This famous allegory of Rumi is different from the meaning that the expression has acquired in English, but it might well have been the source of the idiom. The allegory centers around the story of a group of people who have never seen an elephant before, trying to explain it after touching different parts of the animal in a dark room. The one who has touched its foot describes it as a thick column; the person who has touched the trunk thinks of the beast as a drain pipe, and the one who has touched its ear imagines the elephant as a large fan. Rumi thus concludes that if they only had a candle, all the people would be looking at the same beast. Keshavarz builds on Rumi's allegory to demonstrate that "cultural commentary demands specificity and contextualization" and to elucidate how "a lack of specificity turns *RLT* into a dark house where the reader has little choice but to feel his or her way around the elephant that is post-revolutionary Iran" (37).

7 Unlike Nafisi, Keshavarz's *J&S* is preceded by her pedigree of publications on Persian literature: *A Descriptive and Analytical Catalogue of Persian Manuscripts in the Library of the Wellcome Institute for the History of Medicine* (1986); *Reading Mystical Lyric: The Case of Jalal Al-Din Rumi* (1988); *Recite in the Name of the Red Rose: Poetic Sacred Making in Twentieth-century Iran* (2006); *Lyrics of Life: Sa'di on Love, Cosmopolitanism and Care of the Self* (2014). Also, like *J&S*, all the mentioned works are published by university presses.

8 This, in fact, is often one of the features of Orientalist texts, where the assumption is that the texts are only "natural" or "commonsensical," so there is no need to describe them as such, whereas in recent times, an anti-Orientalist text has more sense of its value as a counter.

9 Later in the chapter I will demonstrate through Keshavarz's personal narratives how this identification has at times been challenging for Keshavarz in the West.

10 This excerpt from one of Farrokhzad's most famous poems, "The Sin," published in her collection *The Wall*, her second volume of verse, is taken from http://www.forughfarrokhzad.org/collectedworks/collectedworks1.htm.

11 The poet, pharmacist/physician, and hagiographer who lived in Iran during the thirteenth century, and is best known for his *The Conference of the Birds* (1177).

12 Unsurprisingly, even after Trump's outrageous claim was debunked by multiple fact-checking sources, he refused to retract the statement.

13 A translation of the poem (by Shahriar Shahriari) can be accessed at: http://www.iranchamber.com/literature/jrumi/masnavi/moses_shepherd.php.

14 The first translation appeared in 1998 by Kamran Talattof and Jocelyn Sharlet (and in 2004 with an Afterword by Persis M. Karim), published by Syracuse University Press. The second translation was published in 2011 by Faridoun Farrokh with a Preface by Shirin Neshat.

Chapter 5

1 There have been far fewer reviews of Nafisi's second book and far fewer citations of it on academic platforms.

2 Until 1992, Mahmoody's memoir had sold some twelve million copies and was translated into more than twenty languages. Sales figures for *RLT* are not exactly known, but figures published in 2007 suggest that since its publication in 2003 *RLT* has sold more than 1.5 million copies (Howell). Also, the irony that despite her deep resentment for her ex-husband Betty Mahmoody has to date maintained her Iranian surname even after her husband's divorce and death should not be lost in the consideration of her fame.
3 Available at: https://windowsoniran.wordpress.com/, but apparently not updated since April 2012.
4 Among such accounts are Afsaneh Moqadam's *Death to the Dictator!: A Young Man Casts a Vote in Iran's 2009 Election and Pays a Devastating Price* (2010), Saideh Pakravan's *Azadi: Protests in the Streets of Tehran* (2011), and Maziar Bahari's *Then They Came for Me: A Family's Story of Love, Captivity, and Survival* (2011).

BIBLIOGRAPHY

Abbott, Charlotte. "Book Lovers of the World Unite." *Publishers Weekly*, 26 Jan. 2004, https://www.publishersweekly.com/pw/print/20040126/29209-book-lovers-of-the-world- unite.html. Accessed 2 Mar. 2022.

Acheraïou, Amar. *Rethinking Postcolonialism: Colonialist Discourse in Modern Literatures and the Legacy of Classical Writers*. Palgrave Macmillan, 2008.

Adams, Lorraine. "Beyond the Burka." *New York Times Book Review*, 6 Jan. 2008, https://www.nytimes.com/2008/01/06/books/review/Adams-t.html. Accessed 2 Mar. 2022.

Ajami, Fouad. *The Foreigner's Gift: The Americans, the Arabs, and the Iraqis in Iraq*. Simon and Schuster, 2006.

Al-Ali, Nadje Sadig, and Nicola Christine Pratt. "Women in Iraq: Beyond the Rhetoric." *Middle East Reports*, no. 239, summer 2006, pp. 18–23.

Ali, Rozina. "The Erasure of Islam from the Poetry of Rumi." 5 Jan. 2017. https://www.newyorker.com/books/page-turner/the-erasure-of-islam-from-the-poetry-of-rumi. Accessed 2 Mar. 2022.

Alsultany, Evelyn. *Arabs and Muslims in the Media: Race and Representation after 9/11*. New York UP, 2012.

Amanat, Abbas. *Hajji Baba of Ispahan. Encyclopædia Iranica*. Bibliotheca Persica Press, 2003, pp. 561–68. Vol. XI, Fasc. 6.

Amiri, Cyrus. *Two Thousand and One Scheherazades: Images of the Father and 'Fatherland' in Post-9/11 Novels and Memoirs by Women of the Iranian Diaspora*. 2013. U of Tehran, PhD Dissertation.

Amirrezvani, Anita, and Persis Karim. "New Windows into the Iranian American Experience: An Interview with Anita Amirrezvani & Persis Karim." Interview by Sara Wilson, World Literature Today, 15 May 2013, https://www.worldliteraturetoday.org/blog/interviews/new-windows-iranian-american-experience-interview-anita-amirrezvani-persis-karim. Accessed 2 Mar. 2022.

———. *Tremors: New Fiction by Iranian American Writers*. U of Arkansas P, 2013.

Ardalan, Davar. *My Name Is Iran: A Memoir*. Henry Holt and Company, 2007.

Asadi, Houshang. *Letters to My Torturer: Love, Revolution, and Imprisonment in Iran*. Oneworld Publications, 2010.

Asha, S. "Reading Lolita in Tehran: Rehashing Orientalist Stereotypes." *IUP Journal of English Studies*, vol. 4, no. 1, 2009, pp. 47–53.

Ashcroft, Bill, Gareth Griffiths, and Helen Tiffin, editors. *The Post-Colonial Studies Reader*. Routledge, 1995.

Atwood, Margaret. "A Book Lover's Tale: A Literary Life Raft on Iran's Fundamentalist Sea." *Amnesty International Magazine*, 2003.

Azadi, Sousan, and Angela Ferrante. *Out of Iran: One Woman's Escape from the Ayatollahs*. Ulverscroft, 1987.

Azam Zanganeh, Lila. *My Sister, Guard Your Veil; My Brother, Guard Your Eyes: Uncensored Iranian Voices*. Beacon Press, 2006.

"Azar Nafisi." *Azar Nafisi Site*, https://www.azarnafisi.com/. Accessed 2 Mar. 2022.

"Azar Nafisi: Reading Lolita in Tehran." *The New Zealand Herald*, 11 Jan. 2004, https://www.nzherald.co.nz/lifestyle/iazar-nafisii-reading-lolita-in-tehran-a-memoir-in-books/ZUY22WFQF6FIIWCH7W5FNIVV3U/. Accessed 2 Mar. 2022.

Bacon, Francis. *The Essays of Francis Bacon*. Project Gutenberg, 2009.

Bahari, Maziar, and Aimee Molloy. *Then They Came for Me: A Family's Story of Love, Captivity, and Survival*. Random House Incorporated, 2011.

Bahramitash, Roksana. "The War on Terror, Feminist Orientalism and Orientalist Feminism: Case Studies of Two North American Bestsellers." *Critique: Critical Middle Eastern Studies*, vol. 14, no. 2, 2005, pp. 221–35.

———. "Orientalist Feminism and Islamophobia/Iranophobia." *The World's Religions after September 11*, edited by Arvind Sharma, vol. 3, Praeger Publishers, 2009, pp. 107–12.

Bahrampour, Tara. *To See and See Again: A Life in Iran and America*. U of California P, 1999.

Balaghi, Shiva, and Chris Toensing. "Let Cooler Heads Prevail on Iran." *Middle East Research and Information Project*, 15 June 2006, https://merip.org/2006/06/let-cooler-heads-prevail-on-iran/. 2 Mar. 2022.

Balasescu, Alec H. "Faces and Bodies: Gendered Modernity and Fashion Photography in Tehran." *Gender & History*, vol. 17, no. 3, 2005, pp. 737–68.

Banita, Georgiana. "Affect, Kitsch and Transnational Literature: Azar Nafisi's Portable Worlds." *Semiotic Encounters: Text, Image and Trans—Nation*, edited by Noha Hamdy, Sarah Säckel, and Walter Göbel, Rodopi, 2009, pp. 87–102.

Bashi, Golbarg "Simply a Stunner." *Iranian.com*, 9 July 2006. 19 June 2015, https://iranian.com/Bashi/2006/July/Parsipur/index.html. Accessed 2 Mar. 2022.

Behbahani, Simin. "The Fortieth Anniversary of Forough's Death: An Interview with Simin Behbahani." Interview by Ladan Parsi. *BBC Persian*, 13 Feb. 2007, https://www.bbc.com/persian/arts/story/2007/02/070213_mv-nm-foroogh. Accessed 2 Mar. 2022.

Behdad, Ali, and Juliet Williams. "Neo-Orientalism." *Globalizing American Studies*, edited by Brian T. Edwards and Gaonkar Dilip Parameshwar, U of Chicago P, 2010, pp. 283–99.

Benhayoun, Jamal Eddine. *Narration, Navigation, and Colonialism: A Critical Account of Seventeenth- and Eighteenth-Century English Narratives of Adventure and Captivity*. Peter Lang, 2006.

Berman, Paul. "Why Germany Isn't Convinced." *Slate*, 14 Feb. 2003, https://slate.com/news-and-politics/2003/02/defending-germany-s-anti-war-foreign-minister.html. Accessed 2 Mar. 2022.

———. *Power and the Idealists, or, the Passion of Joschka Fischer and Its Aftermath*. Soft Skull Press, 2005.

Bhabha, Homi K. *The Location of Culture*. Routledge, 1994.

———. "The Other Question: Difference, Discrimination, and the Discourse of Colonialism." *Black British Cultural Studies: A Reader*, edited by Houston A. Baker Jr., Manthia Diawara, and Ruth H. Lindeborg, U of Chicago P, 1996, pp. 87–106.

Brown, Gillian. "Getting in the Kitchen with Dinah: Domestic Politics in Uncle Tom's Cabin." *American Quarterly*, vol. 36, no. 4, 1984, pp. 503–23.

Burke, Edmund, and David Prochaska, editors. *Genealogies of Orientalism: History, Theory, Politics*. U of Nebraska P, 2008.

Burwell, Catherine, Hilary E. Davis, and Lisa K. Taylor. "Reading Nafisi in the West: Feminist Reading Practices and Ethical Concerns." *TOPIA: Canadian Journal of Cultural Studies*, vol. 19, 2008, 63–84.

Busch, Andrew. *Ronald Reagan and the Politics of Freedom*. Rowman & Littlefield Publishers, 2001.
Bush, George W. "Address to a Joint Session of Congress and the American People." *The White House*, Sept. 2001. 1 May 2013, https://georgewbush-whitehouse.archives.gov/news/releases/2001/09/20010920- 8.html. Accessed 2 Mar. 2022.
———. "State of the Union Address." *The White House*, 29 Jan. 2002, https://georgewbush-hitehouse.archives.gov/news/releases/2002/01/20020129-11.html. Accessed 2 Mar. 2022.
Bush, Trudy. "Bookish Lives." *Christian Century*, vol. 121, no. 10, 2004, pp. 32–35.
Byrne, Richard. "A Collision of Prose and Politics." *The Chronicle of Higher Education*, vol. 53, no. 8, 2006, p. A12.
———. "Peeking under the Cover." *The Chronicle of Higher Education*, vol. 53, no. 8, 2006, p. A16.
Carr, Helen. "Imagism and Empire." *Modernism and Empire*, edited by Howard Booth and Nigel Rigby, Manchester UP, 2000, pp. 64–92.
Carrier, James G. *Occidentalism: Images of the West*. Clarendon Press, 1995.
Carter, Jimmy. "Tehran, Iran Toasts of the President and the Shah at a State Dinner." *The American Presidency Project*, 31 Dec. 1977, https://www.presidency.ucsb.edu/documents/tehran-iran-toasts-the-president-and-the- shah-state-dinner. Accessed 2 Mar. 2022.
Chomsky, Noam. *Turning the Tide: Us Intervention in Central America and the Struggle for Peace*. South End Press, 1985.
———. "Rogue States." *Z Magazine*, 1998, pp. 19–31, https://zcomm.org/zmagazine/rogue-states-by-noam-chomsky/. Accessed 2 Mar. 2022.
Chossudovsky, Michel. *Towards a World War III Scenario: The Dangers of Nuclear War*. Global Research, 2012.
Ciabattari, Jane. "Why Is Rumi the Best-Selling Poet in the US?" *BBC*, 21 Oct. 2014, https://www.bbc.com/culture/article/20140414-americas-best-selling-poet. Accessed 2 Mar. 2022.
Civantos, Christina. *Between Argentines and Arabs: Argentine Orientalism, Arab Immigrants, and the Writing of Identity*. State U of New York P, 2005.
Cole, Juan. "Top Ten Ways Islamic Law Forbids Terrorism." *Informed Comment*, 17 Apr. 2013, https://www.juancole.com/2013/04/islamic-forbids-terrorism.html. Accessed 2 Mar. 2022.
Colley, Linda. "Perceiving Low Literature: The Captivity Narrative." *Essays in Criticism*, vol. 53, no. 3, 2003, pp. 199–218.
Corbella, Walter. "Strategies of Resistance and the Problem of Ambiguity in Azar Nafisi's Reading Lolita in Tehran." *Mosaic: A Journal for the Interdisciplinary Study of Literature*, vol. 39, no. 2, 2006, pp. 107–23.
Cottam, Richard W. *Nationalism in Iran: Updated Through 1978*. vol. 145, U of Pittsburgh P, 1979.
Crawford, Neta C. "Human Cost of the Post-9/11 Wars: Lethality and the Need for Transparency". *Costs of War*, 2018, https://watson.brown.edu/costsofwar/papers/2018/human-cost-post-911-wars-lethality-and-need-transparency. Accessed 2 Mar. 2022.
Dabashi, Hamid. "Native Informers and the Making of the American Empire." *Al-Ahram Weekly*, vol. 797, 2006, pp. 1–7, https://www.meforum.org/campus-watch/10542/native-informers-and-the-making-of-the-american. Accessed 2 Mar. 2022.
———. "Lolita and Beyond." Interview by Foaad Khosmood. *Z Magazine*, 4 Aug. 2006, https://zcomm.org/znetarticle/lolita-and-beyond-by-hamid-dabashi/. Accessed 2 Mar. 2022.

———. *Post-Orientalism: Knowledge and Power in a Time of Terror*. Transaction Publishers, 2011.
Dahmen, Lynne. "Review of *Jasmine and Stars: Reading More Than Lolita in Tehran*, by Fatemeh Keshavarz." *Middle East Studies Association of America*, vol. 41, 2007, pp. 202–03.
Darznik, Jasmin. "The Perils and Seductions of Home: Return Narratives of the Iranian Diaspora." *MELUS*, vol. 33, no. 2, 2008, pp. 55–71.
———. *The Good Daughter: A Memoir of My Mother's Hidden Life*. Grand Central Publishing, 2011.
———. *Song of a Captive Bird: A Novel*. Ballantine Books, 2018.
———. *The Bohemians: A Novel*. Random House Publishing Group, 2021.
De Hart, Betty. "Not Without My Daughter: On Parental Abduction, Orientalism and Maternal Melodrama." *European Journal of Women's Studies*, vol. 8, no. 1, 2001, pp. 51–65.
DePaul, Amy. "Re-Reading Reading Lolita in Tehran." *MELUS*, vol. 33, no. 2, 2008, pp. 73–92.
———. "Reviews: 'Jasmine and Stars: Reading More Than Lolita in Tehran,' by Fatemeh Keshavarz." *MELUS*, vol. 33, no. 2, 2008, pp. 185–86.
Dervis, Zaim. "Representation of the Turkish People in Midnight Express." *Örnek Literary Journal*, 1994, https://www.tallarmeniantale.com/MidExp-academic.htm. Accessed 2 Mar. 2022.
Donadey, Anne, and Huma Ahmed-Ghosh. "Why Americans Love Azar Nafisi's 'Reading Lolita in Tehran.'" *Signs*, vol. 33, no. 3, 2008, pp. 623–46.
Dugdale-Pointon, TDP. "Iran-Iraq War 1980–1988." *Military History Encyclopedia on the Web*, 9 Sept. 2002. http://www.historyofwar.org/articles/wars_iraniraq.html. Accessed 2 Mar. 2022.
Dumas, Firoozeh. *Funny in Farsi: A Memoir of Growing up Iranian in America*. Random House, 2003.
———. "Muslims in the Media - Firoozeh Dumas." *YouTube*, uploaded by Fora.tv, 19 Dec. 2008, www.youtube.com/watch?v=MkfRm6uPrrg. Accessed 2 Mar. 2022.
———. *Laughing Without an Accent: Adventures of an Iranian American, at Home and Abroad*. Random House, 2009.
Ebert, Roger. "'Daughter' Takes Liberties with Anti-Muslim Images." *RogerEbert.com*, 6 Jan. 1991, https://www.rogerebert.com/roger-ebert/daughter-takes-liberties-with-anti-muslim-images. Accessed 2 Mar. 2022.
Eck, Lisa. "From Orientalism to Cosmopolitanism: The Challenges and Rewards of Teaching Foreign Literature." *English Faculty Presentations, Posters and Lectures*, Paper 7, 2013, https://digitalcommons.framingham.edu/download/file/IO_d5a10207-3bda-4bc3-bfe2-0c42bfbe9724. Accessed 2 Mar. 2022.
Edwards, Brian T. "Disorienting Captivity: A Response to Gordon Sayre." *American Literary History*, vol. 22, no. 2, 2010, pp. 360–67.
Egerton, George W. *Political Memoir: Essays on the Politics of Memory*. F. Cass.
Elkholy, Sharin N. "Feminism and Race in the United States." *Internet Encyclopedia of Philosophy*, 2012, 24 Aug. 2015, https://iep.utm.edu/fem-race/. Accessed 2 Mar. 2022.
Ernst, Carl W. *Islamophobia in America: The Anatomy of Intolerance*. Palgrave Macmillan, 2013.
Fanon, Frantz. *Black Skin, White Masks*. Grove Press, 1991.
Fass, Paula S. "The Memoir Problem." *Reviews in American History*, vol. 34, no. 1, 2006, pp. 107–23.

Fernandes, Leela. *Transnational Feminism in the United States: Knowledge, Ethics, Power.* New York UP, 2013.

Fisk, Milton. "Multiculturalism and Neoliberalism." *Praxis Filosofica*, vol. 21, 2005.

Fitzpatrick, Coeli. "New Orientalism in Popular Fiction and Memoir: An Illustration of Type." *Journal of Multicultural Discourses*, vol. 4, no. 3, 2009, pp. 243–56.

Fleming, Kathleen, et al. "The Unveiling of New Orientalism Through Global, Critical Conversations." *The Dragon Lode*, vol. 30, no. 1, 2011, pp. 3–9.

Flint, Kate. "Women and Reading." *Signs*, vol. 31, no. 2, 2006, pp. 511–36.

"For the Love of a Child by Betty Mahmoody." *Kirkus*, 20 May 2010, https://www.kirkusreviews.com/book-reviews/betty-mahmoody/for-the-love-of-a-child/. Accessed 2 Mar. 2022.

Fotouhi, Sanaz. *Ways of Being, Lines of Becoming: A Study of Post-Revolutionary Diasporic Iranian Literature in English.* 2012. U of New South Wales, PhD Dissertation.

Fuchs, Miriam. *The Text Is Myself: Women's Life Writing and Catastrophe.* U of Wisconsin P, 2004.

Gandhi, Leela. *Postcolonial Theory: A Critical Introduction.* Allen & Unwin, 1998.

Genette, Gerard. *Paratexts: Thresholds of Interpretation.* Cambridge UP, 1997.

Gerecht, Reuel Marc. "To Bomb or Not to Bomb, That Is the Iran Question." *The Weekly Standard*, vol. 11, no. 30, 2004. 24 June 2014, https://www.aei.org/articles/to-bomb-or-not-to-bomb/. Accessed 2 Mar. 2022.

Ghasemi Tari, Zeinab. *The Politics of Knowledge and Post-Revolutionary Iran: An Analysis of the Iranian Studies Journal and Iranian-American Memoirs (1979–2012)*, 2015. U of Tehran, PhD Dissertation.

Gide, André. *If It Die: An Autobiography.* Vintage Books, 2001.

Goodman, Amy. "Stephen Kinzer on US-Iranian Relations, the 1953 Cia Coup in Iran and the Roots of Middle East Terror." *Democracy Now*, vol. 3, 2008, https://www.democracynow.org/2008/3/3/stephen_kinzer_on_the_us_iranian. Accessed 2 Mar. 2022.

Grogan, Christine. "'Lolita' Revisited: Reading Azar Nafisi's 'Reading Lolita in Tehran: A Memoir in Books.'" *Women's Studies*, vol. 43, no. 1, 2014, pp. 52–72.

Hakkakiyan, Roya. *Journey from the Land of No: A Girlhood Caught in Revolutionary Iran.* Crown Publishers, 2004.

Hattori, Tomo. "Psycholinguistic Orientalism in Criticism of the Woman Warrior and Obasan." *Other Sisterhoods: Literary Theory and US Women of Color*, edited by Sandra Kumamoto Stanley, U of Illinois P, 1998, pp. 119–38.

Hay, Simon. "Why Read Reading Lolita? Teaching Critical Thinking in a Culture of Choice." *Pedagogy*, vol. 8, no. 1, 2008, pp. 5–24.

Hejazi, Arash. *The Gaze of the Gazelle: The Story of a Generation.* Seagull Books, 2011.

Hendelman-Baavur, Liora. "Guardians of New Spaces: 'Home' and 'Exile' in Azar Nafisi's Reading Lolita in Tehran, Marjane Satrapi's Persepolis Series and Azadeh Moaveni's Lipstick Jihad." *Hagar: Studies in Culture, Polity and Identities*, vol. 8, no. 1, 2008, pp. 45–62.

Henke, Suzette A. *Shattered Subjects: Trauma and Testimony in Women's Life-Writing.* St. Martin's Press, 2000.

Hersh, Seymour. "The Iran Plans." *New Yorker*, 17 Apr. 2006, https://www.newyorker.com/magazine/2006/04/17/the-iran-plans. Accessed 2 Mar. 2022.

Hewett, Heather. "'Bad' Books Hidden under the Veil of Revolution; Iranian Women Resist Oppression by Reading Forbidden Novels." *The Christian Science Monitor*, 27 Mar. 2003, https://www.csmonitor.com/2003/0327/p21s01-bogn.html. Accessed 2 Mar. 2022.

Hiro, Dilip. *The Longest War: The Iran-Iraq Military Conflict*. Routledge, 1991.
Hirsh, Michael. "Bernard Lewis Revisited." *Washington Monthly*, 1 Nov. 2004, https://washingtonmonthly.com/2004/11/01/bernard-lewis-revisited/. Accessed 2 Mar. 2022.
Ho, Christina. "Responding to Orientalist Feminism: Women's Rights and the War on Terror." *Australian Feminist Studies*, vol. 25, no. 66, 2010, pp. 433–39.
Hoberman, J. *Vulgar Modernism: Writing on Movies and Other Media*. Temple UP, 1991.
Hoglund, Emma. *Unveiling New Orientalism: An Exploration in Images*. 2009. Minnesota State U Moorhead, MA Thesis.
Homa, Ava. *Echoes from the Other Land: Stories*. TSAR Publications, 2010.
Hoodfar, Homa. "The Veil in Their Minds and on Our Heads: The Persistence of Colonial Images of Muslim Women." *Resources for Feminist Research*, vol. 22, no. 3/4, 1993, pp. 5–18.
Izadi, Foad, et al. "Iranophobia in the US: An Orientalistic Representation of Iran's Nuclear Program in Iranium Documentary." *Islamic Revolution Studies*, vol. 10, no. 35, 2014, pp. 69–91.
James, Cyril Lionel Robert. *The Black Jacobins*. Penguin, 2001.
Johannsen, Robert Walter. *To the Halls of the Montezumas: The Mexican War in the American Imagination*. Oxford UP, 1985.
Johnson, Jenna, and Abigail Hauslohner. "'I Think Islam Hates Us': A Timeline of Trump's Comments about Islam and Muslims." 20 May 2017, https://www.washingtonpost.com/news/post-politics/wp/2017/05/20/i-think-islam-hates-us-a-timeline-of-trumps-comments-about-islam-and-muslims/. Accessed 2 Mar. 2022.
Jones, Jeffrey M. "Far Fewer Americans Now Say Iran Is No. 1 U.S. Enemy." *Gallup*, 20 Feb. 2014, https://news.gallup.com/poll/167501/far-fewer-americans-say-iran-no-enemy.aspx. Accessed 2 Mar. 2022.
Kahlili, Reza. *A Time to Betray: The Astonishing Double Life of a CIA Agent Inside the Revolutionary Guards of Iran*. Threshold Editions, 2010.
Kakutani, Michiko. "Book Study as Insubordination under the Mullahs." *The New York Times*, 15 Apr. 2003, https://www.nytimes.com/2003/04/15/books/books-of-the-times-book-study-as-insubordination-under-the-mullahs.html. Accessed 2 Mar. 2022.
Kamali Dehghan, Saeed. "Love-Struck Iranians Lose Themselves in World's Biggest Book Labyrinth." *The Sydney Morning Herald*, 5 May 2012, https://www.smh.com.au/entertainment/books/lovestruck-iranians-lose-themselves- in-worlds-biggest-book-labyrinth-20120504-1y49l.html. Accessed 2 Mar. 2022.
Kamran, Cameron. "Review of *Reading Lolita in Tehran: A Memoir in Books* by Azar Nafisi." *Middle East Journal*, vol. 57, no. 3, Summer 2003, p. 505.
Kaplan, E. Ann. *Trauma Culture: The Politics of Terror and Loss in Media and Literature*. Rutgers UP, 2005.
Karim, Persis M., editor. *Let Me Tell You Where I've Been: New Writing by Women of the Iranian Diaspora*. U of Arkansas P, 2006.
Karim, Persis M., and Mohammad Mehdi Khorrami, editors. *A World Between: Poems, Short Stories, and Essays by Iranian-Americans*. George Braziller, 1999.
Kelly, Douglas. "Our Mistake: Note to Readers." *National Post*, 24 May 2006.
Kempley, Rita. "'Not Without My Daughter' (Pg-13)." *The Washington Post*, 11 Jan. 1991, https://www.washingtonpost.com/wp-srv/style/longterm/movies/videos/notwithoutmydaughterpg13kempley_a0a0ca.htm. Accessed 2 Mar. 2022.
Keshavarz, Fatemeh. "An Interview with Fatemeh Keshavarz, Author of Jasmine and Stars: Reading More Than Lolita in Tehran." *MRonline*. 12 Mar. 2007, https://mronline

.org/2007/03/12/reading-more-than-lolita-in-tehran-an-interview-with-fatemeh-keshavarz/. Accessed 2 Mar. 2022.

———. "Jasmine and Stars: An Interview with Fatemeh Keshavarz." Interview by Foaad Khosmood. *ZNET*, 3 Aug. 2007, https://zcomm.org/znetarticle/jasmine-and-stars-by-fatemeh-keshavarz/. Accessed 2 Mar. 2022.

———. *Jasmine and Stars: Reading More Than Lolita in Tehran*. U of North Carolina P, 2007.

Kessler, Glenn. "Trump's Outrageous Claim That 'Thousands' of New Jersey Muslims Celebrated the 9/11 Attacks." *The Washington Post*, 23 Nov. 2015, https://www.washingtonpost.com/news/fact-checker/wp/2015/11/22/donald-trumps-outrageous-claim-that-thousands-of-new-jersey-muslims-celebrated-the-911-attacks/. Accessed 2 Mar. 2022.

Khakpour, Porochista. *Sons and Other Flammable Objects*. Grove Press, 2007.

———. "Essay: Iranians Moving Past Negative Depictions in Pop Culture." *Los Angeles Times*, 2010, https://www.latimes.com/archives/la-xpm-2010-jun-27-la-ca-iran-popculture-20100627-story.html. Accessed 2 Mar. 2022.

Khaz Ali, Ansia *Iranian Women after the Islamic Revolution*. Conflict Forum Monograph, 2010.

Kinglake, Alexander William. *Eothen: Traces of Travel Brought Home from the East*. Oxford UP, 1982.

Kinsley, Michael. "Essay: Rally Round the Flag, Boys." *Time*, 12 Sep. 1988, http://content.time.com/time/subscriber/article/0,33009,968407,00.html. Accessed 2 Mar. 2022.

Kinzer, Stephen. "Inside Iran's Fury." *Smithsonian.com*, Oct. 2008, https://www.smithsonianmag.com/travel/inside-irans-fury-11823881/. Accessed 2 Mar. 2022.

Kirkpatrick, Jeane J. *Dictatorships and Double Standards: Rationalism and Reason in Politics*. Simon and Schuster, 1982.

Koegeler, Martina. *American Scheherazades: Auto-Orientalism, Literature and the Representations of Muslim Women in a Post 9/11 U.S. Context*. 2012. Stony Brook U, MA thesis.

Larson, Thomas. *The Memoir and the Memoirist: Reading and Writing Personal Narrative*. Swallo Press / Ohio UP, 2007.

Latifi, Afschineh, and Pablo F. Fenjves. *Even after All This Time: A Story of Love, Revolution, and Leaving Iran*. HarperCollins, 2005.

Lejeune, Philippe. *On Autobiography*. Translated by Katherine Leary, edited by Paul John Eakin, U of Minnesota P, 1989.

Lewis, Bernard. "Western Culture Must Go." *Wall Street Journal*, 1988, p. 24.

Lie, John. "Theorizing Japanese Uniqueness." *Current Sociology*, vol. 44, no. 1, 1996, pp. 5–13.

Lindstrom, Lamont. "Cargoism and Occidentalism." *Occidentalism: Images of the West*, edited by James G. Carrier, Clarendon Press, 1995, pp. 33–60.

"Lj Bestsellers: The Books Most Borrowed in U.S. Libraries." *Library Journal*, vol. 129, no. 15, 2004, p. 96.

Long, Elizabeth. *Book Clubs: Women and the Uses of Reading in Everyday Life*. U of Chicago P, 2003.

Machlis, Elisheva. "Stars in Her Eyes: The Radiance of Persian Literature." *Women: A Cultural Review*, vol. 20, no. 1, 2009, pp. 103–05.

Mahloujian, Azar. "Phoenix from the Ashes: A Tale of the Book in Iran." *Logos*, vol. 13, no. 4, 2002, pp. 227–29.

Mahmoody, Betty, and Arnold D. Dunchock. *For the Love of a Child*. 1st ed., St. Martin's Press, 1992.

Mahmoody, Betty, and William Hoffer. *Not Without My Daughter*. 1st ed., St. Martin's Press, 1987.
Mahmoody, Sayed. *Lost Without My Daughter*. Thistle Publishing, 2013.
Mailloux, Steven. "Judging and Hoping." *New Directions in American Reception Study*, edited by Philip Goldstein and James L. Machor, Oxford UP, 2007, pp. 23–33.
Majaj, Lisa Suhair. "New Directions: Arab American Writing Today." *ArabAmericas: Literary Entanglements of the American Hemisphere and the Arab World*, edited by Ottmar Ette and Friederike Pannewick, Iberoamericana—Vervuert, 2006, pp. 123–36.
Malcolm, John. *Sketches of Persia*. vol. 9, J. Murray, 1845.
Malcolm, Knox. "Bestseller's Lies Exposed". *The Sydney Morning Herald*, 24 July 2004, https://www.smh.com.au/entertainment/books/bestsellers-lies-exposed-20040724-gdjerm.html. Accessed 2 Mar. 2022.
Malek, Amy. "Memoir as Iranian Exile Cultural Production: A Case Study of Marjane Satrapi's "Persepolis" Series." *Iranian Studies*, vol. 39, no. 3, 2006, pp. 353–80.
Mamdani, Mahmood. "Beyond Settler and Native as Political Identities: Overcoming the Political Legacy of Colonialism." *Comparative Studies in Society and History*, vol. 43, no. 4, 2001, pp. 651–64.
Mannani, Manijeh. "Reading Beyond Jasmine and Stars: Reading More Than Lolita in Tehran." *Comparative Studies of South Asia, Africa and the Middle East*, vol. 29, no. 2, 2009, pp. 322–33.
Marandi, Seyed Mohammad. "Reading Azar Nafisi in Tehran." *Comparative American Studies*, vol. 6, no. 2, 2008, pp. 179–89.
Marandi, Seyed Mohammad, and Hossein Nazari. "Orientalism Beyond Belief: Critiquing the Problematics of V. S. Naipaul's Islamic Excursion." *Journal of Research in Applied Linguistics*, vol. 8, no. 1, 2017, pp. 3–21.
Marandi, Seyed Mohammad, and Hossein Pirnajmuddin. "Constructing an Axis of Evil: Iranian Memoirs in the 'Land of the Free.'" *The American Journal of Islamic Social Sciences*, vol. 26, no. 2, 2009, pp. 23–47.
McAlister, Melani. *Epic Encounters: Culture, Media, and U.S. Interests in the Middle East, 1945-2000*, vol. 6. U of California P, 2001.
Melamed, Jodi. "Reading Tehran in *Lolita*: Making Racialized and Gendered Difference Work for Neoliberal Multiculturalism." *Strange Affinities: The Gender and Sexual Politics of Comparative Racialization*, edited by Jack Halberstam and Lisa Lowe. Duke UP, 2011, pp. 76–109.
Milani, Farzaneh. *Veils and Words: The Emerging Voices of Iranian Women Writers*. Syracuse UP, 1992.
———. "On Women's Captivity in the Islamic World." *Middle East Report*, vol. 38, no. 246, 2008, pp. 40–46.
———. "Iranian Women's Life Narratives." *Journal of Women's History*, vol. 25, no. 2, 2013, pp. 130–52.
Miller, Cheryl. "Theorists and Mullahs." *Policy Review*, vol. 119, 2003, pp. 92–96.
Minter, David L. "By Dens of Lions: Notes on Stylization in Early Puritan Captivity Narratives." *American Literature*, vol. 45, no. 3, 1973, pp. 335–47.
Moaveni, Azadeh. *Lipstick Jihad: A Memoir of Growing up Iranian in America and American in Iran*. PublicAffairs, 2005.
———. *Honeymoon in Tehran: Two Years of Love and Danger in Iran*. Random House Publishing Group, 2009.
Mobasher, Mohsen M. *Iranians in Texas: Migration, Politics, and Ethnic Identity*. U of Texas P, 2012.

Mohanty, Chandra Talpade. "Under Western Eyes: Feminist Scholarship and Colonial Discourses." *Feminist Review*, vol. 30, no. 1, 1988, pp. 61–88.
Molavi, Afshin. *Persian Pilgrimages: Journeys Across Iran*. W. W. Norton & Company, 2002.
———. *The Soul of Iran: A Nation's Journey to Freedom*. W. W. Norton & Company, 2005.
Montagu, Lady Mary Wortley. *The Turkish Embassy Letters*. Broadview Press, 2012.
Moqadam, Afsaneh. *Death to the Dictator!: A Young Man Casts a Vote in Iran's 2009 Election and Pays a Devastating Price*. Macmillan, 2010.
Morello, Nordeen. "Reading Lolita in Tehran by Azar Nafisi." *Larchmont Gazette*, 17 June 2004, http://www.larchmontgazette.org/2004/books/20040613tehran.html. Accessed 2 Mar. 2022.
Morier, James Justinian. *A Journey Through Persia, Armenia and Asia Minor, to Constantinople, in the Years 1808 and 1809*. Longman, Hurst, 1818.
———. *A Second Journey Through Persia, Armenia, and Asia Minor, to Constantinople, Between the Years 1810 and 1816. With a Journal of the Voyage by the Brazils and Bombay to the Persian Gulf. Together with an Account of the Proceedings of His Majesty's Embassy Under ... Sir Gore Ouseley*. Longman, Hurst, 1818.
———. *The Adventures of Hajji Baba of Ispahan*. A. & W. Galignani, 1824.
———. *Zohrab, the Hostage*. R. Bentley, 1832.
———. *Ayesha, the Maid of Kars*. R. Bentley, 1834.
———. *The Mirza*. R. Bentley, 1841. 3 vols.
Morris, Rosalind C., editor. *Can the Subaltern Speak?: Reflections on the History of an Idea*. Columbia UP, 2010.
Mosteshar, Cherry. *Unveiled: One Woman's Nightmare in Iran*. St. Martin's Press, 1995.
Motlagh, Amy. "Towards a Theory of Iranian American Life Writing." *MELUS*, vol. 33, no. 2, 2008, pp. 17–36.
———. "Autobiography and Authority in the Writings of the Iranian Diaspora." *Comparative Studies of South Asia, Africa and the Middle East*, vol. 31, no. 2, 2011, pp. 411–24.
Mottahedeh, Negar. "Off the Grid: Reading Iranian Memoirs in Our Time of Total War." *Middle East Research and Information Project*, 14 Sep. 2004, https://merip.org/2004/09/off-the-grid/ . Accessed 2 Mar. 2022.
Mutlu, Dilek Kaya. "The Midnight Express (1978) Phenomenon and the Image of Turkey." *Historical Journal of Film, Radio and Television*, vol. 25, no. 3, 2005, pp. 475–96.
Nader, Laura. "Orientalism, Occidentalism and the Control of Women." *Cultural Dynamics*, vol. 2, no. 3, 1989, pp. 323–55.
Nafisi, Azar. *Reading Lolita in Tehran: A Memoir in Books*. Random House, 2003.
———. "Monday Interview: Azar Nafisi on Things I've Been Silent About." Interview by Kevin Howell. *Publishers Weekly*, 22 Dec. 2008, https://www.publishersweekly.com/pw/by-topic/authors/interviews/article/13786-monday-interview-azar-nafisi-on-things-i-ve-been-silent-about.html. Accessed 2 Mar. 2022.
———. *Things I've Been Silent About*. Random House, 2008.
———. *The Republic of Imagination: America in Three Books*. Random House, 2014.
Naghibi, Nima. "Revolution, Trauma, and Nostalgia in Diasporic Iranian Women's Autobiographies." *Radical History Review*, vol. 2009, no. 105, 2009, pp. 79–91.
Naipaul, V. S. *Among the Believers*. Random House, 1981.
———. *Beyond Belief*. Random House, 1998.
Najmabadi, Afsaneh, et al. *Women's Autobiographies in Contemporary Iran*. Harvard UP, 1990.

Nazari, Hossein. "The Mad Muslim Mob: De/Mythologising Shi'i Iran in VS Naipaul's 'Islamic' Travelogues." *Journal of Shi'a Islamic Studies*, vol. 9, no. 3, 2016, pp. 273–300.

———. "'A Labor of Love": On the Perils and Seductions of Writing about Iran. An Interview with Jill Worrall." *Studies in Travel Writing*, vol. 22, no. 3, 2018, pp. 325–36.

Newport, Frank. "Americans Still Rate Iran Top U.S. Enemy." *Gallup*, 20 Feb. 2012, https://news.gallup.com/poll/152786/americans-rate-iran-top-enemy.aspx. Accessed 2 Mar. 2022.

Nohlen, Dieter, Florian Grotz, and Christof Hartmann "Iran". *Elections in Asia: A Data Handbook. I*. Oxford UP, 2001.

Not Without My Daughter. Directed by Harry J. Ufland, Pathe Entertainment/Ufland Productions, 1991.

"Not Without My Daughter." *Movieguide*, www.movieguide.org/reviews/not-without-my-daughter.html. Accessed 2 Mar. 2022.

Olson, Elizabeth. "Appeal of Writing Memoirs Grows, as Do Publishing Options." *New York Times*, 12 Oct. 2014, https://www.nytimes.com/2014/10/11/business/appeal-of-penning-memoirs-grows-along-with-publishing-options.html. Accessed 2 Mar. 2022.

Paidar, Parvin. *Women and the Political Process in Twentieth-Century Iran*. vol. 1, Cambridge UP, 1995.

Pakravan, Saideh. *Azadi: Protest in the Streets of Tehran*. Parallel Books, 2011.

Pandey, Swati. "The Latest in Immigrant Lit." *Los Angeles Times*, 2 Dec. 2007, https://www.latimes.com/archives/la-xpm-2007-dec-02-ca-persianwomen2-story.html. Accessed 2 Mar. 2022.

Papan-Matin, Firoozeh. "Reading (and Misreading) Lolita in Tehran." *Common Review*, vol. 6, no. 1, 2007, pp. 28–37.

"Paperback Best Sellers: Mar. 3, 1991." *The New York Times*, 3 Mar. 1991, https://www.nytimes.com/1991/03/03/books/paperback-best-sellers-Mar.-3-1991.html. Accessed 2 Mar. 2022.

Paul, Ron. "Questions That Won't Be Asked About Iraq." *United States House of Representatives*, 11 Sept. 2002. Accessed 6 Aug. 2012.

Pearce, Roy Harvey. "The Significances of the Captivity Narrative." *American Literature*, vol. 19, no. 1, 1947, pp. 1–20.

Peernajmodin, Hossein. *Orientalist Representations of Persia in the Works of Spenser, Marlowe, Milton, Moore and Morier*. 2002. U of Birmingham, PhD Dissertation.

Pitt, David. Review of *Jasmine and Stars: Reading More Than Lolita in Tehran*, by Fatemeh Keshavarz. vol. 103, Booklist Publications, 2007, p. 53.

"Population Increase in Tehran Districts." *Atlas of Tehran Metropolis*, 2012, https://atlas.tehran.ir/en/PopulationMigration/PopulationincreaseinTehrandistricts.aspx. Accessed 2 Mar. 2022.

Porter, Dennis. "Orientalism and its Problems." *Colonial Discourse and Post-Colonial Theory: A Reader*, edited by Patrick Williams, and Laura Chrisman, Columbia UP, 1994, pp. 150–61.

"Public Opinion in Iran and America on Key International Issues." *World Public Opinion .org*, 7 Apr. 2008, https://worldpublicopinion.net/wp-content/uploads/2019/12/Iran_Apr08_rpt.pdf. Accessed 2 Mar. 2022.

Rachlin, Nahid. *Foreigner*. Norton, 1978.

———. *Married to a Stranger*. E, P, Dutton, Inc, 1983.

———. *The Heart's Desire*. City Lights Books, 1995.

———. *Jumping over Fire*. City Lights Books, 2005.

———. *Persian Girls: A Memoir*. Jeremy P. Tarcher/Penguin, 2006.
Rahimieh, Nasrin. "Review of *Jasmine and Stars: Reading More Than Lolita in Tehran*, by Fatemeh Keshavarz." *Middle East Institute*, vol. 61, 2007, pp. 535–36.
Ramazani, Nesta. *The Dance of the Rose and the Nightingale*. Syracuse UP, 2002.
———. "Review of *Persepolis: The Story of a Childhood*, by Marjane Satrapi, and *Reading Lolita in Tehran: A Memoir in Books*, by Azar Nafisi." *Comparative Studies of South Asia, Africa and the Middle East*, vol. 24, no. 1, 2004, pp. 278–80.
Rastegar, Mitra. "Reading Nafisi in the West: Authenticity, Orientalism, and 'Liberating' Iranian Women." *Women's Studies Quarterly*, vol. 34, no. 1/2, 2006, pp. 108–28.
Ross, Clark. "Weapons of Mass Hypocrisy." *The Spectator*, vol. 290, no. 9086, 2002, p. 26.
Rowe, John Carlos. "Reading Reading Lolita in Tehran in Idaho." *American Quarterly*, vol. 59, no. 2, 2007, pp. 253–75.
Rowlandson, Mary White. *The Sovereignty and Goodness of God: A Narrative of the Captivity and Restoration of Mrs. Mary Rowlandson*. Lightning Source Incorporated, 2012.
Said, Edward W. "Islam, Orientalism, and the West: An Attack on Learned Ignorance." *Times*, 16 Apr. 1979, http://content.time.com/time/subscriber/article/0,33009,912409,00.html. Accessed 2 Mar. 2022.
———. "Iran and the Press: Whose Holy War?." *Columbia Journalism Review*, vol. 18, no. 6, 1980, pp. 23–33.
———. "Islam Through Western Eyes." *The Nation*, 26 Apr. 1980, https://www.thenation.com/article/archive/islam-through-western-eyes/. Accessed 2 Mar. 2022.
———. *Covering Islam: How the Media and the Experts Determine How We See the Rest of the World*. Pantheon, 1981.
———. "Inside Islam: How the Press Missed the Story in Iran." *Harper's Magazine*, Jan. 1981, https://harpers.org/archive/1981/01/inside-islam/. Accessed 2 Mar. 2022.
———. *Culture and Imperialism*. Knopf, 1993.
———. "The Clash of Ignorance." *The Nation*, 4 Oct. 2001, https://www.thenation.com/article/archive/clash-ignorance/. Accessed 2 Mar. 2022.
———. *Orientalism*. Penguin Group, 2003.
Saljoughi, Sara. *Whiteness, Orientalism and Immigration: A Critique of Two Iranian Exilic Memoirs*. 2008. Ryerson U, MA Thesis.
Sardar, Ziauddin. *Orientalism*. Open UP, 1999.
Schechter, Danny. "Iran Fulfills America's Need for an Enemy." *Reportergary.com*, Aug. 2012. Accessed 27 July 2015.
Shavarini, Mitra. "Admitted to College, Restricted from Work: A Conflict for Young Iranian Women." *The Teachers College Record*, vol. 108, no. 10, 2006, pp. 1960–82.
Simons, George F. *Keeping Your Personal Journal*. Random House, 1986.
Slotkin, Richard. *Regeneration Through Violence: The Mythology of the American Frontier, 1600–1860*. Wesleyan UP, 1974.
Snider, Ted. "Iranians Have Memories Too." *ZNET*, 10 Apr. 2013, https://zcomm.org/znetarticle/iranians-have-memories-too-by-ted-snider/. Accessed 2 Mar. 2022.
Spelman, Elizabeth V. *Inessential Woman: Problems of Exclusion in Feminist Thought*. Beacon Press, 1988.
Spetalnick, Matt, and Jeffrey Heller. "Obama Says Not Bluffing on Iran Military Option." *Reuters*, 2 Mar. 2012, https://www.reuters.com/article/cnews-us-usa-israel-iran-idCATRE82108520120302. Accessed 2 Mar. 2022.
Spivak, Gayatri Chakravorty. "Can the Subaltern Speak?" *Colonial Discourse and Postcolonial Theory: A Reader*, edited by Patrick Williams and Laura Chrisman, Columbia UP, 1994, pp. 66–111.

Spivak, Gayatri Chakravorty, and Elizabeth Grosz. "Criticism, Feminism and the Institution: An Interview with Gayatri Chakravorty Spivak." *Thesis Eleven*, vol. 10, no. 11, 1985, pp. 175–89.
Spurr, David. *The Rhetoric of Empire: Colonial Discourse in Journalism, Travel Writing, and Imperial Administration*. Post-Contemporary Interventions. Duke UP, 1993.
Stocker, Carol. "Mother's Iran Ordeal Draws Fire at Home." *The Boston Globe*, 24 Jan. 1991.
Stocking, Annie Woodman. "The New Woman in Persia." *The Muslim World*, vol. 2, no. 4, 1912, pp. 367–72.
Stowe, Harriet Beecher. *Uncle Tom's Cabin*. Oxford UP, 1998.
Taheri, Amir. "A Colour Code for Iran's 'Infidels.'" *Canada.com*, 19 May 2006, http://www.canada.com/nationalpost/news/story.html?id=398274b5-9210-43e4-ba59-fa24f4c66ad4&k=28534&p=1. Accessed 9 May 2014.
Tavakoli-Targhi, Mohamad. "Imagining Western Women: Occidentalism and Euro-Eroticism." *Radical America*, vol. 24, no. 3, 1990, pp. 73–87.
Tiffin, Helen. "Post-colonial Literatures and Counter-discourse." *The Post-Colonial Studies Reader*, edited by Bill Ashcroft et al., Routledge, 1995, pp. 95–98.
Tohidi, Nayereh. "Stop Stereotyping Arabs and Iranians." *Los Angeles Times*, 21 Jan. 1991, https://www.latimes.com/archives/la-xpm-1991-01-21-ca-583-story.html. Accessed 2 Mar. 2022.
Tokgöz, Aslıhan. "Representation of Turkishness in American Cinema". https://students.brown.edu/Turkish/old/Gelenler/Turkishness_in_Hollywood.pdf. Accessed 2 Mar. 2022.
"Touba and the Meaning of Night." *The Feminist Press*, 2008, https://www.feministpress.org/books-n-z/touba-and-the. Accessed 2 Mar. 2022.
Tourage, Mahdi. "Written for the West: Reading Three Iranian Women's Memoirs." *American Journal of Islamic Social Sciences*, vol. 25, no. 2, 2008, pp. 100–07.
UN News. "Afghanistan: Civilian Casualties Exceed 10,000 for Sixth Straight Year." 22 Feb. 2020, https://news.un.org/en/story/2020/02/1057921. Accessed 2 Mar. 2022.
Vanderbeets, Richard. "The Indian Captivity Narrative as Ritual." *American Literature*, vol. 43, no. 4, 1972, pp. 548–62.
Vanzan, Anna. "Exploring Identity Through Fiction: Women Writers in the Islamic Republic of Iran Beyond Autobiography." *Pakistan Journal of Women's Studies Alam-e-Niswan*, vol. 17, no. 1, 2010, pp. 15–31.
Viswanathan, Gauri. *Masks of Conquest: Literary Study and British Rule in India*. Columbia UP, 2014.
Walker, Deborah Cunningham. *Veiled Images: Eurocentrism in 'Not Without My Daughter'*. 1999. Florida Atlantic U, MA Thesis.
Ware, Vron. *Beyond the Pale: White Women, Racism, and History*. Verso, 1992.
Watson, H. "Women and the Veil." *Islam, Globalization and Postmodernity*, edited by Akbar S. Ahmed and Hastings Donnan, Routledge, 1994, pp. 141–59.
Weisberg, Jacob. "Party of Defeat: AEI's Weird Celebration." *Slate*, 14 Mar. 2007, https://slate.com/news-and-politics/2007/03/aei-s-weird-celebration.html. Accessed 2 Mar. 2022.
"What They're Reading on College Campuses." *Chronicle of Higher Education*, vol. 50, no. 33, 2004, p. A8.
Whitlock, Gillian. *Soft Weapons: Autobiography in Transit*. U of Chicago P, 2007.
———. "From Tehran to Tehrangeles: The Generic Fix of Iranian Exilic Memoirs." *ARIEL*, vol. 39, no. 1–2, 2008, pp. 7–27.

Wilayto, Phil. *In Defense of Iran: Notes from a U.S. Peace Delegation's Journey Through the Islamic Republic*. Defender's Publications, 2008.

———. "An Open Letter to the Anti-War Movement: How Should We React to the Events in Iran?" *Monthly Review Online*, 8 Jul. 2009, https://mronline.org/2009/07/08/an-open-letter-to-the-anti-war-movement-how-should-we-react-to-the-events-in-iran/. Accessed 2 Mar. 2022.

"William Hoffer." *AuthorsDen.com*, http://www.authorsden.com/williamhoffer. Accessed 2 Mar. 2022.

"Wir Haben Gemeinsam Geatmet." *Der Spiegel 30*, 22 July 1991, https://www.spiegel.de/panorama/wir-haben-gemeinsam-geatmet-a-bfd7651c-0002-0001-0000-000013490005. Accessed 2 Mar. 2022.

Without My Daughter. Directed by Kari Tervo and Alexis Kouros, Dream Catcher Productions, Tarinatalo-Storyhouse Ltd. 2002.

"Women Without Men by Sharhrnush Parsipur." *Kirkus*, 20 May 2010, https://www.kirkusreviews.com/book-reviews/shahrnush-parsipur/women-without-men/. Accessed 2 Mar. 2022.

Worrall, Jill. "Jill Worral's Website."2015, https://jillworrall.com/books-jill-worrall/. Accessed 2 Mar. 2022.

Yardley, Jonathan. "Defiant Words." *The Washington Post*, 10 Apr. 2003, https://www.washingtonpost.com/archive/lifestyle/2003/04/10/defiant-words/c70e48de-a73d-420a-ac68- fd5678ec064a/. Accessed 2 Mar. 2022.

Yeğenoğlu, Meyda. "Sartorial Fabric-Ations: Enlightenment and Western Feminism." *Postcolonialism, Feminism and Religious Discourse*, edited by Kwok Pui-Lan and Laura E. Donaldson, Routledge, 2002, pp. 82–99.

Yohannan, John D. "The Persian Poetry Fad in England, 1770–1825." *Comparative Literature*, vol. 4, no. 2, 1952, pp. 137–60.

Yoneyama, Lisa. "Liberation under Siege: U.S. Military Occupation and Japanese Women's Enfranchisement." *American Quarterly*, vol. 57, no. 3, 2005, pp. 885–910.

Yuval-Davis, Nira. *Gender & Nation*. Sage, 1997.

Zainulbhai, Hani, and Richard Wike. "Iran's Global Image Mostly Negative." *Pew Research Center*, 18 June 2015, https://www.pewresearch.org/wp-content/uploads/sites/2/2015/06/Pew-Research-Center-Iran-Report-June-18-2015- FINAL.pdf . Accessed 2 Mar. 2022.

Zwemer, Samuel Marinus, and Amy E. Zwemer. *Moslem Women*. Gorgias Press, 2009.

INDEX

affirmation. *See under* colonial/Orientalist discourse
ahistorical historicism   23, 141
Ajami, Foad   119
Ale-Ahmad Jalal   7
animalization. *See under* colonial/Orientalist discourse
Arabian Nights   4. *See also One Thousand and One Nights*
Argo   82
Attar (of Nishabur)   173–5, 186
auto-Orientalism   20, 28, 89, 91–4, 154
axis of evil   6, 8, 15, 33, 118

Bahramitash, Roxana   9, 34, 54, 82, 86, 97–113
Behdad, Ali   14, 16, 21–3, 90–4, 100, 107–8
bestialization. *See under* colonial/Orientalist discourse
Bhabha, Homi K.   19–20, 65, 153, 155
binarism (Orientalist/colonial)   21, 23, 30, 44, 57–8, 61, 64, 70, 90, 93, 96, 98–9, 111–14, 127, 140, 143–6, 153–4, 163, 168, 178, 184, 189
binary (opposition)   21, 23, 30, 57–8, 90, 93, 111–14, 127, 140, 143–6, 153–4, 163, 178, 189. *See also* binarism
Bush, George W.   8–9, 33, 57, 118, 120

captivity narratives
  as cautionary tales   44–6
  as propaganda   40, 46, 53, 112, 119, 135, 156, 185
  as religious documents   39–40, 42–4
  as sensational shockers   38, 40–1, 46–8, 71, 80, 97, 182
  stylization in captivity narratives   40–2, 53
Carter, Jimmy   7, 48, 122
citationality   28, 93–4, 154–5, 163
the clash of civilizations   37, 54, 119
collective amnesia   142
colonial/Orientalist discourse
  affirmation   62–6, 86, 112, 127, 143–5
  animalization   63–4
  bestialization   51, 62–3
  contamination   52, 58–9, 61–3, 81
  debasement   58, 64, 66, 68
  defilement   58, 59, 67 (*see also* debasement)
  eroticization (in colonial/Orientalist discourse)
    of Muslim/Iranian women   14, 21
    of Persia   4
  exoticization   4, 21, 23, 182
  infantilization   21, 68, 114
  negation   1, 17, 21, 23, 26, 58, 62–8, 112, 127, 136, 142–6, 153, 162, 186
comprador (intellectual)   30, 105, 133, 135, 137, 154
contamination. *See under* colonial/Orientalist discourse
cross-cultural narratives   82
Culture and Imperialism. See under Edward Said

Dabashi, Hamid   26–7, 89, 94–7, 118–19, 132–42, 147–8
Darznik, Jasmin   11, 27
  The Bohemians   196
  The Good Daughter   196
  Song of a Captive Bird   196
  Writing Outside the Veil   27
debasement. *See under* colonial/Orientalist discourse

decontextualization 21, 142, 153
defilement. *See under* colonial/Orientalist discourse
dehistoricization 21, 142, 153
dehumanization (of Iranians/Muslims/Other) 3, 19, 63–7, 70, 103, 110, 114, 121, 159
deindividualization (of Iranians/Muslims/Other) 19, 66, 104
demonization (of Iranians/Muslims/Other) 1, 17, 24, 26, 36, 56, 70, 72, 81, 89, 114–16, 146, 159, 173, 182, 184–5
dichotomy 64, 70, 98–9, 127, 143. *See also* binarism/binary
dual marginalization 156
dual situatedness/positionality 20, 30, 154–5, 163–4
Dumas, Firoozeh 15, 24
  Funny in Farsi 15
  It Ain't so Awful, Falafel 15
  Laughing Without an Accent 15

eroticization. *See under* colonial/Orientalist discourse
essentialist (auto-)Orientalism 94, 153–4
exoticization. *See under* colonial/Orientalist discourse

Farrokhzad, Forough 168–71, 175–80, 183, 186
feminist Orientalism 98, 100, 113
feminization 21, 93, 200
first Persian Gulf war. *See* Iran-Iraq war
fixity 153, 155
Flight 655 72
Forbidden Love. See under Norma Khouri

ghost authors 52–4
going native 52, 72, 76, 79

harem (Oriental) 4, 23, 96, 105, 113, 115, 138
Honor Lost. See under Norma Khouri
hostage crisis 1, 7, 15, 19, 37, 48–9, 55, 66, 81–2, 84, 130, 156, 189
hostage narratives 38, 48, 49. *See also* captivity narratives
house negro 77. *See also* native informer

in-betweenness 45, 156
infantilization. *See under* colonial/Orientalist discourse
Iranian-American memoirs 10–17, 24–32, 84, 89, 94, 145, 156–61, 181, 191
Iranian literature 176. *See* Persian literature
Iranian/Muslim manhood/Masculinity (in literature) 58–9, 71–2, 100–1, 127, 171–5, 178, 180, 183–6, 192
Iranian/Muslim womanhood/femininity (in literature) 10, 20, 61, 72, 93–4, 98, 100, 169–71, 189
Iranian Revolution 108, 156–7, 176. *See also* Islamic Revolution
Iran-Iraq war 1, 23, 25, 28, 42, 47, 54, 84, 92, 124, 130–1, 164–7
Iranophobia 3, 8, 34, 89, 120
Islamic Revolution 1, 3, 6–10, 19, 23, 28–31, 42, 48, 54, 66, 76, 84, 107, 146–7
Islamophobia 3, 8, 9, 34, 89, 112, 119, 120, 173, 182, 193

Joint Comprehensive Plan of Action (JCPOA) 33, 193

Karim, Persis M. 11, 15, 191
Keshavarz, Fatemeh
  Jasmine and Stars: Reading More than Lolita in Tehran 2, 26, 27, 156, 158, 180
  Lyrics of Life 204
  Reading Mystical Lyric 204
  Recite in the Name of the Red Rose 204
keys to heaven 131, 133
Khomeini, Ayatollah 36, 97, 129, 130, 143
Khouri, Norma
  Forbidden Love/Honor Lost 14, 22
Koegeler, Martina 27, 87–9, 93–4, 109, 141, 145, 153–4

learned amnesia 141
Lewis, Bernard 26, 119–20, 137–8
The Location of Culture. See under Homi K. Bhabha

Lost without My Daughter. See under
    Sayed Bozorg Mahmoody

Mahmoody, Betty   1, 9, 25, 28, 34, 36,
    42–4, 47, 49–83, 114, 148, 189,
    190
  For the Love of a Child   36, 37, 46,
    53–7, 71, 74
  Not Without My Daughter   1, 25,
    28–31, 33–84, 89, 90, 148
Mahmoody, Sayed Bozorg   34, 70, 190
  Lost without My Daughter   81
Marandi, Seyed Mohammad   7, 47, 83,
    89, 123, 131, 191
marginalization   1, 3, 15, 17, 26, 62, 66,
    98, 141, 152, 156, 173, 185
Marlowe, Christopher
  Tamburlaine the Great   4
masses (in Iranian-American
    memoirs)   19, 51, 66–7, 114,
    121, 167, 193. *See also* mobs
Midnight Express   53
Milani, Farzaneh   11, 30, 33, 35, 38, 51,
    78
Milton, John
  Paradise Lost   4
  Paradise Regained   4
mimicry   19–20, 65
mobs (in Iranian-American
    memoirs)   19, 51, 66–7, 167,
    193. *See also* masses
Moore, Thomas
  Lalla Rookh   4
Morier, James   5
  *The Adventures of Hajji Baba of
    Ispahan*   5
  The Mirza   5
Mosaddeq, Mohammad   6, 48, 122
mythmaking (in Iranian-American
    memoirs)   31, 42, 46–7, 52, 57,
    131, 133, 164

Nafisi, Azar
  Anti-Terra   142
  Reading Lolita in Tehran   1, 10, 20, 22,
    23, 25, 26, 28, 29, 31, 83–149,
    156, 158, 177, 180, 190, 192
  The Republic of Imagination   191
  Things I've Been Silent About   191

Naipaul, V. S.   115
  Among the Believers   7
  Beyond Belief   7
native informers/native informants   118,
    133–5, 179
negation. *See under* colonial/Orientalist
    discourse
neo-conservatism   8, 117, 119, 132, 185
neoliberal multiculturalism   87–8, 127,
    154
neo-Orientalism   2, 17, 21–2, 87–93, 116,
    121, 179
new Orientalism   21, 26, 32, 90, 117, 158,
    160, 172–6, 180–1, 186. *See also*
    neo-Orientalism
9/11   1–2, 8–11, 14–16, 19, 22, 24, 25, 27,
    28, 30, 31, 34, 83–5, 87, 89–90,
    94, 100–1, 112, 118, 131, 132,
    135, 137, 141, 158, 159, 162,
    173, 179, 189, 190, 191, 194
1953 coup d'état   6, 48, 49, 122, 142

Obama, Barack   33, 193
Obama, Michelle   82
One Thousand and One Nights   4, 23, 145
Orientalism   2, 17–22, 24, 53, 56–7,
    68, 81–2, 88–94, 98–100, 148,
    151–5, 162, 190, 194
  latent   35
  manifest   35
Orientalism. See under Edward Said
Orientalist exclusionism   151, 153
Orientalist feminism   9, 24, 31, 98–100,
    112, 113, 116

Pahlavi, Mohammad Reza (the shah of
    Iran)   6, 48, 76, 107, 129, 136,
    148, 169, 170
Pahlavi, Reza (the shah of Iran)   103,
    106, 109
Paidar, Parvin   24, 98–100, 103, 107
Parsipur, Sharnush   175–80, 183, 186
  Touba and the Meaning of Night   179
  Women Without Men   176–9, 192
Persia
  representations in literature   3–5, 19
Persian literature   31, 144–7, 158–9,
    161–2, 168, 170, 173, 177, 184–5
Persian poetry fad   4

The Persians (play by Aeschylus)   4, 19
Pirnajmuddin/Peernajmodin, Hossein   4, 191
post-9/11
   atmosphere/anxieties/apprehensions   9–11, 15, 25, 30, 31, 83, 85, 100, 112, 131
   Islamophobia   8, 9, 89
   memoirs/literature   2, 13, 16, 19, 25, 27, 28, 30, 90, 94, 101, 102, 132, 141, 194
   US literary market   9

reception (of Iranian-American memoirs)
   Jasmine and Stars   152, 156, 164
   Not Without My Daughter   35–8
   Reading Lolita in Tehran   84–9
resistance
   discourse of   13, 20, 24, 28, 29, 31, 151, 152, 156, 187, 192
   to foreign hegemony   7, 133, 152, 187
   of Iranian women   17, 94, 99, 106, 107, 113, 114, 122
   of Western women   77, 79
Rumi   32, 144, 159, 161, 173–5, 186

Said, Edward W.
   The Clash of Ignorance   119
   Covering Islam   66
   Culture and Imperialism   24, 124, 127, 132–48, 151–3, 187, 194
   Orientalism   2, 4, 17–22, 35, 56–7, 66–8, 73–5, 78, 83, 91, 98–9, 119, 190
Sardar, Ziauddin   18–19, 71
SAVAK   6, 170
Scheherazade   10, 115, 134, 145, 175
scriptotherapy   12

selective memory   142
self-Orientalism   91
September 11 attacks. *See* 9/11
sexualization   182
Spencer, Edmund
   The Faerie Queene   4
Spivak, Gayatri Chakravorty   8, 9, 20, 103, 118, 153
Spurr, David
   The Rhetoric of Empire   52, 57–69, 76
strategic auto-Orientalism   20, 94, 153–5

the third space   155
Trump, Donald   33, 55, 112, 119, 173, 182, 193

unveiling   103–5, 115
   mandatory (in Iran)   106–7, 109
US occupation of Afghanistan   8, 9, 26, 98, 116, 119, 186
US occupation of Iraq   8, 9, 26, 98, 116, 119, 186

veiling
   mandatory (in Iran)   51, 106–9
vicarious trauma   40, 89, 159

the war on terror   8, 9, 16, 118, 135, 173
Westoxication   7
the white man's burden   62
white/western supremacy   67, 112, 116, 117, 135, 139, 143
Whitlock, Gillian   83, 113
   Soft Weapons   5, 11
Wilayto, Phil   117, 190
Without my Daughter (documentary)   70
Wolfowitz, Paul   56, 120
Worrall, Jill
   Two Wings of a Nightingale   1, 16

www.ingramcontent.com/pod-product-compliance
Lightning Source LLC
Chambersburg PA
CBHW062220300426
44115CB00012BA/2152